Christmas 2010

For Father Stephen Bierschenk,

From Mark Mueller and me.

William A. Barnowsky

THE MALIBU MIRACLE

WILLIAM S. BANOWSKY

PRESIDENT EMERITUS, PEPPERDINE UNIVERSITY

THE MALIBU MIRACLE

A MEMOIR

Published by Pepperdine University Press

24255 Pacific Coast Highway

Malibu, CA 90263

www.themalibumiracle.com

Consultant: Stephen D. Giddens, The Book Foundry

Photography from the Pepperdine University Archives and private collections

LA Times photo used with permission.

Printer: Regency Publishing Services, Ltd.

ISBN: 978-0-9824627-3-7

Printed in China

First printing 2010

FOR

Gay Barnes Banowsky

AND

OUR FOUR SONS

David ✤ *Britton* ✤ *Bill* ✤ *Baxter*

CONTENTS

FOREWORD

ANDREW K. BENTON

President, Pepperdine University
January 2010

There are many great stories in higher education. I am moved by the resolve of the Stanford family to honor their fallen son with the founding of a college and I find the rise of Emory in the last century to be nothing short of inspiring. There are many, many more. The Pepperdine story is uniquely compelling.

As I write this introduction to the historical account of Pepperdine's move to Malibu and its ascent to the national stage, I realize it is a story that will never be complete. As each graduating class leaves and a new one takes its place, a new chapter begins in a remarkable story that continues to unfold.

Only a few days ago, I looked into the young faces of the entering class of Seaver College—my tenth class as a Pepperdine president, and the 72nd undergraduate class since the opening of George Pepperdine College in 1937. I spoke to these wide-eyed young students and their parents of dreams, hopes and higher things. It was also my first opportunity to introduce them to some of what makes Pepperdine so special. It is, after all, a unique institution within higher education, blending the tangible and intangible elements of faith, scholarship and culture. Telling this story takes time, for as you will read, ours is a complex tale supported by powerful ideas that many in academia find to be incompatible or even contradictory. At Pepperdine, these ideas live in harmonious tension.

Perhaps the grand Pepperdine design cannot be fully understood unless experienced. For example, there truly is, as then president Banowsky declared in 1970, "a Spirit of Place" on the Malibu campus. I want our students to sense the palpable presence of the courage, creativity and sacrifice of our founders and friends who made "the Malibu miracle" possible.

When I recently welcomed the class of 2013, I impressed upon them that their own history now merges with the larger Pepperdine story and creates a new dimension to our "spirit of place." It will help every student—all of us—to know the history of which we are now a part. While their experience will be measured in just a few, short years of time, they are lifetime heirs to a legacy now nearly 75 years old, and they are part of what is arguably the most dynamic segment of our history—*The Malibu Miracle*—begun in the late 1960s.

It's important for our students to know the distance traveled by this university so they can understand our trajectory and why we believe, with all our hearts, that we can reach our goals. I want them to know, amid so many things, that it was not always like this and that what they see and experience today was "bought with a price" and that the high price paid can be viewed as both brilliant and tragic.

Remarkably, Pepperdine has kept its balance on the tightrope strung between being *good* as perceived by traditional academic lights and being *true* to our founding 1937 principles.

A few years ago, just before George Pepperdine II passed away, I sat at his bedside and asked him what he thought his father—our founder—would think about Pepperdine today. His response was simply, "He would be very, very proud. You have done more than even he dreamed." I hope so; indeed, I suspect every one of the seven presidents of Pepperdine would hope so, as well.

In the middle of those seven presidents, serving as the fourth, is William Slater Banowsky. His role then was pivotal and his perspective today is fresh and full of insight into times that must never be forgotten in order to understand this university. Preceded by the courageous M. Norvel Young and followed by the venerable Howard A. White, President Emeritus Banowsky was a president that Madison Avenue would like to have created. Handsome, youthful, bold, willing to take a risk and able to back it up, Bill Banowsky played a leading role in the complete and utter transformation of much of what is Pepperdine today.

As you read the following pages you will meet other heroes; but the voice is Dr. Banowsky's and this compelling story is written largely in the first person, for he was there.

Our colleagues in higher education have really been quite generous as I consider how many of their major friends and donors opted to join the Pepperdine cause with its bold and audacious vision of what could be. Those friends and their generous support and confidence are still a critical part of our future.

The following account of all that led to the move to Malibu and our present circumstances, with the drama now unfolded, begs the question: given all that we know now, would we do it all again? I would like to think so, but could we? In this regulatory environment, I doubt it. Thus, we are doubly grateful for the courage and vision of each of the six presidents who has guided our journey so far: Batsell Baxter, Hugh Tiner, M. Norvel Young, Howard A. White, David Davenport and, of course, the one who chronicles the journey in these pages, President Banowsky.

Writing with a certainty and confidence that was a hallmark of his administration, Dr. Banowsky takes us into conversations and deliberations that shape Pepperdine today. From the nascent hopes of a Kansas entrepreneur, George Pepperdine, to the historic institutional romance with one of the great ladies of Los Angeles, Blanche Ebert Seaver, both our dreams and our provenance are detailed. The stories and insights are many, nuanced, told well and with fervor.

George Pepperdine's decision in 1936 to open his college in 1937 set the pace for a school that would always be in a hurry to surprise, to please, to inspire and to outperform any reasonable predictors of likely success or outcome. Along the way, 80,000 alumni have added their respective stories to enrich and enliven all that was George Pepperdine College located at 79th and Vermont in Los Angeles and now is Pepperdine University located primarily in Malibu, but with graduate campuses throughout greater Los Angeles and permanent foreign campuses in London, Heidelberg, Florence, Buenos Aires, Lausanne and Shanghai. All of this developed in just 73 years and without losing touch with the dreams and spiritual convictions of our founder.

It has been reported that when a small boy once asked George Pepperdine how much money he had, he replied, "All I have left is what I have given away." Along with Mr. Pepperdine, this book also introduces Mrs. Frank R. Seaver, the maker of Pepperdine's Malibu miracle. I am but one of many who stands in awe of their generosity and its impact on the lives of so many.

What follows is a compelling and complex story told by one blessed with clear vision and depth of courage rarely seen. To understand Pepperdine University, one must understand the Malibu miracle.

"It is difficult for us to imagine how the university could have advanced so substantially in its rather brief history unless we consider God in the equation of our firm and certain mission."

ANDREW K. BENTON
President
Pepperdine University

McCARTY PROCLAIMED IT "THE MALIBU MIRACLE"

John T. McCarty, shown here during campus construction with Chancellor M. Norvel Young, christened "The Malibu Miracle" in 1969. John embodied the broad national conservative base that rallied around the new campus. Assistant to Chancellor Young, he was the president of the prestigious American Conservative Union.

"MIRACLES STILL HAPPEN!"

The Malibu miracle!

Those three words were first spoken to me in mid-July 1969 by Pepperdine colleague John T. McCarty. We were standing in construction dirt high up on the Malibu mountain being transformed into the home of Pepperdine University.

President of the American Conservative Union, John moved from Rockford College in Illinois to be Pepperdine assistant chancellor, raise money for the Malibu campus and "evangelize his anti-big-government gospel."[1] All who benefit from Pepperdine owe John a debt and this book reports many such debts.

On that memorable Malibu day, John—surveying endless ocean and sparkling islands, surging surf with pristine sand hugging big beach houses, majestic hills reaching the heavens and framed in front by the Los Angeles skyline—spread out his arms like Moses on the mountain and proclaimed, "Bill, this is *the Malibu miracle!*"

"MANIFEST DESTINY"

This three-word phrase captured the glory of the new campus and Pepperdine's mantra was born—but barely so. "I will not attempt elaborate explanations about legal 'timing' and 'coincidence,'" submitted highly esteemed Latham and Watkins attorney Joseph L. Bentley in 1981. "After more than ten years of continuous work on this project, all of the 'miracles' confirm my personal testimony of Pepperdine's 'manifest destiny' in moving from Los Angeles to Malibu." Bentley cited "four miraculous proofs."[2]

Today, decades later, people still ponder the supernatural "hows." "How did that dying little college do it? How did they get that priceless ocean property? How did they raise millions to pull it off overnight?" Of course, a case could be made for sheer luck. Such an advance may have flowed naturally from human causes without any supernatural how. Nonetheless, for thousands of us only one answer satisfies ineffably unrequited questions. The Malibu campus came in fulfillment of the will of God.

AMERICA'S REBELLIOUS DECADE

This miracle materialized from 1968 to 1978. That was also the decade of unrivaled rebellion in American higher education, zenith of the civil rights movement and vortex of the Vietnam War. NBC news anchor Tom Brokaw's book on this decade said, "It was time to 'Turn on, Tune in and Drop out.' Americans were walking on the moon but also dying in Vietnam. Nothing was beyond question and there were far fewer answers than ever before."[3]

In August 1968 the miracle at Malibu first emerged against the backdrop of the student rebellion at the Democratic National Convention in Chicago. Cordoned streets were choked with tear gas, shattered glass and *PEACE NOW!* signs. American flags flamed everywhere. Foul bags of urine and feces flew from high hotel windows, followed by foul televised screams. Long-haired students waved Vietcong flags and yelled "Pigs, pigs!" and "Oink, oink!" until warlike cops clubbed all in sight. Scores of students were injured and hundreds arrested. The official investigation ruled it "a police riot."

Tom Brokaw propounded: "Has there ever been, before or since, a week when so many lives were set off on so many different courses?"[4]

Watching television all week in my Malibu den, I sensed the call to set my own course. I knew Americans hungered to hear about another kind of college and a different kind of student. At that precise moment, in that violent summer of 1968, Pepperdine College was just acquiring its new Malibu land. Pepperdine seized the moment and set its course in pursuit of the Malibu miracle.

Paradoxically, tragedy for other schools opened an opportunity for Pepperdine. The case for law and order became more compelling with each day's news. In May 1970, the semester before I became Pepperdine College president, six students were shot to death and 24 others injured by police at Kent State in Ohio and Jackson State in Mississippi. Days later, on June 13, 1970, President Nixon formed the Commission on Campus Unrest that held its first hearing at our Los Angeles doorstep.

Higher education was so paralyzed that Dr. Jerry E. Hudson, president of Hamline University and Willamette University, pointed to Pepperdine at Malibu as "the only academic institution of its size to be built in the United States during the entire 1968–1978 decade."[5] The *Los Angeles Times* pointed to Pepperdine as the "only private institution of higher learning to be built in Los Angeles County in more than 30 years."[6] Dr. R. Gerald Turner, president of Southern Methodist University and former chancellor of the University of Mississippi, observed: "In American higher education during the last third of the twentieth century Pepperdine was among those universities achieving the greatest growth in the fastest time."[7]

"THEY CALLED IT PARADISE"

Pepperdine suffered the results of the national anarchy, facing the after-effects of the historic 1965 Watts riots not far from its peaceful promenade. The college was soon cast in the role of community oppressor when its sole security guard shot a neighborhood teenager to death.

Racial tension was compounded by criticisms, both internal and external, that the institution was abandoning its neighborhood just when it was most needed. As the pathway to Malibu opened, vigorous idealistic resistance came from trustees, faculty and students. Southwest Los Angeles residents resented Pepperdine's trade of its inner-city mission for the ocean. Malibu residents resented Pepperdine's push into their exclusive outpost at the northern reaches of Los Angeles County.

Against all opposition, defying daunting costs, and right on schedule, a campus opened in Malibu to education's usual rhythms and routines. Except for a few embittered Malibuites, the opponents quieted down. Faculty and students settled into the shining campus by the sea. People took it for granted as though it had somehow rolled in off the ocean like a misty Malibu morning.

When we opened Pepperdine in Malibu, the Eagles rock band rolled out a 1972 song about Malibu that some said was inspired by the campus: "They all called it paradise, the place to be. They watched the hazy sun sinking in the sea."[8]

PEPPERDINE'S MIRACLE DECADE

It is not easy to explain how a dwindling college with a local reputation could have suddenly emerged as a major university with international standing. Pepperdine's fifth president, Howard A. White, in a 1986 letter to me, agreed with McCarty that it was a miracle. "You presided over the Malibu miracle which has now become a routine and regular part of our vocabulary."[9]

From its 1937 founding until 1972 the school struggled for survival on a tiny island in the city's changing ocean. It had absolutely no endowment. It competed with larger and more reputable institutions. It fought on its own campus against radical elements that drew support from national terrorist groups in the larger community.

THE A-TEAM

Chancellor Young, President Banowsky, Provost Hudson and Vice President Hornbaker huddled in the Brock House several times a week.

TWO TOP AIDES

Phyllis A. Dorman, Bill's executive assistant for 25 years, and JoAnn McLin Carlson, the director of university publications, worked closely with President Banowsky.

BILL AND GAY IN 1973

Entering the historic Adamson Beach House, for several years the residence of Norvel and
Helen Young. Gay and Bill have now celebrated 54 wedding anniversaries, and have four
sons (all attorneys) and 14 grandchildren (some of whom are Pepperdine students).

The world's esteem for Pepperdine rose with its Malibu campus. Famed *Saturday Review* editor Norman Cousins quipped: "The Malibu campus of Pepperdine University is the campus God would build if he had the money."[10] Its 830-acre campus was voted "the most beautiful in the United States."[11]

For 50 years I have served Pepperdine: as junior faculty, dean of students, assistant to the president, executive vice president, chancellor of the Malibu campus, president and regent. My 40-plus years on the board is now the longest tenure of any board member in Pepperdine history. Three of seven Pepperdine presidents to date—Batsell Baxter, Hugh M. Tiner and M. Norvel Young—preceded me. And three—Howard A. White, David Davenport and Andrew K. Benton—succeeded me. I worked with all six.

Dr. Baxter, after his Pepperdine presidency, was my David Lipscomb College Bible professor. I sat in the second pew, on my 20th birthday, at his 1956 Nashville funeral. I restored Dr. Tiner as a regent in 1976 and we served together as regents until his 1981 death. I worked for 40 years with Dr. Young and Dr. White. Under Dr. Davenport and Dr. Benton I was president emeritus and regent. George Pepperdine, born in 1886, and Andrew K. Benton, born in 1952, lived lifetimes apart but I served with both.

My presidency demanded transformational decisions. These included acquiring the Malibu land and designing, funding and constructing the campus; moving out of Los Angeles to Malibu; advancing from a college to a university; acquiring the school of law and moving it out of Orange County to Malibu; founding the graduate school of business and management and the graduate school of education; building Seaver College of liberal arts; founding *Pepperdine People* magazine and the Pepperdine University Associates; and founding the expanded ecumenical board of regents. "It is safe to say," wrote Pepperdine historian Richard T. Hughes, "that Dr. William S. Banowsky provided the crucial leadership during the all-important decade from 1968 to 1978."[12]

My wife, Gay Barnes Banowsky, designed our first art gallery and co-designed the Malibu president's home, the Brock House.[13]

Meanwhile, Pepperdine's permanent endowment approached one billion dollars. That endowment was based almost entirely on trusts executed during my presidency by Mrs. Frank R. Seaver in the 1970s. Her Pepperdine gifts grew to one-half billion dollars, spotlighting the Seaver family—with the Stanfords, Dukes and Vanderbilts—on the short list of largest contributors to higher education in American history.[14]

THE EARLIEST MIRACLE MAKERS
As Firestone Fieldhouse rises beneath Seaver College in 1972, Mrs. Frank Roger Seaver,
the Malibu campus founder, holds aloft plans for the Raleigh Runnels Memorial Pool.
She is flanked by Helen and Norvel Young; Charles, Amy Jo and Susan Runnels;
John Hall and Richard Seaver of the Hydril Company; and Bill Banowsky.

MERELY MY MEMOIR

Millions of words have been written about the Malibu miracle, but no one
has told the inside story. Few are left who know it. The circle of "miracle
makers" has dwindled to a dot. I tell this story because if I do not, much of it
will die with me. Pursuing institutional self-awareness, I write to enrich our
tradition. "Know thyself" is wise counsel for institutions as well as individuals.
An institution as great as ours, with lofty spiritual ideals, must cherish its
history.

I am humbled to bear witness for so many who love Pepperdine so much.
I have wondered, "How would Norvel Young say this?" Or Blanche Seaver,
or Howard White, or scores of others with whom I've communed. Seeking
scrupulous accuracy, I felt the eyes of 80,000 alumni looking over my shoulder,
along with scores of staff and faculty families who have given their lives to
Pepperdine.

I'm a builder, not a historian. It took me longer to write this book than it did to build the campus. Therefore, this is no comprehensive history of Pepperdine University. It is a memoir of personal perspectives, no doubt recounted subjectively, during that pivotal 1968 to 1978 decade. What most commends my memoir is that I was there. "Write what you know about," advised Mark Twain. This is what I know about Pepperdine's rags to riches reincarnation.

Because this story should enrich our corporate memory I felt called to record it, but feared jousting with miracles. The supernatural takes one's breath away. There's much to be said for silence. My soul mate of 50 years inspired me to tell it as it happened. That's what I have done. Gay and I lived these events together, clinging to one another as they washed over us wave upon wave. If I dreaded jousting, she emboldened me. If I wearied, she revived me. If I dillydallied, she spurred me on. My sharpest critic, keenest editor and dearest friend, Gay and I alone know how much she contributed—and suffered. Without her there would be no book and, conceivably, no miracle. Mrs. Seaver, our childless miracle-maker-in-chief, loved Gay as her own daughter.

Memory tends to be inaccurately vain. I disciplined mine by researching thousands of primary documents tied to the 1968–1978 decade. Phyllis A. Dorman, for a quarter century my executive assistant, saved every scrap of paper that crossed my desk. These Banowsky Papers were processed and indexed in the Payson Library by Provost Steven Lemley and Archivist James Smythe. Bill Henegar and Ana Rodriguez-Garat Banowsky edited the final text.

Therefore, this book is neither autobiography, hagiography nor histor-iography. It is my best effort to explain how a few flawed people, acting ineffably beyond their abilities, empowered an institution of Christian higher education to bless future generations, perhaps until the end of time.[15]

As Pepperdine moved tons of Malibu earth, Chancellor Young cited tons of supporting scripture. "If you have faith as small as a mustard seed, you can say to this mountain, 'Move from here to there' and it will move. Nothing will be impossible for you."[16]

1. Obituary of John T. McCarty, *National Review*, October 4, 1985. John was also a General Electric executive, executive director of the American Association of Presidents of Independent Colleges and trustee of the Philadelphia Society with William F. Buckley Jr., Russell Kirk and Milton Friedman.
2. Joseph L. Bentley, personal letter to Howard A. White, May 7, 1981. The Banowsky Papers. Manifest Destiny is the nineteenth-century doctrine that the United States must dominate the Western hemisphere. Bentley summarized four Pepperdine proofs for a Malibu Manifest Destiny: "(1) *Environmental Impact Review*. Two weeks after the campus opened, on September 21, 1972,

the California Supreme Court ruled in *Friends of Mammoth* to apply the California Environmental Quality Act of 1970 to *private* projects. But after CEQA's 1970 passage, Pepperdine received dozens of permits, moved tons of dirt and built the campus. Only on July 14, 1972, (two weeks before we opened) did the county issue our final Conditional Use Permit. It is certain no permits would ever have been issued if that 1970 law had been applied even a few days sooner. (2) *County General Plan*. California Government Code Section 65563, enacted December 30, 1971, ruled that beginning August 31, 1972 (one week before we opened), no building permit or subdivision map would be approved unless consistent with the new Environmental Development Guide designed 'to slow, stop and reverse the loss of open space.' Our campus was all vulnerable 'open space' but, in 1971 and 1972 when our permits were issued, the EDG did not quite yet have the force of law. (3) *Coastal Permits*. On November 7, 1972 (precisely 60 days after we opened), Proposition 20 passed, creating the California Coastal Commission. If adopted any earlier, it would have prohibited the development of our campus. (4) *Coastal Appeal of Sewage Plant*. Most dramatic was the failure of the appeal of the Regional Commission's issuance of a Coastal Permit for our sewage disposal system. We got that permit, on June 13, 1977, by a 10 to 1 vote, despite a literal busload of Malibuites opposing us at the hearing. Those opponents had until 5:00 p.m. of the tenth working day after that decision to appeal it to the California Coastal Commission. On that tenth day the appeal arrived—at 5:15 p.m. It was declared 'untimely and void' by 15 minutes! If their denial of that permit had been allowed, it would have defeated our permanent sewage system just as temporary arrangements with Las Virgenes were expiring. The law school, fine arts building and additional housing would never have been built and the county would have closed the entire campus as a health hazard."

3. Tom Brokaw, *Boom! Voices of the Sixties* (New York: Random House, 2007), 1.
4. Ibid., 96–102. Brokaw, a personal friend of 40 years, began work on the air with me at KNBC-TV in 1969.
5. Jerry Hudson, in Jerry Rushford, ed., *Crest of a Golden Wave: Pepperdine University, 1937–1987* (Malibu: Pepperdine University Press, 1987), 163. Howard A. White christened chapter four of his pictorial history, "The Miracle at Malibu, 1972–1980."
6. Robert Kistler, article in the *Los Angeles Times*, Tuesday, February 10, 1970.
7. R. Gerald Turner, personal interview with the author, January 10, 2007. The Banowsky Papers. "At Pepperdine and OU during the years from 1965 to 1975," President Turner added, "nobody in America was better behind a microphone than Bill Banowsky."
8. There was also the song "Malibu" by Hole. And then there was Shelley West's, "You're the Reason God Made Oklahoma." West sang: ". . . when the wind blows you can see all the way to Malibu."
9. Howard A. White, personal letter to the author, March 4, 1986. The Banowsky Papers.
10. Judy Pasternak, "Pepperdine: Party School by the Shore (Republican, That Is)," *Los Angeles Times*, September 19, 1987.
11. *The Best 361 Colleges, 2006 Edition* (The Princeton Review: Random House, 2006). The annual survey by The Princeton Review asked 110,000 students at 361 colleges to rate the top 20 colleges in 62 categories. "The most beautiful campus in the United States is Pepperdine University, overlooking the Pacific Ocean at Malibu." http://www.princetonreview.com/college/research/articles/rankingspr.asp. As for academic distinction, in the year 2000 Pepperdine University was ranked by *U.S. News and World Report* as the 49th best in the country.
12. Richard T. Hughes, "Faith and Learning at Pepperdine University," in Richard T. Hughes and William B. Adrian, eds., *Models for Christian Higher Education: Strategies for Survival and Success in the Twenty-First Century* (Grand Rapids, MI: William B. Eerdmans, 1997).
13. Gay also designed our official orange, white and blue Pepperdine Waves flag. The official flag debuted with the Brock House dedication during President Ford's campus visit, September 25, 1975.
14. John T. Mosley, "Pepperdine charismatic President William S. Banowsky almost single-handedly raised the funds for the Malibu campus." *Pepperdine Tennis Classic*, March 26, 1976, 1.
15. Marshal Berges, *Los Angeles Times Home*, Sunday, June 4, 1978. "Once scorned and now widely admired, Pepperdine University is in a class by itself. A tacky rhinestone of a school when it was put together in southwest Los Angeles during the 1930s, its Malibu campus has become a glittering diamond set on 650 acres. The sparkle runs deep, and to many observers it symbolizes the university's academic progress. The man most responsible for Pepperdine's improvement in recent years is its president William S. Banowsky, 42. Bright, charming and demanding, he projects strength, honesty and sincerity."
16. Matthew 17:20 (NIV).

"Demographic changes and social unrest erupting in the Watts Riots near the campus sealed our fate in that location."

DONALD V. MILLER

Chairman
Pepperdine College
Board of Trustees

PART I

THE LOS ANGELES
DEATH

"I treasure our unique friendship. It's chemistry I've never known with anybody else, and doubt I'll ever experience again. I cherish our partnership most highly."

M. NORVEL YOUNG
Third President
Pepperdine University

THE PROVIDENTIAL PARTNERSHIP

President William S. Banowsky and Chancellor M. Norvel Young in deepest meditation during the design, funding and construction of Pepperdine University at Malibu.

CHAPTER 1

THE PROVIDENTIAL PARTNERSHIP

"Wow!" came the ebullient shout and extended hand. "I'm President M. Norvel Young of George Pepperdine College," as if that were his full name. "Young man, that was a masterpiece! Let's sit down and talk as soon as you finish shaking hands."

My lifetime relationship with Norvel Young began Saturday, February 15, 1958, at a banquet in the student center of David Lipscomb College in Nashville, Tennessee. I was the student speaker. Norvel was the brand-new college president in my audience. He was 42 years old. I was 22 and three months from graduation. The moment we met our lives began to change. I became his protegé and alter ego. He became my mentor and guide. At that banquet the Malibu miracle was conceived, a decade before it visibly appeared.

FATEFUL NASHVILLE BANQUET

Norvel, never given to understatement, called my ten-minute lamentation on America's moral decline "a masterpiece." I first delivered the speech three weeks earlier to win the coveted Lipscomb's Founder's Day Oratorical Contest.[1] Lipscomb's president, Athens Clay Pullias, congratulated my win and described the upcoming convention of Church of Christ college presidents. It was Lipscomb's turn to host the annual gathering and Dr. Pullias booked me to repeat my oration at the closing banquet. He only intended "to show these presidents the kind of preachers Lipscomb produces." No one imagined that the banquet would alter the destiny of another college 3,000 miles away.

Presidents from everywhere packed the student center. A. M. Burton, founder of Life and Casualty Insurance Company, gave out $5,000 or $10,000 checks at this meeting, according to college size. Richest churchman east of the Mississippi, Burton was the counterpoint to George Pepperdine out west. When wrestling with whether to establish his college, Mr. Pepperdine had traveled by train in 1935 to consult A. M. Burton and inspect Lipscomb.

On this night Burton's generosity drew many presidents. Norvel's brother-in-law, F. W. Mattox, came from Lubbock Christian College in Texas. Norvel's cousin, James O. Baird, came from Oklahoma Christian College. George S. Benson came from Harding College in Arkansas. A dozen more, including H. A. Dixon, Jack Bates, Rex Turner Sr. and James Cope, came from smaller colleges. Claude A. Guild, my Fort Worth boyhood preacher, traveled from Oregon as president of Columbia Christian College. From Abilene Christian College came the venerable Don H. Morris, who had recruited hard for me to stay in Texas. Thanks to Pepperdine's pacesetting, all these schools are now universities.[2]

Sitting at the head table between President Pullias and my wife, Gay, I surveyed the dignitaries. (Gay Barnes came to Lipscomb from North Carolina. We had been married two years and had an infant son.)[3] I spotted Lipscomb professors Howard A. White and Jennings Davis, who would soon go with Norvel to Pepperdine. They sat alongside Nashville preachers Batsell Barrett Baxter, Carroll B. Ellis, Ira A. North, B. C. Goodpasture, Marshall Keeble and Jim Bill McInteer. President Pullias whispered to me eerie coincidences about two attendees I did not know.

"That's Norvel Young over there, Pepperdine's new president. Norvel won Lipscomb's 1934 oratorical contest," he said. "I hear he's recruited Frank Pack to leave Abilene and head Pepperdine's religion department. Dr. Pack won it in 1935." I was awed to be listed in such a lineage.

NORVEL AND HELEN AT PEPPERDINE

I finished my address. Dr. Pullias closed the proceedings with a prayer. I basked in congratulations and President Young was first in line.

Though just selected Pepperdine president, he had deep roots with the institution. In 1937, as a young scholar with a Vanderbilt University master's, he addressed the Pepperdine College founding faculty. The next year he joined that faculty and taught history from 1938 through 1941. Helen Mattox, a member of the founding student body, enrolled in his class, and the rest is history.

Norvel connected with Pepperdine to define his life—and with Helen to perfect it. They married in 1939. Historian Richard T. Hughes crowns Helen as "perhaps the most visible and influential woman among Churches of Christ in the second half of the twentieth century."[4] Without Helen

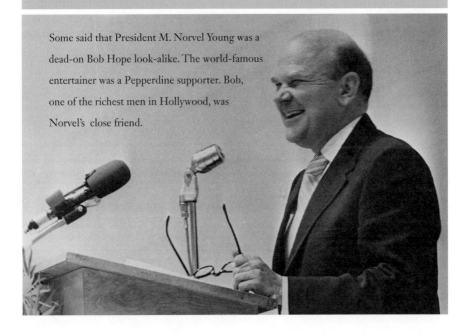

Some said that President M. Norvel Young was a dead-on Bob Hope look-alike. The world-famous entertainer was a Pepperdine supporter. Bob, one of the richest men in Hollywood, was Norvel's close friend.

Mattox Young there could have been no M. Norvel Young, as we knew him, and without M. Norvel Young there would have been no Malibu miracle.

In 1941 the Youngs left Pepperdine to pursue Helen's master's and Norvel's doctorate at Peabody College in Nashville.[5] His dissertation, *The History of Colleges Established and Supported by Members of the Churches of Christ*, featured Pepperdine College in chapter 6.[6] Deciding not to return to Pepperdine—"because of its liberal drift"—they instead chose ministry, succeeding the great G. C. Brewer at the historic Broadway Church of Christ in Lubbock, Texas.

Norvel, a dynamic occasional speaker, found homiletics tedious. "Bill, I was a mediocre pulpit man," he chortled. "If Helen could have done the preaching, I could have done the promoting, and that church would have really taken off."[7] As it was, under his promotional leadership for 13 years from 1944 through 1957, that church did take off. Located at the gate of Texas Tech University, the Youngs built it into the largest Church of Christ congregation in the world, with the nicest building. Committing himself early, and confirming it profoundly in partnering with Helen, Norvel contributed his career as America's unsurpassed Church of Christ leader.

In 1957 they left Lubbock for Pepperdine. National media celebrated the West Texas preacher riding out to save the troubled West Coast college. *Time* magazine's August 5, 1957, issue featured Norvel, Bible in hand, in front of the Broadway building. *Time* headlined the article, "The Nondenomination," Norvel's principal plea.[8]

Time caught my attention when Lipscomb history professor Dr. Howard A. White brought it to class on the opening day of my senior year. Ten years later, Dr. White providentially became my key Malibu miracle administrator and, ultimately, my Pepperdine presidential successor. Dr. White's early Pepperdine perceptions, which he poured out to our 1957 Lipscomb class, included Norvel's commitment "to save the school for the church"; "faculty outrage at a new president they considered a fundamentalist"; and "alumni alienation over the resignation of Dean E. V. Pullias," who was, coincidentally, the brother of Lipscomb's president.

CONTRASTS AND COMMONALITIES

Six months after *Time* publicized Norvel's new job, he and I met at that Nashville banquet. "An amazing team was formed," the Young-Banowsky watchers noticed. "Young and Banowsky were a matched pair that spanned two generations. Both were visionaries, both were exceptional speakers, both were motivators, both were charming promoters. It would take all that talent and more to accomplish the task set before them." That task meant the Malibu miracle and our partnership's financial foundation. "In the heyday of fundraising for the new Malibu campus, Bill Banowsky and Norvel Young made a good team for several reasons. Bill was younger and more aggressive. Norvel was experienced and more human. Bill had urgency. Norvel had patience. It was a good combination."[9]

Commonalities shared, differences accommodated, we compounded our opposites with a unified force greater than our individualities. An alchemy of deepest friendship and shared vision turned our labors into pure gold. "Bill Banowsky was not only Norvel's great friend, but in so many ways like a son to him."[10]

Norvel, born in Nashville in 1915, was 20 years older than I, born in Abilene, Texas, in 1936. If not much time or geographic difference, it was a full generation with keen distinctions between West Texas and Middle Tennessee. Old enough to be my father, Norvel was never fatherly but a wiser brother. "Hey brother!" we greeted one another, whether alone or in groups, in person or by telephone, day and night. "Hey brother! How are ya?"

The particular two decades Norvel experienced before I was born—encompassing World War I, the Roaring Twenties and the Great Depression—made a huge difference in men. From his "Greatest Generation," Norvel had much to teach a protegé. Friendship feeds on communication, and whether in the car, on a plane or at the beach, it was continuous casual conversation

BLANCHE AND BOB

Chancellor Young invited his friend Bob Hope to deliver the first Malibu commencement address in December 1972. The Malibu campus founder, Mrs. Frank R. Seaver, assisted in conferring an honorary degree on Dr. Hope.

with serious implications. We held nothing back, with many a truth being uttered in jest. He ridiculed my political lust as "the devil's tug." I deflected, "Oh yes, philosopher Young! Just as Socrates taught Plato, Plato taught Aristotle and Aristotle taught Alexander the Great, you're always trying to teach something profound to me!"

"Yes, Bill, but stay humble," he would say, smiling sardonically but good-naturedly. "Remember, an arrogant Alexander broke the classic tradition, abandoned philosophy for politics, didn't teach anybody anything, died drunk at an early age and left no legacy but war!" Norvel almost always won our friendly philosophical fights.

PATRICIAN AND COWBOY

We carried social, economic and geographic differences but contrasted most in psychological temperament. Norvel, a raging extrovert, gained energy from working a crowd, conversation and banter—and the more "others" there were, the more energy he gained.

Norvel was a southern gentlemen with an air of aristocracy that drew him easily to other aristocratic men of old money like Richard Carlton Seaver of Los Angeles, Richard Mellon Scaife of Pittsburgh, Edward L. Gaylord of Oklahoma City, Charles S. Payson of New York and Robert Coe of Cody, Wyoming. I could drop the names of a dozen others who, while maintaining patrician reserve, granted Norvel instant access as a comfortable peer.

I confess to a touch of Texas redneck, and some friends called me a cowboy. My heroes, like John Wayne and Ronald Reagan, had always been cowboys. As much money as I raised, I somehow felt a class difference with the big rich. Oh, if they were first-generation rich like Blanche Seaver, or self-made men like Fritz Huntsinger or good old boys like "Tex" Thornton, I enjoyed profound intimacy. "Bill," Norvel pondered, "how do you manage to get so much closer to some of our friends than I do?"

Norvel's gregarious soul encircled a center of ultimate privacy. Never withdrawn, he protected an intimate space away from familiarity. His modesty occasionally astonished Helen. Like Ronald Reagan was with Nancy, he was ultimately alone only with Helen. But perhaps to no other friend would he have written as he did to me in 1974: "You know me better than any other person on this planet."[11]

Norvel's personality had no sharp edges. With a perfect sense of timing, he eschewed conflict. Noncombatant to a fault, he was always conciliatory, always unifying. He wasted no energy on negativity, nursed no grudges and had no anger in him. He was irenic. I was dogmatic. He spoke softly. I got intense. He read fiction and nonfiction voraciously for pleasure. I read nonfiction strictly for facts. He was philosophical. I was theological. He was a churchman. I was a preacher. Gay loved Norvel and coined the term "Norvelian" to capture his capacity to smooth out rough edges. I caught his enthusiasm, he captured my energy, and God used our differences in ways that are yet unfolding.

Norvel loved life in all its fullness more than any other person I have known. A hardheaded sentimentalist, he celebrated being alive because he knew soon none of us would be. Conducting countless funerals—wrestling with what Tennyson called "being my own corpse coffin at last"—his duel with death fired volcanic energy to make every hour of every day count for good. "Boy, it's a great day to be alive!" he rejoiced morning, noon and night. It wasn't death Norvel dreaded to experience but life he hated to lose.

He was arrestingly reflective. Driving home after the elite Newcomen Society's California Club black-tie dinner, he said out of nowhere, "Bill, for these good men tonight it's life or death to be in this Los Angeles social circle. But in Phoenix or Dallas or Chicago they've got entirely different circles. We don't care about theirs. They don't care about ours. Silly little game we play, isn't it?" Another day, walking on the beach, he said out of nowhere, "Bill, the world needs more service and cooperation, less selfishness and competition." Yes, we were equally ambitious. But his accepting personality and genius for empowering others left us noncompetitive with one another. Sitting on an airplane he said out of the blue, "Bill, like Rodgers and Hammerstein, we make music together!"

No plaster saint, the irrepressibly optimistic Norvel Young was a complicated "man of sorrows and acquainted with grief." His favorite hymn was Cardinal J. H. Newman's "Lead, Kindly Light, Amid the Encircling Gloom." Incorrigibly happy, he was at the same time profoundly serious. Making the Malibu miracle, he experienced a devastating automobile accident. Watching him rebound inspired me to respect him all the more.

COLLEGES, MONEY AND MOTHERS

Before Norvel and I met, deep roots of Christian education predestined our bond. Each with an older brother, we answered the competitive call as flag-bearing second sons for illustrious multi-generational families who wanted our lives to count for Christ. Pepperdine counted quintessentially because Christian education, for both the Young and the Banowsky families, came first.

Our parents and grandparents glorified colleges as the pinnacle of our faith tradition. Norvel's parents, Matt Norvel Young Sr. and Mary Ruby Morrow, met at David Lipscomb College and were married on campus by famous evangelist T. B. Larimore. My parents, Wade Lowell Banowsky and Thelma Beatrice Slater, met at Abilene Christian College and were married on campus by famous evangelist Homer Hailey. Norvel and Helen met at Pepperdine College in 1938. Gay and I met at David Lipscomb College in 1954. Along with the church, our families esteemed Christian education above all.

On the matter of money we may have lived on different sides of town. Norvel's dad was a prosperous Nashville real estate developer who was able to send Norvel on a trip around the world in the 1930s. My school-teacher dad worried about paying monthly bills. What our fathers had in common was dedication to church and family leadership. With biblical piety, sweetened by earthy humor, they were inspirational models for Norvel and me.[12]

Our mothers lit the spiritual fire in our hearts. Ruby Morrow and Thelma Slater, cut from the same cloth, were firstborn daughters of big, proud families. Both belonged to the Stone-Campbell movement that issued in the twentieth-century Church of Christ. But opposite economic experiences instilled conflicting convictions about the purpose of the church in the world.

S. F. Morrow, Ruby's father, was probably the richest member of the Church of Christ in Tennessee at the time. He was generous in his support of evangelism but, on principle, he left his adult children very much on their own and declined Matt's request for help getting started in the real estate business.

GRACE VERSUS LEGALISM

Historian Richard Hughes said geography shaped doctrinal differences. "Unlike Norvel Young, who grew up in Tennessee congregations often marked by tolerance and grace, Banowsky grew up in Fort Worth, Texas, where Churches of Christ were known for their legalism and their claims to be the one true church. In time, Banowsky found such claims to be repugnant and came to resist any form of legalism."[13]

Equalizing geographic influences, Norvel came out to be educated in my bucolic West Texas, while I crossed the Mississippi to be educated in his urbane Nashville, "the Athens of the South."[14] Hughes added, "With a few notable exceptions, even most Texas congregations have now completed their sect-to-denomination transition."[15] While I am gratified that Churches of Christ are no longer a sect, I feel a little churchless. "In the 1960s, the church was heralded as the fastest growing in America," reported the *Christian Chronicle* in February 2009. "Now membership has dwindled down to the lowest level since records began being kept 50 years ago, according to the 2009 edition of the *Churches of Christ in the United States*. Failing even to keep pace with population growth, we're down to 12,629 congregations and 1,598,281 adherents."[16] Our twentieth-century church was defined by denominational doctrine. But, in my opinion, the high price we paid for selling out sectarian exclusivity was that the Church of Christ mutated into just another disordered denomination whose amorphous evangelicalism may lead us into historical oblivion.

Norvel modeled church leadership. Before replacing him as president of Pepperdine, I succeeded him in the pulpit of the Broadway Church of Christ in Lubbock, Texas. When we partnered to transplant Pepperdine from Los Angeles to Malibu we rejuvenated its church roots. During the late 1960s and '70s our families helped found a congregation in the Malibu Civic Center that today is the University Church of Christ.

With Emersonian spirituality, Norvel conversed with God as if citing the morning paper. In the office, on a beach, before a restaurant meal, he'd say, "Bill, let's have a little prayer." He would praise the deity without closed eyes, bowed head or changed tone. For both of us, throughout our long and bumpy lives, the center of reality remained the Person of Christ.

NO COMPETITION BETWEEN LIGHTHOUSES

Norvel held an enigmatic power. With balding head, impish grin and Bob Hope nose, if you knew Norvel those unremarkable features radiated wisdom, intuition and ambition. [17] If you believed in reincarnation you'd think here was an old soul who had done this before. To the uninitiated, his radiance remained concealed behind twinkling, mischievous brown eyes. Joviality illuminated his wry smile. Endlessly speaking in prose, he overflowed with epigrams.

"There's no telling how much you can get done if you don't care who gets the credit!" "There's no competition between lighthouses!" "You can't be big and little at the same time!" "Crying is the refuge of plain women but the ruin of pretty ones." "Never curse the bridge that carries you over!" "You'll be surprised by the bridges you'll never have to cross!" "You're doing more good than you know!" "The future's as bright as the promises of God!" "I stand on tiptoe looking forward to what God will do in the years ahead!" "The rising tide lifts all ships!" "Wow!"

On the 1972 day we opened the undergraduate campus of Pepperdine in Malibu, he created his masterpiece: "Malibu's 830 acres are smog free, sun kissed, ocean washed, island girded and mountain guarded!" On the 1998 day of his funeral, Pepperdine president David Davenport "smiled as he remembered . . . that only Norvel Young could get away with such blatant hyperbole. If anyone else were to use such language it would be laughable, but when Norvel used these phrases—repeatedly—he was greeted with cheers."[18]

Norvel created a new epigram for that Nashville night we met. "During the compelling speech, Norvel felt 'a strange connection with Bill,' as he later put it. When he got home he told Helen, 'I want this young man. He's a leader!' Later, Norvel said of Banowsky, 'He was obviously what we call in Tennessee *a five-gaited horse*—a man of many talents.'"[19] I never knew why Norvel compared me to a horse until he explained it to Patricia Yomantas. "He could think clearly, he could plan intuitively, he could act decisively, he could write persuasively, and he could speak like a Demosthenes. Pepperdine needed him, and when we invited him to come we had in mind the thrust of his leadership. Our dream for Bill was more than fulfilled."[20]

On that Nashville night, after pats on the back from others, the world-class recruiter cornered me. I learned later, at the University of Oklahoma, what counted was not Barry Switzer's coaching of recruited Sooners. What counted was the Sooners Switzer recruited. Recruitment was everything. Everyone at Pepperdine was recruited directly by Norvel. Or, he or she was recruited by the man or woman who was recruited directly by Norvel. Or, he or she was recruited by the man or woman who was recruited by the man or woman who was recruited directly by Norvel. Pepperdine is people. Norvel was the fountainhead from which the Malibu miracle people flowed.[21]

THE INSTANT BONDING

In our initial Nashville meeting Norvel needed a personal assistant to share his crushing load. Leading me aside, sitting down and selling hard, after 20 minutes he cut to the chase.

"So, Bill, you'll graduate and come to Pepperdine as my assistant, get your USC master's and I'll fix a preaching place. You'll have a nice salary. Bill, what do ya say? You and Gay will love California!"

I was only 22, not even a college graduate. I knew little about this man, Pepperdine or California. Until that moment I saw myself as someone who might spend his life in preaching and church leadership while teaching speech at my Tennessee alma mater. I had signed an agreement with President Pullias to teach three years at Lipscomb in exchange for graduate tuition in a masters' program at the University of New Mexico. I had agreed to preach for Albuquerque's Netherwood Park Church of Christ while doing graduate work. I couldn't just walk away from those commitments because this compelling man wanted me to.

"I'd like to say yes, Dr. Young," I said. "But I'm committed for a year in Albuquerque."

"Well," replied Norvel, "Albuquerque isn't far from Los Angeles. We can visit one another and work out details. A year passes fast. I want you to think of yourself as being on the way to help me at Pepperdine."

Neither of us could have known, but the push I felt from Norvel's enthusiasm was the first stirring of the Malibu miracle. Over the year that followed, our frequent visits together solidified the bond that began on that night. When Gay and I moved to California in 1959, Norvel and I had formed a loyal friendship.

He gave me every opportunity to learn. In my first "tour of duty" at Pepperdine, he assigned me to teach speech, work as his assistant to give me exposure to college administration, and direct the Bible Lectures. I even worked as dean of students for a year. When we moved to Lubbock to work with the Broadway Church of Christ—the church Norvel and Helen had led prior to their coming to Pepperdine—those five years away didn't diminish our constant communication and mutual admiration. Our relationship matured.

By the time I came back to Pepperdine in 1968, we were a ready-made fundraising team. We responded in the same way to the nerve-shattering responsibility of keeping the institution alive and the Malibu miracle unfolding; we both startled our wives in the same way by bolting upright in the middle of many nights, wondering how at each month's end we could meet gargantuan construction bills on top of growing faculty payrolls. Setting aside the pain and anxiety, we would put on our game faces and go out to sit, side by side, across from some millionaire whose help we desperately needed. While attentive to the millionaire, we were reading each other too. We were "in the flow" together, knowing exactly what should be said next and who should say it. We went out many nights with our wives to working dinners after working all day in the office or downtown. Magically, none of it seemed much like work because it was so energizing to do it together. It was common for us to compose proposals, letters and articles for each other—"Here's what you should say, Norvel." And he might hand me a piece of paper, saying, "And here's what you should say, Bill." We even talked simultaneously on separate telephone extensions to the same prospects or to a board member about some problem.

Two people never talked more with each other than we did during those days. We sometimes traveled all day by car or by plane, talking all the while. In the early years, while the Malibu campus was under construction, we rode horses for hours high above the campus. We took breaks sitting by the ocean, watching the eternal waves roll in. And we talked about everything—history, philosophy, theology, psychology, literature, our families, friends, donors, national and state politics, church politics and Pepperdine politics. We

THE NEW PRESIDENT AND FIRST LADY

M. Norvel Young and Helen M. Young, after moving from Lubbock, Texas,

to Los Angeles and Pepperdine, September 1, 1957.

didn't see everything alike but we each knew how the other thought about everything. We knew each other's moods.

Norvel was a peace-loving man and, thanks to him, we never had an emotional argument. I tended to defer to him on long-range strategy. He gladly gave me the lead on day-to-day fundraising and public relations tactics. He often said I thought like an architect and so, when it came time to make decisions about the campus design, he deferred to me. We cooperated perfectly on faculty and student issues. We were of one mind on everything that was important for the future of Pepperdine. We were each aware of what we owed the other, forgave each other when necessary and never sweated the small stuff. We loved each other faithfully, as brothers do when at their best, all the time.

"I WANT THIS YOUNG MAN!"

Norvel had the gift of discovering what people had to offer and of bringing it out. In my case, he saw something in me that moved him to issue such a direct and impassioned offer to me, a graduating senior, in February 1958. I will never know what I might have done had I never met Norvel. But it is possible that I would never have been president of anything.

Perhaps I made good on that debt. In the 1980s, he reflected with me on Pepperdine's—and ultimately his own—delivery from the purgatory brought on by the Watts riots and, then, his catastrophic 1975 accident. "Bill," he said, "how do I thank you for two second chances?" He believed that. According to two of his children, he privately told his family, more than once, "We have Bill to thank for saving my life."

Without both of us, it is difficult to imagine how Pepperdine might have gone after 1965. There is a very real possibility it might even have ceased to exist. I'm compelled to say that without us, or someone very much like us, there would have been no Malibu miracle. A combination of the two of us is what made the singular and crucial difference for Pepperdine.

"Norvel did not belong in this century," Dr. Jerry Rushford eulogized at Dr. Young's 1998 funeral. "He was, I think, maybe from the sixteenth century. He was a Shakespearean character."[22] It was the sixteenth-century essayist Montaigne, in 1582, who perfectly pictured the providential partnership between Norvel and me: "In the friendship I speak of our souls mingle and blend so completely they efface the seam that joined them. Press me to say why I loved him and I can only answer, because it was he and because it was I. So many coincidences are required for such a friendship that fortune can do it only once in three centuries."[23]

Standing to leave for California in 1958, his hands holding mine, Norvel was near tears. "Bill, I feel a providential connection. I'll send you a letter and put it in writing." We said goodbye and God bless you. I found Gay, across the banquet room, with some stragglers. We walked out into the cold February night, across the Lipscomb campus to our two-room Granny White Pike apartment.

Norvel, his biographers say, returned to Los Angeles telling Helen, "I want this young man! He's a leader!"

"Honey," I kept Gay awake, "I just never met a man like Norvel." But, of course, we had no notion of the three big Pepperdine problems Norvel flew back to face.

1. James Withers, "Fort Worth Student Wins Oratory Prize," *Fort Worth Press*, January 31, 1958. "Bill Banowsky, son of Mr. and Mrs. Wade L. Banowsky, 1421 Robinwood Dr., is winner of the annual Founder's Day Oratorical Contest at David Lipscomb College, Nashville, Tennessee, where he is a senior. He won the annual Gold Medal Award, speaking on 'America's Religion—Faith or Fad?' Banowsky is president of the Lipscomb student body, a varsity baseball player and consistently on the honor roll." The contest was Monday, January 27, 1958. One day earlier the first of our four sons, David Wade Banowsky, was born in Nashville's St. Francis Hospital.

2. Four years earlier, President Morris dispatched his top assistants, Dr. William J. Teague and Dr. Jack A. Scott, to beat Lipscomb's offer of a baseball scholarship. Teague and Scott became my lifelong friends. We served together in the Malibu miracle and they became college presidents. No agency authorized Pepperdine to graduate from college to university status. No rules prescribed it. Norvel and I mustered the nerve to proclaim it in 1971 and audaciously printed a new letterhead announcing it. Others also soon mustered the nerve and printed a letterhead. If not most conventional, among Church of Christ institutions Pepperdine was always in the academic and spiritual vanguard.

3. We married September 7, 1956, at Nashville's Acklin Avenue Church of Christ, Dr. Howard A. White, minister.

4. Richard T. Hughes, *Reviving the Ancient Faith: The Story of Churches of Christ in America* (Grand Rapids, MI: William B. Eerdmans, 1996), 383.

5. They cut costs living with Norvel's parents at 1904 Blakemore where Norvel had grown up after age 12. A short walk from Vanderbilt and Peabody, and a short drive from Lipscomb, the *20th Century Christian* was founded there. Today it headquarters the Academy of Recording Arts and Sciences, which presents the Grammy Awards.

6. M. Norvel Young, *A History of Colleges Established and Controlled by Members of the Churches of Christ* (Nashville: Old Paths Book Club, 1946).

7. Bill Henegar and Jerry Rushford, *Forever Young: The Life and Times of M. Norvel Young and Helen M. Young* (Nashville: 21st Century Christian, 1999), 100. The Youngs also created *20th Century Christian* and *Power for Today*, founded Lubbock Children's Home and launched Lubbock Christian University.

8. *Time*, August 5, 1957, 58.

9. Henegar and Rushford, *Forever Young*, 205–206, 283.

10. Ibid., 336.

11. M. Norvel Young, personal letter to the author, February 14, 1974. The Banowsky Papers.

12. Majoring in Bible, dad feared financially to preach. He went to work, with his degree, in Abilene's Cox Grocery Store for 60 cents an hour. With a TCU master's, he became a top administrator in Fort Worth's public schools, filled the pulpit, taught the big Bible class and, like Matt Norvel Young

Sr., was the strongest elder. I preached the 1970 funeral for Norvel's dad. Norvel preached my mother's 1989 funeral, attended, on a cold February afternoon, by one thousand mourners. At 94, dad's 2005 funeral was at Richland Hills, the world's largest Church of Christ. When Dad left a small estate, I remembered Norvel's epigraph: "Every man I've known ran out of time before he ran out of money."

13. Richard T. Hughes and William B. Adrian, eds., *Models for Christian Higher Education: Strategies for Survival and Success in the Twenty-First Century* (Grand Rapids, MI: William B. Eerdmans, 1997), 425. Supporting Hughes' geographical thesis, Leroy Brownlow of Fort Worth wrote in 1945 that only our church was biblical in name, organization, baptism, music, missionary work and communion, concluding: "All of the lost are non-members of the Church of Christ, and all of the saved are members of the Church of Christ." Leroy Brownlow, *Why I Am a Member of the Church of Christ* (Fort Worth: Leroy Brownlow Publications, 1945), 188. As George Pepperdine established his college in 1937, he published his famous booklet, *More Than Life!* Circulating more than three million copies, it is Brownlow's sectarian twin. "The true church of Christ today is the same in name, faith, worship and doctrine as in the days of the Apostles . . . The church of Christ is not one of the denominations and it does not affiliate with them because it cannot endorse, or even appear to condone, their divisive, unscriptural teachings . . . May all be satisfied to wear only the name of Christ and belong only to the church of Christ." George Pepperdine, *More Than Life!* in Richard L. Clark and Jack W. Bates, *Faith is My Fortune* (Los Angeles: George Pepperdine College Press, 1959), 226–228. George Pepperdine and I were reared in precisely the same way; Norvel was the exception.

14. Norvel arrived in Abilene within months of my parents' marriage in the lobby of Zelnar Hall, the girl's dormitory. Two months before Norvel graduated in 1936 as student body president, I was born in a nearby rented house at 2834 South 3rd Street, a stone's throw from the original Abilene Christian College campus and the Highland Church of Christ that I first attended when only five days old. Norvel liked my windblown plains enough to spend 13 years in Lubbock. I spent four in Nashville.

15. Hughes, *Reviving Faith*, 5. Hughes argues that my Texas sect "stood over against the dominant culture . . . as the exclusive domain of both truth and salvation, from which . . . other religious bodies and the culture at large have departed. Moreover it was bellicose in the prophetic judgments it hurled against the culture and its handmaidens, the popular denominations." Hughes argues that Norvel's Tennessee "denomination made its peace with the dominant culture, abandoned its exclusivist rhetoric, muted its prophetic voice, and came to behave as a well-mannered, compliant member of the larger culture and of the larger Christian community."

16. *Christian Chronicle*, February 2009. 1, 18 and 23.

17. Accompanied by Loretta Young, Bob Hope delivered our first commencement address to the premier Malibu graduates in May 1973. We conferred an honorary doctorate, hoping he would reciprocate with a major gift. At a later Beverly Wilshire black-tie dinner he winked at Norvel, "Don't worry! I've got Pepperdine on my conscience!" Norvel never got any of Bob's money but they looked enough alike to be brothers.

18. Henegar and Rushford, *Forever Young*, 333.

19. Ibid., 203.

20. Jerry Rushford, ed., *Crest of a Golden Wave: Pepperdine University, 1937–1987* (Malibu: Pepperdine University Press, 1987), 179.

21. Thomas G. Bost serves as one of countless examples. Raised in the church, Bost knew of Norvel but first met him accidentally in 1967 on a bus at New York's Kennedy Airport. A third-year Vanderbilt law student, Bost was there for job interviews with several New York firms. But after introducing himself to Norvel, he became the riveted subject of Norvel's California sales pitch. From that providential recruitment meeting, Bost ended up at Latham and Watkins in Los Angeles. He and his wife, Sheila, became one of the most dynamic leadership teams in Pepperdine history. Both served on the board of regents and Tom served as its chairman and as a distinguished professor of law.

22. Henegar and Rushford, *Forever Young*, 338.

23. Donald M. Frame, translator, *The Complete Essays of Montaigne* (Stanford, CA: The Stanford University Press), 136.

"Do you suppose that we could do something in the framework of education without becoming strictly a Christian college?"

GEORGE PEPPERDINE
Founder
George Pepperdine College

"FAITH IS MY FORTUNE"

Mr. George Pepperdine, the founder of the original college in Los Angeles and of the Western Auto Supply Company, was a devout Christian businessman.

CHAPTER 2

THE FACULTY AND CHURCH CONFLICT

Only three months after meeting Norvel Young in Nashville I did, indeed, make it halfway to Pepperdine College. Gay, our little son David and I moved to Albuquerque for my University of New Mexico master's degree and Netherwood Park Church of Christ ministry.

Through the months, Norvel and I got acquainted. His constant calls and correspondence pictured California as a veritable cornucopia. But, occasionally, his guard came down enough to give me a glimpse of a grim reality.

NORVEL'S THREE PROBLEMS

His guard came all the way down when the time came for our second face-to-face meeting. That was on December 1, 1958—ten months after our first meeting in Nashville. Norvel traveled to Albuquerque "to address a leadership dinner for Churches of Christ of Northern New Mexico at the University of New Mexico student union," the *Albuquerque Journal* announced.[1] As master of ceremonies for the occasion, I introduced him and we sat together at the head table.

After the dinner, he went home with Gay and me to spend the night. He kept us awake half the night closing the deal for us to join hands with Helen and him at Pepperdine. We agreed to do so, beginning just a few months away in August 1959. Then, he completely shifted gears. He kept us awake the other half of the night pouring out what he called "my three big Pepperdine problems."

Norvel was renowned for combining a sunny smile with a stiff upper lip. But on this night he lost both. His sales pitch was punctured by expressions of discouragement concerning those three big problems. For months he had needed to talk to someone outside the tense situation. Once he started talking he couldn't stop. It was a catharsis.

Norvel went to Pepperdine, as he so often put it, "to save the college for the church." He arrived to discover that what he thought was the major challenge had tripled. In addition to the problem of church alienation, which he anticipated, he was also confronted with a virulent faculty revolt and a desperately threatening financial crisis.

As essential brief background, a clear understanding of these three historic George Pepperdine College problems is keenly relevant. If Norvel Young had not gone to Pepperdine in 1957 there would have been no Malibu miracle in 1968. His heroic confrontation of these three problems is the indispensable prelude to the Malibu miracle.

The first two of those three big problems, church alienation and faculty revolt, seemed to have developed directly from George Pepperdine's uncertainty about the nature of the college he would create. The third problem, the college's threatening financial crisis, developed primarily as a result of Mr. Pepperdine's catastrophic personal bankruptcy.

CALIFORNIA'S "CORRUPTING INFLUENCE"

Norvel's church and faculty problems were deeply interrelated. Antagonism between some California Churches of Christ and much of the college faculty was an early Pepperdine College personality trait. The church and faculty problems were literally two sides of the same coin. But some people concluded that the whole coin was geographic location. It seemed obvious that the culprit of Pepperdine's doctrinal division was "the slippery slope of California."[2]

"In 1937, I came to Pepperdine and found a college of transplanted Southerners, both faculty and students," complained popular founding faculty member Dr. Wade Ruby.[3] "People in Texas," Norvel's biographers fully agreed, "believed that Pepperdine College had moved far beyond its affiliation with Churches of Christ and no longer had the support of church members in California or across the nation." They pinpointed the cause of apostasy: "It was located in California, a place known for its corrupting influence on faith!" The biographers also accurately tied the church and faculty conflicts tightly together into two sides of the same problem. "Convinced that the board made a major blunder in selecting Norvel Young as president, many faculty members, including the scholarly and popular Dean E. V. Pullias, had resigned in the summer."[4]

While emphasizing "California's corrupting influence on faith," Norvel's biographers could also have pointed to simple church population pressures. Contrasted with Bible Belt states, relatively few Church of Christ members resided in California. In the 1970s, James D. Bales of Harding University clearly proved this demographic reality with surveys. Dr. Bales reported that Texas, with a population of less than 20 million, "had a booming 750,000 Church of Christ members." On the other hand California, with a population of 30 million, "had only a tiny 40,000 Church of Christ members. The small size of the Church of Christ in California," Dr. Bales concluded, "kept the percentage of the students who were members of the Church of Christ low throughout Pepperdine's existence."[5]

Indeed, the first class in 1937 consisted largely of Church of Christ students imported from other Christian colleges. Later, Pepperdine recruited many non-Church of Christ students from Southern California. Therefore, if we apply the geographic theory to explain Pepperdine's church problem, simple demographics may explain as much as California's "corrupting influence on faith." Dr. Bales concluded that it was all a matter of math. The Church of Christ-related Bible Belt schools enrolled more than 90 percent of their students from the church. Pepperdine, Dr. Bales reported, was fortunate to enroll around 20 percent. In a few bad years, the percentage dropped below ten.[6]

"NONINSTITUTIONAL" MR. PEPPERDINE

But, insofar as the college's confusing relationship to the church can be attributed to geography, it may be as much the fault of Kansas as of California. That is because the unwitting creator of confusion was the founder himself. In 1916, when George Pepperdine moved from Kansas to California, he carried with him deep boyhood "noninstitutional" religious doctrines, including anti-Christian college convictions.

"Noninstitutional"? What does that mean? Auburn University historian David Edwin Harrell Jr. defined it: "In the history of the Church of Christ in America 'noninstitutional' designated an attitude of profound respect for local congregational authority. It was an aggressive theological position opposing all extra-congregational institutions such as Christian colleges, orphan's homes and homes for the aged."[7] In 2007, out of approximately 60,000 total congregations of the Church of Christ, about 2,000 of them were "noninstitutional" congregations.[8]

George Pepperdine's anti-Christian-college convictions did not signal secular leanings. Quite the opposite. They came out of his legalistic Bible study. Nevertheless, his ambivalence about how the church should relate to the college bred ecclesiastical ambiguity into Pepperdine's DNA. Ambiguity alienated much of the church and divided most of the faculty. All of that is a piece of Pepperdine College history badly in need of revision. Pepperdine's church alienation and campus division did not come after 20 years of sliding down California's "corrupting" slippery slope. They came to school on the very first day.

A lifelong Church of Christ member, George Pepperdine was born out on the Kansas prairie and reared in a small noninstitutional congregation. "Inevitably," emphasized Professor Harrell, "because of their importance, the colleges operated by members of the Church of Christ became the center of the institutional debate."[9]

George Pepperdine's rural Kansas congregation was at the geographic epicenter of that institutional debate. It prohibited even Sunday school Bible classes, believing Bible study should be conducted in the home instead. Therefore, they were branded by the mainstream churches as "anti-Sunday school." They were also slurred as "Sommerites" because they followed a powerful leader, Daniel Sommer of Indianapolis. "Sommer became a ruthless foe of higher education among Churches of Christ," Richard Hughes wrote, and he "routinely objected to church-related colleges on the same grounds that he objected to missionary societies: both institutions usurped the power of the local church."[10]

Young George Pepperdine admired Sommer and read everything he wrote. Sommer's pugilistic paper, the *American Christian Review*, could be found in every pew of George's little Kansas congregation. He also relished Sommer's famous 1901 and 1908 debates against mainstream church and college leaders J. N. Armstrong and B. F. Rhodes on the proposition: "Can Christians scripturally operate colleges in which the Bible is taught?" Young George Pepperdine early—and profoundly—answered, "No!"[11]

"George's parents," reported Audrey Gardner's scholarly thesis on early Pepperdine history, "rigidly followed the teachings of Daniel Sommer, an arch-conservative anti-Christian college advocate."[12]

All of this created the colossal paradox in Pepperdine's DNA. George Pepperdine was rigidly reared, and devoutly churched, to oppose Christian colleges as evil instruments of Satan. He held as much contempt for church-related colleges as he held for alcohol, dishonesty and adultery. He continued to hold reservations about Christian colleges right up until the last hour when he finally bit the bullet and decided to found one. He envisioned a college with a Christian environment that would assiduously avoid any official church relationship. It was a high tightrope to walk. Ambivalence and ambiguity were inevitable. Indeed, both were bred into the Pepperdine theological DNA.

THE TINER CONTRIBUTION

Pepperdine was a man starting out with deep Biblical conviction opposing Christian colleges and he ended up founding one. When and how did he change his mind?

"The idea of founding a Christian college didn't come with a clap of thunder or a voice speaking through a burning bush," his biographers explained, "but through the vision and enthusiasm of a young man George knew, Hugh M. Tiner."[13]

A Texan, Tiner earned degrees at Abilene Christian College, Stanford University and the University of Southern California. In 1934, at age 26, he was appointed a Los Angeles County high-school supervisor. Serving also as minister of the Sichel Street Church of Christ, Tiner conducted a Sunday radio program, *Take Time to Be Holy*. One of his ardent listeners was George Pepperdine.[14]

About this time, Pepperdine began considering how he might donate large amounts of his fortune and have a greater impact, rather than giving smaller amounts to many charities. "But in 1935, when Dr. Tiner first suggested to George the idea of the establishment of a Christian college," Bill Youngs accurately reports, "George approached it very cautiously," conditioned to view any kind of Christian college with suspicion. Then those incredibly shocking words came out of Mr. Pepperdine's mouth: "Do you suppose we could do something in the framework of education without becoming strictly

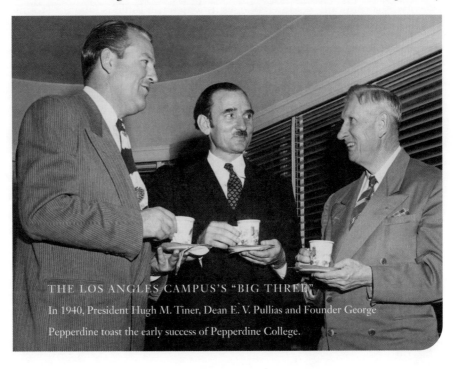

THE LOS ANGELES CAMPUS'S "BIG THREE"

In 1940, President Hugh M. Tiner, Dean E. V. Pullias and Founder George Pepperdine toast the early success of Pepperdine College.

a Christian college?"[15] Pepperdine was not an educator. He was a churchman. For him this was not an academic question about the nature of the college. It was a theological question about the nature of the church. Given his background, it was an inevitable question.

Nonetheless, most people today can't imagine how the founder of Pepperdine University ever said such a thing. But it was no isolated, off-the-cuff comment lifted out of context. He repeated it often over the two years of 1935 and 1936 as he wrestled mightily with whether to found a college. And if so, what kind of college?

Bill Youngs gives Pepperdine's question clear context. "George's reticence about a 'strictly Christian college' came out of his own religious background. As a youth, many members of the Churches of Christ felt that Bible education should be confined to the home and the church and thus they frowned on established 'Bible schools.' George grew up among that persuasion. So instead of envisioning a traditional Christian college, they talked about a college offering 'the best academic training in a Christian environment.'"[16] With all of Pepperdine's ups and downs through all of these years, I am awestruck by how identically the founder's first instincts resembled the ultimate mission statement. Pepperdine University's official 1999 self-definition featured "academic excellence and Christian values."

BIBLE AND CHAPEL DOUBTS

Many fail to appreciate the impact of the founder's doctrinal hesitation on the character of today's institution. Dr. Tiner recalled how serious it seemed at the time. "How close the church can be to the college, and whether we can allow this, but we can't permit that, may seem like pretty fine points to us now. But you have to remember that, at that time, in 1935, Mr. Pepperdine even had doubts about making Bible teaching and chapel a part of the program. He felt that such spiritual activities would bring criticism from some of the brethren."[17]

Therefore, in his ultimately persuasive move, Dr. Tiner called in reinforcement. He arranged for Batsell Baxter, the most experienced Christian educator in the church, to meet with Mr. Pepperdine in Los Angeles. Baxter had already served as president of David Lipscomb College and also of Abilene Christian College, when Tiner was an Abilene undergraduate. "But don't get your hopes up too much," Pepperdine cautioned Tiner when he consented to meet with Baxter.[18]

This historic meeting, in February 1937, convinced Pepperdine to found George Pepperdine College. He and Batsell Baxter, both born in 1886, cherished the church, held many values in common and connected over three brainstorming days of work. Pepperdine not only determined to go forward but also persuaded Baxter to be the George Pepperdine College founding president. Pepperdine and Baxter joyfully anointed Tiner, the elated maestro directing at their side, as the founding dean.

Even such rapid progress did not remove from Mr. Pepperdine's mind all institutional doubt. He now clearly wanted to start a school. But he envisioned what was called "a non-institutional institution like Florida Christian College" established just seven years later to serve non-institutional Churches of Christ until this day.[19] He hesitated to mix the work and worship of the church with the teaching program of the college.

When Pepperdine gave the word to go forward, Baxter probed. "Well," he asked, "just what did you have in mind?" Even up to this last hour at the altar, the decision from the founder continued to be ambiguous about his college's relationship to the church. "That's the whole trouble, Dr. Baxter. I don't know exactly what I want!" He emphasized, "I know one or two things I don't want. I don't want another college that will be dependent upon the churches for support," distinguishing Pepperdine College from all Church of Christ-related Bible Belt colleges then included in church budgets. "I have in mind a four-year liberal arts college where any worthy boy or girl, regardless of religion, can get an education."[20]

If slow deciding to build his college, Pepperdine was breathtakingly fast getting it built. Deciding in February, he opened in September, ambiguity and all. His dizzying pace created a paradigm for the Malibu miracle, which would come 37 years later. In seven months, he acquired 30 acres for $150,000, built four buildings, hired 20 faculty, recruited 167 students from 22 states and dedicated the college on September 21, 1937. From the beginning, Pepperdine College was a dynamic, entrepreneurial enterprise on the fast track. Always facing serious problems and peculiar ambiguities, Pepperdine would never be staid and boring.

NOT CHURCH CONNECTED

At the dedication, California governor Frank Merriam, Los Angeles mayor Frank L. Shaw and President Batsell Baxter spoke. Then the founder gave his famous address, reinforcing the theme of church and college separation. "This college shall be a private enterprise, not connected with any church, and shall not solicit contributions from the churches."[21] Gifts, he added parenthetically, "from individual members of the churches are gratefully accepted." Days later, on November 30, 1937, he repeated this theme in his first chapel speech. "Students entering this school are not required to belong to any church, or to subscribe to any religious doctrine . . . We want this school to operate not as an extension of the church but as an extension of the Christian home."[22]

Within a few months of the college's operation, Mr. Pepperdine grew comfortable with required chapel and Bible classes and outgrew most traces of his anti-Christian-college upbringing. But the damage had been done. Indigenous campus disunity was the price paid for the early seeds of ambiguity already sown. As a result, the founding Pepperdine faculty did not begin with a unified spiritual sense of the way Pepperdine College should relate to the Church of Christ.

In higher education, two kinds of "Christian affiliation" are common. One is denominational—Baylor (Baptist), SMU (Methodist), Notre Dame (Catholic). Some interdenominational colleges, such as Westmont and Wheaton, maintain evangelical ties through mandatory statements of faith and conduct signed by all faculty, staff and students. Neither Mr. Pepperdine nor the founding faculty would have accepted any such creedal requirement. Therefore, only the Church of Christ affiliation assured that the college would remain Christian.

Mr. Pepperdine did not create confusion by what he said, but by what he did not say. Today's revised Pepperdine bylaws stipulate tight restrictions to closely tie the university to the church and to guarantee church control. The president of the university, the chairman of the board, the chairman of the executive committee and a majority of the regents must be Church of Christ members who exercise control over most matters affecting faculty, staff and students.

In contrast, Mr. Pepperdine's original constitution had only one restriction: "Members of the board of trustees shall be members in good standing of the Church of Christ." The college was founded in religious silence. There were no requirements for president, administrators, faculty, students or curriculum. Mr. Pepperdine was chairman of the board of trustees and intended to oversee the religious direction of the school. He did not foresee the need for church requirements beyond his lifetime. However, his silence led to constant questions by those who inherited the leadership of the institution.

This vacuum left the founding faculty free to fight it out among themselves for answers to key questions. Must the president be a church member? Should non-church faculty be hired? If so, how many? Should a mandatory percentage of church students be enrolled? If so, what percentage? How many Bible courses should be required? How many days a week should chapel be required? Meanwhile, the *Los Angeles Times* branded it, "the fundamentalist Church of Christ."[23]

There were sensitive unanswered questions. For instance, no Church of Christ-related college had ever before been racially integrated. Pepperdine enrolled black students but, "due to lack of space," prohibited their dormitory residence until 1943.

BAXTER VERSUS PULLIAS

Dr. Steven Lemley, a close observer of Pepperdine's history, believes the faculty divided along the lines of the differing visions of founding president Batsell Baxter and Dean E. V. Pullias. Church historian Richard T. Hughes elaborated: "George Pepperdine created the ambiguity Batsell Baxter exploited on behalf of an exclusive relationship with the Churches of Christ and which Earl Pullias exploited on behalf of diversity and strong academics."[24]

Earl V. Pullias came in the school's first year, with academic credentials a cut above most. A PhD in psychology from Duke University, he fulfilled post-graduate medical internships at the University of London and Oxford University Institute of Medical Psychology. "Always, there existed a mysterious energy I call 'the Pepperdine spirit,'" Archivist James Smythe testified. "Dean Pullias was the quintessential embodiment of 'the Pepperdine Spirit' of modesty, service and faith. He lived in a little house. He drove an old car. He gave his money to the poor."[25]

In 1938, Norvel Young joined the Baxter camp against the Pullias camp. He campaigned for his close friend, J. P. Sanders, to be appointed religion department chair. "I believed that Pepperdine College at that point," Norvel emphasized, "was in danger of leaving its connections with the church, and the school was under some criticism at that time. I thought J. P. would lend a lot of credibility." Deploring church criticism, "Norvel's most important consideration," said his biographers, "was always the way in which he would be perceived by his church brotherhood."[26]

After 18 months, an embattled Baxter abruptly resigned and instantly left California in the middle of his third semester. The official record says, "He was pressed into resigning." But it doesn't say who pressed him. The Baxter camp blamed the Pullias camp. The Pullias camp pointed to Baxter's personal behavior. Whatever the real story, it was an acrimonious passage.

With Baxter out, Chairman Pepperdine instantly appointed Hugh Tiner president. Together, they empowered Dean Pullias. When Pullias came to power, Norvel and Helen left. They had "already decided never to return. Norvel had become disenchanted with the school's direction and didn't want to go back as a professor. He and his whole family were sad about the treatment of President Baxter . . . They were now afraid that Pepperdine would lose all connections with the church and become a secular college."[27]

PRESIDENT YOUNG AND
FOUNDER PEPPERDINE
The two key leaders celebrate Young's first
1959 graduation ceremony as president.

This administrative and faculty wrangling came in the first two years of the college's existence. It is impossible to know what was in the minds of the divided faculty. Some may have been confused about Mr. Pepperdine's vision for his college. Others may have exploited the founder's ambiguity to promote their own particular vision. Regardless, the absence of a clearly stated mission statement from the founder set the stage for controversy and President Young's agonizing problems faced in the late 1950s.

After President Baxter's departure, President Tiner presided for the next 18 years, the longest tenure of all seven presidents to date. But, during all of the Tiner years, Dr. Pullias ran the college from the inside. "Next to Mr. Pepperdine," concluded historian Howard White, "Hugh Tiner had done the most to start Pepperdine."[28]

CHURCH AND FACULTY WHIPSAW

Norvel and Helen returned to Pepperdine in 1957 because they sought "to save the college for the church." What they got upon arrival was simmering hostility between some California congregations and some Pepperdine faculty branded by the brethren as "liberals." Caught in a continuous whipsaw, whatever the Youngs did to cultivate the church was resented by some faculty. Whatever they did to placate faculty was resented by some congregations. Damned if they did and damned if they didn't, the Youngs were caught in an all-encompassing vise of the faculty versus the church.

During year one the Youngs regained church confidence, only to pay dearly for it in year two with intense faculty reaction. Many faculty resigned with the Youngs' August 1957 arrival. On April 16, 1958, Los Angeles newspapers headlined: "Mass Exodus of Pepperdine Faculty." In one stealthily orchestrated blow, designed to cripple the college, 15 of the 60 full-time Pepperdine professors quit at one time in mid-semester. Blaming Norvel's church outreach, they confessed "fear that nonsectarian Pepperdine will now come under complete Church of Christ control."[29]

The wily faculty strategically abandoned their posts at the end of the term. That gave President Young and the new dean, J. P. Sanders, only the three summer months to replace one-fourth of the faculty. Before Norvel's first two tumultuous years were finished, one-half of the Pepperdine faculty had resigned, including eight department heads.

FADING BLUE BUILDINGS

In March 1959, three months after Norvel visited us in Albuquerque, Gay and I visited him and Helen in Los Angeles. We were awed to see Pepperdine and California for the first time. We attended the annual Pepperdine Bible

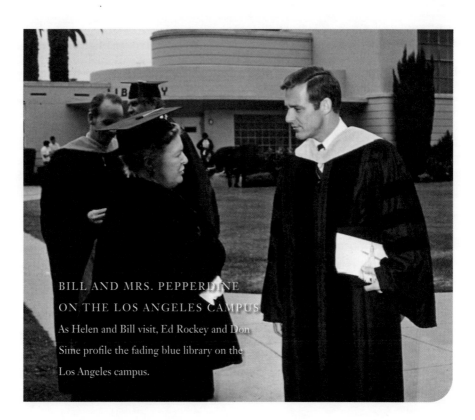

BILL AND MRS. PEPPERDINE
ON THE LOS ANGELES CAMPUS
As Helen and Bill visit, Ed Rockey and Don
Sime profile the fading blue library on the
Los Angeles campus.

Lectures, inspected the college and concluded arrangements for a preaching job when we moved in August. Taking little David with us, we stayed with dearest friends Betty and Walter Glass. Malibu miracle pioneers, they came from Lipscomb with Norvel's original church crusade and gave 50 years to Pepperdine, personifying faculty families about whom a whole book should be written.[30]

Norvel was ready for us. He showed off my future office next to his at the top of a remodeled grocery store building on Vermont Avenue that everyone called the "Tower of Power." After booking me for a USC graduate-school appointment, he orchestrated a meeting with the five elders of the nearby South Gate Church. After the evening lecture one night, we circled up with the elders in folding chairs behind the stage curtain in the college auditorium and cut the deal, then and there. Without hearing me preach, they hired me on Norvel's word. Without seeing South Gate, we agreed to move into their parsonage in August for a salary of $107 per week.

Gay and I loved the charm of 1950s Pepperdine. A tiny oasis in the flat, congested megalopolis, its architecture was not Ivy League but boasted a Southern California beauty all its own. Its half dozen low-lying two-story buildings hugged 30 palm-tree-appointed acres. Its 1930s modern art deco architecture featured streamlined glass, curving corners and stucco façade. Every inch of every stucco building was painted Mr. Pepperdine's favorite blue, the specialized color carried in local stores as "Pepperdine Blue." The buildings unfolded into a stunning landscape when freshly painted but faded fast in California sun.

These fading blue buildings symbolized Pepperdine's fading hopes. Gay and I were impressed with the school but pessimistic about its future. Even as we agreed to join Norvel and Helen in August 1959, we already planned to get the doctorate as quickly as possible and return to some Texas pulpit.

Gay and I began our first Pepperdine year; Norvel and Helen began their third. They were already prevailing on two of their three big problems. They were victorious with the church. They were also strengthened with faculty and staff after replacing the resignations with strong faculty and staff from the church. But so little progress had been made on the financial crisis that the school's future still seemed at stake. "Norvel," his biographers reveal, "admitted he was 'reckless' to have taken the job." He confided to me. "Bill, if I'd known how bad things were financially I'd have never come."[31]

But how could a man like Norvel, who could read a balance sheet like the morning paper, not have known that the school was on the brink of bankruptcy?

THREE PEPPERDINE FIRST LADIES

Gay Banowsky, Maxine White and Helen Young in 1959 on the lawn of the president's home on the Los Angeles campus.

1. *Albuquerque Journal*, December 1, 1958. "Dr. William Mattox, president of Lubbock Christian College, will introduce the speaker . . . Church leaders are expected from Santa Fe, Gallup, Raton and Socorro . . . Dr. Teague, vice president of Pepperdine, will be honored."

2. David Lamb, *Down the Slippery Slope* (London: Croom Helm Ltd, 1988), vii. "The 'slippery slope' argument can be found in all areas of policy-making and is sometimes called 'the domino theory,' 'the floodgates,' 'the tip of the iceberg,' or 'the camel's nose in the tent.' All these metaphors suggest a series of gradual steps from an acceptable to an unacceptable position, where it is difficult to determine the exact point at which the crucial transition is made."

3. Audrey Gardner, "A Brief History of Pepperdine College" (master's thesis, Pepperdine College, 1968), 36.

4. Bill Henegar and Jerry Rushford, *Forever Young: The Life and Times of M. Norvel Young and Helen M. Young* (Nashville: 21st Century Christian, 1999), 138–139, 147. Years later, Charles B. Runnels moved from Houston, Texas, to Pepperdine with the same apprehensions about California's corrupting influence. "The elders at our Houston congregation were afraid for us because they had heard all of the unpleasant stories about Los Angeles." Ibid., 191.

5. James D. Bales, "An Evaluation of Pepperdine University," *Firm Foundation*, October 17, 1978, 6. Because of California, Pepperdine was the first, and only, Church of Christ-related college to integrate. From its 1937 founding Pepperdine allowed African Americans and other racial minorities to enroll but "only Caucasians could live in the dormitories and engage in social clubs because of limited space."

6. Ibid., 14.

7. David Edwin Harrell Jr., *The Churches of Christ in the Twentieth Century: Homer Hailey's Personal Journey of Faith* (Tuscaloosa: University of Alabama Press, 2000), 85.

8. Bobby Ross Jr., "Who Are We?" *Christian Chronicle*, March 2007, 17.

9. Harrell, *Journey of Faith*, 75–76.

10. Richard T. Hughes, *Reviving the Ancient Faith: The Story of Churches of Christ in America* (Grand Rapids, MI: William B. Eerdmans, 1996), 229.

11. James Stephen Wolfgang, "Daniel Sommer (1850–1940)," in *The Encyclopedia of the Stone-Campbell Movement,* ed. Douglas A. Foster and others (Grand Rapids, MI: William B. Eerdmans, 2004), 692–694. Sommer's journal was later renamed the *Octographic Review*, after the eight authors of the New Testament, and finally named the *Apostolic Review*.

12. Gardner, "A Brief History," 1.

13. Richard L. Clark and Jack W. Bates, *Faith is My Fortune* (Los Angeles: George Pepperdine College Press, 1959), 174.

14. Before television, *Take Time to Be Holy* was a half-hour radio program featuring announcements of church activities in Southern California, a capella congregational hymns and a brief Bible message. Pepperdine's Dr. James Smythe preached on it monthly during the five years he was a minister of the Southwest Church of Christ where Mr. Pepperdine was an elder. James Smythe, personal interview with the author, August 5, 2005. The Banowsky Papers.

15. Bill Youngs, *Faith Was His Fortune: The Life Story of George Pepperdine* (Malibu: Pepperdine University Press, 1976), 198.

16. Ibid.

17. Ibid., 199.

18. Clark and Bates, *Fortune*, 176. Also see James L. Lovell, personal letter to G. E. Brewer, March 23, 1937. The Lovell Papers. "George's convictions about the work of the church can scripturally undertake our broadening and his going to build a college."

19. Bobby Ross Jr., "A Non-Institutional Institution," *Christian Chronicle*, April 2008, 3, 17. In 2008, there were 9,801 "Mainstream" Churches of Christ, 1,974 "Non-Institutional," 554 "One Cup," 510 "Non-Sunday School," and 124 "Mutual edification."

20. Clark and Bates, *Fortune*, 176.

21. Ibid., 184.

22. Ibid., 186.

23. William Trombley, "Pepperdine Torn by Internal Dissent," *Los Angeles Times*, Part II, Sunday, April 18, 1976.

24. Richard T. Hughes and William B. Adrian, eds., *Models for Christian Higher Education: Strategies for Survival and Success in the Twenty-First Century* (Grand Rapids, MI: William B. Eerdmans, 1997), 419.

25. James Smythe, personal interview with the author, January 23, 2003. The Banowsky Papers. "The very cruel dismantling of the original Pepperdine obviously made me resentful," wrote former Dean Pullias in 1987. "But I'm over that now, and deeply proud of Pepperdine." Earl V. Pullias, personal letter to Patsie Trowbridge, February 15, 1987. The Pullias Papers.
26. Henegar and Rushford, *Forever Young*, 89, 93.
27. Ibid., 93.
28. Jerry Rushford, ed., *Crest of a Golden Wave: Pepperdine University, 1937–1987* (Malibu: Pepperdine University Press, 1987), 72.
29. Henegar and Rushford, *Forever Young*, 147.
30. We were the first Pepperdine family, in March 1968, to buy a Malibu residence. The Glasses were second in 1969. For three years during campus construction, Walter Glass raised and lowered the 20- by 30-foot American flag up and down the 65-foot pole. Betty Glass endlessly sewed its frayed edges, calling herself the "Betsy Ross of Pepperdine."
31. Henegar and Rushford, *Forever Young*, 139.

"Some were convinced the dream known as
George Pepperdine College was over.
The picture was grim.
Only a few knew just how grim."

HENEGAR AND RUSHFORD
Biographers
Pepperdine University

"THE SEAVER LEARNING CENTER" LOS ANGELES
Shown here between Helen Pepperdine and President Banowsky,
one of Mrs. Seaver's earliest big gifts was not to Malibu but to the
Los Angeles campus in 1969 to build "the Seaver Learning Center."
Everyone seemed determined to continue forever in Los Angeles.

CHAPTER 3

THE IMPENDING FINANCIAL FAILURE

In August 1959, "Dr. Banowsky accepted the newly-created position of Assistant to the President, an extension of the Pepperdine President's office," reported the *Fort Worth Star-Telegram*. "Dr. Banowsky's duties will include coordination of plans for the college's Silver Anniversary, direction of the Spring Bible Lectures, conduct of monthly church fellowship dinners and service as a member of the Religion faculty."[1]

We found Norvel and Helen almost exhausted after bearing 24 months with church, faculty and financial burdens. "Norvel and Helen had to endure the deep valleys of discouragement," reported their biographers.[2] As they gained on the first two problems, they struggled under the unexpected magnitude of the third. They felt themselves to be shockingly alone in the saving of Pepperdine financially.

The college owed all to Mr. Pepperdine. But in a fateful twist of fate his financial failure caused the financial crisis. His 1951 bankruptcy put Norvel and Helen in a purgatory that set the stage for the Malibu miracle.

HELEN WEPT, NORVEL GNASHED

Before describing the miraculous days we must understand the dire circumstances. In the late 1950s, Pepperdine College faced imminent bankruptcy. The Youngs' biographers twice chose the word "grim" to describe the crisis. Helen said, "When we returned to Pepperdine I shed more tears in two years than in the rest of my life."[3]

Helen, remembering "occasions when she simply sat down and wept," summarized in one paragraph the three problems: "We . . . felt very unloved for the first time in our lives. I would sit in the Vermont Avenue Church and cry every Sunday because I felt many of the faculty resented our coming. But that was just part of it. We had to take that, and we still had to get out and raise money. The most disappointing thing to Norvel was that, though the churches were wonderful to welcome us, they really didn't have the means to support the school."[4]

Helen's tears were especially for Norvel. She had never before seen him depressed. "All of Norvel's life," she said, "Wherever he went he always whistled. But when we returned to Pepperdine he simply stopped."[5] One thing daughter Emily missed was her father's Lubbock piano playing. "Daddy even had time to play the piano," she said. "I remember that he would play a march, and the kids would march all around the house."[6] Sadly, the president's home on the Los Angeles campus of Pepperdine displayed a grand piano that Norvel never played.

Norvel tended to grind his teeth. The dentist diagnosed it as bruxism and devised a night guard, advising Norvel to also wear it during daytime stress like bumper-to-bumper freeway traffic. Gay noticed Norvel's worry stone, a small gem with a thumb-sized indentation that he rubbed between his index finger and thumb. "In those crazy California 1960s," Gay recalled, "worry stones were the rage." Loving endless literary turns of phrase, Norvel cited *The Pilgrim's Progress*. "I've entered the Slough of Despond," he sighed.

NORVEL'S UNBALANCED BUDGET

After a full year of backbreaking begging, Norvel and Helen were still losing the money battle. The board had fired President Tiner because of seven unbalanced budgets and had hired Norvel to balance that runaway budget. Friend and foe alike just assumed he would. But when the fiscal year ending August 31, 1958, was audited, it reported a big $30,000 deficit. When friend and foe realized the highly praised and publicized new president had made it eight straight deficits, his school hit rock bottom.

Norvel's own spirit smoldered down to the "embers of hope," reported his biographers. "There were others who were convinced that the dream known as George Pepperdine College was over. That was especially true after Norvel's first year when it was found that the school was still in the red. Board of trustees members George Evans and Bob Jones both were convinced the cause was lost. After all, the college could no longer borrow money and Mr. Pepperdine had a number of notes floating around . . . The school had to pay cash for every single purchase . . . Even Norvel Young thought they might have to pare back and become a small Bible college."[7]

But the indomitable Norvel quickly recovered. How? By analyzing the defeat and recognizing two resolvable reasons for his budget deficit.

First, he had squandered the year running around California trying to raise money from churches. "He would spend the weekends as a traveling salesman, on the road to places like Bakersfield and Riverside, Fresno and Redlands," reported Patricia Yomantas. "While Norvel slept, Helen would drive to the next destination."[8]

Norvel repented of his naïve barnstorming and hat-passing at small churches and made the most strategic fundraising move in Pepperdine history. He drove five miles to downtown Los Angeles every day to cultivate and solicit, one-on-one, his growing circle of conservative business friends. "Our relationship with the business community has been a great factor in our success," Norvel understatedly rejoiced in 1971.[9] Pepperdine's unparalleled business relationship balanced all future operating budgets and fully financed the Malibu miracle.

NO FUNDRAISING HISTORY

In addition to misplaced energies, there was an even bigger reason for Norvel's unbalanced budget. He had inherited a 1957 unfunded deficit of $200,000 from his predecessor. He had to pay that off, with interest, before addressing his own first budget.

Norvel's 1957 unfunded deficit nakedly exposed the most bizarre perpetual Pepperdine failure of them all. Since tuition and fees never cover operating expenses of an institution of higher education, the budget must be balanced by fundraising. For its first two decades Pepperdine College conducted virtually no fundraising and raised virtually no money. There was no development office, no alumni or business solicitation and no organized fundraising of any kind whatsoever. Not a single dollar was ever raised during President Baxter's brief 18-month tenure. No more than $25,000 was raised during the biggest and best year of President Tiner's 18-year tenure. "President Tiner was a wonderful man and great in public relations," reported faculty member and later dean Olaf F. Tegner. "But he just couldn't seem to raise money."[10] Alumnus Walter King added, "Hugh could not ask people directly for money."[11] Tegner and King were, perhaps, Tiner's two best friends. While Tiner did not have the fundraising gift, he made friends for a Pepperdine future in which hundreds of millions would be raised. Why wasn't he inclined to just ask them for himself?

NO BALANCED BUDGETS

He didn't have to ask them because Pepperdine College had devised a highly unconventional accounting expedient. It instantly transformed actual unbalanced budgets into audited balanced budgets. How did that work?

In hard fiscal reality, from 1937 to 1957 the college accumulated not seven but twenty actual unbalanced budgets. As mentioned above, colleges are not simply nonprofit institutions, they are profit-*losing* ventures! With normal operating expenses—and without any fundraising—the college never actually balanced its budget conventionally. It always ran operating deficits. The deficits were always covered by extraordinary year-end emergency subsidies from Mr. Pepperdine or his foundation.

For the first 13 years, Mr. Pepperdine wrote personal or foundation checks to pay for all operating deficits. In effect, this was like "retroactive fundraising"—instead of raising the funds necessary to balance accounts as the college went along, Mr. Pepperdine simply settled accounts by giving one gift at the end of the fiscal year.

Before taking on the presidency, Dr. Tiner unwittingly tipped his hand about his financial plans: "I wouldn't touch it unless Mr. Pepperdine puts at least one million dollars into an endowment for the college."[12] Tiner told me that he and Mr. Pepperdine took money out of the foundation at the end of every fiscal year to cover all of the deficits.

But in 1951 Mr. Pepperdine went bankrupt. George Pepperdine, as he told Norvel Young in 1957, was no longer able to make any gifts to balance the budget. "The administrators had used endowment money to make ends meet, but obviously that was a dead-end strategy."[13] Suddenly, he could no longer perform his year-end rescue. "What will we do without George?" asked the panicked administration and board. They answered with a technically legal, but fiducially reprehensible, set of actions. Though perhaps not fully conscious of what was going on and the long-term consequences, for the next six years they committed the unforgivable sin of fiduciary trust. They balanced all of the operating budgets by robbing the permanent endowment fund until it was utterly gone.

PEPPERDINE'S DEEPEST SECRET

We don't know what the trustees were thinking. Perhaps they reasoned Mr. Pepperdine had given the endowment and, now that he was unable to give his usual year-end gift, they could balance the budget by using the endowment he had given. But in reality, they hocked the family jewels to pay for lunch. Surely the board knew the endowment money would eventually run out. Yet amazingly, for a half dozen years only weak and insipid attempts were made to raise any money.

For each fiscal year, from 1951 through 1956, the college "borrowed" an annual average of $170,000 from the endowment to cover the deficit. These endowment invasions entered the books as "gifts." Therefore, the budgets all technically balanced.

But for fiscal year 1957, with no fundraising and the endowment stripped to zero, the beleaguered trustees were finally forced to declare a $200,000 unfunded deficit. They mortgaged college property, borrowed from the bank, fired President Tiner and hired President Young. But this was too little, too late. By the time Norvel paid back the bank, with interest, he had no hope of balancing his own 1957–58 budget.

George Pepperdine supplemented the operational budget for 13 years, just as he had planned from the founding of the college. He never wanted to burden the churches or others with the cost of running his school. There was no reason to make public the means of year-end budget-balancing. But with his bankruptcy, everything changed. Mr. Pepperdine resigned as board chairman. The following six years of financial management were kept completely private by the president and, presumably, the board. In these latter years, especially, "the prolonged financial crisis was Pepperdine's best kept secret. The trustees apparently looked the other way to hide it even from themselves," said Archivist James Smythe.[14]

Dr. Young, definitely, was totally unaware. He thought he was coming "to save the college for the church," and he was utterly ambushed by the life-threatening financial crisis. But God works in mysterious ways. Only because Norvel and Helen, somewhat blindly, went to Pepperdine in 1957 did the Malibu miracle emerge in 1968. More than once in this story, part of the miraculous mix was a touch of ignorance and a dash of recklessness.

But the key question remains: how could such gross financial ignorance have been possible? How could men like banker Don Miller and CPA Bob Jones, men of highest intelligence and integrity, not have known? How could a fully accredited, annually audited college operate with seven years of budget deficits—desperately balanced only by the consumption of its own seed corn—without everyone on the board, at the banks and in the media knowing all about it?

FOUNDER'S SYNDROME

How did this deadly fiscal crisis arise? Why was there no serious attempt to seek resources from a carefully crafted donor base? Norvel and I retained John Andrew Bolinger as a consultant in 1968. Bolinger was a national authority on fundraising and diagnosed the school's first two decades as having been infected by "founder's syndrome." He pointed out how those crucial years actually put the institution in grave condition by what he called "one-man financial rule."[15]

Founding president Batsell Baxter, previously president of two financially challenged colleges, was thrilled by Mr. Pepperdine's generosity. He "expressed a pleasant surprise concerning two features of George Pepperdine College: . . . it was the only college with which he ever had experience where the founder had money enough to build and operate it without asking anyone for help."[16] Donald V. Miller, who followed Mr. Pepperdine as chair of the board of trustees, confirmed this impression: "He [Pepperdine] intended always to be the sole source of funds for the college," Miller said.[17] It is unlikely that Baxter or Miller suspected that this "feature" might ultimately lead the institution to near ruin.

Bolinger theorized that the worst thing about founder's syndrome was its neutering effect on governing boards. One-man financial rule, he said, erodes a board's sense of fiduciary responsibility and tends to make them mere advisors. "At Pepperdine," Bolinger said, "you are still fighting the effects of those days when it came to money and everyone just said, 'Let George do it!'"[18]

Bolinger's diagnosis squares with the testimony of trustees. "Early on we were mostly rubber stamps when it came to the money," Bob Jones painfully admitted. "George and Hugh, with the help of a one-man accounting firm, ran the finances by themselves. They reported few financial details to the rest of us, except to say that the annual budget was balanced. I didn't worry about it. It was that way before I came on board and I just accepted it."[19]

In replacing Mr. Pepperdine as chairman Mr. Miller later confessed: "After serving passively under George for many years I was too slow to take ownership. Even after George went down, President Tiner and his auditor continued to handle finances by themselves until the big 1957 operating deficit."[20] The board's passivity came from founder's syndrome but, even after the downfall of the founder, the board continued to devour the small college endowment until it was gone.

"The faculty knew absolutely nothing about the college's finances," added Archivist Smythe. "Fearing that the college would become a glorified Sunday school, the faculty fought Norvel on church issues. If the faculty had known what a financial fight Norvel was waging for their survival they would have given him more support."[21]

MR. PEPPERDINE WITH THE FIRST FOUR 1938 GRADUATES

Students Malcom Hinckley, Carmen Landrum, Paul Tucker and Richard Gibson transferred to
Pepperdine College as seniors. Here they're seen standing with Mr. Pepperdine on graduation day.

THE BOARD OF TRUSTEES

Mr. Pepperdine, no control freak, was by nature non-authoritarian except on those few religious matters that seemed to come directly from God. He never micromanaged the college, stayed out of campus controversy and deferred academic issues to others.

Even on money he never worried about how his administrators spent it. He worried only about where they got it. Lingering religious noninstitutionalism left him wanting to give all of it himself. Instinctive naïveté made him think he could. On the day of its dedication he proclaimed, "I am endowing this institution,"[22] a naïvely presumptuous claim. "George was a sweet and gentle man, but naïve and credulous," chairman Miller added. "He believed God guided him financially."

Mr. Pepperdine operated his board like the steady eldership of a congregation, meeting monthly, often in his own living room, without much paperwork beyond his own handwritten notes. He believed five to be a good board size. Tellingly, his first appointee was then dean Tiner. Few knew why he would bypass President Baxter altogether to empower the school's second man. But Dean Tiner wielded enormous power and, together with the chairman, controlled the finances. The other three trustees were Clarence Shattuck, A. J. Drumm and Donald V. Miller, who became one of Pepperdine's great leaders. Chairman Pepperdine soon appointed as sixth trustee his wife, Helen, perhaps an inappropriate arrangement in education today.

With no standing committees, the board operated as a committee of the whole on all matters except finance. Chairman Pepperdine and President Tiner comprised the finance committee, convened confidentially and communicated little information beyond the perennially balanced annual budget. The college issued no annual financial report and, through years of conditioning, the trustees never worried about the college's financial health. When the founder went bankrupt President Tiner, aided by his auditor, quietly continued to run the finances privately. At year's end he calculated the needed cash to balance the budget and drew it out of the endowment. Although less at first, then $100,000 a year, this was the beginning of the tailspin. Suddenly in 1957, the whole endowment was gone and the operating deficit exploded right in the faces of the board. How else could chairman and Pasadena banker Don Miller say with a straight face: "The tragedy of the whole issue was that neither the board, Norvel nor [dean] J. P. [Sanders] was aware of the crucial financial state the school was actually in."[23]

WESTERN AUTO SUPPLY COMPANY

How did George Pepperdine acquire his fortune and how did he lose it? At the turn of the twentieth century he and his first wife, Lena Rose Baker Pepperdine, founded one of America's earliest commercial store chains to serve the emerging automobile industry. In March 1909, they launched from their rented Kansas City home a mail order automobile parts catalog business. This home-based business eventually developed into the Western Auto Supply Company, with 374 stores nationwide. In 1916, the Pepperdines moved their headquarters from Kansas to Los Angeles.

Lena Baker Pepperdine, with a keen business mind, was the company's vice president and treasurer. Her three Baker brothers—Hal, Ernest and Herbert—worked right alongside her and George in building the business. The Baker contribution to the Western Auto success cannot be overstated. When Lena died suddenly in 1929 of a rare infection, George's friends worried about how he would manage without her.

BUSINESS TO PHILANTHROPY

Thanks to the Bakers, Mr. Pepperdine's fortune was fully formed. His life without Lena took a sharp turn. Deeply religious, he counted his blessings and decided to give back to the Lord and to society much of what he had received. His business interests waned as his attention turned toward charity. He turned away from the making of money toward giving it away.

"I felt a calling," Mr. Pepperdine testified, "to a ministry not of sermons, but of money." From 1930 to 1936, his charitable instincts were quickened by the Great Depression "when so many people were in desperate need."[24] His biographer said that he became "obsessed with how to go about giving away [his] money."[25]

This was the gilded age of philanthropy. Carnegie, Mellon and Vanderbilt were celebrated for giving money away. Watching their foundations at work, George felt the need for his own philanthropic vehicle. He created in 1931 the George Pepperdine Foundation, a generous gesture that turned out to be his life's greatest mistake. Twenty years later, in 1951, it was the foundation's financial failure that forced him into catastrophic personal bankruptcy. "George made the mistake so many men in business make," analyzed Dr. Tiner. "Having made a fortune in one field, he believed he could do it in another. One in which he had no experience."

As his business interests ebbed, a new romantic interest arose to complement his charitable career. In 1932 he met Helen Louise Davis at the Arlington Christian Church. He courted her in the Protestant Welfare Association and they married in 1934. Together, they dived into dozens of community causes. With her "keen interest in welfare work . . . natural inclination toward benevolence and . . . concern for the unfortunate . . . Helen became an integral part of his giving ways."[26] The first Mrs. Pepperdine had partnered in his business career. The second Mrs. Pepperdine partnered in his philanthropy.

In early marriage, George and Helen made two monumental money decisions. Number one: their 1937 decision to found George Pepperdine College assures the fame of their name for centuries to come. Altogether, over the ten years from 1937 to 1947, they gave Pepperdine College a total of $3 million, not an extraordinary amount today but a considerable figure coming out of the Great Depression. Number two: their 1939 decision to sell Western Auto for another $3 million—and to put all of it into their foundation rather than into their college endowment—led to financial disaster.

DEBT AND CONFLICTS OF INTEREST

"The story of George's financial difficulties centered in the Pepperdine Foundation and its operation," recorded Clark and Bates. "Within the period of less than a decade during the late 1940s and early 1950s George was to see the funds of the foundation, and his own personal fortune as well, disappear in a vortex of financial disaster. Only the College remained free and clear, and creditors of the Foundation attempted, unsuccessfully, to attach the college assets. This period of merciless trial was a supreme test of his unconquerable faith. The years of legal battles were very trying . . . and involved the irretrievable loss of money."[27]

The foundation did not go wrong from the gifts it made. Aside from massive gifts to Pepperdine, the other gifts were small and few, to charities and churches. The foundation's first five years were hobbled by the Great Depression. Then came the demanding capital needs of the college. The foundation's failure came not from giving its money away, but from its desperate attempt to make more.

Mr. Pepperdine's total lifetime fortune came to about $7 million. Over time, he gave $3 million directly to his college. He placed another $4 million in his foundation. It was overseen by trustees not directly involved in the college management. Delegating his foundation resources to others, he expanded his involvement in community causes on whose boards he served. His charity work became nearly a full-time occupation. He placed his faith in the directors of his foundation, who turned out to be incompetent and unscrupulous.

In the early 1940s, under the economic stimulus of World War II, "industries began to boom and the opportunities to invest in various enterprises were most alluring . . . Eventually the Foundation held investment in more than twenty firms." The climate proved to be irresistibly tempting as "the executives of the Foundation, in some instances, served as officers or board members of the various firms" in which they were investing.[28] "They were guilty of grave conflicts of interest by putting foundation money into businesses of which they were owners, officers or directors."[29]

THE PEPPERDINE BANKRUPTCY

"George focused on community work and completely entrusted his major assets to the foundation managers," Dr. Bill Stivers, a lifetime Pepperdine servant, testified. "They plunged into risky start-up companies—all with George's permission, mind you—like oil wells, mines and exploratory chemicals. By this time, Mr. Pepperdine was not hoping for more personal wealth; he was giving money away. He believed successful foundation investments would insure the college's future. The foundation managers convinced George to get in on the ground floor of many highly risky ventures for great profits. They got only great expenses. They threw good money after bad. They crashed in ruinous failure."[30]

"When additional capital could not be supplied, great losses occurred," added biographer Youngs. "The foundation, with George's endorsement, borrowed large sums . . . and found themselves unable to pay the banks."[31] Unpaid interest came due. Loans were called. Banks foreclosed. Unpaid creditors dissolved George Pepperdine Foundation. In February 1951, Mr. Pepperdine declared bankruptcy and resigned as chairman of the board.

THE AFTERMATH

For years its only solution, Mr. Pepperdine now became the college's biggest problem. The media went wild. "He created a small, tacky campus in Southwest Los Angeles, dotted with palm trees and a thousand or so students, financially stable but largely uninspired intellectually, esthetically or athletically," *Sports Illustrated* wildly exaggerated.[32] But this was the age when any behavior that demanded bankruptcy was scandalous. Mr. Pepperdine's suffering splashed across Los Angeles newspapers. Prolonged publicity tied his school's name to allegations of fraud. Protracted litigation was humiliating and expensive.

Six years later, Norvel arrived on an unfinished campus. Mr. Pepperdine's final capital gift came in 1945 for the business administration building. With only half of his master plan in place, all construction was canceled for science, engineering, a student union, administration and a football stadium. The stadium was no longer needed since, in a bitterly divisive 1961 decision for which some still have not forgiven us, Norvel and I abolished football. Norvel's biographers note: "After all, the college could no longer borrow money, and Mr. Pepperdine had a number of notes floating around . . . The school had to pay cash for every single purchase."[33]

For years after the debacle, "George suffered many indignities, insults and rough treatment in going through the ordeal of dissolution of the Foundation, defending numerous law suits brought by creditors whom he would like to have paid," recorded his biographers. "It was painful and distressing to George, not only to owe people funds which he could not pay, but to realize that the assets which he placed in the Foundation, for the purpose of building a large endowment for the college, had been swept away."[34]

NAÏVE AND CREDULOUS

Mr. Pepperdine, an American original, mastered the automobile parts business but at midlife cashed out and plunged into capital management. He chose hard words to compare his own suffering to Job, acknowledging that "the Lord did not actually take away my wealth, but He allowed me to be naïve and credulous enough to fall for some very unwise and speculative investments . . . Often a man will make an outstanding success in one business, then fail miserably in other endeavors where he lacks experience."[35]

This is the chastened, charismatic man Gay and I got to know. Our first four Los Angeles years coincided with his final four. He appreciated my church leadership on the annual Bible Lectures and monthly fellowship dinners in the gymnasium. He and Helen drove over one Sunday for my South Gate sermon and lunch with Gay and me.

"A BEAUTIFUL SUNSET"

For his final and I think finest address, the 1957 graduating class invited Mr. Pepperdine to speak at their commencement: "During the last 20 years we have had both successes and failures, joys and sorrows, trials and errors . . . I made millions in business, but I also lost part of those millions through unwise investments . . . I will not allow the sorrow of the losses to prevent me from enjoying the good that is being done . . . God has been good to me in spite of my mistakes and shortcomings, my faults and failures. I . . . blame myself rather than other people for my disappointments and troubles . . . I cannot wish you life without sorrow or trouble, for they are a part of human existence. We must expect . . . rain with the sunshine; pain with the comfort; sorrow with the happiness . . . I cannot wish you a life without clouds, but may there be only enough clouds in your life to make a beautiful sunset."[36]

Sunset for Mr. Pepperdine came on July 31, 1962. As Norvel's assistant, I helped Helen Pepperdine with arrangements for the memorial service, held in the college's packed auditorium. Four months earlier I had directed the historic Los Angeles Sports Arena Lectureship meeting where Mr. Pepperdine made his final appearance before an assembly of 12,000.

After Mr. Pepperdine's passing, I completed my PhD work. At about the same time, Norvel most reluctantly informed me of an opening in the pulpit of the 2,000-member Broadway Church of Christ in Lubbock, Texas. Norvel and Helen had served Broadway for 14 years before accepting the Pepperdine presidency. Gay and I set off for a rewarding five-year stint as their minister. It was a providential opportunity for a 27-year-old man with a young family.

We were burrowed in the inner city with three jobs and three little boys—Britton and Bill Jr. joined David during those first Los Angeles years. (Baxter is a Lubbock-born native Texan.) We had no time for what Southern California had to offer. The beaches and mountains were faraway places and Malibu was the name of a place we had never been. Gay, who taught in a Watts school, claims she never once saw the snow-covered San Gabriel Mountains to the east.

Even then, living on 79th Street next to the campus, we dead-bolted doors, barred windows and worried a lot about our little boys playing in the front yard across from the campus. All of us were worried about the rising crime rate. Hubert G. Derrick, a founding faculty member and our neighbor during those years, described that 1963 atmosphere: "Several of our students were mugged," he wrote. "My home across the street from the campus had been robbed twice," continued his memoir.[37]

LEAVING FOR LUBBOCK

On the day of my doctoral graduation, house sold and furniture sent, we drove straight from the USC campus to Lubbock. We left Los Angeles with feelings of relief. Having been born in Abilene and grown up in Ft. Worth, I knew our little family would really be at home in Lubbock. Two happy years later we watched in shock the televised pictures of the worst race riot in American history in Watts, near the Pepperdine campus. We telephoned frenzied friends. We learned that, though the burning and looting only grazed the area around Pepperdine, they felt nervous and very vulnerable.

Dr. Derrick's summary of those times came down to a short cause-and-effect interpretation: "Since we were a dormitory school, we were forced to find another area where this unsolvable problem did not exist. Fortunately, a wealthy family that favored our ideals came to our rescue by giving us land in Malibu."[38] It wasn't that simple, of course, but it is the way a lot of people have seen it ever since. That's why they call it a miracle.

In Los Angeles, years of tension and uncertainty followed. Helen recalls telephone conversations with anxious families in the Midwest and South who were about to send their children off to Pepperdine in just a few short weeks. Among them were the Lemleys from New Mexico. They called to ask, "Is it safe for our son to come?" Steven, anxious to enroll as a transfer student from Lubbock Christian College, remembers hearing Helen's voice echoing through the receiver, "Oh, yes. Everything is just fine. Things are under control. The Police and National Guard are handling the situation. Our campus is far from the actual riot and we won't be affected one bit!" Helen also sometimes spoke Norvelian. That was the message for dozens of concerned families. But Norvel and Helen faced an unanticipated challenge they could not control, as we shall see.

1. "Dr. Banowsky Appointed to Pepperdine Position," *Fort Worth Star-Telegram*, June 1, 1968, 16.
2. Bill Henegar and Jerry Rushford, *Forever Young: The Life and Times of M. Norvel Young and Helen M. Young* (Nashville: 21st Century Christian, 1999), 146.
3. Helen Mattox Young, personal interview with the author, June 2, 2006. The Banowsky Papers.
4. Henegar and Rushford, *Forever Young*, 146.
5. Helen Mattox Young, personal interview with the author, June 2, 2006. The Banowsky Papers.
6. Henegar and Rushford, *Forever Young*, 140.

7. Ibid., 150–151.
8. Jerry Rushford, ed., *Crest of a Golden Wave* (Malibu: Pepperdine University Press, 1987), 117.
9. Ibid., 118.
10. Henegar and Rushford, *Forever Young*, 172
11. Rushford, *Golden Wave*, 76.
12. Audrey Gardner, "A Brief History of Pepperdine College," (master's thesis, Pepperdine College, 1968), 33.
13. Henegar and Rushford, *Forever Young*, 130.
14. James Smythe, personal interview with the author, January 14, 2006. The Banowsky Papers.
15. "John Andrew Bolinger: Fundraiser and Health Advocate," *Claremont Courier*, November 19, 2005.
16. Richard L. Clark and Jack W. Bates, *Faith is My Fortune: The Life Story of George Pepperdine* (Los Angeles: George Pepperdine College Press, 1959), 180.
17. Henegar and Rushford, *Forever Young*, 156.
18. "Bolinger: Fundraiser and Health Advocate," *Claremont Courier*, November 19, 2005.
19. Robert P. Jones, personal interview with the author, February 20, 1991. The Banowsky Papers.
20. Donald V. Miller, personal interview with the author, January 23, 1999. The Banowsky Papers.
21. James Smythe, personal interview with the author, March 24, 2007. The Banowsky Papers.
22. Clark and Bates, *Fortune*, 209
23. Henegar and Rushford, *Forever Young*, 151.
24. Clark and Bates, *Fortune*, 162.
25. Bill Youngs, *Faith Was His Fortune: The Life Story of George Pepperdine* (Malibu: Pepperdine University Press, 1976), 197.
26. Ibid., 173–185.
27. Clark and Bates, *Fortune*, 230–231.
28. Ibid., 233.
29. Donald V. Miller, personal interview with the author, January 23, 1999. The Banowsky Papers.
30. William T. Stivers, personal interview with the author. February 15, 1999. The Banowsky Papers.
31. Youngs, *Life Story*, 222.
32. "The School of Soft Knocks," *Sports Illustrated*, May 23, 1977, 102.
33. Henegar and Rushford, *Forever Young*, 151.
34. Clark and Bates, *Fortune*, 236.
35. Ibid., 237.
36. Ibid., 190–197.
37. Hubert G. Derrick, *Why I Have to Believe: With an Early Pepperdine University History* (Huntington Beach, CA: Geocopy Educational Materials, 1994), 15–16. Dr. Derrick was elected to the board of regents in 1974.
38. Ibid., 16.

"When the Watts riots of 1965 created the perception of South Central Los Angeles as a violent, crime-ridden and undesirable inner city, M. Norvel Young commissioned William S. Banowsky to secure funds for a new campus."

CANDACE DENISE JONES
2003 Master's Thesis
Pepperdine University

GEORGE PEPPERDINE COLLEGE
79th and Vermont, Los Angeles, 1937–1980

CHAPTER 4

THE WATTS RIOTS DEATHBLOW

Heaven may have predestined the Malibu miracle but the 1965 Watts riots determined its timing. Pepperdine had prevailed through 28 years of church, faculty and financial fighting. But the worst race riot in American history finally delivered the Los Angeles deathblow. Was the Malibu miracle destined to be a resurrection that required a corpse?

If so, it was emphatically no sudden death. Seven stunning years were required to acquire, fund and create the Malibu campus. It would not open until 1972. The Los Angeles campus would not be disposed of, by bargain sale, until 1981.

In the Watts riots funeral wake President Young "commissioned" me to lead the creation of a new campus. He quietly launched the process, in late 1966, with a somewhat veiled search for potential sites. In the tensely confidential post-riots climate, the site selection committee performed its crucial work.

WORST RACE RIOT

After months of mounting conflict between the Los Angeles Police Department and its south central L. A. citizens, a single match lit the explosion. At 7:22 p.m., Wednesday, August 11, 1965, what seemed like a routine traffic stop at 116th and Avalon ignited the holocaust.[1]

African-American driver Marquette Frye and his car full of friends were pulled over by white officers Lee W. Minikus and Robert T. Johnston. Following field sobriety tests, five men were charged with inebriation. But when officers radioed for the wagon to take them to the 79th Street Station they refused to be handcuffed. They resisted arrest.

One thing led to another. Everything went from bad to worse. An unhappy neighborhood crowd of 50 soon saw blood on Frye's forehead from a police baton cut. "Frye's mother jumped on an officer's back and ripped his shirt. Within three hours scores of police vehicles on the ground and helicopters overhead circled "a rampaging mob of more than five hundred."[2]

Dozens of fires blazed for three miles all around. Bricks and sticks were thrown at police cars and fire trucks. Scores of stores were trashed and robbed of everything on the shelves, including knives and guns. For six days, concealed snipers targeted police and firefighters, killing three and injuring others. Pent-up ghetto anger exploded into a lawless all-night orgy of vandalism, arson and murder.

"I will be truthful with you," confessed a rioter. "Everybody was getting what they could get; I figured, well, I might as well get what I could get. They was running into the pawnshops, getting guns, rifles, and machetes ... People was running with new suits in their hands; I never owned a suit in my life, and this just excited me. Even little kids was pushing washing machines down the streets."[3]

Looters commandeered area gas stations and stole the fuel for Molotov cocktails. "They started taking gas out of the pump, putting 'em in Coca-Cola bottles, and beer bottles and bomb a car on fire in a matter of seconds, and people just lost their whole car, and some people even lost their lives in the car because they couldn't get out."[4]

The Watts riots raged for six straight days and nights, Wednesday through Monday. An army of almost 10,000 was called out to quell it, including 3,900 National Guardsmen, 934 policemen, 719 sheriff's deputies and 2,500 firefighters. The rioting killed 34 people and injured thousands more, hundreds of them seriously. Dead law enforcers were a Long Beach police officer, a deputy sheriff and a Los Angeles firefighter. Seriously injured were 136 firefighters, 90 policemen and 10 National Guardsmen.

In the African-American community the toll was higher, with 31 killed and 731 seriously injured. Altogether, 4,000 blacks were jailed, including 500 juveniles ages 7 to 17.[5]

PEPPERDINE POLICE STATION

This largest and most destructive race riot in American history caused, in 1960s dollars, $100 million in property damage to 600 buildings, 200 of them burned to the ground. Thousands of automobiles were destroyed or damaged.

The destruction intensely frightened Pepperdine College. During six days of death and damage, millions around the world watched on live television. Pepperdine people also watched. "Betty and I, on our August vacation, watched from Alabama," recalled English department chair Dr. James Smythe, who had lived at Pepperdine College since 1943. "Just three years earlier, to feel safer, we had left our longtime residence one block from the campus on 79th Street. We moved three miles away to Morningside Park in Inglewood. But, even at that distance, as we watched from Alabama, we were desperately afraid that our new house would surely be burned to the ground. It was horrendously frightening."[6]

President Young was another horrified Pepperdine television watcher. Caught away in Washington, D. C., on a fundraising trip, he watched the first three days and nights nonstop from his hotel room. Helen, who fled their campus residence on the rioting's first day, insisted he stay in Washington and not even attempt to return. In the president's absence Vice President William J. Teague, a take-charge kind of guy, managed the college crisis. He closed the campus, evacuated students and faculty, and assisted families residing around the campus to move elsewhere with friends. He and his wife, Peggy, welcomed to their Inglewood home fundraising colleague Robert L. Walker and his family. Helen Young and her three daughters moved in with Spanish professor William Stivers and his wife, Frances. Helen's son, Matt, slept next to longtime Pepperdine leader George Hill, and a score more, on a pew at the Inglewood church. Everyone on or around the campus fled to somewhere else.

After the total evacuation the Pepperdine campus did not stay empty for long. As the faculty and students moved out the National Guard moved in. Ground zero of the rioting centered south of the campus. But the rioters rampaged north, fantasizing the ruin of central Los Angeles. That drove their destruction, day and night, ever closer to the campus. The flames eventually leaped 30 blocks north of the campus, as far as 46th Street, where an entire block of commercial buildings was burned to the ground. Pepperdine College, if not the battle epicenter, made the ideal strategic center for battlefield operations.

TERRIFYING AFTERMATH

More than 400 National Guardsmen bivouacked in Pepperdine's dormitories for four days and nights. Day and night, Guardsmen manned sandbagged machine-gun batteries in a 79th Street battlement line atop the sturdy flat roofs of the two-storied auditorium, academic life and business buildings. Guardsmen were determined to corral the culprits in their own southern neighborhoods and, for the most part, succeeded.

Rioting died down. Death and suffering remained south of the campus. Other than massive cleanup, Pepperdine sustained no loss of life, injury or property damage. The damage was psychological. James C. (Chip) Moore, later Pepperdine's director of human resources, had lived across from the campus for many years. Then an awed eyewitness student, he reported broken windows in all of the buildings along Vermont Avenue leading up to the campus. If the students and faculty were frightened, the trustees were terrified. One Dallas trustee simply mailed in his resignation and never again came to the campus. The escalated fear level would never subside to pre-riot days.

The greatest fear was enrollment. Steven Lemley, a new transfer student and later president of Lubbock Christian University and provost of Pepperdine University, arrived before the smoke settled. Turning off of the Harbor Freeway he saw National Guardsmen protecting every quadrant of the campus and wondered what he was getting into.[7]

Students and faculty returned to the disheveled campus in heightened anxiety. Many feared that it could all blaze up again on any given day. Every day something burned at Berkeley or Columbia and many wondered how Pepperdine could avoid being next. To reassure worried parents, President Young took several security measures. He doubled campus security which meant growing the staff from one full-time officer to two. Prior to the rioting, campus security was managed by one lone guard. That highlights how unprepared the college was for what was coming. To discourage students from leaving campus after dark, President Young kept the popular Oasis snack bar open until midnight. To keep all others out, in 1969 he erected a six-foot chain-link security fence around the campus. If nothing else, it symbolized the escalating fear.

WHITE FLIGHT?

After the Watts riots President Young redoubled student recruitment. But it grew difficult, and expensive, to coax parents in the Midwest and South to send sons and daughters to a campus many considered to be at the center of America's racial woes. The smoke in Watts cleared but Pepperdine's pathway darkened into months of confusion. Was the college dead in Los Angeles? Or, with renewed resolution, could it continue to fulfill its mission in the inner city?

The sociological phrase "white flight" was aimed early at Pepperdine by some neighbors, media, student body and faculty. Twentieth-century white flight memorialized the move of tens of millions of white Americans from deteriorating inner cities to shining suburbia. The media relished the pejorative phrase because it depicted a demographic evolution driven by race. "The direct and indirect consequences of the Watts Riots," one white flight researcher concluded, "brought about the college's move to Malibu . . . The Watts riots served as the catalyst generating a desire by the Pepperdine administration to leave the perceived chaotic and unpredictable urban setting."[8] White flight theorists argued that the danger was always only a perception.

Can they reduce the Malibu miracle to a pedestrian case of twentieth century racial reaction? I don't think so. For one thing, this may not have been the first time God used mixed human motives to work His will. But theology aside, the white flight theorists of academia and media grossly simplified; the Malibu move was far more complicated than they imagined. They theorized a swift, sinisterly planned, shrewdly sweeping move of the entire institution out of the ghetto to the beach. Reality on the ground revealed a fumbling, stumbling process over a pathway of 20 turbulently ambiguous years. It was not a flight but a slow train with many stops.

White flight theorists also reduced Pepperdine's *perceived* predicament to a choice between two irreconcilable options. They asked, "Would Pepperdine fulfill its inner city mission or abandon it for safety?" But, with respect to the Los Angeles campus, Pepperdine people held not merely two but three positions. "Pepperdine is dying and must move," said some. "Pepperdine is alive and well and must stay put," said most. "Pepperdine is some of both," said President Young. "The undergraduate college must move but the rest can stay."

Given the proper presuppositions, a reasonable case could have been made for any one of those three positions. I will explain them and make the case for the road taken.

I. PEPPERDINE IS DYING AND MUST MOVE

The real-life debate was whether or not the Los Angeles campus of Pepperdine College was truly terminal. The debate was heated, much like one of those questions as to whether or not a family should unplug a loved one from the life-support system. But who would want to make such a decision? Therefore, the debate waged hot academically but most players stayed cool strategically. Nobody made any big moves.

I early and always held the least popular of the three positions. After 1965, I came to believe that the Los Angeles campus was terminally ill. I truly felt that Pepperdine should pull the plug and move on to someplace else. Those committed to the survival of the Los Angeles campus at any cost resented my influence. I stayed publicly quiet.

But I was aware that in American history most private colleges had died. In 1963 Norvel himself wrote: "An army of 'educational experts' gloomily predict that the next 25 years will witness the demise of the private liberal arts colleges."[9] A few private colleges became the longest-living human institutions. But, in American history, 90 percent of church-related colleges died young. Within the Stone-Campbell movement, in Texas alone, "23 colleges were founded between 1865 and 1929, 12 by the Churches of Christ and 11 by the Disciples of Christ. The Churches of Christ colleges averaged ten years of life. The Disciples colleges averaged 22 years. Only three of these 23 institutions exist today."[10] The 28-year-old Pepperdine College was precariously vulnerable when the Watts riots struck. It would have been less the exception and more the rule had Pepperdine College died, then and there. In my studied opinion, had Pepperdine not moved it would be dead today.[11]

The area around the old Pepperdine campus had grown "more untenably violent," Tom Brokaw wrote in 2007. "In my youthful idealism, I imagined the area would be transformed. But before long I began to see that the problems in Watts were far more systemic on both sides of the racial barrier than I had realized. Twenty years later in 1985, I returned to do a documentary on the sad, violent takeover of those neighborhoods by large, well-organized, and ruthless street gangs," lamented Brokaw.[12]

THE DEEPER REALITY

White flight theorists also utterly ignore the compelling economic mandate for moving. Pepperdine, with no endowment and totally dependent on tuition, was financially jeopardized when the undergraduate enrollment began to fall. Moreover, Pepperdine's terrifying predicament was not merely "perceived," as the white flight theorists put it. In 1969, Pepperdine alumnus Bob Andrews laid out the terrifying reality in the Long Beach *Independent*: "For a decade now Pepperdine College has been the boundary line for an ever-deepening ghetto."[13] That same year Catherine Meeks, an African-American student who became a distinguished author, agreed: "Protests, bomb threats and student unrest confirmed that the decision to secure another undergraduate campus, made after the Watts Riots, was indeed the right choice," echoed the thesis of Candace Denise Jones.[14]

The demise of the campus proceeded slowly, almost imperceptibly. There was no poignant moment of expiration. There was no precise day of death. There was no autopsy. Complete closure came in 1981 when the campus was sold to Crenshaw Christian Center for $12 million.[15] Fear had already caused erection of the six-foot security fence. That fence stood until Crenshaw Christian Center established its 10,000-seat "Faith Dome" sanctuary, a school and multitudinous services designed by and for African Americans. The campus perseveres as a Christian center, its buildings and grounds intact as they always were. But surrounding them now is not a six-foot but a *12-foot* high security fence. Crenshaw Christian Center lives to serve its black community, but it also lives in unrelieved danger.

II. PEPPERDINE IS ALIVE AND WELL AND MUST STAY PUT

Mechanisms of death-denial abound. Naturally, the last to acknowledge the death of the Los Angeles campus were those closest to it. Soon, an odd partnership of death-deniers made strange bedfellows of two otherwise opposite forces, the idealists and the pragmatists. They coalesced to form the loud majority.

Idealists condemned death-talk as non-Christian racial rationalization. Pragmatists condemned death-talk as utter nonsense because flat-broke Pepperdine wasn't going anywhere. Whether out of spirituality or practicality, both the idealists and the pragmatists believed that Pepperdine was alive and well. "Chairman of the Bible Department Frank Pack believed that the College should just build a taller fence and stay put," according to Henegar and Rushford. Over the course of 36 months, this coalition passed three faculty senate resolutions against leaving Los Angeles. Norvel's biographers reported: "Quite a number of the faculty were not sold on finding a new undergraduate campus."[16] Neither were most administrators, including Dean J. P. Sanders, Dean of Graduate Studies Howard A. White and Dean of Students Jennings Davis.

For these good men, serving the underprivileged was not only in the Bible; it was also in the 1960s air. "Ask not what your country can do for you," rang President Kennedy's Peace Corps call to tens of thousands. "Inasmuch as ye have done it unto one of the least of these my brethren," rang Christ's words in Sunday sermons. "O Master, let me walk with Thee in lowly paths of service free," rang Washington Gladden's social gospel song from Sunday pews. "Bill," said the gentle J. P. Sanders, "remember how comfortable it was back in Tennessee? Gloria and I came out here with Norvel and Helen to serve Christ by serving the needy." The courageous Howard White added, "Bill, do you think we should just cut and run? What would Christ do?"

Deep convictions like these ran from the sublime to the ridiculous. Dr. Lemley, who was to become the Youngs' son-in-law, was visiting in their home in 1966 when Norvel returned from a trustees meeting. Steve listened in astonishment as Norvel described the latest outrageous idea for saving the campus. "For two hours," laughed Norvel, "the trustees talked seriously about raising billions to buy out and clear away all of the scores of deteriorated business and residential blocks between the campus and the Harbor Freeway. Like USC, they reasoned, this would provide Pepperdine direct access off of the Harbor Freeway onto the completely controlled campus." Dr. Lemley shared this story to show the desperation to save the campus, even if by means of the absurd and fantastic.

MOVING THE CEMETERY

Coalescing with woozy idealists, who fantasized about buying out three square miles of the city, were the practical people. They just wanted to stay put. Their motive was, perhaps, more material than spiritual. Some trustees, administrators and faculty resisted death talk not because they didn't fear it, but because they saw no way to avoid it. In his written requiem, board chairman Donald V. Miller seemed hopelessly reconciled to staying put when he calculated the impossibility of moving. "Dr. Young once compared the feat of relocating a college campus to moving a 'cemetery' in complexity," Miller wrote. "It would involve seeking a suitable site, inducing those owners to make a land gift, and the massive job of raising millions of dollars for land development and building the necessary buildings, a super-human task."[17]

"A super-human task," said the top man in 1968. Perhaps that's why by 1972 they called it a miracle.

But Norvel's cemetery cliché, an unapologetic death analogy, was a keeper. He repeated it endlessly. Few of the idealists or the pragmatists around him ever actually believed that they could escape their 79th and Vermont grave. And President Young, for reasons both idealistic and practical, joined the crowd of doubters. "But as bad as the situation seemed, Norvel was not ready," his biographers emphasized. "He did not believe the riots would destroy the school . . . Norvel was hopeful that the ugly situation would wane and finally disappear . . . It seemed out of the question to think about moving to another location."[18]

Conservative Norvel disliked ambiguous change. Because of his innate idealism, he was deeply disinclined to leave Los Angeles. Our partnership ran on private code. His congenital conservatism we coded as "tractor-tread shoes." Since the 1930s he nurtured for outdoor activity an aged pair of low-cut brown boots with thick, grooved soles. We both lost old friends the day he set them up on top of his car and drove off unaware. Those tractor-tread shoes were a metaphor for Norvel's dogged determination to hang on to whatever he truly cared about. Norvel truly cared about the Los Angeles campus.

As a practical man Norvel cared equally for a bird in hand. It was worth two in the bush. In accord with Chairman Miller, to President Young it seemed impractical, if not impossible, to raise the untold millions necessary to construct a whole new campus completely from scratch. It seemed out of the question to think about moving to an entirely different location. "We were a little slow in joining with those who advocated finding new property," said Norvel. "I kept thinking, 'This will all go away.'"[19]

Norvel was tired. Deep down he doubted that the cemetery could be moved. It was the most turbulent time in the history of higher education. The average college president's tenure was less than four years. Norvel had already pushed himself for ten turbulent years. He was now in no mood to risk all of his gains on some quixotic move to some unknown place that he had no practical way to finance.

Despite Norvel's wishful thinking, none of it went away. But the raging *perception* of danger began to drive people away in droves. Donors who later gave generously to the new campus refused to give anything at all to the old. First-rate students who later lined up to enroll at Malibu would never have enrolled in Los Angeles.

In 2004, 47 years later, *Seventeen* magazine ran a nationwide survey to seek "America's Top Ten Safest Campuses." Guess what? Pepperdine at Malibu was ranked first! Number one! "The safest campus in America." The Naval Academy and the Air Force Academy ranked second and seventh, respectively.[20] After the 1965 Watts riots, safety mattered. After the 2001 World Trade Center, safety mattered almost more than anything else. Where would Pepperdine be today had it hunkered down and stayed put?

III. THE UNDERGRADUATE, RESIDENTIAL LIBERAL ARTS COLLEGE MUST MOVE

Meanwhile, however, Norvel set Pepperdine on the adventurous path to Malibu. Feeling pressure from all sides, he made a courageous decision. Pushed by me and some potential donors to go, pushed by most to stay, Norvel took half the loaf, as was his nature. He conceived of a university whose central administrative headquarters, graduate programs and commuter and part-time curricula would remain forever on the Los Angeles campus. A new second campus would be built to serve only undergraduate, residential, full-time students. Norvel tended to believe in the best of both worlds.

Although entrenched opposition persisted, Norvel generated support for his grand compromise. For one thing, to those who looked objectively it was apparent that the residential, full-time, undergraduate program was dying in Los Angeles. As Hubert G. Derrick, the founding professor of Spanish and tennis coach, wrote in his memoir: "Since we were largely a dormitory school, we were forced to find another area where the presently unsolvable problem [of losing the full-time, undergraduate, residential base] did not exist."[21]

Pepperdine's Los Angeles survival was never about overall enrollment. It was about the viability of the undergraduate, residential liberal arts college. In 1969, I commissioned the new Los Angeles campus provost, Jerry E. Hudson, to execute an enrollment study. His finding? "The number of part-time, evening, graduate and commuter students was growing. But the number of full-time residential students—the heart of the liberal arts college—was declining."[22] I conceded as much to the *Los Angeles Times*: "We were deeply concerned with a possible retreat of white church students."[23] My concern was for the church relationship. Most of our Church of Christ students were white. Although the majority of undergraduate students were never affiliated with the Church of Christ, for the first time in Pepperdine history the percentage fell below ten percent.

Therefore, Norvel's compromise gained traction. Pepperdine could keep its residential Christian college alive in another location, he preached. But Pepperdine must always maintain a vital program in Los Angeles, he also preached. As the days passed, that part of Norvel's vision faded, and failed.

SITE SELECTION COMMITTEE

"In 1966 President Young appointed a committee to investigate various prospective sites for an additional campus," reported Henegar and Rushford.[24] With his trustees divided, and mostly opposed to a second campus, Norvel turned discreetly to the leading businessmen on his president's board. He also turned in confidentiality to me in my Lubbock, Texas, ministry. "Young asked Dr. William S. Banowsky, the man who would become the school's fourth president, to head the search committee for a second campus," Pepperdine's Patricia Yomantas reported in 1987 for the official record.[25]

In Norvelian style, President Young organized the site selection committee under the radar. It quietly operated for two years. Its work led to the acquisition of the Malibu land.

1. Paul Bullock, *Watts: The Aftermath; An Inside View of the Ghetto* (New York: Grove Press Inc., 1969,) 12. Standard sources providing concurring documentation and detail for this chapter include: David Sears, *The Politics of Violence: The New Urban Blacks and the Watts Riot* (Boston: Houghton Mifflin Publishers, 1974); Robert Conot, *Rivers of Blood, Years of Darkness: The Unforgettable Classic Account of the Watts Riot* (New York: Morrow, 1968); Robert Fogelson, *The Los Angeles Riots* (New York: The Arno Press, Inc., 1969). Gregory Alan Williams, *A Gathering of Heroes: Reflections in Rage and Responsibility; A Memoir of the Los Angeles Riots* (Chicago:

Chicago Academy Publishers, 1994); Mark Baldassare, ed., *The Los Angeles Riots: Lessons for the Urban Future* (Boulder, CO: Westview Press, 1994); Lynn Bowman, *Los Angeles: Epic of a City* (Berkeley: Howell-North Books, 1974), 346–47.

2. Fogelson, *L.A. Riots*, 14–21.
3. Williams, *Heroes*, 116.
4. Candace Denise Jones, "White Flight? George Pepperdine College's Move to Malibu, 1965–1972" (master's thesis, Pepperdine University, 2003), 40–41.
5. Conot, *Rivers of Blood*, 81.
6. James Smythe, personal interview with the author, December 6, 2007. The Banowsky Papers.
7. Steven Lemley, personal interview with the author, August 15, 2009. The Banowsky Papers.
8. Jones, "White Flight," 1–2.
9. M. Norvel Young, "Beginning A Second Quarter Century of Christian Education," *Firm Foundation*, February 5, 1963, 1.
10. D. Duane Cummings, "Higher Education, Views of the Movement," in Douglas A. Foster and others, eds., *The Encyclopedia of the Stone-Campbell Movement* (Grand Rapids, MI: William B. Eerdmans, 2004), 393.
11. Don Crisp, personal interview with the author, January 3, 2007, The Banowsky Papers. Crisp, chairman of the Abilene Christian University board of trustees and recipient of a Pepperdine University honorary doctorate, said at Gay's mother's funeral: "Bill, we all now know that if you had not moved Pepperdine out of Los Angeles the school would be dead."
12. Tom Brokaw, *Boom! Voices of the Sixties* (New York: Random House, 2007), 22.
13. Bob Andrews, "Portrait of a Campus Guard in Trouble," *Independent*, March 17, 1969, 8.
14. Jones, "White Flight," 45.
15. President Howard A. White called me at the University of Oklahoma, March 15, 1981. "Bill, I've got great news. We've finally sold the old campus to Crenshaw Christian Center. Their leader, with whom I've worked for months, is Fred Price. He's great on TV. No shouting or sweating, holds his Bible open and talks conversationally like a big class. We can feel good about where the campus ended up and I'm greatly relieved to get if off our hands." The Banowsky Papers.
16. Bill Henegar and Jerry Rushford, *Forever Young: The Life and Times of M. Norvel Young and Helen M. Young* (Nashville: 21st Century Christian, 1999), 188.
17. Donald V. Miller, in Henegar and Rushford, *Forever Young*, 188.
18. Henegar and Rushford, *Forever Young*, 186-187.
19. Ibid., 187.
20. *Seventeen*, September 25, 2004, 4.
21. Hubert G. Derrick, *Why I Have to Believe: With An Early Pepperdine University History* (Huntington Beach, CA: Geocopy Educational Materials, 1994), 15.
22. Jerry Hudson, email to Candace Denise Jones, July 9, 2002. Jerry Hudson Papers.
23. Lee Dye, "Pepperdine Will Handle Student Discipline Itself," *Los Angeles Times*, June 2, 1969, 12.
24. Henegar and Rushford, *Forever Young*, 188.
25. Jerry Rushford, ed., *Crest of a Golden Wave: Pepperdine University, 1937–1987* (Malibu: Pepperdine University Press, 1987), 119.

"Naturally I first fell in love with
Pepperdine University because of
its magnificent situation between
the western end of the Santa Monica
Mountains and an eastern cover
of an apparently endless sea.
Here any soul might be challenged
to greatness, and disciplined to
modesty. Oh to be young again
and listen to Plato and Christ
in these halls, perched on
these hills, under these skies."

 WILL DURANT

Twentieth-century
Philosopher and Historian

PART II

THE MALIBU
RESURRECTION

"The Watts riots near the campus in 1965 discouraged potential students. Dr. Young asked Dr. William S. Banowsky, the man who would become the school's fourth president, to head the search committee for a second campus."

PATRICIA YOMANTAS
Historian
Pepperdine University

MALIBU DREAMING

This is the way the Malibu miracle looked on October 2, 1969, when the Adamson family donated the first 138 acres.

CHAPTER 5

THE MAGNIFICENT MALIBU LAND GIFT

"Malibu is arguably the most desirable real estate on planet earth," proclaimed Morley Safer in 2007 on CBS's *60 Minutes*.[1]

Forty years earlier, this real estate description appeared on the cover of the 1968 *Malibu Chamber of Commerce Business Guide and Directory*: "Twenty-five miles from downtown Los Angeles Malibu runs smog-free along the Pacific coastline for 26 miles in an east to west direction relaxing its population of 16,000 in an ideal Mediterranean southern exposure with high of 80 and low of 60 degrees, a water temperature of 70 and annual rainfall of 15 inches."

How did Pepperdine acquire 830 acres of Malibu real estate?

RINDGE-ADAMSON FAMILY

For centuries the California coast, from Santa Monica to San Luis Obispo, was home for the Chumash Indians. Their coveted enclave was Humaliwo village in the mouth of Malibu canyon where the lagoon at Malibu Creek meets the ocean. "Malibu" meant "where the surf sounds loudly and mountains rise to the sky."[2]

Earliest Malibu written accounts came from Juan Rodriguez Cabrillo, a Portuguese explorer sailing for Spain. On October 10, 1542, he anchored in the Malibu Lagoon. He claimed the entire coast for Spain and named it "Pueblo de Las Canoas" because of the fleet of Chumash canoes that rowed out to greet his ships.

In 1804 the King of Spain decreed to Don José Bartolomé Tapia a "land use concession" of 13,315 acres. It was recorded as Rancho Malibu Topanga

Sequit. That was the first historical use of the "Malibu" name.[3] An 1864 court detailed Malibu's legal description: "It extends from a place called 'Topanga,' the dividing line between these lands at the 'Rancho Santa Monica' on the southeast, running along the Pacific to a point called 'Mogu' on the northwest, and bounded on the northeast by a range of mountains extending the length back to 'Topanga,' and adjoining the ranchos of 'Las Virgenes,' 'Triunfo,' 'Santa Ysabel' and 'Conejo.'"[4]

Following two other private owners, in 1892 Frederick Hastings Rindge, a Massachusetts-born Harvard graduate, bought the entire Rancho Malibu for ten dollars an acre.[5] For half a century the Rindge family controlled Malibu and expanded it to 17,000 acres. In 1887, Rindge married Rhoda May Knight and moved to Los Angeles. "When I first sought a country home," goes the 1890 Rindge classic, *Happy Days in Southern California*, "I told a friend I wished to find a farm near the ocean, and under the lee of the mountains; with a trout brook, wild trees, a lake, good soil, and excellent climate, one not too hot in summer. To this hope my good wife demurred, saying, 'You ask too much.' Such, however, was my picture of the ideal farm. But my friend said, 'I know such a place, I think, but I would like to refresh an old memory and see it again.' So he went, and came back to me, reporting it just as he had thought, and that it was for sale."[6]

With passing decades the Rindge family struggled to keep Rancho Malibu intact. When Mr. Rindge died in 1905, his widow, Rhoda May Rindge, gained fame as the indomitable "Queen of Malibu." Her victorious fights kept the Southern Pacific Railroad and a modern freeway from crossing Rancho Malibu.

Soaring property taxes forced the Rindge family into bankruptcy. Rancho Malibu was subdivided, but prime parts reverted back to the Rindges.[7] They hired foreman Merritt Adamson to supervise their huge ranch. In 1915 Adamson married their daughter, Rhoda Agatha Rindge.

In the late 1960s when Pepperdine searched for a new site it was Rhoda Rindge Adamson's three children—Merritt Huntley Adamson Jr., Sylvia Rindge Adamson Neville and Rhoda-May Adamson Dallas—who had inherited hundreds of virginal acres where Malibu Canyon pushes through the Santa Monica Mountains to the sea. That legendary plateau above the Malibu Lagoon that was the central Chumash camp and very heart of the original Spanish land grant became the home of Pepperdine University.

In October 1968, Pepperdine announced the Adamsons' gift of 138 acres. It soon mushroomed to 830 acres. "Our family long has felt this prime Rancho Malibu land should be held for an outstanding and special use," Merritt Adamson announced at the October 2, 1968, news conference. "My sisters and I feel that in making this gift of land to Pepperdine we are helping to fulfill the destiny of this property. Pepperdine will fulfill this outstanding and special use."[8]

The Adamson family had not previously been among Pepperdine's supporters. What motivated them to give Pepperdine the priceless land?

SITE SELECTION COMMITTEE

In August 1966, one year after the Watts riots, Norvel came to Lubbock for a confidential two-day conference with me. Pepperdine had withstood the pressure in all academic programs but one. Gravely, that one was its definitive undergraduate program for full-time residential students. The percentage of Church of Christ students plummeted and Norvel was unwilling to sustain further bleeding at the very heart of the Pepperdine mission.

After an agonizing post-riots year, Norvel knew he had no choice but to build "a second campus somewhere safe to serve full-time undergraduate residential students." But he knew not where and he knew not how. Therefore, he appointed a four-man site selection committee to search for a second campus and came to Lubbock to retain me as a modestly paid committee consultant. Norvel loved consultants. From 1965 through 1968 he put three others on his payroll. They were John R. Bollinger, Walter Burch and Robert Johnson. "The three fundraising steps are *identification*, *cultivation* and *solicitation*," they preached to Norvel. "You succeed at one and two but falter on three."

Contrariwise, I specialized in solicitation. "Bill Banowsky had the poise and courage," recorded Norvel's biographers "to ask friends of the university for the 'big gift.'"[9] Resisting all consultants I said, "You're either working or meeting but you're not doing both simultaneously." Pepperdine consulted about raising money without ever raising much. Without any consultants the Malibu miracle raised hundreds of millions. But for a time there, I was a consultant.

In our Lubbock meeting Norvel stressed the need for confidentiality. "The trustees and faculty are troubled about a second campus," he said. "It's a risky move and we shouldn't meet in your church office." When I suggested the nearby motel, Norvel knew a more private place. "Ya know, Bill, it'd be ideal to meet at your home in that little separate guest bedroom out by the garage."

Norvel was at home at 3210 27th Street, the church parsonage that served as his own last Lubbock residence. It included a detached room he and Helen christened "the prophet's chamber" because Ira North, Jim Bill McInteer and Batsell Barrett Baxter stayed there while guest preaching at the Broadway church. Now, in 1966, Norvel and I stayed there for two days without looking up. Gay brought meals and he spent the night right there. The serious search for a second campus launched in the Lubbock prophet's chamber landed 24 months later on the Malibu shore.

STRUCTURING THE COMMITTEE

Norvel and I grew close. I served on Pepperdine's president's board, he and Helen visited the Broadway church frequently and they appointed me associate editor of the *Twentieth Century Christian* magazine. For two years every article was assigned, and edited for publication, at my Lubbock desk. I coordinated by telephone with the Youngs in Los Angeles and the production office in Nashville.

In Lubbock Norvel opened our "prophet's chamber" summit with a nice surprise. Several promising sites were already surfacing from developers eager to donate land if the college committed to moving onto it. Norvel wisely appointed "a committee to investigate various prospective sites."[10] Bypassing trustees, Norvel recruited from the president's board. In Lubbock he pulled out his list and we evaluated the prospects for a full day. Norvel decided to go with Donald Darnell as chairman. The other three were Walter Knott, famed founder of Knott's Berry Farm near Disneyland; Bryant Essick, Los Angeles businessman; and Henry Salvatori, an oilman, Reagan intimate and titular head of the California Republican Party. When Salvatori demurred, "I'll do all I can but don't need any more committees," banker Miles Flint became the fourth member. But Salvatori was "very influential in steering the school toward the 'seaside paradise.'"[11]

I consulted with the committee from November 1966 until February 1968, working by phone and mail. Every other month I flew to Los Angeles for committee meetings. Pepperdine paid $250 per trip, plus travel, and I stayed with Norvel and Helen, or Walter and Betty Glass. The committee lunch meetings were conducted in a secluded room at the California Club. Before meetings Mabel Bean, Norvel's secretary, circulated paperwork. The committee convened for lunch with full details of all sites under any kind of consideration. The committee also made excursions to 10 or 12 developments in Los Angeles, Orange, Riverside, Ventura and San Bernardino counties.

Norvel distanced faculty and trustees from this potentially controversial process and worked exclusively with the committee. The committee approached its task professionally, with no attachment to the Los Angeles campus, no church distractions and no need to worry about whether Malibu was more worldly than ordinary places. The committee supported Pepperdine's Christian and free-enterprise values and judged all options only on the three rules of real estate: "location, location, location."

CHARLES B. RUNNELS

Finding a location to fit Pepperdine's pressing needs but paltry means was a daunting task. Norvel recruited for professional assistance a man destined to become one of the most popular personalities in Pepperdine history.

In 1963 Charles B. Runnels, a young Texas lawyer and Church of Christ leader, moved from Houston to California to work for the Tenneco Corporation. In the process of acquiring gas pipeline approvals, he got acquainted with many development projects. This was back when construction throughout California was exploding. In 1967 Norvel convinced Tenneco chairman Gardiner Simon to grant Runnels a one-year leave to

OUT ON THE TOWN
In what seemed an almost nightly ritual in sparkling Los Angeles ballrooms, a 39ish Charlie Runnels escorted a spry-at-80 Blanche Seaver into black-tie dinner after black-tie dinner. Blanche loved life in all of its fullness.

work full-time with the committee. When the year ended Runnels resigned at Tenneco and signed on for 40 more at Pepperdine. He was assistant to the president, vice president for business relations, vice chancellor, chancellor and chancellor emeritus. Charlie, Pepperdine's all-star utility player, was the beloved pastor of the board of regents.

Revered for total loyalty to the five presidents with whom he so closely served, Charlie partnered with his brilliant and beautiful wife, Amy Jo. Perennially sparkling personalities in elegant Los Angeles banquet halls, they cultivated friendships with scores of financial leaders. Norvel's biographers note that in 1978, when I moved to the presidency of the University of Oklahoma, the Runnels family "filled the gap" to become Mrs. Seaver's adopted family.[12] Mrs. Frank Roger Seaver, of course, was destined to be the founder of Seaver College and the donor of $300 million. The Runnels family honored her in their home for every Thanksgiving and Christmas and scores of other days. They traveled with her. Amy Jo massaged her feet in hotel rooms everywhere. She joined them for worship every Sunday at the Inglewood Church of Christ where Dr. Runnels served as an elder. In 1978, thanks perhaps largely to Charlie, she was baptized there. Charlie was Pepperdine's "chief friend-raiser." Aside from the presidents themselves, he generated more Pepperdine support than any other person.[13]

The site selection committee first convened November 16, 1966, with eight hands on deck: the committee members plus Norvel, Charlie, Mabel and me. I challenged Norvel one last time—but for the first time in front of others—about the site for which we should be searching. It was our only strategic disagreement.

I urged a search for a new site for the entire institution. I argued Pepperdine could not raise money, attract students or succeed with its church constituency in its Los Angeles location. I argued Pepperdine had neither manpower nor money to operate two diametrically opposite campuses.

Norvel would have none of it. He argued for a permanent and primary base in Los Angeles. He conceded insurmountable difficulties for a traditional liberal arts, full-time, residential Christian college, but believed it could always serve as a commuter campus for part-time and graduate students. He believed such a multiple-campus model would be forever administered from headquarters on Vermont Avenue. He limited the search for a second campus to a safe suburban beachhead of 50 to 150 acres of free, flat, buildable land for a small undergraduate college.

Duly commissioned, the committee went to work with sites already on its agenda. In 60 days it was well enough established for Norvel to announce its mission and composition.

"THE MULTICAMPUS CONCEPT"

With the site search Norvel launched "the multicampus concept." Putting the best face on the worst case and producing positive explanations for complicated situations was the gift Gay called Norvelian. "Our Los Angeles campus was admirably suited to education for life in the city, but . . . we did not have adequate space for additional residential programs," Norvel said, thus euphemizing the dwindling dorms. "We decided to take the college to the people rather than attempt to bring all the people we wished to serve to one central location."[14]

On January 25, 1967, Vice President Teague announced in a press release "that the college was considering additional locations. He emphasized that the Los Angeles campus would not be abandoned, but that the institution was moving toward a multicampus concept. He stated that more than forty sites were under consideration for additional work of the college."[15] It sounded like an advance, not a retreat; an addition, not a desertion; an expansion, not an extinction.

The media ignored it and Teague soon left. Everyone else stayed silent. Almost two more years passed before another word was uttered on the multicampus concept.

THE FINAL THREE

After a year of searching, the committee's choices boiled down to three. "More than 40 fine locations were studied, some as far away as Temecula and San Diego. The more promising ones were in places like Palos Verdes, Calabasas and Westlake Village."[16] Forty developers, motivated by land appreciation caused by the presence of a private college, courted Pepperdine. Most offers were informal. Some sparked sufficient curiosity for a California Club committee luncheon. But no site ever challenged Palos Verdes, Calabasas and Westlake Village, the top three contenders on the committee table from the get go.

Calabasas and Westlake Village were a matched set located nearby in an upscale area off the 101 Freeway at the Ventura County line. Both offered 250 flat acres with modern roads and utilities. Calabasas and Westlake Village were safe, accessible and free. They were favorites.

The third ocean site was offered, not by developers, but by Blanche Seaver. "I want to combat America's moral decline by donating my land to build a conservative Christian college," she said. Her gracefully sloping land panoramically overlooked the Pacific at Palos Verdes peninsula. Accessible, with all utilities, its defeating drawback was its 60-acre size. Although twice that of the Los Angeles campus, 60 acres seemed inadequate compared to the 250 acres offered by both Calabasas and Westlake Village. Mrs. Seaver soon donated her magnificent land to help finance the Malibu miracle. Had she owned 200 acres, fate may have led to Pepperdine University at Palos Verdes—"PU at PV."

With Palos Verdes out, the choice came down to the two practical but pedestrian sites on the 101 Freeway. Norvel prayed for a site to tempt my return to build the campus. I felt no temptation. Privately I wondered if Norvel made a noble, but questionable, career move ten years earlier to take on Pepperdine's endemic problems. I had no desire to duplicate his dilemma. I felt no call to a California return.

THE LIFE-CHANGING CALL

I felt no call, that is, until Norvel telephoned at 10:15 a.m., Monday, September 18, 1967. I was at my Lubbock desk.

"Bill, we've just been offered land in Malibu!" A long pause followed his shouted exclamation. I wasn't sure what I had heard.

"Whad'ya say, Norvel?" I stumbled.

"I said, we've just been offered land in Malibu. I know that's a shocker. But it's for real!" Another long pause.

"It's right on the ocean. It's in the heart of Malibu!" he continued. "I first saw it only yesterday and couldn't sleep all night. Helen and I stayed awake rejoicing. It's just beautiful. It overlooks the Pacific. Huge mountains rise up behind it. Catalina floats like a fishing cork way out in front of you. Bill, God has answered our prayers. This Malibu site will solve all our problems!" Norvel seemed over the top.

"That's crazy. Malibu? Nobody's gonna give us any ocean property in Malibu. Why would they? We don't even know anybody in Malibu!"

"George Evans knows these people." he explained. "They're his clients. It's a family named Adamson. They've been in Malibu forever. They own lots of ocean land. They're proposing to give us the most beautiful spot of all."

Hearing the name George Evans, I straightened up in my chair. I had known him briefly during my 1959–1963 Pepperdine sojourn and my assessment was that George was a man of few words whose promises could be taken to the bank.

"But why, Norvel? Why would this Adamson family give us priceless ocean property?" I questioned.

"George's proposal came so fast I have few details," confessed Norvel. "And there's one huge negative. It's rough and mountainous without any of the basic utilities whatsoever. Some trustees already say site development costs are prohibitive."

My red flag flew up. I pressed to learn how unbuildable this site was. Norvel conceded we'd have to move hundreds of tons of dirt. "There are no roads or sidewalks. Only snakes, coyotes and contented cows grazing in a meadow," he chuckled. "It's rough, but beautiful. You won't believe it 'til you see it, so come now!"

"OK, Norvel. Let me talk it over with Gay. I'll call right back."

UNSUNG HERO GEORGE EVANS

I telephoned Gay to report Norvel's call and told her I felt inclined to go because of George. Gay admired George and agreed. I called George, the Adamson money manager in the catbird seat. From his Santa Monica office, through their Marblehead Development Corporation, he ran the business interests of Merritt, Sylvia and Rhoda-May. Financially creative, he conceived a plan to "save the Adamsons and put Pepperdine on the map." George lived in tony Bel-Air whose 1920s developers donated a thousand acres to build UCLA. The university, in turn, enhanced the value of surrounding Bel-Air home sites. Meanwhile, in Malibu, the land-poor Adamsons were unable to sustain any development. They were forced to sell much of Malibu to pay property taxes. George negotiated for the Adamsons a gift to Pepperdine of 138 acres and a joint venture with Alcoa, the Pittsburgh company of Richard Mellon Scaife, to develop adjoining acreage, Bel-Air style.

A Price Waterhouse CPA, George zoomed to the business apex as executive vice president of the Purex Corporation. He and his parents were longtime members of the Southwest Church of Christ where George Pepperdine was an elder. "He always made a generous year-end contribution," said minister James Smythe. In 1960 Norvel positioned George with the businessmen on the president's board and elevated him in 1965 to the board of trustees. That's how, 36 months later, Pepperdine ended up with the Malibu land.[17]

Meanwhile, the Adamson-Alcoa Malibu Country Estates project failed. On November 7, 1972, 60 days after Pepperdine opened the Malibu campus, California voters created the California Coastal Commission. Pepperdine saw the environmental train coming, darted out early and ran fast to stay a step ahead. The Adamsons, one step behind, got hit by the train. They built a few homes before being completely shut down by the new commission. Paradoxically, the Adamson defeat became Pepperdine's blessing as the university quietly acquired hundreds more acres in its uncrowded neighborhood.

I dialed Norvel back to say I was on the way. "I'm booked in the morning on that early TWA flight arriving at 9:00. I'm straight back tomorrow night.

We'll have all day. Brother, sounds like you may finally have found yourself a winner."

LOVE AT FIRST SIGHT

Tuesday, September 19, 1967, I flew out to see the Malibu land for the first time. Norvel met me at LAX. We drove 20 winding miles north along the ocean. Talking nonstop, we sped past Sunset Boulevard, Topanga Canyon, Big Rock and La Costa and Carbon beaches to Malibu's civic center. The highway's tight topography then blossomed wide open into a spectacular three-dimensional landscape for miles around. On the left, the regal Malibu Colony spread movie-star mansions along the beach. But Norvel turned my attention to the right, pointing up to the mile-wide opening of Malibu Canyon soaring up through the Santa Monica Mountains.

"Well, Bill, there it is," he said softly.

"Where?" I puzzled, with a high-up and far-away squint. "Is that it?" pointing to a big white building on the high skyline.

"Oh no, that's the Hughes Research Laboratory. Look further left."

I looked and found the center of the Malibu miracle: tall rugged mountains meandering gracefully down across the verdant meadow and melting into the sea. Point Dume and the Santa Barbara Channel Islands sparkled in the distance. In the soft foreground were the 138 acres destined to be Pepperdine's home. The creative canvas defined my career.

Norvel drove up the highway hill a half mile farther and edged off onto the gravel shoulder. Today, that spot marks the major intersection of Pacific Coast Highway and Malibu Canyon Road. Then, there was no intersection. The canyon road turned a half mile east, into the civic center. Norvel and I quickly inspired the county to extend the canyon road to intersect the highway. That created Pepperdine's front corner and southern border. It also created much goodwill among Malibu and San Fernando Valley drivers.

Norvel maneuvered off of the highway onto a dirt path leading 150 yards from the highway, to a barbed wire fence enclosing a cattle field. The car rolled up to a ramshackle gate girded by a cattle guard. Norvel set the brake and rolled down the windows. We sat silently, looking through the gate and over the cows to green hills in the foreground and dark, rocky mountains behind. Two spectacular canyons framed the scene, right and left, like a dreamy early-California landscape. Winter Canyon on the right flamed out at its top into bright red rocks. Norvel and I renamed it "Red Rock Canyon." On the left the much larger Marie Canyon zoomed up to a height of 1,500 feet and stretched a half mile wide at its pinnacle. In the sweet center of the whole scene sat

In 1968, Bill arrives in the background, Norvel is
already in the foreground with Merritt and Sharon
Adamson, who gave the land, and Blanche Seaver, who
would ultimately give most of the cash.

the 138 acres offered by the Adamsons, surrounded by three thousand more.
Norvel and I sat enthroned in the car, monarchs of all we surveyed.

I broke the silence to ask about the specific boundary lines for those 138
acres. Norvel suggested a quick hike. We stepped out into an exhilarating
ocean breeze wafting from northwest to southeast across the picturesque
ranch scene of cow licks, water troughs and barbed wire fence. Facing the
ocean, Norvel swept his right arm from Santa Monica on the left toward
Ventura on the right. "Bill, those 138 acres start down here and run along the
highway to Marie Canyon," pointing northwest.

"How far do they extend up into the mountains?" I asked.

"Not all the way to the top, but that'll never pose a problem," Norvel
answered. "No one will ever be able to build in the precipitous mountains
above us. We're protected above by rugged peaks and below by the highway.
Hughes buffers us on the east and the Adamsons' luxury houses will buffer

us on the west. We're nestled into a topographical haven of safety, comfort and beauty."

It was beautiful, indeed, but very rugged. It was dramatically apparent why it would cost extra millions to build here and why some trustees already opposed it. Norvel, lamenting the costs, pointed to the complete absence of roads, water, gas and electricity. Then came the clincher: "Bill, there's no public sewer system anywhere in Malibu!"

"Come on Norvel," I pointed down to the beach. "How do all those movie stars live in those million-dollar houses without a sewer?"

"Every residence and business in Malibu must operate its own private septic tank," Norvel explained. "We would have to gain government permission to build the biggest private sewer system in all of Malibu and face horrendous costs of construction and perpetual operation. Little wonder some trustees are spooked."

"Can we walk up there?" I asked, pointing almost straight up the central mountain to the soft plateau flattening out above the cows.

"Sure," Norvel said. Apologizing for no key to unlock the gate, he pulled the barbed wire fence apart, eased through and I followed suit.

"Bill, watch out for cow dung. It's everywhere, especially where you're not looking. You'll stink for a week!" Norvel led in his trademark tractor-tread shoes as we picked our way across the meadow and up the hill. We puffed to the first plateau and paused where Stauffer Chapel now stands. We spent quiet minutes drinking in the scene. We walked 50 yards farther to where Tyler Campus Center now stands and edged to the bluff, pausing where the big fireplace now rises in the corner of the dining room. We were silent again.

"Norvel," I asked, breaking the reverie and turning to look up the steep hill behind us, "can we go up there?" I pointed to the jeep road that wound up the hill to the rocky bluffs where the big flagpole now stands.

"Sure," Norvel shouted, charging ahead in those tractor-tread shoes.

Halfway up I puffed, "Is this all still part of those 138 acres?"

"It sure is!" Norvel huffed. "All of this would be our new campus."

The steep jeep road, curving right, circled straight up to the top of the mountain where the Brock House now stands. This was our third level since starting at the car. We had ascended to the central plateau where Seaver College now stands and then on up to the sweet spot destined to become the Banowsky family residence. The most spectacular panorama on the planet swept out across the ocean for a hundred miles from right to left.

"Norvel, this is the place," I quietly said. "I think God is calling us to build Pepperdine here."[18]

"I'm thrilled to hear that," he replied. "Does that mean you'll commit now to come back out here and take the lead to build this second campus?"

"Yes, Norvel. There's no way I can say no if, but only if, the trustees say yes and approve this site." Awaiting his reply, I got a loud scream instead.

"Watch out!" screamed Norvel, standing behind me on the bluff where the flagpole now stands.

"Watch out for what?" I twisted around.

"For that rattlesnake you're about to step on!" Norvel yelled again.

My heart in my throat, I jumped away from a silver-gray circle of poised rattlers coiled beside me. We scrambled off the rocks, caught our breath and walked back down to the car. Was the snake an omen of unseen obstacles ahead?

HIGH SIERRA SUMMIT

Norvel and I met 30 days later to consummate my commitment. "In 1967, Bill Banowsky and Norvel Young met again," recorded his biographers, "in Fresno, California, at the ranch of Marion and Lois Edmonds. Bill knew the Edmondses from the days when he served as preacher for the South Gate Church of Christ and Marion Edmonds was an elder. Banowsky and Young were both in Fresno for a church function."

I was preaching for a week to a nightly assembly of 6,000 in an area-wide "Crusade for Christ" at the Fresno Convention Center. At this peak in my preaching career, I frequently conducted evangelistic meetings in major cities. Deep fulfillment in the ministry made it painful to leave the pulpit. But Norvel had come up for the week to convince me. The Malibu trump card gave him the winning hand.

After the preaching we took off for two days of camping and fishing in the neighboring Sierra Nevada Mountains. Guided by the Edmondses' son-in-law, Pepperdine alumnus Merlyn Lund, we fished and talked at 8,000 feet in soft sunshine around a placid mountain lake. On the second night, around our blazing campfire, Norvel and I sealed the deal.

"Norvel shared his dream for a new undergraduate campus, *which he hoped would be at Malibu*," the biographers wrote. But I was deafened by the Malibu madness, and did not hear the incertitude of mere "hope." I heard only the certain sounds of the surf with campus construction resonating in the Malibu mountains. I went with my heart. "And Bill caught the dream," reported the official record, adding that, "while he did not have an interest in returning to the Los Angeles campus, the idea of building a whole new school in a place like Malibu excited him."[19]

In the campfire's warmth, I pledged, "Norvel, it's a done deal. With Merlyn here as our witness, I will take the lead to design, fund and construct

A MIRACLE IN THE MAKING

This December 1969 panorama reveals the miracle of moving more than three million cubic yards of earth and rock. It especially dramatizes the Marie Canyon fill, which ran 120 feet deep at the Pacific Coast Highway. With twenty-first century ecological protections and prohibitions along the California coastline, such a massive movement of earth would be utterly impossible today.

"BUT I KNEW . . .

Even then, that it was the most ecologically perfect thing that could be put here."

—Bill Banowsky

the new Malibu campus, but first you must promise that the trustees will approve the Malibu site."

"You've got a deal," Norvel replied. "I promise, with Merlyn here as our witness, that we're going to Malibu." The three of us shook hands around the fire.

TRUSTEES REJECT MALIBU

At that magical fireside moment no one could have known that keeping Norvel's promise would demand an Armageddon battle with the board. After the meeting in Fresno, I returned to Texas, and Norvel's biographers recount: " The board received a letter from Bill Banowsky . . . [who] wrote powerfully on why he believed that Malibu was the right location."[20] I closed that five-page "powerful" letter urgently: "Norvel, if you and I must confront the board sooner or later, sooner would be better than later."[21]

Norvel agreed. We scheduled two decisive meetings to secure the Malibu site approval. On Thursday, February 15, 1968, the site selection committee convened for lunch at the California Club and included George Evans. Norvel opened in eloquent encomium on Malibu glories. George followed with assurance that the Adamsons would donate the land. All four committee members were completely sold. Chairman Darnell called for the motion and vote: "The site selection committee hereby unanimously recommends to the Pepperdine College trustees that the second campus should be built on the Malibu site." After 15 months of meetings the site selection committee adjourned and never met again.

With Pepperdine at Malibu dancing in our minds, Gay and I secretly went house shopping. We found the perfect Sunset Mesa residence where Malibu meets Pacific Palisades at the Getty Museum. The backyard pool at 18335 Clifftop Way cantilevered over Topanga Canyon with the ocean stretching to the horizon beyond. Out front, at night, an endless procession of airliners twinkled like fireflies to their LAX landings. The Banowsky family was first to move to Malibu. We bought our home four years before we opened the campus. That's the good news. The bad news is that, almost immediately after we bought it, the trustees turned Malibu down.

During the search process the big president's board performed perfectly but the little board of trustees performed pitifully. Their most pitiful day was Monday, March 11, 1968. "The 15 members of the board of trustees finally met to decide the future direction of undergraduate study at Pepperdine. After much discussion, they decided to decline the offer of the Malibu property because the College simply did not have the money to invest in moving the thousands of tons of earth to build on the hillsides." On top of the money concerns, others "opposed the Malibu site, believing that the celebrity village's reputation made it an unsuitable place for a Christian college."[22] Malibu was "just too worldly," some said.

That coalition of idealists and pragmatists that had formed in Los Angeles to defend the old campus now determined to kill off the Malibu campus in embryo. The 15 to 0 vote would have been Pepperdine's obituary if the board of trustees had been permitted to write it. But Norvel and I did not permit them. We dug in deeply to defeat them.

Personally, after preparing for months, buying our new residence and scheduling a television resignation for Sunday, March 17, 1968, I was now forced to announce my move back to Pepperdine just when Malibu seemed anything but certain. I edited the press release to replace all of the Malibu references with vagueness. "Dr. Banowsky will become the executive vice president of Pepperdine College," Texas and California newspapers reported, "to lead development of a new campus whose location, expected to be selected within 30 days, is to be in another part of Los Angeles County."[23] That vague reference to Los Angeles County merely meant to the trustees Calabasas or Westlake Village. But for Norvel and me it meant only Malibu. I, therefore, publicly predicted a 30-day location decision. But it took six grueling months to win the Malibu victory on October 2, 1968.

"PEPPERDINE UNIVERSITY
THE MALIBU CAMPUS"
The brand-new major intersection at Pacific Coast Highway and
Malibu Canyon Road—December 1969.

CHRISTMAS 1968

Governor Ronald Reagan brings "Season's Greetings" by congratulating President Young and Executive Vice President Banowsky on the acquisition of the land for the Malibu campus.

RALLY ROUND THE FLAG

The first thing to go up at Malibu was the 100-foot tall flagpole. The American flag flew every day until the campus opened three years later. That first Malibu miracle inner circle of eight included Charles Runnels, Gay and Bill Banowsky, Blanche and Richard Seaver, Norvel and Helen Young talking to Hydril's John Hall. In the background are the scorched but virginal Malibu hills.

10:00 A.M., WEDNESDAY, OCTOBER 2, 1968

Setting aside worldliness worries, Norvel and I addressed the trustees' financial terror. We quickly raised $2 million in cash for Malibu site preparation. That $2 million marked the conception of the historic capital campaign that eventually raised more than $400 million. Norvel and I worked all summer with our two top prospects, Richard Mellon Scaife and Mrs. Frank Roger Seaver. Mr. Scaife came through with $500,000, making him—aside from Mr. Pepperdine—the largest donor in Pepperdine history. But only for a few days.

"[Mrs. Seaver] made the greatest pacesetting gift—$1,350,000—when it was announced that Pepperdine had received a gift of land in beautiful Malibu and was going to build a second campus there," reported her biographer, Bill Youngs. "She has multiplied that gift many times since with a commitment which may very well be one of the greatest donations ever made to private education."[24] Mrs. Seaver's check was the largest single gift yet received in Pepperdine history, Mr. Pepperdine included.

Along with the Scaife and Seaver gifts, Norvel and I garnered $150,000 more from a few others and called a trustees meeting. We laid the $2 million on the table. We got unanimous approval of the Malibu land. We got permission to proceed full speed ahead with campus construction.

The historic press conference unveiling the Adamson family gift was set for 10:00 a.m., Wednesday, October 2, 1968. "I am pleased to also announce," added Norvel, "that the board of trustees approved the appointment of the executive vice president of the College, Dr. William S. Banowsky, to be the director of the Malibu Campus. He has been challenged to take the lead in constructing a truly innovative master plan that will directly influence the shape of brick and mortar."[25] Fancier Malibu titles would follow but "director of the Malibu Campus" came first.

THE BIG THREE

During the press conference a gratified George Evans, the shy Adamson consigliere, stood quietly aside. His marriage of Pepperdine to Malibu would be a lasting legacy, but George was no legacy man. "This quiet diffidence is how George appeared every Sunday for worship at the Southwest church," said minister James Smythe. Timing is all. When George Evans died in 2003 at the age of 90, Norvel publicly christened him the "unsung hero of the Malibu miracle".[26] He was one of the three big stars God used uniquely to perform it. Many lesser stars adorned the Malibu heavens but God lined these three big stars up at the quintessentially perfect time and place. George got the land. Without George there would be no Malibu. Blanche gave the money. Without her there would be no campus. Norvel, the greatest person in Pepperdine history, pulled it all together.

Blanche, a celebrated professional musician, loved classic opera at the Dorothy Chandler Pavilion. Suppose the Malibu miracle were grand opera. With dramatic pathos it awaits a creative composer to set it to music. In the Malibu miracle opera Blanche was the diva. George was the set designer. Norvel was the impresario. I played the part of musical conductor. And there was one more major player. His name was Ronald Reagan.

"REAGAN REPUBLICANS"

At the majestic Hilton Hotel press conference, Merritt, Sylvia and Rhoda-May Adamson were positioned before microphones on one side of a formal table. Norvel and Bill Teague were positioned before microphones on the other side. It was high drama. Many media were present. Having learned already just *how* the Adamson family decided to give their Malibu land away we now learned precisely *why* they decided to give it to Pepperdine College.[27]

"The choice of Pepperdine for this gift," proclaimed Merritt Adamson, "was prompted, in large part, by the *conservative nature of the college* (emphasis mine)."[28]

Merritt and his sisters were "fiercely loyal Reagan Republicans." In publicly announcing their main motive for making the Pepperdine gift, they unveiled the indispensable Malibu miracle component. One of the greatest leaders of the twentieth century happened, perhaps miraculously, to be the "patron saint of Pepperdine."

1. Morley Safer, "The Malibu Canine Protection Farm—A Documentary," *60 Minutes*, CBS, July 15, 2007.
2. *The Story of Malibu* (Malibu: The Malibu Lagoon Museum, 1978), 14.
3. Ibid., 22. "Under the law during the Spanish period, the absolute ownership of land was unknown. Concessions of land, however, could be granted by the territorial governors in the name of the king of Spain for farming and cattle grazing." This "use concession" and not an outright land grant was the status of Tapia's title.
4. Ibid., 2.
5. "Spanish Exploration and Early Owners of Malibu," http://www.malibucomplete.com/mc_history_spanish.php. "Thirty-five years earlier in 1857, Leon Victor Prudhomme sold Rancho Malibu to Don Mateo Keller for ten cents per acre. His son, Henry Keller, sold it to Rindge for ten dollars an acre." Malibu land inflation was underway early.
6. Frederick Hastings Rindge, *Happy Days in Southern California* (Cambridge: Frederick H. Rindge, 1898), 116–124.

7. Lawrence Clark Powell, "On Republishing Frederick Hasting Rindge's *Happy Days in Southern California*." Address delivered at a breakfast meeting sponsored by the Malibu Historical Society, at Pepperdine University, November 11, 1972. Powell was the dean emeritus of the UCLA Libraries.

8. Ron Stump, "Adamsons Donate 138 Valuable Acres," *Pepperdine Graphic*, October 10, 1968, 1, 4. Stump was editor-in-chief of Pepperdine's student newspaper.

9. Bill Henegar and Jerry Rushford, *Forever Young: The Life and Times of M. Norvel Young and Helen M. Young* (Nashville: 21st Century Christian, 1999), 214.

10. Ibid., 188.

11. Ibid., 193.

12. Ibid., 225.

13. "Celebrating Charlie," *Pepperdine People*, Spring 2008, 31.

14. Henegar and Rushford, *Forever Young*, 189.

15. Jerry Rushford, ed., *Crest of a Golden Wave: Pepperdine University, 1937–1987* (Malibu: Pepperdine University Press, 1987), 111.

16. Henegar and Rushford, *Forever Young*, 191.

17. Michael F. Adams, Pepperdine inter-office communication, to Larry D. Hornbaker, January 21, 1985. According to Adams, by 1985 George Evans had discontinued his Pepperdine gifts because "he is still disappointed with Dr. O'Neal over our investment policies."

18. See Dorothy D. Stotsenberg, *My Fifty Years in Malibu* (Malibu: Pepperdine University Press, 2005). This book pictures the beauty and grace of the virgin site. Especially see Chapter 22, "Then Came Pepperdine!", 125–130.

19. Henegar and Rushford, *Forever Young*, 204.

20. Ibid., 193.

21. William S. Banowsky, personal letter to M. Norvel Young, October 26, 1967. The Banowsky Papers. This letter remains, today, the strongest possible case for Malibu. It presciently predicted in detail the miraculous transformation of Pepperdine University at Malibu.

22. Henegar and Rushford, *Forever Young*, 192–193.

23. *Los Angeles Times*, March 17, 1968.

24. Bill Youngs, *The Legacy of Frank Roger Seaver* (Malibu: Pepperdine University Press, 1976), 116.

25. M. Norvel Young, "Banowsky Named Director of Malibu Campus," press release, October 2, 1968. The Banowsky Papers.

26. Henegar and Rushford, *Forever Young*, 192, 329.

27. "Malibu Chosen as Site," *Pepperdine News*, October 1968. Here was the official 1983 Pepperdine University Malibu land acquisition record: (1) Original Adamson 138 acres in 1968; (2) Additional Adamson and Alcoa 284 acres from 1969 through 1973; (3) Two Senial Ostrow gifts of 210 acres in 1969 and 1972; and Howard A. White's "Louisiana Purchase" of 198 acres for the Drescher campus site in 1983. Today's campus totals 830 acres.

28. "Malibu Chosen as Site," *Pepperdine News*, October 1968.

"Pepperdine's principles attracted Ronnie and me many years ago. We love the Malibu campus and support the university."

NANCY REAGAN
The First Lady
May 1, 1983

THE REAGAN REDWOOD TREE

Governor and Mrs. Reagan personally selected, and planted, a rare specimen redwood tree on December 15, 1972. As Nancy Reagan lectures Bill about how to tend and care for the tree, Bill and Governor Reagan seemed almost amused, if not chagrined.

CHAPTER 6

RIDING THE REAGAN REVOLUTION

I left our Sunset Mesa residence at 8:15 a.m. Saturday morning to drive five miles north. The date was January 18, 1969. At the center of Malibu I pulled off the highway onto the dirt apron at Pepperdine's brand-new property.

The 9:00 a.m. meeting was with trustee George A. Evans and construction coordinator Andrew K. Rawn.[1] They were already there and excited. Six days earlier—Monday, January 13, 1969—we launched massive grading to move mountains and begin to build Pepperdine's new campus. "Construction," reported the *Santa Monica Evening Outlook* "has begun with brush clearing operation on the 138-acre hillside campus. Phase one of the self-contained residential college will cost $24.6 million, including a theme tower to rise 125 feet offering views from Palos Verdes to Pt. Conception."[2]

OUR "PATRON SAINT"

The three of us chatted beside Andy's truck and watched the conception of Seaver College. Huge yellow scrapers, bulldozers and big dump trucks hummed like bees in a hive.

Suddenly, a black limousine edged off the highway and eased alongside us. We squinted through tinted windows, wondering who it was. The back window slid down. A handshaking arm stuck out. To our joyful surprise, it was the governor of California. He came, as he often did on Saturdays, from his home in nearby Pacific Palisades to ride horses on his ranch sprawling just over the hill from the campus.

"Hey, Bill," he said, shaking my hand as he cocked his head into that immortal crooked grin. "Boy, I'm thrilled to see you guys at work on this new campus!"

Ronald and Nancy Reagan lived nearby and loved Pepperdine.

"Let me say I have a strong proprietary interest in this new Malibu campus," Reagan told Pepperdine students four years later in December 1972, when he and Nancy came to plant a redwood tree. "For many years I've owned a ranch near here. I've ridden all over these hills above the campus. I hope you students will absorb the beauty and love of Malibu. It will never leave you."[3]

The Malibu miracle materialized in the mighty winds of the "Reagan Revolution." Lyn Nofziger, Reagan's irascible communications director in Sacramento and White House political director, was a Pepperdine visiting professor.[4] In 1977–78, Nofziger taught a two-unit political science course, Communicating in Politics. "Ronald Reagan," he informed his classes, "is the patron saint of Pepperdine!"[5]

REPUBLICAN PARTY SCHOOL

The *Los Angeles Times* dramatized the Reagan relationship in a 1987 exposé headlined: "Pepperdine: Party School by the Shore (Republican, That Is)."

> In less than two decades, Pepperdine has transformed itself from an obscure South-Central Los Angeles college of 1,500 to a thriving seaside university with 2,500 students and satellite schools pushing total enrollment past 6,000. There is little dispute that the changes are directly related to administrators' solid ties to the Republican Party in general and the Reagan Administration in particular—ties that are at least as strong as the school's links with the Churches of Christ. The rise of Pepperdine parallels the rise to national power of Ronald Reagan and the California Republicans. They were first courted by Pepperdine officials in the late 1960s and early 1970s, a time when other campuses were engulfed in turmoil over the Vietnam War and an assortment of radical causes.

The *Los Angeles Times* also divulged that, along with the Reagans and Nofziger, recent Pepperdine Republican speakers included Supreme Court Chief Justice William H. Rehnquist, Justice Antonin Scalia, Secretary of State Alexander Haig, Attorney General Edwin Meese III and members of the President's Council of Economic Advisors, Arthur Laffer and Beryl Sprinkel.[6]

But by 1987 the intimate Reagan relationship was an ancient accusation. Fifteen years earlier, editor-in-chief Bob Eisberg of the *Graphic*, the student newspaper, leveled the charge more caustically. The year was 1973 and "Pep Watergate" is how Eisberg titled his early editorial. "Pepperdine has become the darling of the conservative wing of the GOP. The word 'independent' should be stricken from Pepperdine's self-description as an 'independent, liberal arts, Christian college,'" lampooned Eisberg.

"When FBI Director L. Patrick Gray was asked by Senator Sam Ervin, on the televised Watergate hearings, where he was on the break-in night of June 17, 1972, Gray responded he was in Los Angeles to speak at a Pepperdine 'Great Issues' dinner and the university law school graduation," Eisberg continued. He also lamented the early 1970s list of speakers. "They include Attorney General Richard Kleindeinst, White House henchman John Ehrlichman, Secretary of Agriculture Earl Butz, economists Arthur Burns, Jean Pierre Rinfret and Herbert Stein, Senator Barry Goldwater and, of course, Governor Reagan himself."[7]

IT'S BANOWSKY'S FAULT

Both the *Los Angeles Times* and the *Graphic* blamed me for launching Pepperdine deep into Republican waters. "In case you haven't noticed, all of those people are Republicans just like Pepperdine President William S. Banowsky is a high-profile Republican," agonized student editor Eisberg. "Right in the middle of Ervin's televised Watergate hearings, Dr. Banowsky announced that Governor Reagan had appointed him to the position of Republican National Committeeman for California. Two weeks ago, Dr. Banowsky took four Pepperdine students to the state GOP Convention to make them official members of the California Republican Central Committee.

"Last year," lamented Eisberg, "Reagan appointed Dr. Banowsky the Southern California Chairman of the Nixon Reelection Committee and delegate to the Republican National Convention in Miami. On national television, Dr. Banowsky escorted Spiro Agnew to the convention platform for Agnew's renomination as vice president of the United States. Where does it all end?"

"It probably won't end," as Eisberg answered his own question, "until Banowsky runs for Governor in 1974 or the U.S. Senate in 1976. And if you don't think Banowsky is running for high office you're in a smaller minority than the people who will now admit they voted for Nixon-Agnew in 1972."

"But the worst thing of all," erupted Eisberg with ironic accuracy, "is that Pepperdine doesn't seem to mind its GOP reputation!"[8] That reputation was at the heart of the Malibu miracle. Along with the criticism came the congratulations. "Congratulations on the great reelection victory that you helped shape for President Nixon," wrote my friend Billy Graham at the same 1972 moment.[9]

By 1987, the *Los Angeles Times* commemorated Pepperdine's meteoric rise "from right-wing extremism to national academic prestige." But the newspaper also cited a surprising detractor: "'I think it would be a mistake to characterize Pepperdine as a right-wing university,' said Norman Cousins, a Pepperdine advisory board member and former editor of the liberal *Saturday Review*."

To explain the phenomenal mainstream progress, the *Los Angeles Times* called me out in 1987 as the central conservative culprit from the 1960s and '70s. "'Pepperdine didn't change its politics,' said William S. Banowsky who was university president in the 1970s. 'Its politics just became less disreputable.'"[10] By translation, that meant Pepperdine's patron saint had become the popular two-term president of the United States.

WHAT'S THE RELEVANCE?

Why is all this political minutiae relevant? Because the national media targeted this controversial question at the heart of the Malibu miracle: Was Pepperdine transformed by a supernatural spiritual phenomenon? Or by a calculated political operation? Was it an educational or an ideological achievement? Was it caused by God or Reagan? According to historian Howard A. White, it was a combustible combination of both. "Joining to produce the 'Malibu miracle' were . . . the American system of free enterprise . . . and . . . the overarching providence of God."[11]

The Malibu miracle did not occur in a vacuum but was part and parcel of the Reagan revolution. Guided by providence, it centered on higher education and conservative public policy. As if choreographed by a company of angels, Reagan's 1966 gubernatorial election and the formation of Pepperdine's 1966 site selection committee could not have been more perfectly timed. President Reagan's rise to power and Pepperdine's rise to prestige could not have been more synchronized. In the second half of the twentieth century, Reagan's place among great leaders and Pepperdine's place among great universities were mutually reinforcing. Without Ronald Reagan the Malibu miracle is inconceivable.

Despite media insinuation, there was nothing sinister about the symbiotic relationship. It unfolded naturally. In its earliest years the Reagan revolution headquartered in the family's residence at 16695 San Onofre in Pacific Palisades, on Malibu's border, minutes from Pepperdine. Reagan was a General Electric spokesman and the company designed and equipped his model electric home. Gay and I were frequent guests, often escorting Blanche Seaver, Dick Scaife and others.

In addition to their residence and ranch near the campus, the Reagans vacationed two weeks every summer at nearby Trancas in the Broad Beach home of friends. Our family owned a Broad Beach house and visited with the Reagans at the surf.

When Reagan became governor he inherited rioting campuses statewide. Some of the presidents publicly denounced him. Imagine his relief to escape the battlefield by driving a few miles from Pacific Palisades to the Malibu campus to be welcomed, honored and adored. Pepperdine became the favorite school of one of the most powerful men on the planet.

When the governor became "a hiss and a byword" on most California campuses, Pepperdine always remained "Reagan's school."[12] Long before the Reagans entered politics Pepperdine people were among their friends. Such friendships would have continued had they stayed in show business. There was nothing superficial about it.

"The roots of Pepperdine's Republican tradition were planted by the founder himself, George Pepperdine," the *Los Angeles Times* observed. "George Pepperdine established the college in 1937 to train business leaders."[13] Mr. Pepperdine was a fierce free-enterprise economic and social conservative who supported Republicans from Teddy Roosevelt and Herbert Hoover to Dwight Eisenhower and Barry Goldwater. With the coming of President Young in 1957, that conservative taproot took total control of Pepperdine. When Reagan became governor, an early appointment put his personal friend, President Young, on the powerful California Commission on Higher Education. Pepperdine's conservative image, no predatory fundraising façade, was genuine to the core.

GEORGE S. BENSON

Pepperdine's conservatism, however, in no way implied the absence of calculation. A strategy was crafted to identify, cultivate and solicit donors. Pepperdine learned to package and present the powerful case for conservative higher education from America's fundraising master himself—Dr. George Stuart Benson.

In 1936, a year prior to Pepperdine's founding, Dr. Benson left missionary work at Sun Yat-sen University in China to become president of "a small, unknown Church of Christ college in the little, sleepy town of Searcy, Arkansas, with a $68,000 mortgage against its campus."[14] Thanks to a 1936 cash gift of $50,000 from his friend George Pepperdine, Benson paid the debt, built a campus bonfire, burned the mortgage papers and celebrated the joy of fundraising.[15] George S. Benson put Harding University on the map by becoming one of the great fundraisers of all time.

Chastened by his China experience, Benson was inspired and equipped to warn America, early and earnestly, about the emerging threat of world communism. Addressing conservatives everywhere, he added to his trinity of devils big-government abuse and free-enterprise suppression. George Benson pioneered the precise formula that 40 years later catapulted Ronald Reagan to the presidency.[16]

Benson's stardom struck with his 1941 appearance before the Congressional House Ways and Means Committee. His presentation of a detailed plan to cut "$2 billion of FDR boondoggles from the federal budget" was ballyhooed by the media into a sensational national story. Overnight, Dr. Benson gained fame and Harding got a flood of students. Money flowed into the Arkansas school from big-government haters everywhere. Benson's church critics claimed that he diverted attention from the church "to affirmations of Americanism, support for patriotic nationalism, and a preoccupation with the threat of international Communism."[17]

By 1943 Benson had moved from politics into American educational history. He established his renowned National Education Program. The NEP was no extracurricular adjunct. It was a Harding College for-credit academic department to promote Americanism for adult students nationwide. It featured faith in God, fiscal conservatism, anti-communism, limited government and free enterprise. "This program," concluded *The Encyclopedia of the Stone-Campbell Movement*, "was widely regarded as an important intellectual center for the 'New Right' movement in American politics that helped foster the conservative resurgence culminating in the election of Ronald Reagan in 1980."[18]

Long before bloggers, cable television or radio talk shows, George Benson became the Rush Limbaugh of his day. He broadcast weekly on 183 radio stations in 43 states. He published a weekly column in 2,600 newspapers. He edited a hard-hitting monthly newsletter for forty thousand subscribers. He professionally produced cartoon-style conservative motion pictures seen by 35 million Americans. He shrewdly consolidated his base by founding the famous "Harding Freedom Forum." It attracted to his campus thousands of businessmen, educators and industrial workers from across America.

PEPPERDINE EMULATES HARDING

Benson's bold program was a conservative call to arms. Its primary purpose was to gain business backing and financial support for Harding College. It established a fundraising model for many private institutions. Ambitious young conservatives everywhere observed Benson's operation in awe.[19] Two of the most awed and ambitious were M. Norvel Young, who watched from his Lubbock, Texas, pulpit and William J. Teague, who watched from his Abilene Christian College fundraising vice presidency. Young and Teague

Top: Preeminent twentieth-century British philosopher, theologian and journalist Malcom Muggeridge speaks at the 1975 Pepperdine University Great Issues Series.

Bottom: In 1973, George Herbert Walker Bush visited the Malibu campus as chairman of the Republican National Committee. As the Republican National Committeeman from California, Dr. Banowsky served on Chairman Bush's executive committee.

were destined soon to join forces at Pepperdine College in Los Angeles, where they would make historic use of Benson's fundraising model.

In 1957, Dr. Young was summoned to save Pepperdine from bankruptcy. He instantly entered into months of consultation with Dr. Benson. The aging Arkansas genius admired Pepperdine and made several Los Angeles trips to stay for days with Dr. and Mrs. Young. Emulating Dr. Benson, Dr. Young founded the Pepperdine Freedom Forum in 1958. He soon changed its name to the Great Issues Series, about which the *Los Angeles Times* concluded: "This powerful annual event drew experts in many fields to examine the full spectrum of monetary, foreign and social problems underlying the nation's unrest." Speakers included Barry Goldwater, Milton Friedman, Irvin Kristol, William F. Buckley, Malcolm Muggeridge and Ronald Reagan. Most of the Malibu miracle funding was first conceived by the prolific Pepperdine Great Issues Series.[20]

Meanwhile Teague, his presidential ambitions disillusioned at Abilene Christian College, decided to move to the Harding College vice presidency. He could sit at master Benson's feet, hopefully, as his heir apparent.[21]

Young initially tried a talented Texas friend, O. T. (Skipper) Shipp, as his first Pepperdine fundraising vice president.[22] With no fundraising program in place from the Tiner years, Shipp labored mightily. After two years produced little money and an unbalanced budget, Shipp returned to the familiar fertile field of Texas.

In 1958, Benson retired at Harding College. As earlier in Abilene, Teague's presidential ambitions were again frustrated. Therefore, in 1959, Young recruited Teague. He had gained a world-class fundraising education in Texas and Arkansas. Norvel crowned him vice president and heir apparent. Working together, Young and Teague adopted Benson's model and multiplied it mightily.

Gay and I were Bill and Peggy Teague's lifelong friends. He and I bonded early as West Texas pals, he from Nocona and I from Abilene. For our first Pepperdine sojourn Gay and I arrived in Los Angeles from Albuquerque on the same August 1959 day Bill and Peggy arrived from Arkansas. For four years, 1959 through 1963, we worked side by side in adjoining Tower of Power offices. Teague was Norvel's vice president and I was Norvel's assistant.

WILLIAM J. TEAGUE

Bill Teague made a largely overlooked Pepperdine contribution. During the decade from 1958 to 1968, though not raising much cash, he erected brick by brick the financial foundation upon which Norvel and I subsequently established Malibu miracle fundraising.

1968 REPUBLICANS FOR
GEORGE PEPPERDINE COLLEGE

Vice President William J. Teague and Peggy Teague out on the town with Mrs. Seaver. The Teagues, although largely uncelebrated, devoted the difficult decade from 1958 to 1968 to the building of the Malibu miracle financial foundation.

Teague was one of those hard-right, cutting-edge conservatives described in philosopher Eric Hoffer's popular book of the day, *The True Believer*.[23] Today's "true believers" are social and evangelical new-right conservatives. Back then many were members of the John Birch Society. The true believers, then and now, sense one another's shared convictions. They bond in fellowship and trust. They can smell a liberal a mile away. If, like Norvel and me, one is only an ordinary conservative with an occasional moderate streak, they sense that too. They often have as little regard for moderates as for outright liberals. The true-believing Teague earned credibility with the conservative Pepperdine donors who eventually made the major Malibu gifts. When Mr. Pepperdine passed away in 1963, Dr. Teague, who served as an elder for three Church of Christ congregations, was one of three men chosen by the family to officiate at the founder's funeral.

At Pepperdine, under Norvel's careful coaching, Teague unleashed a volley of 1960s right-wing artillery. His arsenal included the Pat Boone–USA radio show; a series of anticommunist films shown in hundreds of school rooms; and the fabulous Pepperdine Freedom Forum.[24]

Off campus, Teague was publicly highly popular. He was honored, for instance, as one of the judges for the 1968 Tournament of Roses Parade in Pasadena. A peripatetic Republican speaker, Teague was a superior master of ceremonies. Brisk and witty at the podium, he was paired so often to preside and introduce Governor Reagan that adoring Republicans dubbed them "the gold dust twins." But despite his off-campus popularity, Teague's combative conservatism created faculty conflict at Abilene, Harding and Pepperdine. "Vice President Teague's flagrant courtship of the right wing perturbed many faculty," Dr. James Smythe recalled. "Norvel always found a way to get along. But Teague and the faculty were at war. He seemed to shove his conservatism into their faces."[25]

Teague's adversarial relationship did not apply to all faculty. Some were Republicans and a few were as active in the party as Teague. Dr. Fred L. Casmir, longtime Pepperdine speech professor, joined Teague as a Republican candidate for Congress.[26]

"NORVELIAN"

"It wasn't popular then to be 'Conservative' or patriotic or even 'anti-Communist,' but we dared to be different,"[27] Norvel reflected on Teague's faculty tensions. In truth, Pepperdine's conservative campaign required less courage than common sense. "Daring to be different meant public disagreement with the mainline media and elite academy. But the silent majority loved us for it," Norvel shamelessly confessed.

With Norvelian finesse the non-pugnacious Norvel sacrificed popular media coverage for quiet financial support from grateful conservatives proud of Pepperdine for waving the flag. He assiduously avoided offending the faculty. Instead, he adroitly unleashed the combative Teague to build a conservative base.

With slightly tweaked timing and less faculty opposition, Dr. Teague and not I would have succeeded Norvel as fourth president of the college and first of the university. But, after ten years warring in Los Angeles with scant hope for a new campus, Teague traded Pepperdine equity for a fling at congressional politics, leaving others to pull together his foundational financial work. He never enjoyed a day at Malibu. But it's possible that without him no one else would have either.

Norvel brought me back to Pepperdine in 1968 to replace Teague, with an enlarged title of executive vice president. I piloted the voyage to Malibu. "I reaped," in Christ's words, "where I had not sown." I could never have harvested so many millions from so many conservatives in such short time without Teague's ten years of tilling the soil. Millions of dollars solicited for Malibu came from scores of conservatives cultivated by Teague, including Blanche Seaver and Dick Scaife. The biggest donors admired Bill most and missed him much. But he received no Pepperdine recognition, not even a ritualistic honorary doctorate. Few today appreciate how much he and Peggy gave.

After losing the 1968 congressional race by the narrowest margin in any district that year, Teague ultimately achieved his goal. In 1981 he was elected president of Abilene Christian University. The Teague Activities Center memorializes his years of Abilene service with passable faculty serenity.

THE REAGAN CONTRIBUTION

Historic leaders Richard M. Nixon, Gerald R. Ford, George H. W. Bush and George W. Bush visited the Malibu campus at one time or another. All were Pepperdine friends. But Ronald Reagan blessed the Malibu miracle in three unique ways. First, Reagan addresses at early Malibu events generated momentum. Second, being recognized as "Reagan's school" created credibility. Third, personal endorsement by Ronald and Nancy Reagan lubricated fundraising. Momentum, credibility and fundraising were the three indispensable Reagan contributions. After several campus visits to boost construction, on February 9, 1970, Reagan delivered the "Birth of a College" address, "one of the most memorable occasions in the history of Pepperdine College."[28] Through the years, on both campuses, Reagan delivered several stirring addresses. But he capped it all off on April 20, 1975, with his address to dedicate Frank R. Seaver College.

First Lady Nancy Reagan, on May 1, 1983, also delivered a major Malibu address and received an honorary doctorate.[29] Pepperdine had bestowed a doctorate on her husband 12 years earlier. Reagan ultimately received 27 doctorates, including one from Oxford University. The Pepperdine doctorate was number two, following the one from his Eureka College alma mater. I don't know of a dollar the Reagan friendship ever cost us. But I know of hundreds of millions of dollars it helped raise. Reagan introduced new prospects and he assisted with their cultivation. He came personally, in his own words, "to be your bait."

Pepperdine friends on the other side of the aisle included Senator Alan Cranston, California governor "Jerry" Brown and Los Angeles mayor Tom Bradley. But very little cash came from Democrats. The biggest Democrat donor to the Malibu miracle was Jewish business genius Seniel Ostrow, president of Sealy Mattress Company. Mr. Ostrow's Rancho Malibu acreage included some that joined the Malibu campus and he made two enormous land donations at its northwest corner. In 1969 he gave 50 acres. In 1972 he gave 160 more.[30] "I gave Pepperdine my 210 acres primarily because I'm proud to be a Reagan Democrat."[31]

KNOWING RONALD REAGAN

I first met Reagan on March 18, 1963. He spoke at Pepperdine in Los Angeles at the required 10:00 a.m. Monday chapel. As dean of students, I sat beside him. He was introduced by his friend Bill Teague. Norvel closed the packed-house event. A youthful 52, Reagan knew who he was and where he was. He addressed our students with a winsome blend of humor and scripture. Reagan had attended the Disciples of Christ Eureka College in Illinois. From 1928 to 1932, he enjoyed daily compulsory chapel and required Bible classes. Reagan's vibrant embrace of Pepperdine naturally developed as a reminder of his cherished Eureka days.[32]

Months later, in October 1964, after moving to the Broadway Church of Christ, I watched on my Lubbock bedroom television as Reagan delivered his famous fundraising speech for Goldwater's presidential campaign. That positioned him for the California governorship. When Norvel campaigned for my return to build a second campus, it was, of course, Malibu that sealed the deal. But the chance to work politically with Reagan was also appealing. Norvel pointed to Teague's dynamic mix of Pepperdine and politics as the ideal model for me.

Friday, June 7, 1968, I delivered my Pepperdine coming-out speech. Norvel booked me before the world's largest Rotary Club at its Hilton Hotel weekly luncheon. The Malibu miracle was mightily encouraged by

FRIENDS AND BROTHERS

Ron and Bill enjoy a moment of private
conversation in January 1973. It is
a beautiful Sunday afternoon in the
backyard of Reagan's Pacific Palisades
neighbors. Name tags in place, Bill gets
set to introduce the governor for his
25-minute inspirational speech.

two historic Los Angeles mayors, Sam Yorty (1961–1973) and Tom Bradley (1973–1993). For the Rotary speech I was introduced by Mayor Yorty in one of the most tumultuous moments of American history. Only 60 days earlier Martin Luther King had been assassinated. Just two days earlier, at the nearby Ambassador Hotel, Robert F. Kennedy was assassinated. "The nation, shocked and grieving, seemed to be coming apart at the seams," recalled NBC anchor Tom Brokaw.[33]

The social and rhetorical moment called for law-and-order oratory. My stem-winder, "The Abuse of Freedom," condemned "long-haired hippie campus demonstrators, inner-city racial rioters and outright assassins," and I called for "discipline, restraint and spiritual faith." The Rotarians gave the speech a standing ovation. Freedoms Foundation at Valley Forge gave it a George Washington Honor Medal. Norvel mailed it to 40,000 people. Under my picture on the corner came this captioned endorsement: "'This is a great address and should receive wide distribution.'—The Honorable Ronald Reagan, Governor of California." On the personal stationery of "Mrs. Ronald Reagan, Executive Residence, Sacramento, California" came this handwritten note: "Dear Bill, Thank you so much for sending your great speech, 'The Abuse of Freedom.' Ronnie and I really appreciated it. Sincerely, Nancy."[34]

My speeches to schools and colleges, corporations and conventions, civic clubs and community groups fueled political persona, media celebrity and close relationships with dozens of wealthy Pepperdine supporters, including Blanche Seaver. She accompanied me to scores of speeches as we perfected a communications shorthand that made our friendship lots of fun. During the 1968–78 decade I averaged 3 formal speeches per week, 12 per month, 150 per year.

I usually spoke pro bono though Reagan advised that I institute a modest honorarium for business and professional appearances. The speeches brought appointments to high Republican posts and election as director of 12 publicly traded corporations wanting an educator for outside director. Mrs. Seaver accompanied me around the state. We bonded, communing on tiny bags of peanuts passed out on PSA flights. Speeches resulted in two years of my own weekly KNBC-TV interview program, *Now with Banowsky*, and three years of an opinion column for the *Los Angeles Herald Examiner*.

President Nixon's 1972 reelection put a feather in our cap. On election night Gay and I huddled alone with the Reagans around a backstage table at the Century Plaza Hotel. We awaited the cue to appear together from behind the curtain, proclaim victory and take the television bows. We chatted for 15 minutes then walked, arm-in-arm, out on stage. Reagan presented me as the California chairman for Nixon's reelection. The hackneyed election night scene was memorable for Gay and me. The one time we stood before the cameras in political victory we stood beside the Governor and Mrs. Reagan. Many witnessed the warm friendship. Credibility soared and Malibu miracle fundraising accelerated.

Months later, in 1973, the four of us circled again around the same Century Plaza backstage table. This time we were awaiting grand entry into the Republican Party of California annual fundraising dinner. At Reagan's request, I served as chairman. Christening it "The Governor Reagan Appreciation Dinner," we raised $500,000. The Reagans were gracious to Gay and me in backstage intimacy and later sent this warm personal note: "Nancy and I cannot adequately express our thanks to you and Gay for the outstanding job you did. It was a moving and gratifying experience and one of the most unforgettable nights of our lives. Thank you for making it all possible and for your continuing special friendship. Sincerely, Ron."[35]

Going forward, politics for me was as up and down as a roller-coaster ride. On the upside, on Wednesday, June 26, 1974, I served as chairman of the Governor Ronald Reagan Appreciation Dinner at the Century Plaza Hotel. We raised funds, at $250 per plate, for the Republican Party of California. On the downside, two years later the Democrats got the Attorney General of California to sue me and the dinner committee for a minor technical violation in response to a new political funding law.[36] It was but another distractive hassle.

NOT KNOWING REAGAN

Reagan interactions revealed his legendary capacity to combine cordiality with emotional distance. "Although he was completely cordial," Tom Brokaw wrote of his 1963 introduction to Reagan in Nebraska, "he was not noticeably warm. That part of his personality remained an enigma even to his closest friends and advisors throughout his historically successful political career."[37] Except for alter ego Nancy, it also remained an enigma to his family. His daughter, Patti Davis, disparaged the enigma in three anguished novels and in her autobiography. "Indeed," shocks that dust jacket cover, "Patti creates a portrait of the former president as a man so scarred by his own childhood in an alcoholic home that he emotionally abandoned his children."[38] All fathers cut Reagan lots of slack.

"Bill, rule one of politics is you don't think out loud," Reagan once advised me. As Mike Deaver himself early discovered, "Reagan was maddeningly evasive ..." An aide who had worked for him at close quarters for eight years complained, "Every time I see the Governor I have to remind him who I am."[39]

With me, Reagan risked candid conversation in the solemn sanctitude of the Bohemian Grove. The summer encampment of the Bohemian Club of San Francisco nestles along the Russian River, between Santa Rosa and the Pacific Ocean, under the world's tallest redwood trees. The club's thousand members divide themselves up like college fraternities, into 50 camps. It is the ultimate in male bonding. Presidents Herbert Hoover, Richard M. Nixon and Pepperdine's own David Davenport holed up in the Caveman Camp, Norvel was in Camp Bromley. Charles Runnels was in Cuckoo's Nest. Edgar Bergan, Art Linkletter, Dennis Day, Hernando Courtright and I were Dragons. Norvel, Charlie and I raised lots of Malibu miracle money from Bohemian brethren.

I found Reagan relaxing one 1972 afternoon in front of the fireplace at the Lost Angels Camp. "Governor, I've wanted to get your advice on that John Tunney senate race next year. Deaver, Mease and Nofziger are pushing me to run. I'm sure you know Nancy called last week to assure that the party will rally behind me for the nomination. But I love what I'm doing and don't want to leave Pepperdine. What do you advise?"

"Well, Bill, it's sure a sacrifice. I thought my acting career was a fishbowl but nothing compares to politics," Reagan chuckled.

"Governor, you love Pepperdine. Should I give up Pepperdine leadership for the senate?" I agonized.

"Bill," he said, "that's a question only you can answer. You can't go wrong building Pepperdine. But you could be meant for national service. Don't do it unless you want it gut deep. It's up to you." Someone joined us at the fireplace. Conversation drifted. Strolling away under the redwoods that sheltered the Lost Angels Camp, I felt yet again the mystery of penetrating Reagan's profound privacy.

He left me, and millions more, in the dark when he audaciously challenged President Ford in the 1976 primary. Only after publicly declaring support for Ford did I realize that the self-contained Reagan had tried to tip me off. I missed his subtle signal. It happened when Gay and I flew to Sacramento, March 15, 1975, for the California Republican Party annual convention. President Ford spoke at lunch. Governor Reagan introduced him. Gay and I sat nearby at the head table. As we lined up to march in with Ford and Reagan, Mike Deaver said, "Bill, after lunch, do you and Gay want to fly home with the boss?" Mike, in Sacramento for the three-day convention, knew we were headed home and, thoughtfully, arranged for us to fly straight to Santa Monica on Reagan's Learjet.

We were alone for the one-hour flight. Gay and I sat facing forward with Reagan across facing back. After small talk he opened his briefcase for paperwork. Halfway home he closed it and seemed suddenly serious. "Well, what do you guys make of our new president?" he asked out of the blue. "He's no public speaker, is he? He just doesn't seem to have it," said the show-business-wise Reagan in shocking candor. "Remember, he's only an accidental president!" I was stunned. Reagan never spoke more sharply. "I seriously doubt if Ford can win an election," he closed. "What do you guys think?"

Taken aback, I didn't know what to think. Months later, after declaring support for Ford, I finally realized that, at that very moment in the intimate jet, Reagan was thinking the unthinkable. "He would try the most aggressive move in American politics," recorded biographer Richard Reeves, "that of challenging the incumbent president of his own party."[40] Reagan was turning 65. He knew such a challenge would be bitterly controversial. But privately pushed by Nancy and a handful of others, Reagan's ambition was inestimably greater than I imagined.

I failed to grasp his candid hint and I missed the opportunity to respond in kind. He had, for the first time, permitted me into his most private place. He had made himself vulnerable in the hope that I could provide reasons why he should challenge President Ford. Habituated to Reagan's renowned indirection, I was asleep at the switch.

"No, he's not publicly impressive," I replied matter-of-factly, "but he seems to be a good guy." I responded at the level I assumed Reagan wanted to hear. He stared briefly, nodded his head and reopened his briefcase. The Learjet landed in Santa Monica and we said goodbye. When Reagan came to campus one month later, April 20, 1975, to address the Seaver College dedication, I still had no sense of the grand plan now sizzling in his head.

But the Ford White House sensed it and set out to stop him. Bo Calloway, the pushy former Georgia governor, called me on Saturday, May 10, 1975. "Bill, President Ford wants you to declare today, along with 40 other California Republican leaders, your support for his election." I agreed. It never occurred to me to do otherwise. One of the saddest phone calls of my life came to the Brock House that night.

"Hey, Bill, this is Ron. How are ya? Bill, I'm calling because I know this Ford crowd's been calling you and everybody else. Bill, don't fall for their pitch. They're just putting pressure on all my best friends to try and cut me off!" pled Reagan. "Just do what Ted Cummings did. He told them that he was a Reagan man!"

Those plaintive words still hurt today. Reagan worked the phones all weekend in damage control, urging his supporters to stay loyal. My heart sank. "Governor, I had absolutely no idea you were interested in this race. I'd give anything if I could retract what I told the White House this morning. With Ted Cummings I'd shout to the world I'm a Reagan man. But it's too late. The *Los Angeles Times* has printed this story for street circulation. It'll soon be at every door, announcing I back Ford. It breaks my heart. There's nothing I can do but get completely out of politics because I'll never oppose you."

We said polite good-byes. That's the last time I talked to Reagan for four years.

"Forty Republican Leaders Back Ford," ran the next day's headline.[41] I wasn't the only Reagan stalwart who got sucked in. Pepperdine's Margaret Brock, known as "Miss Republican of California," was on the list, along with a dozen other Malibu miracle supporters. Considered "amateur volunteers who just got snookered," they were all soon forgiven. I was "an insider, too smart to just get snookered," said Mike Deaver. "Bill, you look like just another political whore," Ed Meese indelicately put it. I resigned instantly as the Republican National Committeeman from California. Except for a lingering pernicious itch, I got completely out of politics.

TOP FIVE PRESIDENTS

When I gave President Ford such a timely boost we became very close friends. "President Ford's utter lack of pretension and guile was a refreshing change from the aloofness and paranoia of his predecessor," wrote Pepperdine public policy professor Robert G. Kaufman. "Ford was a fine man whose greatest achievement was to restore confidence in American political institutions at a particularly difficult and dismal time for the nation."[42]

I arranged for President Ford's Malibu campus campaign appearance on September 25, 1975. After that historic event he summoned me, in January 1976, to the Oval Office. "Bill," he stunned me, "I want you to join my cabinet as Secretary of the Interior Department. Secretary Hathaway's in the hospital now and won't return. I'll put you in as undersecretary and within weeks you'll step in as secretary."

Astonished, I asked President Ford for a few days to talk to Gay and think it over. Walking out of the White House my heart was not in it. I would not leave Pepperdine to be an appointed Washington bureaucrat. I telephoned regrets to President Ford but the word was already out and, as usual in politics, it was premature. "Banowsky to Be Named to Top Interior Post," headlined the *Los Angeles Times*.[43] The *New York Times* editorialized: "The last man we need to protect our environment is a major fundraiser for the governor who wanted to cut down the redwood trees."[44] Horace W. Busby Jr., from a Texas Church of Christ background and, coincidentally, uncle to Pepperdine history professor John Busby McClung, was Ford's White House advisor. "Don't worry, Bill," Busby advised, "you haven't lived until you've survived a negative *New York Times* editorial."[45] President Ford understood. I sent out a "Dear Friends of Pepperdine" letter to take the "no politics" pledge.

I heard next from Reagan in 1979, after becoming president of the University of Oklahoma. "Bill," he telephoned from Los Angeles. "I'm calling about that open Oklahoma 1980 Senate seat. I want you to run. I plan to be in the White House and I need your help in the Senate. Holmes Tuttle's been talking to his sister in Tuttle, Oklahoma. She says you're perfect to win. We'll give you all the organizational backing from our presidential campaign in Oklahoma."

A month later I announced my decision to stay at OU. I couldn't have made it in politics anymore than Samson made it when he compromised and cut his hair.

THE AGE OF REAGAN

In March 1982, President Reagan traveled from Washington D.C. to address the Oklahoma State Legislature. We hugged. I sat on the front row. "I'm so happy to be here in Oklahoma today with my old Pepperdine friend, Bill Banowsky, who's doing his usual great job now here at OU," Reagan opened. The big-spirited Reagan never once held my accidental defection against me but Nancy may still have me on her bad list.

"Just as the first half of the twentieth century has been called the age of Roosevelt, the last half of the twentieth century will be called the age of Reagan," predicted a presidential historian.[46]

Like other early insiders I underestimated Reagan. Here is what actually happened on his watch: the end of the Cold War; the collapse of communism; the liberation of Eastern Europe; the largest tax cuts in American history; the strengthening of the military; supply-side Reaganomics; NASDAQ; and the Silicone Valley. One presidential historian already ranks Reagan in the top five, "that small group of the greatest presidents generally deemed to comprise Washington, Lincoln, Franklin D. Roosevelt with some argument to be made for Jefferson and now Reagan."[47]

The Malibu miracle was yet another major Reagan revolution result. We now meet an original Reagan revolutionary, "the miracle-making Mrs. Seaver."

1. Chairman Rawn of Topodynamics, Inc., was retained—at the insistence of George A. Evans and Robert P. Jones—to coordinate campus construction. (See chapter 13).
2. "Pepperdine Begins Construction," *Santa Monica Evening Outlook*, January 19, 1969, 1.

3. Virginia A. Garrison, "Nationally-Known Leaders Take Special Interest in Pepperdine University," *The Capital Letter* 13, no. 33, August 15, 1973, 1–2. Dramatizing the national impact of the Malibu miracle, the Church of Christ, Sixteenth and Decatur Streets, Northwest, Washington, D. C, adapted the entire issue of the February 1973 *Pepperdine News* to fill its weekly bulletin.
4. Jon Thurber, "Lyn Nofziger, 81, Key Aide Helped Groom Reagan for the White House," *Los Angeles Times*, March 28, 2006, 14B.
5. "Seaver College Faculty News," *Pepperdine People*, Summer 1978, 19.
6. Judy Pasternak, "Pepperdine: Party School by the Shore (Republican, That Is)," *Los Angeles Times*, September 19, 1987, 16.
7. Bob Eisberg, "Pep Watergate," *Pepperdine Graphic*, September 15, 1974, 1.
8. Ibid.
9. Billy Graham, personal letter to the author, November 13, 1972. The Banowsky Papers.
10. See note 6 above.
11. Jerry Rushford, ed., *Crest of a Golden Wave: Pepperdine University, 1937–1987* (Malibu: Pepperdine University Press, 1987), 165
12. Jack Mulkey and Chris Parker, "President Banowsky, Politics and Pepperdine," *Pepperdine Graphic*, October 4, 1974.
13. See note 6 above.
14. David B. Burks, ed., *Against the Grain: The Mission of Harding University* (Searcy, AR: Harding University Press, 1998), 56.
15. Bill Youngs, *Faith Was His Fortune: The Life Story of George Pepperdine* (Malibu: Pepperdine University Press, 1976), 183. George Pepperdine's 1936 Harding College gift of $50,000, only one year prior to founding his own Pepperdine College, is a solid piece of material evidence to prove that after 20 years in California his early Kansas opposition to Church of Christ-related colleges was waning.
16. John C. Stevens, *Before Any Were Willing: The Story of George S. Benson* (Abilene, TX: Abilene Christian University Press, 1991), 62.
17. Richard T Hughes, "Churches of Christ, The Lure of Christian America, and the Loss of the Kingdom of God," *Leaven: A Journal of Christian Ministry* 13, no. 4, Fourth Quarter 2005, 204–205.
18. L. Edward Hicks, "Benson, George Stuart (1898–1991)," in Douglas A. Foster and others, eds., *The Encyclopedia of the Stone-Campbell Movement* (Grand Rapids, MI: William B. Eerdmans, 2004), 73.
19. Ibid., 73. "Today Benson's teachings on traditional American values and free enterprise economics are being carried on through dozens of educational organizations run by his disciples."
20. Richard Bergholz, "Forum Will Probe Into U. S. Woes," *Los Angeles Times*, March 24, 1968, 12.
21. In the months before I left the pulpit in Lubbock, Texas, to return to Pepperdine, I hosted Bill Teague in Lubbock to preach at the Broadway Church of Christ on November 14, 1967, and at Texas Tech University on November 15, 1967.
22. Bill Henegar and Jerry Rushford, *Forever Young: The Life and Times of M. Norvel Young and Helen M. Young* (Nashville: 21st Century Christian, 1999), 279.
23. Erick Hoffer, *The True Believer* (New York: Random House, 1960).
24. Bill Youngs, *The Legacy of Frank Roger Seaver* (Malibu: Pepperdine University Press, 1976), 114.
25. James Smythe, personal interview with the author, December 6, 2007. The Banowsky Papers.
26. "Political Briefs," *Santa Monica Evening Outlook*, October 1, 1970. "Dr. William S. Banowsky, chancellor of Pepperdine College's Malibu campus will be featured speaker Saturday at a dinner honoring Fred L. Casmir, Republican candidate for congress in the 31st District. Casmir is a longtime Pepperdine professor," 10.
27. Henegar and Rushford, *Forever Young*, 207.
28. Rushford, *Golden Wave*, 112.
29. Ibid., 231.
30. The original 138 acres, Ostrow's 210 acres and an addition 284 Adamson-Alcoa acres created the total 632-acre Malibu campus achieved during my presidency. President White acquired another 198 acres to reach today's 830-acre campus.
31. Garrison, *Capital Letter*, 2.
32. Edmund Morris, *Dutch: A Memoir of Ronald Reagan* (New York: Random House, 1999), 64–91.
33. Tom Brokaw, *Boom! Voices of the Sixties* (New York: Random House, 2007), 27.
34. Nancy Reagan, personal letter to the author, November 19, 1968. The Banowsky Papers.

35. Governor Ronald Reagan, personal letter to the author, July 2, 1973. The Banowsky Papers.
36. Larry Kramer, "Big Reagan Funds Dinner Scrutinized," *San Francisco Examiner*, August 29, 1975, 1. My executive committee was Margaret Martin Brock, Theodore E. Cummings, Justin Dart, Paul Hearle, Robert F. Hatch, Earle Jorgensen, Raymond E. Lee, Gordon C. Luce, Edward Mills, Frank Thomas Murphy, Holmes Tuttle and Jack D. Wrather Jr.

    Michael K. Deaver, Assistant to the Governor, wrote: "You have my sincere congratulations and admiration . . . A financial success on such a high plane with such a warm glow . . . You set the tone during the weeks of preparation ..."
37. Brokaw, *Boom!*, 9.
38. Patti Davis, *The Way I See It: An Autobiography* (New York: G. P. Putnam's Sons, 1992).
39. Morris, *Dutch*, 387.
40. Richard Reeves, "My Years With Ronald Reagan," *American Heritage*, February/March 2008, 51. (Reeves' biography, *President Reagan: The Triumph of Imagination*, was published by Simon and Schuster in 2006.)
41. *Los Angeles Times*, May 11, 1975.
42. Robert G. Kaufman, "President Gerald R. Ford," *Pepperdine People*, Spring 2007, 16.
43. *Los Angeles Times*, January 31, 1976, 1. "What's this call I got from the FBI about a high White House position?" wrote John C. Stevens, President of Abilene Christian University. "I just talked to FBI Agent Merton Anderson saying you are in line for a big presidential appointment," Pepperdine basketball coach Gary Colson wrote me.
44. *New York Times*, February 2, 1976, 22.
45. Horace W. Busby Jr., personal letter to the author, February 3, 1976. The Banowsky Papers.
46. Lee Edwards, "The Origins of the Modern American Conservative Movement," *Heritage Lectures*, November 21, 2003, 6.
47. Conrad Black, *Richard M. Nixon: A Life In Full* (New York: Public Affairs Publishing, 2007), 1057. Black, author of the highly acclaimed best seller, *Franklin Delano Roosevelt: Champion of Freedom*, is the former chairman of the *London Daily* and the *Sunday Telegraph*.

"Without Mrs. Seaver's rare generosity
'the Malibu miracle' would have been impossible.
Her gifts more than matched all others combined."

HOWARD A. WHITE
Fifth President
Pepperdine University

"MAMA DEAR"
In 1916, Blanche Theodora Ebert married Frank Roger Seaver,
who christened her "Mama Dear."

CHAPTER 7

THE MIRACLE-MAKING MRS. SEAVER

"Mrs. Seaver," beamed M. Norvel Young. "I'm honored to introduce to you Dr. Bill Banowsky, the young Texas minister I've been telling you all about." That was it. That was the conception of the Malibu miracle's embryonic fiscal heartbeat.

My introduction to Mrs. Frank Roger Seaver occurred on her front porch. It was 9:00 a.m., Tuesday, November 28, 1967. The introduction was part of the preparation Norvel and I made after deciding that I would return to Pepperdine but before announcing it publicly.

AUSPICIOUS INTRODUCTION

Rapturous over the Malibu land acquisition, I had no idea how to raise enough money to pay for the construction of a campus from scratch. Norvel, commendably, balanced his operating budgets with scores of modest gifts. He had not yet received a major gift from any source or set aside a single dollar for a capital campaign. When I met Mrs. Seaver, anything like a million-dollar contribution seemed inconceivable.

Slight fundraising experience, in a pre-Internet age, taught me it was easier to raise a million dollars from one person than one dollar from a million persons. Anxious about being trumpeted as the man to create the campus and wondering how to corner enough cash, I pressed Norvel to name prospects who could give a million. He listed six: Richard Mellon Scaife, Charles M. Payson, Mrs. Frank R. Seaver, Clint Murchison, Fritz Huntsinger and Walter Knott. We agreed I should get well acquainted with all six before going public. Norvel and Bill Teague had already introduced me to Scaife in Pittsburgh and to Payson in New York.[1] Clint Murchison was a Dallas acquaintance and I knew Walter Knott from the site search committee. The day arrived

THE REAGAN AND SEAVER CONNECTION

For the 1972 dedication of the Huntsinger Academic Center, Norvel and Helen gather with Governor and Mrs. Reagan and prominent members of the Seaver family. Standing behind Blanche is her sister, Mabel Ebert Marks, and her nephew, Theodore Spencer. Family friend Odell McConnell, contributor of the McConnell Law Center, stands to the left.

CHURCH AND STATE

In a 1969 Beverly Wilshire Hotel receiving line, Blanche greets her longtime political friend, President Richard M. Nixon, and her longtime spiritual advisor, Cardinal James McIntyre. Mrs. Seaver moved about town in the highest circles.

for me to meet Blanche Seaver. Norvel arranged a drive to the Palos Verdes Peninsula to tour her property as a possible second campus site.

In 1967 Mrs. Seaver had superficial Pepperdine involvement. She had never set foot on Pepperdine's campus, six miles south of her residence. Norvel had a relationship with her late husband, Frank R. Seaver, before his 1964 death. After a few small Pepperdine gifts, Frank surprisingly remembered Pepperdine modestly in his will. Norvel considered Blanche the primest of the prime prospects, but he did not know her well.

Although Blanche had not made a Pepperdine gift she liked what she saw and she loved Vice President Teague. He had cultivated her for Pepperdine. They traveled together to Republican Party functions in a close friendship fueled by Bill's fiery, free-enterprise speeches. He had just announced his 1968 congressional candidacy. Blanche signed on as a member of his campaign finance committee. Norvel, nervous over Teague's departure, was anxious for me to move into position quickly to keep step with her and two dozen more wealthy conservatives. To most of them, Pepperdine simply meant Bill Teague. They didn't know the decaying Los Angeles college. They knew Bill Teague, the Pepperdine vice president. Norvel knew that people don't give money to institutions. People give money to people. He pushed me hard to get on board fast.

Sizing folks up like a psychologist, Norvel knew Blanche and I were made for one another. He and my mother were close and he teased out my attention: "Bill, I've got a sense of destiny about you and Blanche. She reminds me of your mother—spiritual, musically gifted, dedicated to God. Bill, Blanche could become Pepperdine's guardian angel."

At five minutes before nine, Norvel and I arrived at number 20 Chester Place, Mrs. Seaver's mellowing 1920s mansion in the heart of early Los Angeles.[2] We straightened our ties, fixed American flag pins in our lapels and rang the doorbell. Decades before TV talk-show flag pins Mrs. Seaver expected any men, women or children in her company to wear one. "When Blanche spoke," revealed the *Los Angeles Times*, "she would urge students in attendance to join the Young Americans for Freedom, a conservative youth group."[3]

COMPELLING CONSERVATIVE FORCE

Blanche appeared at the door with a warm smile framed by pink cheeks. She was adorned in her standard pink suit decorated with a jeweled American flag. In an era of the properly dressed lady she wore a soft pink pillbox hat with crisp white gloves. She greeted Norvel with a warm handshake and he formally introduced us.

"Mrs. Seaver," I said, extending my hand and biggest smile. "I'm honored to meet you. I've heard many wonderful things about you!"

"Well, thank you very much, young man," came her matching hand and smile. "I'm happy to meet you too. You've been well introduced. Dr. Young and Dr. Teague praise you to the heavens. I'm glad to get a look at you for myself."

Mrs. Seaver looked everyone in the eye and her deep blue ones penetrated my matching ones as our hands clutched in contact. We held the handshake gaze for what seemed like minutes, perhaps to see who might blink first.

At 77, Mrs. Seaver appeared and acted 25 years younger. I was 31, about the age of the grandson she never had. Exquisitely feminine, Blanche was middle-class born, Midwest raised, sweet, soft and sentimental. With no college education she sat on several college boards.[4] With no business experience she inherited hundreds of millions in her husband's business. With no political training she devoured piles of political literature in her daily mail. She was a key supporter of many conservative causes and an intimate insider with Richard M. Nixon and Ronald Reagan, the two most powerful Republican leaders of the day.

Blanche was a compelling force in 20 educational, civic and religious organizations "in memory of my beloved Frank." She elevated Mr. Seaver to a living monument in her daily life. Never has a widow lived more passionately to celebrate the love and glorify the life of her late husband. She recited like a mantra Mr. Seaver's famous saying: "If you want to do something for the future of your country do something for the youth, for they are the future of the country."[5] A proud prima donna, Blanche was humble at heart.

"Blanche, Dr. Banowsky came all the way from Texas today just to meet you," Norvel beamed. "In a few weeks he's coming permanently to build our new campus. I knew you'd want to meet him as soon as possible. And, since you've suggested your beautiful Palos Verdes land as a possible site for the campus, I thought we'd go down there together to see it."

BANOWSKY FAMILY MEMBER

We three lingered on the large, elevated stone porch that extended across the front of her old mansion. Blanche did all of the talking. Entranced by her animated conversation I later processed this as one of the highest moments in my life and, for Pepperdine, providential. The Malibu miracle meant hundreds of fundraising introductions but Mrs. Seaver produced the mother lode. Her gifts more than tripled all other contributors combined.

For the Banowsky family, Mrs. Seaver transfigured into a prized personal relationship. Blanche held front-row season tickets to every artistic, musical and theatrical event in Los Angeles. She ticketed and tutored our family's social and political education. During that decade of dazzling nights out on the town with her we achieved our cultural zenith. At the Dorothy Chandler Pavilion she awakened us night after night to elegant grand opera. At the Hollywood Bowl she enlarged us under the stars in her stage-side box with scores of inspirational performances. At the Los Angeles Museum of Art she refined us with the world's celebrated exhibitions. In Hollywood she feasted us at festive opening nights of *The Sound of Music*, *Patton* and other classics. At endless political events she honored us at her front and center tables.

Our four young sons were cultured by all those times they got haircuts, donned suits and ties, and put flag pins in their lapels. We often gathered round Mrs. Seaver's Chester Place dining table for a formal five-course meal complete with finger bowls. She tested and interrogated the boys. Today they still taste Mrs. Seaver's split pea soup and savor her challenging conversation.[6]

THE DOHENY CONNECTION

That morning we met, Blanche stopped talking and declared: "Well, gentlemen, time's wasting. Are we all ready to go?" She pointed to the black Cadillac in her driveway and Sandy, her uniformed chauffeur, standing at attention near its rear door.

"Bill, you sit here in back with Blanche," Norvel directed as we reached the car. "I'll sit up front with Sandy." Norvel was always happy to take the second seat and sit alongside the chauffeur. For now, during our half-hour drive south down the Harbor Freeway, Norvel intended for Blanche and me to get well acquainted. "There's no limit to what you can accomplish if you don't care who gets the credit," was Norvel's beloved mantra.

Sandy, a six-foot Asian man, was the Hydril Company employee who drove Mrs. Seaver all around town. At her age, with robust health and volcanic energy, she pursued a frenetic schedule of day and night activities. Some said Frank, in his final years, seemed frail and weary in the hotel ballrooms night after night on his wife's spry arm. Blanche compensated for Frank's death by sharply escalating her activities, in his memory.

When we settled into the Cadillac, Norvel launched the conversation. "Blanche, tell Bill about this big Doheny compound, Chester Place," he suggested as Sandy backed out of her driveway.

"Well, that's the Doheny House right there." Blanche pointed to the magnificent three-story mansion across the street. "It's been declared an official California Historical Monument. This whole private Chester Place Park of ten houses was created at the turn of the century by 'Pa D and Ma D,'

LIFE IN LOS ANGELES

Bill and Gay at Christmas 1972, in the president's residence on the Los Angeles campus, with four sons, David, 14; Britton, 12; Billy, 11 and Baxter, 7.

as everybody called Mr. and Mrs. Doheny. Their huge mansion is number 8. Our much smaller one is number 10."[7]

In the robber-baron age of Rockefellers and Mellons, Edward L. Doheny was, "reportedly, the wealthiest man in America."[8] He is most remembered for high shenanigans in the Teapot Dome Scandal of the Harding administration during the 1920s.[9] Harding's secretary of the interior, Albert B. Fall, achieved the dishonor of being the first cabinet member in American history to be sent to prison. He was convicted of taking Doheny bribes in exchange for lucrative government leases in a Wyoming oil field called Teapot Dome. Doheny escaped prison but suffered years of legal trials and paid $47 million in fines. "The man labeled the icon of unbridled American greed" put his name on Doheny Drive in Hollywood, built the Doheny Memorial Library at USC, inspired Upton Sinclair's novel, *Oil!*, and was loosely portrayed by Daniel Day-Lewis in the 2007 film *There Will Be Blood*.[10] Edward Doheny and Frank Seaver were close personal friends and business colleagues.

Frank Seaver's long life had no hint of scandal. But during those scandalous years, his fabulous petroleum career was launched in professional affiliation with Doheny. In 1919, Frank joined Doheny's empire at the top. His big break came two years later in 1921 when he moved to Mexico to manage Doheny's Huasteca Petroleum Company, the Mexican government's largest taxpayer. "Frank Seaver recalls personally delivering advance taxes in the form of gold on at least one occasion to make it possible for the government to meet the army payroll."[11] The United States imports more oil from Mexico than any other nation and the Doheny-Seaver partnership pioneered the Mexican industry.

During this raucous Pancho Villa period Frank and Blanche spent six fabulous years in Mexico City. From 1921 until 1927 they regularly rattled back and forth from Mexico City to Los Angeles on trains routinely robbed by banditos. They returned fluent in Spanish and devoted to California's indigenous and exploding Hispanic culture. Blanche, adoring the sharply defined rhythms and haunting melodies of Mexican music, quickly mastered the guitar. Every year her September 15 birthday was celebrated with a colorful fiesta called "The Paisano Party," covered routinely by the *Los Angeles Times* society page.[12]

The Seavers returned to Los Angeles in 1930 and moved into one of ten houses comprising Doheny's Chester Place. Protected by a stone and steel fence, with three guarded gates, it hunkered between downtown Los Angeles and the University of Southern California. Doheny granted the Seavers life residency and Frank lived there 34 years. Blanche lived there 64 years.

"The Dohenys were extremely devout Catholics," Blanche said with delight. "They built their beautiful sacred chapel on the third floor. The cardinal came to conduct their private family mass." A large contribution to the Vatican brought Mrs. Doheny the title of "papal countess." Countess Estelle Doheny "played royalty to the hilt in her chapel with a vaulted ceiling of Tiffany glass supported by columns of Sienna marble and walls inlaid with pure gold leaf. Seated on a throne-like chair, she received her guests," recorded Doheny biographer Stanford J. Mock.[13]

The Dohenys eventually bequeathed their Chester Place compound to the Archdiocese of Los Angeles for the campus of Mount St. Mary's College for Women. "Oh, yes," said Blanche as Sandy drove out of Chester Place, "my dear Cardinal McIntyre owns all of this and every month I mail him a rental check."

FRANK AND BLANCHE

Frank Roger Seaver was a native Californian by a hair. In 1883 his parents, Carlton and Estella Seaver, migrated from New York to California. Ten days after their train arrived, Frank was born in San Jose on April 12, 1883. After living briefly in Los Angeles, when the town's population was 20,000, they settled in rural Pomona. Carlton founded the First National Bank of Pomona and later merged it with United California Bank. The Seavers loved Pomona College and Frank graduated with honors as the 1905 student body president. He attended Harvard Law School, passed the bar and was admitted to practice before the United States Supreme Court.[14]

Frank was drawn to politics and in 1910 was elected president of the Pomona College Alumni Association. After being defeated for the state legislature he was elected, in 1912, to the Los Angeles County Board of Freeholders, now the Board of Supervisors. He was the principal draftsman of the original Los Angeles County Charter. The charter is virtually unchanged today as written a hundred years ago.[15] "Frank Seaver was credited with being the genius behind the drafting of the charter, the one who almost single-handedly wrote it," says the official record.[16]

Perhaps the most important Malibu miracle personality was Frank's wife of 48 years, Blanche Ellen Theodora Ebert. Born in Chicago, September 15, 1891, she was the youngest of ten children whose parents migrated from Bergen, Norway. A musical prodigy, she had to be lifted onto the piano stool for her earliest recitals. She was recruited as a child into instruction at Jane Addams' famous Chicago Hull House and began teaching her own pupils at age 13.

At age 21, in 1912, music led Blanche to the burgeoning mecca of Los Angeles. She opened her own piano studio in the Majestic Building and her name and face began to appear in Southern California newspapers. "The piano solo by Miss Blanche Ebert," commented a critic in 1914 about a Whittier Choral Society concert, "was one of the best numbers of the evening."[17] Blanche was a rising star and nearly any night in the 1920s she could be heard on the radio. She was piano accompanist for contralto Estelle Heart Dreyfus, violinist Ignaz Haroldi, Oskar Seiling, Louise Rieger, Anna Kopetsky, Marie B. Tiffany, Axel Simonson, Juan de la Cruz, Anthony Carlson, Ettore Campana and Marguerite Stevenson.

Blanche was a teetotaler with a scrupulous diet and no bad habits who preached the gospel of clean living to others. An interview in the January 15, 1914, issue of the *Los Angeles Daily Tribune* captured the idealism of 23-year-old Blanche, a vision she cherished until her death, 80 years later, at the age of 102:

> Life is short but art is long . . . I am trying to express . . . the masters of music . . . it requires many things to do this—command of languages, feeling, sympathy, suffering, joy and . . . the great desire to express music, not merely to play the piano, but . . . to comprehend the souls of the musicians who received the gift of music from the Greatest Musician. It is a rather difficult thing in this day of commercialism to keep always in the atmosphere of real art; there are so many chances to solve the bread and butter question with less work and less art . . . I have tried to associate myself with . . . the music that lives forever . . . Simplicity and greatness go together.[18]

Innately spiritual, Blanche communed with God in informal conversational meditation. "Sometimes I feel as if I must be worrying God to death," she often said. For her God was present, never fearful, always loving, not a doctrine, a reality as natural as breathing in and out. Blanche lived joyfully without anxiety in a spirit of trust and zest and felt the direct guidance of God in her daily life.

THE MYSTICAL MEETING

Frank Seaver and Blanche Ebert met, almost mystically, in 1915 on the Los Angeles Hill Street trolley. They married within months on September 16, 1916, at the Ebert family's North Shore Congregational Church in Chicago. Their long love life could fuel a romance novel.

Now Mrs. Frank Roger Seaver, Blanche continued her creative career but shifted interest from musical performance to original composition. Her 1919 arrangement of "The Battle Hymn of the Republic" was performed by the Philadelphia Orchestra conducted by Leopold Stokowski in a memorial

AT TWENTY CHESTER PLACE

Returning from seven years in Mexico, Frank and Blanche Seaver settled in 1930 into their mellow Chester Place mansion.

AT POMONA COLLEGE

In 1957 Frank and Blanche stroll the Pomona College campus. By 1960, they were the largest donors in the history of Frank's alma mater.

COUNTY CHARTER AUTHOR

Supervisor Kenneth H. Hahn honors friend and
constituent, Frank R. Seaver, on the 50th anniversary
of the Los Angeles county charter, which was authored
by Mr. Seaver. Blanche Seaver approves.

THE SEAVER LEARNING CENTER

Supervisor Hahn and officials of the city of Los Angeles honor Mrs. Seaver in 1971 for the
"Seaver Learning Center" on the Pepperdine College Los Angeles campus.

concert honoring President Theodore Roosevelt. She also composed widely popular songs of the day such as "Calling Me Back To You" and "Just For Today," both made famous on 1920s national radio by beloved Irish tenor, John McCormack. After composing "two dozen other published songs"[19] Blanche turned her attention to Frank's career.

Frank, with brilliant natural business gifts, was trained immaculately in the law at Harvard. After serving in World War I as a naval officer, he joined Doheny's oil and gas empire at the top. But after that first profitable Doheny decade, with its many Mexico City successes, he wanted to own and operate his own ship. In 1928 he bought the Doheny Stone and Drill Company and reorganized it into the Hydril Company. It specialized in exquisite quality oil-field tools and equipment and soon became a major supplier of petroleum industry accessories worldwide.

Frank was also an inventive engineering genius who created, and patented, the planet's most sought-after oil-well blowout preventer. Any serious oil-well driller from Texas to Teheran insisted on the installation of the Hydril Blowout Preventer. "In every oil field in the world you will find Hydril Blowout Preventers," biographer Bill Youngs testified 50 years ago. The Malibu miracle was fueled by Frank's famous invention that was praised not only as a fabulous money maker but also as an early ecological innovation that saved the global environment from even more pollution.

SEAVER PHILANTHROPIC LEGACY

The huge Seaver fortune did not flow easily to Pepperdine early on. Long before even meeting any Pepperdine people the Seavers committed to a prodigious philanthropic program. Pepperdine was at the end of the line behind Pomona College, the University of Southern California, Loyola Marymount University, the First Congregational Church of Los Angeles, the Pilgrim School, the Harvard School for Boys, Don Bosco Technical Institute, Freedoms Foundation at Valley Forge and others.

Frank's first loyalty was to his Pomona College alma mater. He joined its board of trustees in 1947 and led with such power and popularity that Pomona College commissioned *The Seaver Story*, a 1960 biography, in his honor. Biographer Jane Werner Watson praised Frank in lofty language that presaged convictions still echoing in today's meetings of the Pepperdine University board of regents assembled in the Seaver Board Room. "Frank Seaver was by no means a board figurehead," Watson emphasized. "He was an articulate spokesman for strongly held views on the real purpose and goals of a private college, on the proper assumption of responsibility by its trustees and on the necessity of avoiding unconscious imitation of other institutions

BLANCHE AND BILL

At the heart of the Malibu miracle was the profound friendship between the Malibu campus founder, Mrs. Frank R. Seaver, and its builder, Bill Banowsky.

with lesser or divergent objectives."[20] Today, one or another Pepperdine regent makes that same speech at every quarterly board meeting.

Frank's profoundly deep ideological convictions about what an academically excellent private college ought to be was precisely why the huge Seaver fortune finally found its perfect place in Seaver College of Pepperdine University at Malibu.

Frank's first Pepperdine friend way back in the 1950s was Los Angeles County Supervisor Kenneth H. Hahn, a devoted Pepperdine alumnus. Kenny revered Frank. Frank was Kenny's distinguished second supervisorial district constituent who served on the original Los Angeles County Board of Freeholders. Frank had drafted the county charter. Kenny and Frank lunched together throughout the 1950s, "usually at the Union Station cafeteria because Mr. Seaver enjoyed getting a full meal for a dollar."[21] In 1962, the supervisors staged a 50th anniversary celebration of the drafting of the county charter. Frank, as the only surviving draftsman, and Blanche paraded in a line of 1912 automobiles from Chester Place to be honored at the County Hall of Administration.[22]

To Pomona College, Frank gave, and gave, until he became the largest donor in its history. He began at graduation by naming his alma mater beneficiary of his first $30,000 life insurance policy. He concluded by giving, from 1956 through 1964, $7.5 million to create the monumental three-building Seaver Science Center, "unsurpassed in quality and character on any campus in America."[23]

THE SEAVER-HAHN CONNECTION

Thanks mostly to Supervisor Hahn, Frank Seaver was primed for Pepperdine when Norvel Young arrived in 1957. In 1960, Henry Salvatori, a powerful member of Norvel's president's board, brought Frank to the annual Pepperdine Freedom Forum at the Biltmore Hotel. The keynote speaker was Senator Barry Goldwater, soon to be nominated for president. Salvatori, president of Grant Oil Tool Company, and Seaver were close friends in the same petroleum equipment business. Furthermore, Henry and Blanche sat together at meetings of the USC board of trustees.

By intriguing contrast, during that period Pepperdine also received its first Seaver gift. "I'll never forget the first time . . . I asked [Frank Seaver] to help on a film project illustrating the difference between Communism and the private enterprise system," said Norvel. "He wrote out a check for $7,500."[24] Norvel was thrilled. But a check for $7,500—against Pomona's for $7.5 million—dramatized Pepperdine's severe 1960s underdog position. As Pomona's Seaver Science Center soared, Pepperdine's much-ballyhooed

Los Angeles science building was dedicated three times but never got off the ground.[25]

POMONA AND USC

In addition to his historic leadership at Pomona College, Frank also served on the board of trustees of Loyola Marymount University of Los Angeles and contributed millions to that Catholic-related institution. The nonsectarian Seavers, Protestant patriarchs at the First Congregational Church of Los Angeles, were ecumenically devoted to all expressions of conservative Christianity. They moved about town in Catholic circles, with Cardinal McIntyre as their personal spiritual counselor and landlord. When Pomona awarded Frank an honorary doctorate in 1958, Loyola quickly followed suit in 1959.

Before Frank's 1964 death, Blanche was revered in her own right for educational contributions. "In June 1960, she was elected to the Board of Trustees of the University of Southern California—the third woman in the history of the University to sit as a member of the Board and the first woman to be so honored in the last twenty-five years," the Watson biography reports.[26] In 1964, she immediately filled Frank's seat on the Pomona board and continued his contributions. In 1970, Pomona College conferred Mrs. Seaver's first honorary doctorate.

But if Pomona was first love for Frank, for Blanche it was the University of Southern California. The Seavers' nearest neighbor at number 9 Chester Place was Rufus von Kleinsmid, USC's all-powerful president from 1921 through 1946, and then its chancellor. The von Kleinsmid connection caused the Seavers to give USC several million dollars in the 1950s to build the Seaver Commons and Residence Halls and major medical school facilities. In 1960, when Blanche joined the USC board, they gave millions more. In 1965 she gave a $1.2 million check that President Norman Topping enlarged into a three-by-six foot poster and displayed in the USC board room to inspire others. Had Pepperdine not received Mrs. Seaver's vast fortune USC undoubtedly would have.

VIEWING PALOS VERDES

Meanwhile, on the morning we met, chauffeur Sandy pulled through the Chester Place gate and onto the Harbor Freeway. "Oh, look, there's USC," Blanche instantly pointed with pride to the right. "I'm on the board of trustees there, you know."

"Yes, Blanche," Norvel regained initiative. "Bill's also a USC alumnus and got his doctorate there."

"Wonderful, young man." she said glowingly. "I've also got several doctorates. We've got USC in common."

Three miles south of USC at Florence Avenue we saw the green freeway sign announcing Pepperdine College Next Exit.

"Look, Blanche," said Norvel. "That's our sign! You can't see our campus but it's just a couple of miles over there," pointing west through endless smog, traffic and tiny bungalows.

"Yes, Norvel, I've seen your sign but never your campus. Let's do that. It seems odd for us to drive past your old campus that I've never seen while on our way to see my property for a new campus," she chuckled. There was good reason for that. After the 1965 Watts riots, fundraising strategy had dictated that Young and Teague should never bring donor prospects to campus but meet them at a private club or prestigious hotel, for fear they would be frightened away by the deterioration along Vermont Avenue and the access streets between the campus and the Harbor Freeway.

WILL AND TESTAMENT

On October 30, 1964, at age 81, Frank Roger Seaver "graduated into the larger life," as his Forest Lawn marble headstone memorialized. In his last hours, from his Good Samaritan Hospital bed, he gazed out across Wilshire Boulevard at a big billboard: Barry Goldwater for President! He sighed to Blanche, "Mama dear, I'm so happy we're finally getting a great American for president," and died before suffering the Lyndon Johnson landslide.

Mr. Seaver's last will and testament was the rainbow that led Pepperdine to the pot of gold. After knowing him only 48 months, Norvel Young and Bill Teague earned a modest place for Pepperdine in Mr. Seaver's will. He divided the Hydril Company in half and named 16 institutions to receive shares of stock. Pomona received most and Pepperdine least. He then bequeathed the other half of the Hydril Company to Blanche. His modest Pepperdine bequest aroused her interest in "that little Christian college my beloved Frank cared about enough to remember in his will."

The Seavers had no children and Blanche determined to give her entire estate to the causes to which she was committed. Mrs. Seaver and I soon developed a deep relationship in which neither of us would ever say no to the other. My challenge was to convince her to contribute her entire Hydril Company inheritance to Seaver College and Pepperdine University. The pot at the end of the rainbow was the half of Hydril Company she inherited and,

Several nights every single week were selflessly devoted by Blanche to countless local events in support of her many political and charitable causes.

eventually, contributed to make the Malibu miracle. It amounted to more than $300 million.

PEPPERDINE AT PALOS VERDES?

A unique Seaver estate asset was the beautiful 60-acre site on the Pacific Ocean at the western slope of the Palos Verdes Peninsula. During the Depression Frank picked up the matchless property for the taxes owed on it. Six miles past Pepperdine, Sandy exited the freeway and wound west on a curving hillside drive carved around magnificent multi-acre mansions. As we neared the ocean he pulled onto the Seaver property. It nestled against the soft green hill like an emerald. It matched Malibu aesthetically and came complete with roads, utilities and sewer. In contrast with Malibu "worldliness," worrying some trustees, this conservative residential community was the home of trustee James L. Lovell, who lobbied hard for its selection.

"Blanche, your land is beautiful," said Norvel as the three of us stood together on the hillside overlooking the ocean. "It's easy to see why Frank loved it."

"Yes," Blanche replied nostalgically. "My beloved Frank found this spot in 1933 and we drove down here to watch the sunset." Blanche grew sentimental at sunset. "Just look at Catalina Island out there in front of us!" Blanche loved the ocean and her favorite vacations were Hawaiian cruises with Frank.

Norvel got down to business. "Blanche, we'd love to build our second campus here but Richard Seaver and the other men on our board think it's just a bit too small," he gingerly ventured. Richard Seaver was, of course, Mrs. Seaver's nephew and money manager.

"Yes," Blanche agreed. "Think of huge USC we just passed. I can see this beautiful space is too small for a whole college." Then she uttered those magic words.

"I can't wait to see that Malibu property you and Charles Runnels have been raving about. I've got a lot of great friends in Malibu, especially Mae West and Maureen O'Sullivan.[27] I visited Mae's beach house for dinner only last month. Last week Sandy drove me out to see Maureen's daughter, Mia Farrow, in the Colony on the beach. She just gave birth to twins.[28] So, is that Adamson property everybody's talking about anywhere near there? I've got a lot of old friends in the Colony."

Norvel and I grinned at one another in a wave of joy. "Yes, Blanche!" he joyfully replied. "That beautiful Malibu property looks out over the ocean right on top of the Colony. It's absolutely perfect. And we've got lots of land there too—138 acres."

"Great, Norvel," she said enthusiastically. "When can we go out to Malibu so I can see it for myself?"

"Well, how about tomorrow, Blanche, same time, 9:00 a.m.?" Norvel eagerly suggested.

"Sounds good to me." she responded enthusiastically. "How about you, Bill? Will you be able to go with us again tomorrow out to Malibu?"

"I sure will, Mrs. Seaver." I grinned. "That's one trip I wouldn't miss for the world and, if you agree, we'll bring Charlie Runnels. He's been working with our site selection committee, you know."

"Great!" Mrs. Seaver exclaimed. "Charles has been pushing me for weeks to drive out with him to Malibu."

A SPIRIT OF PLACE

The next day Norvel, Charles and I picked up Mrs. Seaver again at Chester Place. This time Charles drove his car, with Norvel again in the passenger's seat and Blanche and me again in the back. It was a beautiful day and Charles drove easily off the highway and up the dirt path to the central pad right where Seaver College was destined to be built. Blanche was overwhelmed as we stepped out of the car.

"Norvel and Charles and Bill, this is the place!" she quite literally exclaimed within seconds. "The search is over. Look at this. I want to help you in every way I can to build a Christian college right here. I'll talk to Richard Seaver today about giving you our Palos Verdes land to get started!" she exclaimed.

"After the Watts Riots in 1965," reported the *Los Angeles Times* years later, "Mrs. Frank R. Seaver made the Malibu campus possible by donating land on the Palos Verdes Peninsula that could be sold to raise the money to build at Malibu."[29] That transaction brought $4 million to Pepperdine.

Norvel, Charles and I stood suddenly stunned and speechless. "Mrs. Seaver," I finally sighed. "Everybody loves this place but some terrified trustees fear it'll cost too much to build the college here. Just look around at how rugged this place is. There are no roads, no utilities, no sewer, only this unspoiled and beautiful place." I sighed again, hoping for a positive response and it came.

"Yes, Bill. But God is on our side. The college is meant to be here. We'll all go to work and do it together." Then she repeated the profound pledge that changed Pepperdine forever. "I promise to do everything I can to help. I'll talk to Richard Seaver today and tell him this Malibu campus is my number one priority. More than that, I'll tell him it's my only priority. I'm tired of scattering my money here and there. I want to focus on this place. I want to focus all of my contributions on something that will last for the ages. I'll tell

"THREE PEAS IN A POD"

That's precisely what Bill's mother, Thelma Slater Banowsky, said when she met Blanche Seaver. Blanche and Thelma were close. They shared the same deep devotion to God, to family and to music. They equally energized Bill to make his life count for some lasting good.

Richard that, from now on, I want to concentrate all our gifts right here in Malibu. Let's roll up our sleeves and go to work."

Norvel fought back tears and hugged Mrs. Seaver, saying, as he often did, "Why don't we have a little prayer, and Charlie, why don't you lead it."

"OK," Charlie said. "We'll just hold hands." The four of us circled snugly in the soft noonday sun, tightly holding hands, high on the hill where Seaver College would soon rise with Pepperdine University all around it. Charles thanked God for Mrs. Seaver and asked for His blessings on the Malibu campus. "As you know," Blanche wrote of that moment years later, "I leave everything to God. I bother the life out of Him with my prayers."[30]

Our foursome pronounced the amen in unison as Blanche dabbed gently at her eyes. "Boys, I can't wait to come back up here to this very same place at sunset." Blanche and I often sat in the car on campus at sundown, entranced as the big orange ball melted into the sea, softly singing together, "Beyond the sunset, earth's blissful morning, when with our loved ones heaven is begun."

Blanche Seaver's life radiated another 30 years, until her sunset came April 9, 1994, at the rich old age of 102. Blanche lived the twentieth century to the hilt, savoring every second of the Malibu miracle. She remained in the middle of the Banowsky family. Her nephew Richard invited me to officiate at her 1994 First Congregational Church of Los Angeles funeral. I composed these words and titled them, "The Malibu Miracle."[31]

> We lowered our flags when the one who loved
> This place the most went away from us for a moment.
> But she lives forever in Seaver College.
>
> Two equal things bind a third thing too.
> We're bound together by a dream come true.
> She lives today in Seaver College.
>
> We're most at home in this Spirit of Place
> Where God comes down to touch this space.
> She lives forever in Seaver College.

Nephew Richard Carlton Seaver empowered his Aunt Blanche's every Malibu miracle move. Who was he? Why did Blanche endlessly exclaim, "I'll call Richard about that today!" We turn there now.

1. Personal letters from the author to Richard M. Scaife and Charles M. Payson, October 18, 1967, The Banowsky Papers. Young, Teague and I traveled to Pittsburgh and New York for the purpose of introducing me to these two men.
2. Stanford J. Mock, *Edward L. Doheny* (New York: Museum of American Finance, 2005), 2. "Doheny bought a secluded, fashionable two-block street called Chester Place, near the University of Southern California and created a huge private park of Victorian mansions."
3. Judy Pasternak, "Pepperdine: Party School by the Shore (Republican, That Is)," *Los Angeles Times*, September 19, 1987, 16.
4. Mrs. Seaver was a trustee, or regent, at the University of Southern California, Pepperdine University, Pomona College, Freedoms Foundation at Valley Forge and a score of civic, charitable and educational organizations.
5. Mrs. Frank R. Seaver, address delivered at the dedication of Frank R. Seaver College, Malibu, April 20, 1975. The Banowsky Papers.
6. Mrs. Seaver overflowed with preachments. "My beloved Frank went to Harvard Law School and said, if you finish college and know what you want to do, go and do it. If you're not sure, go to law school! That best prepares you for every opportunity." Our four sons, who heard that preachment for ten years, all went to law school. Not all chose to practice law but all, indeed, were "best prepared for every opportunity."
7. "Edward L. Doheny," *Wikipedia Encyclopedia*. Retrieved from http://en.wikipedia.org/wiki/Edward_Doheny.
8. Mock, *Doheny*, 1.
9. Margaret Leslie Davis, *The Dark Side of Fortune: Triumph and Scandal in the Life of Oil Tycoon Edward L. Doheny* (Berkeley, CA: University of California Press, 1998,) 16–17.
10. Martin L. Ansell, *Oil Baron of the Southwest* (Columbus: Ohio State University Press, 1998), 22–43.
11. Jane Werner Watson, *The Seaver Story* (Claremont, CA: Pomona College Press, 1960), 11. In 1960, Pomona College commissioned a Seaver biography, *The Seaver Story*. R. J. Wig, president of the Pomona College board of trustees, praised "the three-building Seaver Science Center unsurpassed on any campus in America. For those pursuing the Seavers' life and times the

Watson biography is a must read, as is *The Legacy of Frank Roger Seaver*, published in 1976 by the Pepperdine University Press. I assigned Dr. James R. Wilburn the task of working with creative writer Bill Youngs on this, the most extensive source on the Seavers in print.

12. *Los Angeles Times*, September 16, 1973.
13. Mock, *Doheny*, 3.
14. Bill Youngs, *The Legacy of Frank Roger Seaver* (Malibu: Pepperdine University Press, 1976), 9–27.
15. Watson, *Seaver Story*, 21–22.
16. Youngs, *Legacy of Seaver*, 32.
17. Ibid., 43.
18. Ibid., 44–45.
19. Watson, *Seaver Story*, 10, 15, 25.
20. Ibid., 27.
21. James Smythe, personal interview with the author, January 6, 2006. The Banowsky Papers.
22. Youngs, *Legacy of Seaver*, 32–33.
23. R. J. Wig, "Foreword," in Watson, *Seaver Story*. Wig was president of the board of trustees, Pomona College.
24. Bill Henegar and Jerry Rushford, *Forever Young: The Life and Times of M. Norvel Young and Helen M. Young* (Nashville: 21st Century Christian, 1999), 206–207.
25. In 1959, President Young recruited distinguished University of Georgia chemist, Loyd Frashier, with the promise of a new science building. After the third abortive ground breaking, Dr. Frashier coined a joke. "When asked, 'What's that open space by the business building used for?' he answered: 'Oh, that's where we practice breaking ground for the science building!'"
26. Watson, *Seaver Story*, 26–27.
27. On the evening of March 5, 1970, Mrs. Seaver, Gay and I were Mae West's dinner guests at her Malibu beach house, along with 20 others, for a séance led by a spiritualist who claimed to communicate with the dead. Blanche was open to that sort of spirituality.
28. Gay and I also accompanied Mrs. Seaver to Mia Farrow's Colony residence to see her young twins.
29. See note 3 above.
30. Mrs. Frank Roger Seaver, personal letter to Richard C. Seaver, June 20, 1979. The Banowsky Papers.
31. William S. Banowsky, "The Malibu Miracle," written for the funeral of Mrs. Frank R. Seaver, April 18, 1994. The Banowsky Papers.

"Richard Seaver is a humble man
who underplays his powerful position."

ZAN THOMPSON
Los Angeles Times
July 10, 1978

BILL, BLANCHE AND RICHARD SEAVER

A divine bond of love and trust blessed the dynamic Malibu miracle relationship between Mrs.

Seaver, her guardian nephew, Richard Seaver, and the ambitious, young Pepperdine president.

CHAPTER 8

RICHARD C. SEAVER AND HYDRIL

Following Frank Seaver's 1964 funeral, nephew Richard telephoned: "Aunt Blanche, what do you know about Pepperdine?"

"Not much," she answered. "I've never been down to their campus. It's not far away but in the wrong direction. I've been downtown to their Freedom Forum and gotten well acquainted with Doctors Teague and Young. Why do you ask, Richard?"

"Because it must have been important to Uncle Frank," Richard informed her. "He named Pepperdine College one of 16 institutions to benefit from his will."

HORATIO ALGER TALES

George Pepperdine and Frank R. Seaver were personal friends and a perfectly matched set. The Western Auto Supply Company, founded by Mr. Pepperdine, built George Pepperdine College in Los Angeles. The Hydril Company, founded by Mr. Seaver, built Seaver College and Pepperdine University at Malibu.

Without the vitality of the American free enterprise system, and the generosity of the men who created these two companies, there would be no Pepperdine in either place. The lives of both men read like Horatio Alger tales of ordinary American boys who made it big.

"Every great enterprise was started by some man. George is glad he started ... the Western Auto Supply Company ... working under the American Free Enterprise System," Mr. Pepperdine's 1959 biographers emphasized with capital letters.[1]

"Frank Seaver, in the depths of the Great Depression, courageously organized the Hydril Company. Today it is the center of a firmly knit web of factories, products and subsidiary companies," emphasized Mr. Seaver's biographer with equal 1960 fervor.[2] Pepperdine University and Seaver College glorify the great achievement of twentieth-century American capitalism.

To maximize and fulfill this creative capitalism, the nephew of Frank Seaver became the financial enabler and expediter of the Malibu miracle. He was the second generation Hydril leader and Frank's business successor. He was Richard Carlton Seaver.

NEPHEW AND "SON"

Mr. and Mrs. Seaver had no children. But Blanche had nine older siblings and Frank one younger brother. Between them they enjoyed a small army of relatives. I knew several of their nephews well. Throughout their lives Frank and Blanche cherished an especially intimate relationship with one gifted nephew. More than nephew, Richard blossomed into the beloved son they never had. Like a son, he reciprocated with unconditional love, lifelong loyalty and impeccable stewardship of their vast fortune.

Providence prepared Richard's aunt, Mrs. Frank R. Seaver, to facilitate the Malibu miracle by providing three necessary preconditions. First, Blanche's familial disappointment paradoxically became Pepperdine's blessing. Blanche Seaver adored children, and if had she been blessed with her own houseful of heirs—children, grandchildren, great-grandchildren—they surely would have received all her time, attention and treasure.

Blanche compensated for her own empty nest by service to other people's children. She supported St. John's Hospital Guild for Pediatric Care, Sisters Servants of Mary, Children's Hospital Convalescent Home, the Los Angeles Orphanage Guild, St. Vincent's Hospital Auxiliary for Children, Social Service Auxiliary, St. Elizabeth Day Nursery, the Children's Guild of St. Anne's Hospital and the Salvation Army.[3] She also supported a long list of educational institutions. Denied her own covey, she created Seaver College to educate tens of thousands of other people's children.

FACILITATING ANGEL

Second, along with miraculous motive God also provided necessary means. Providence financially qualified Mrs. Seaver to execute the Malibu miracle. Seaver College and Pepperdine University could live, along with Oxford and Cambridge, for another thousand years. But, insofar as I know, there were no other Blanche Seavers running around Los Angeles in the 1960s and '70s who could have made it happen. There was no long list of childless candidates qualified to give a local college $300 million. My intense preparation had produced a list of one. There was, quite literally, only one Blanche Seaver.

Third, along with motive and means, God also provided the money manager. Malibu miracle realities required such synchronistic harmony of too many opposing personalities and disparate circumstances to have been fortuitously coincidental. Except for her initial Palos Verdes property, Blanche wrapped all gifts to Pepperdine in packages of the earnings, dividends and stock of the Hydril Company. The consummate cooperation of the Hydril Company was a providentially predestined Malibu miracle necessity. A Seaver family Hydril financial facilitator like Richard was essential. Blanche signed all of the Pepperdine checks but Richard covered all of them.

BORN TO LEAD

Third generation Californian, Richard was born at the Good Samaritan Hospital in Los Angeles on June 10, 1922. "By an odd coincidence," he said, "I served as a trustee and member of the board's executive committee at Good Samaritan for 40 years."[4] With Richard Seaver nothing was ever merely coincidental.

Richard was the namesake of his grandfather, Carlton Seaver, who came to California in 1883. Carlton and his wife, Estella, had two sons.

Frank Roger was first and Richard's father, Byron Dick, was the younger. The Seaver brothers graduated with honors in the earliest days of Pomona College and both studied at the Harvard University Law School. In 1908, they opened a two-man firm at the Hollingsworth Building in Los Angeles. Practice thrived and for ten years they worked side by side on all sorts of legal cases.

Frank left his brother in 1918 to enter business with oil tycoon Edward L. Doheny. But Byron Dick practiced law at that same address and kept Frank's name on the door for 50 years. Byron Dick predeceased his older brother in 1954 by a decade.

Richard followed from birth in his famous family's footsteps. He graduated from Fairfax High School and in 1940 enrolled at Pomona College with his eye fixed, like his father and Uncle Frank, on law school to follow. But World War II intervened. Just as Uncle Frank had served as a World War I naval officer, on the day Japan attacked Pearl Harbor Richard joined the Pomona College ROTC. With the Seaver name in Southern California synonymous with patriotism, he soon left college to be commissioned as an army infantry officer. From 1942 to 1946 he served in the Pacific theater of war, rose to the rank of captain and received the Bronze Star for bravery in combat on the Philippine Islands. Richard Seaver personified "The Greatest Generation."[5]

After the war, chuckled Richard, "I had to make up for lost time."[6] In 1947 he married Sallie Suzanne Tierman, the mother of his five children. He completed his Pomona bachelor's degree in mathematics and received a law degree from the University of California at Berkeley in 1949. He was admitted to the bar in 1950. "As for Berkeley," Richard explained, "I later sent my sons and daughters to the private Stanford University Law School. But after my years overseas in the army, I was eager for an experience at a prestigious public university."[7] Richard was always kind but could also be tough.

After law school, Richard signed on with the San Francisco firm of Thelan, Marrin, Johnson and Bridges and headed the Los Angeles office.

FRANK'S RECRUITMENT CAMPAIGN

Meanwhile, Frank developed his own vision of his favorite nephew's future. Before Richard was "scarcely dry behind the ears," Frank envisioned him as his successor.[8] Frank observed Richard's exemplary military and academic careers. On the day he graduated, Frank enlisted his talents to serve Hydril Company and safeguard Mrs. Seaver. It turned into an unrelenting seven-year recruitment campaign. Richard knew his uncle's imperiousness and savored his own independence. He demurred and joined the big law firm.

Undaunted, the persistent Frank tied his nephew to Hydril in three ways: he dismissed his own lawyers and hired Richard's firm to represent Hydril; he appointed Richard to the Hydril board; and he caused the other directors to elect Richard board secretary. If not yet fully aboard, Frank tied his nephew to the towrope and pulled him toward the Hydril ship.

"He didn't press me [to come full time]," Richard recalled, "or make any kind of issue about it. But he kept bringing it up from time to time. And I kept turning him down. For one thing, I felt I was worth more money than he was inclined to pay me. If I went to work for him I knew he would fix my salary; whereas, as an attorney, I could set my own limits."[9]

Finally, in August 1957, Frank persuaded Richard to give up his other legal practice to join the Hydril Company full-time as heir apparent. "This time I sat myself down and really gave it serious consideration," said Richard. "I got to thinking that if he was not my uncle I would have leaped at the opportunity. So I decided I shouldn't let that prejudice me toward the job."[10]

August 1957 was momentous. That month, in yet another Malibu miracle "coincidence," another young man about Richard's age was elected president of George Pepperdine College. President M. Norvel Young's office on the Pepperdine campus was six miles from Richard C. Seaver's office at Hydril. George Pepperdine and Frank Seaver were already good friends. Norvel and

Richard soon became intimate friends. Twenty-four months later, in August 1959, I joined Pepperdine as President Young's assistant and became Richard Seaver's close friend. Fifteen years before the Malibu miracle emerged, the indispensable personalities to perform it were providentially pulled together.

But in 1957 Richard moved full time into the tiny room adjacent to Frank's big office and sensed nothing miraculous. "I did almost everything," Richard recalled. "I accompanied him nearly everywhere business took him. I did all the legal matters—pension plan, contracts and so on. A lot of people tried to buy Hydril in those days, and I sat in on all those discussions. I wrote my own resignation once a month—but, of course, I never turned one in!"[11]

ASCENSION AND SUCCESSION

In November 1964, a month after the death of Frank Roger Seaver, the Hydril Company board of directors elected Richard Carlton Seaver chairman, president and chief executive officer. He was 42 and would lead Hydril for the next 43 years. Hydril soon developed far beyond a family owned and regionally focused company. In a shrewd strategic move, Richard transferred manufacturing and distribution from Los Angeles to Houston, the world petroleum headquarters. The Hydril Company went public as an international oil industry provider of premium connection and pressure control products. Like a Hollywood movie with a happy ending, in May 2007—one month before his death—Richard sold the Hydril Company to Tenaris S. A. of Buenos Aires, Argentina, for $2.2 billion.[12]

In addition to running Hydril, Richard directed his aunt's personal, household and financial affairs. He managed the ubiquitous live-in Mexican maid Carmella, the tireless chauffeur Sandy and Mrs. C. A. Anderson, Blanche's three-day a week secretary. Everyone reported to Richard. He paid all the bills. Blanche did not maintain a bank checking account, keep or carry any cash, hold a credit card or drive a car—ever.

To help manage her affairs, Richard hired two top attorneys. John Hall, a UCLA product, was Hydril Company assistant to the president and Richard's right-hand man. Hall, Mrs. Seaver's confessor, visited Chester Place several times a week. Myron Harpole, Richard's estate-planning confidant, expedited Mrs. Seaver's routine gifts, structured her multi-year contributions and wrote, and rewrote, her will. Together, Hall and Harpole took the lead throughout the 1970s, engineering the long-term irrevocable trusts that transferred Mrs. Seaver's estate to Pepperdine and created the Malibu miracle.

Richard also worked to enrich the community of Southern California. He was counselor and benefactor to the arts and higher education and a lifelong leader in the Episcopal Church. He served as altar boy, junior warden, treasurer, vestryman and trustee of the Diocesan Investment Trust. In 2006 he received the "Angel Award," one of only four presented "for extraordinary service to the church" in the history of the Episcopalian Diocese of Los Angeles.

Richard shared his aunt's devotion to high opera. In 1986, he became a founding member of the Los Angeles Opera board of directors and served as its president and chairman. Richard Seaver's "passion for opera," said the opera's chief executive, Marc Stern, "and commitment to our city played a central role in making the [opera] company what it is today."[13] Richard also made onstage contributions, appearing in his favorite non-singing role of the Cardinal in *Tosca* in 2001, and reprising it in 2005.[14]

An avid sailor, he was a member of the Saint Francis Yacht Club in San Francisco and the Newport Harbor Yacht Club, where in 1970 he served as Commodore. Along with his monumental business career, Richard was a patron of the arts and director of prestigious institutions, including the Los Angeles Museum of Natural History.

In 1970, Pepperdine conferred on Richard the honorary doctor of laws degree and for more than 30 years he served on Pepperdine's advisory university board. He also served for 25 years on the Pomona College board of trustees where he was awarded the honorary doctor of fine arts degree in 1997. He was instrumental in relocating his grandfather's Pomona home, built in 1900, to the college campus where it now serves as the Alumni House. The college's theater complex is named for his father. In 2004, Pomona College christened the fourth world-class building in the Seaver Science Center: the Richard C. Seaver Biology Building.

RICHARD'S FIVE ACES

That's quite a legacy but nothing gratified Richard like his five children. In January 1975, Richard, Norvel and I—flush with Malibu miracle success—met to plan the dedication of Seaver College three months later on April 20, 1975. Relaxing in the men's card room on the California Club second floor, we quickly concurred that Governor Reagan had to address the historic celebration. Suddenly, we got sidetracked and a bit argumentative. We neglected the dedication. We debated who had the best and brightest children. Norvel bragged on his son and three daughters. I bragged on our four sons. Richard trumped us. "Yes boys, you've each got four aces," he exclaimed. "But I've got five!"

"Richard Seaver's dynamism literally crackles when he talks about his children," is the way Zan Thompson put it.[15] I commissioned Zan, who wrote for the *Los Angeles Times*, to prepare a cover story profiling Richard for the summer 1978 issue of *Pepperdine People* magazine. It was the third issue of this now prestigious publication I had founded nine months earlier. Its colorful nautical cover featured Richard commanding the *Liberty*. His magnificent 36-foot sloop was docked in front of his residence at the Newport Beach Yacht Club, of which he was president.

"Richard looks much younger than his 56 years when he talks about his children," wrote Thompson. "When I visited his office he picked up the latest issue of *Sea* magazine and flipped it open to a picture of two little girls in bathing suits holding a trophy. 'There's a picture of Martha and Victoria when they were younger. Our family all sailed a great deal in the sixties. We still do some.' The caption said the Seaver children had won most of the junior races at Newport Beach that summer in the early sixties."

"My children have always been a big part of my life," Richard told Zan. "At least once a year, once a semester when I could, I spent a day with each one of them at college, attending classes and staying in the dormitories. I visited them at Smith, Princeton, Yale, Stanford, and Stanford Law, all of them many times."[16]

His sons and daughters earned a dean's list of life honors. Carlton graduated from Princeton, served four years as a naval officer and, after Stanford Law School, practices in Los Angeles. Patrick graduated from Yale and from both the Stanford law and business schools and practices law in Los Angeles. Martha, a systems engineer, graduated from Stanford.

Becoming the third generation of Seavers to impact Pepperdine, Christopher replaced his father as Hydril president and Victoria replaced him as president of the Seaver Institute. Chris graduated from Yale and served four years with the State Department in Africa. In 1976 my friend, Frank Shakespeare, chairman of the United States Information Agency, appointed me public member of the agency's Zaire Inspection Team. Chris guided the Banowsky family on a frightening four-day tour of the former Congo and the war-torn city of Kinshasa. Hydril was sold in 2007 to an Argentine company for $2.2 billion. With that sale Christopher Seaver influenced the appreciation of Pepperdine's endowment portfolio. Victoria graduated from Smith College and the UCLA School of Architecture and Urban Planning. The Seaver Institute was incorporated in 1955. Victoria is president and continues to manage, on Pepperdine's behalf, more than $100 million in irrevocable trusts signed and sealed during my presidency, but not yet delivered.[17]

In 1978 Richard proclaimed, "Mrs. Frank Roger Seaver's gifts have made Pepperdine University, and its new Frank R. Seaver College at Malibu, the Hydril Company's biggest stockholders."[18] As the price of oil soared from $15 to $150 a barrel, the value of Pepperdine's Hydril holding soared through

THE BROCK HOUSE

Bill greets his stalwart and intimate friend, Richard, at the Brock House. The bond between these two men held the Malibu miracle together.

THE WHITE HOUSE

Richard Seaver stood at the right hand of President Jimmy Carter in a 1978 Oval Office meeting with Pepperdine supporters. Bob and Peggy Bales stand to the left, Bill in the middle and Gay to the right.

the roof. How could such a propitious set of circumstances fortuitously fall together without divine premeditation?

GUARDIAN AT THE GATE

"Aunt Blanche decides who gets the gift, and I handle the money,"[19] Richard self-deprecatingly understated. Blanche was the philanthropist; the *Los Angeles Herald-Examiner* called her, "'Mrs. Philanthropy' which should be Mrs. Seaver's other name."[20] Her nephew never took initiatives with her coffers, but he was the stern keeper of the coffers who "handled the money." If "Aunt Blanche decides who gets the gift," as Richard said, he himself decided whether it was practical, prudent and possible. "My nephew Richard C. Seaver often says to me," Blanche told the *Los Angeles Herald-Examiner* in 1970, "'Auntie, you can't give any more money away for a while; you must let Hydril have time to catch up.'"[21]

Mrs. Seaver, an idealistic musical genius without business expertise, was besieged by scores of suitors. If they smiled, wore an American lapel flag and came for a conservative cause, she wanted to help. Without comprehension of the size of her fortune, she assumed it to be inexhaustible. That put her nephew in a powerful but unpleasant position. Since her gifts were tied to Hydril stock, the valuation, liquidity and timing—matters about which she cared little—were constantly crucial. She was the donor but he was the expediter, the guardian at the gate. It was her purse but he controlled the strings. To paraphrase Scripture, whatever he loosed would be loosed but whatever he bound wouldn't get a dollar.

Richard inspired his aunt to follow her heart so long as its leading was reasonable. He felt called to please but also to protect her. He processed the small checks for charity and politics. Then came institutions seeking large gifts. He conscientiously discouraged her on causes he considered weak or weird. She pushed, pled and pestered until he usually relented. But, when push came to shove, Blanche always bowed to Richard's ultimate judgment. He vigilantly protected her interests, in honor of his uncle Frank.

PERSUADING RICHARD

"I will not allow Aunt Blanche to be pauperized!" Richard almost shouted at Norvel and me on a few occasions. It took awhile to persuade this "high-church" Episcopalian and aficionado of the fine arts that our little financially strapped college could eventually make it to Malibu.

Richard was congenitally cautious. More than 100 distinguished leaders eagerly accepted a seat on the Pepperdine University board of regents, including former United States President Gerald R. Ford. The only one ever to decline was Richard. His declination marked no disrespect. Nor was it because, for 25 years, he chaired the Pomona College trustees' buildings and grounds committee and directed the development of that campus.[22] He declined out of an abundance of caution to avoid even the appearance of a fiduciary conflict of interest. In finally allowing his aunt to give her entire estate to Pepperdine, and implementing its transfer, he would not simultaneously govern its subsequent investment by Pepperdine. While encouraging his aunt, and others, to join Pepperdine's governing board, he protected his independence as her financial manager.

Richard had the capacity to say no. After approving two early gifts, for two years he resisted his aunt's pressure to give her entire estate. He said no to Norvel and me because he desperately feared for Pepperdine financially.

As a member of the advisory board he saw the financial statements. He worried about the balance sheet. He watched anxiously as bank borrowing for construction soared to the limit. He was nervous not only about how the huge notes would be repaid but also whether the monthly interest could be managed. He apprehensively watched the ravenous additional acreage acquisition and rapacious construction. What if Blanche hitched her wagon to Pepperdine's shooting star and the whole thing fell to earth? "All would be lost," he sighed, "and I'd look like a fool."

By June 1972, Malibu campus construction created a cash flow crisis. "Pepperdine's impending bankruptcy" was whispered throughout the financial community.[23] I was on the Litton Industries board of directors, and Chairman Charles B. "Tex" Thornton, for whom Pepperdine's administrative center is named, asked aside at a Litton meeting, "Bill, what's all this I hear about Pepperdine's big financial problems?" But Richard Seaver and Richard Scaife joined hands to go further. They opened the door for a full year so that McKinsey and Company, a business consulting firm, could come into Pepperdine's finance office to assure our solvency and their peace of mind. We survived within months the Malibu miracle's gravest cash crisis and both Richards relaxed.[24]

The more Pepperdine succeeded, the more aggressively Richard supported Norvel and me. The more he saw the Malibu campus emerging, the more he agreed with his aunt about the wisdom of concentrating on one great cause rather than scattering resources among many. After assuring sufficient cash flow to complete the college construction, he and his aunt committed $6 million to name it Frank R. Seaver College. Richard ultimately executed irrevocable trusts for Pepperdine to inherit Mrs. Seaver's entire fortune, exceeding $300 million.

Which came first, the chicken or the egg? When Richard saw we might make it he committed all. But if he had not committed all we might not have made it. Richard came to believe that Blanche could make the difference between success and failure. He allowed her to give all for the Malibu miracle. "We took a very high risk for a very high return," Richard reflected. "Norvel, Bill and I joined hands, bonded like the three musketeers and got it done!"[25]

ADVENTURES IN IRAN

We bonded like triplets from April 6 through 15, 1977. We traveled with our wives and Oly and Allie Tegner throughout the nation of Iran. As official guests of the Shah, we were provided the king's private jet and personal crew. It was a fabulous ten-day guided tour of every Iranian nook and cranny including Kharg Island, the world's largest offshore crude-oil terminal. Iran, at that moment, was the number one U.S. ally in the Middle East.

"Iran has always been one of Hydril's best oil business customers," Richard explained on the flight from New York to Tehran. "The Shah is doing a lot of really good things for his people in education and health care. Hydril sends an instructor every year to the Abadan Technical Institute, 'a little Cal Tech' on the Persian Gulf."[26]

Our trip climaxed in the historic Winter Palace with an academic-style cap and gown ceremony. The palace guard positioned the men before the Shah at the throne. The women crept in quietly from the side, heads modestly covered in solemn reverence. To honor Hydril's contribution to Iranian industry, the Shah decorated Richard with the Order of the Crown. To recognize the Shah's leadership, I conferred on him Pepperdine's doctor of laws degree. To support Iranian professors and students in our school of education—including Dr. Chillingar who engineered our trip—the Shah gave Pepperdine $1 million.

All of that caused quite a stir back home. *Newsweek* magazine, in a major article headlined "Petrograms," published a big cap-and-gown picture of me conferring an honorary doctorate on the Shah of Iran and loudly trumpeting the $1 million grant.

"Officials at Pepperdine University, a church-run institution in Los Angeles, had heard that oil-rich nations like Iran wanted to tap U.S. academic resources—and were willing to pay," *Newsweek* ominously reported. "So, in April, Pepperdine president William S. Banowsky traveled to Tehran, detailed the virtues of his school and presented an honorary doctor of laws degree to His Imperial Majesty Shah Mohammed Reza Pahlavi. Last month, Banowsky's diligence paid off. The Shah of Iran gave Pepperdine the largest

"PEPPERDINE AND PETROGRANTS"

This picture and caption, which appeared in *Newsweek* magazine on April 22, 1977, showed Pepperdine University conferring on the Shah of Iran an honorary doctor of laws degree in that country's fabled Winter Palace. To Norvel's right is Oly Tegner, dean of the School of Education. To Bill's left is Richard Seaver. The Shah handed Oly a Pepperdine gift of $1 million, according to *Newsweek*.

academic grant it has ever received: $1 million for the university's school of education."

Newsweek then questioned the impact on American foreign policy of the 50 institutions of higher education—including Georgetown, MIT, Montana State University, Michigan State University and the University of Houston— "who have established similar pipelines to the OPEC nations of the Middle East." After revealing Pepperdine's $1 million "pay off as the largest yet reported," *Newsweek* cut us lots of slack. "Some petrogrants, like Pepperdine's deal with the Shah, have the simplest of quid pro quos: an agreement to set aside scholarship money for qualified Iranian students."[27]

To our great sadness *Newsweek* also reported that, after generations of his family's leadership, the Shah was in political peril. He was soon overthrown by regressive Mullahs in the Iranian Revolution of 1979.

NORVEL, RICHARD AND BILL

Everyone knew Norvel and I were close. Few knew Richard Seaver was the third member of our intimate fellowship. Mixing Tennessee metaphors, Norvel called us "birds of a feather who gee and haw together!" We trusted and confided like brothers with spaced birthdays—Norvel, born in 1916; Richard, 1922; Bill, 1936. On March 4, 1972, my 36th birthday, Richard retained us as "advisors to the management of Hydril Company" with a generous "monthly consulting fee." It was a gesture of friendship in appreciation for the creation of Seaver College.[28]

Richard and I were soul mates. We hung out together, sailing on his yacht and philosophizing at my beach house. We held the same worldview and agreed on religion and politics. I hosted him at the Bohemian Grove and he hosted me at the downtown Episcopal church. No matter how painful or punishing, we always "spoke the truth in love" (Ephesians 4:15).

"Richard Seaver doesn't merely like Bill Banowsky," smiled President David Davenport during his official president's report to Pepperdine regents assembled on Friday, June 12, 1998, in the Seaver Board Room. "Richard Seaver *loves* Bill Banowsky. Richard Seaver and Bill Banowsky share very many very deep values in common."

Be that as it may, there would have been no Malibu miracle without the unique friendship between Norvel Young and Richard Seaver. It was really something special. Richard loved me like a younger brother. He respected and trusted Norvel like a sagacious older brother.

Eerily prescient long-range thinkers, Richard and Norvel bonded in an uncanny capacity to perceive and shape the future. They equally invoked the word "judgment," by which they meant "discrimination and discernment."

They intuitively agreed upon the future, almost clairvoyantly, as if they shared a crystal ball.

"Best, I like the creative part of my job, the planning, envisioning what will happen in years to come," Richard candidly revealed about himself. "I like to shape a concept of something bigger and worth doing, and then put together today the parts that will fall in place tomorrow," he said, describing his reasons for making a total commitment to the Malibu campus. "I try to hold the long-range view and the independence that my Uncle Frank did. In my job, it is not the short run that brings the satisfaction. I don't just solve a problem or make a sale. The things I accomplish are building blocks for a greater achievement down the line."[29]

In the next breath Richard explained that those words were spoken with Norvel in mind. "I often think that Dr. Young must feel like that. Norvel has a tremendous following in this town! He must have looked years ahead to see the great potential for Pepperdine, and to recognize the needed leadership and ability in young Bill Banowsky. In less than ten years, Bill has developed into one of the most versatile, energetic, and effective university presidents in the country."[30]

Richard loved and respected me in my own right but also as a creation of Norvel. "Bill's success," he added, "must be very gratifying to Norvel." He often heard Norvel say, "There's no telling how much you can get done if you don't care who gets the credit." Richard concluded, "We needed them both. Norvel is the builder of Pepperdine University and Bill is the builder of the Malibu campus."[31]

Farsighted Richard looked at the Pepperdine looming beyond Norvel and me. "I enjoy knowing the people who are running Pepperdine. They're an unusually able bunch. Jim Wilburn, for instance, the vice president for university affairs, brings added intellect and organizational talent to the mix."[32] But Norvel Young provided Richard deepest reassurance. Voracious readers, Richard and Norvel traded obscure literary citations as if it were secret code. Hardheaded intellectuals, they relished one another's quiet company. Both men were big in spirit. Their deep fellowship was bigness communing with bigness.

Norvel called Richard, "God's gentleman." The Malibu miracle relied on their sanctified relationship. Without it, we would never have earned the Seaver fortune, yet another reason why Norvel is, in a real sense, the miracle maker. We could not have done it without Blanche. Blanche would not have done it without Richard. Richard would not have done it without Norvel. Pepperdine University is tied forever to the integrity of M. Norvel Young.

NORVEL AND RICHARD AND BILL

Like three closely loyal brothers—with comfortable spaces between their ages—
Norvel and Richard and Bill enjoyed, trusted and promoted one another.

TWINKLE IN HIS EYE

Richard Carlton Seaver died on his 85th birthday, June 10, 2007. He "fought the good fight, kept the faith and finished the course," in the words of 2 Timothy 4:7, luminously alive to the last hour. "Los Angeles Opera," said the world-famous Placido Domingo, the opera's general director, "has lost one of its most important and influential friends."[33]

A few months earlier Richard and his fiancée, Sara Jayne Kimm, relaxed for a week with Gay and me at our home on the Pacific Ocean in Puerto Vallarta, Mexico. In animated joy, he reflected on our four decades of friendship and historic work together. "Bill and Gay," he chortled, that perpetual twinkle in his eye, "we done good, didn't we!" I agreed—we had indeed "done good."

Seaver College had been dedicated 30 years earlier. He rejoiced in its national academic prestige, perceived its permanence and was gratified to leave a lasting Seaver family legacy for the ages. "Bill, you know, this will be the most important and enduring work of our lives," he humbly forecast as we walked the beach encircling the Bay of Banderas. I reflected on his prophecy and agreed again with my old friend. Among his last words to me were these:

> At the end of the day, I'm grateful to God that we could make this quantum leap in unity without a major dispute or the loss of one. Norvel came back and finished strong. Blanche died fulfilled. We kept the whole team together— the Pepperdines, the Seavers, the faculties, the Churches of Christ, both of the boards, the students—everybody! As the Bible says, "We kept the unity of the Spirit in the bond of peace." I'm gonna go to my reward feeling real good about what we've done!

On Saturday, July 8, 2007, all of us packed the St. John's Episcopal Church in Los Angeles to celebrate the life of Richard Carlton Seaver. The Right Reverend J. Jon Bruno, Bishop of the Diocese of Los Angeles, officiated. "Known as 'Chief' to his family and friends," read the commemorative program, "Richard's wise counsel, ready wit, generous and encouraging spirit and twinkle in his eye will be missed."[34]

During the Malibu miracle some of us had sleepless nights. Richard Seaver may have had the most. Had he ever awakened resolved, "No! I just can't let Aunt Blanche take this big risk!" there would have been no Seaver College and probably no Malibu miracle. Centuries to come will celebrate the Seaver name. They will do so in honor of Frank Seaver who made the fortune, Blanche Seaver who gave the fortune and Richard Seaver who delivered the fortune intact to Pepperdine.

After several close calls, some real scares and a few very sad hours, with Richard's push Pepperdine made miraculous progress. Suddenly, in March 1969, Pepperdine suffered tragedy in its campus guard's shooting of a 15-year-old neighborhood boy. We turn to that sad hour.

1. Richard L. Clark and Jack W. Bates, *Faith is My Fortune* (Los Angeles: George Pepperdine College Press, 1959), 161.
2. Jane Werner Watson, *The Seaver Story* (Claremont, CA: Pomona College Press, 1960), 22.
3. Anne Thompson Smith, "One Woman's Patriotism: Millions for Education," *Los Angeles Herald-Examiner*, May 3, 1970, 12B.
4. "In Celebration of the Life of Richard Carlton Seaver, June 10, 1922–June 10, 2007," memorial service brochure, July 8, 2007.
5. Bill Youngs, *The Legacy of Frank Roger Seaver* (Malibu: Pepperdine University Press, 1976), 97.
6. Ibid.
7. Richard C. Seaver, personal letter to the author, February 22, 1970. The Banowsky Papers.
8. Youngs, *Legacy of Seaver*, 96.
9. Ibid., 98.
10. Ibid., 99.
11. Ibid.
12. Valerie J. Nelson, "Richard C. Seaver, 85; Oil-drilling Executive, Donor to L. A. Opera," *Los Angeles Times*, June 14, 2007, 33.
13. Ibid.
14. See note 4 above.
15. Zan Thompson, "Richard C. Seaver: His Vision and Industry," *Pepperdine People*, Summer 1978.
16. Ibid.
17. Larry Hornbaker, confidential memorandum to Howard A. White, William S. Banowsky and M. Norvel Young, May 5, 1984. The Banowsky Papers. President Andrew K. Benton continues to work on the maturation of Seaver Institute trusts held to benefit Pepperdine.
18. See note 15 above.
19. Youngs, *Legacy of Seaver*, 101.
20. See note 3 above.
21. Ibid.
22. See note 4 above.
23. Larry Hornbaker, confidential memorandum to Vice President Francis Frank, "Re: Hydril Stock Loan," June 16, 1972. The Banowsky Papers. "Because of our cash flow crisis, Dr. Banowsky has requested that I try to work out a loan utilizing the shares of Hydril stock we own, plus the shares Mrs. Seaver has in a 12-year trust designated for Pepperdine University. This is a highly confidential arrangement, and any discussions beyond ourselves and the banks we are dealing with could be extremely damaging . . . In our discussions with the banks it must be clearly understood that they *cannot* discuss this matter with the Hydril Company or with the Seavers."
24. Steve Gray, "Pep Management Study Gets Funds" *Pepperdine News*, March 1976, 1.
25. See note 15 above.
26. Ibid.
27. Raymond Sokolov, "Petrogrants," *Newsweek*, July 4, 1977, 75–76. Although possibly the largest purely "academic grant," it was far from the largest contribution Pepperdine "had ever received."
28. Richard C. Seaver, personal and confidential letter to William S. Banowsky, March 4, 1972. The Banowsky Papers. "Effective as of January 1, 1972, and continuing during our mutual pleasure until terminated or changed by either you or the company, Hydril will pay you a retainer fee of $500 each month. It is understood that your relationship with the company will be as independent contractor and not as an employee or agent. No attention or action on your part is expected unless and until you are called upon by the President of the Company. If the stipend should seem inadequate it will be altered for our mutual benefit." Richard kept me on the Hydril payroll as a

consultant for the next 25 years throughout my tenure as president of Pepperdine, the University of Oklahoma, Gaylord Broadcasting Company and as executive vice president of Tenet Healthcare Company.

29. See note 15 above.
30. Ibid.
31. Ibid.
32. Ibid.
33. See note 12 above.
34. See note 4 above.

"Wait a minute, Charlie! I ain't done nothin'!"

LARRY DONNELL KIMMONS
15-year-old Pepperdine Victim
Los Angeles Sentinel

THE 1969 CAMPUS

The 30-acre open campus is surrounded by tight little houses. A
teenager from one of those tight little houses came over to play
basketball in the gym. (Budlong Street slices through the center of
the campus with the white-bottom, round-top gym at the left.) The
neighborhood boy was shot to death by the Pepperdine security guard.

CHAPTER 9

THE LARRY KIMMONS TRAGEDY

Our third son, Bill Jr., will never forget that telephone call. "Dad," Billy shouted down the hall, "it's Dr. Young for you."

It was 6:00 p.m., March 12, 1969. Driving 40 minutes in heavy traffic from the Los Angeles campus I had arrived at our Sunset Mesa home near the Getty Museum in Malibu. Crashing into the den chair in front of the TV news, I heard the phone ring and Billy's shout and picked up the extension.

"Hey, Norvel, what's up?"

"Bill," he said voice quivering, "I need you to get back down here fast. Something horrible's happened!"

The imperturbable Norvel seemed extremely agitated. "What Norvel? What's horrible?"

"Charlie Lane just shot a teenage black boy to death! The ambulance is picking up his body now. Police and reporters are flooding in. Students are mixing with dangerous neighborhood people. We're meeting here at my house with police to decide what to do. Bill, this could be the holocaust we've dreaded!"

His biographers record that "Norvel said, 'When I ran up, Larry was lying on the ground dying. Blood was all over and around him. The woman screaming was Larry's mother, and my heart went out to her.'"[1]

TALE OF TWO CAMPUSES

Larry Donnell Kimmons, a local Washington High School student, was pronounced dead on arrival at Morningside Hospital. And Pepperdine's worst nightmare was now a horrible reality. After the Watts riots that hit the community like an earthquake three years earlier, Norvel and I lived in dread of aftershocks. With acquisition of the Malibu property six months before this shooting, Pepperdine had become the tale of two radically different campuses. The Malibu campus was under construction. But, as Henegar and Rushford's chapter subhead proclaimed in capital letters, Pepperdine Los Angeles was "A CAMPUS UNDER SIEGE."[2]

Norvel and I were rapidly building the Malibu campus with one hand. We were barely keeping the lid on the Los Angeles campus with the other. "Protests, bomb threats and student unrest," an academic critic admitted, "confirmed that the decision to secure another undergraduate campus, made after the Watts Riots, was indeed the right choice."[3]

In the spring of 1969, racial and anti-Vietnam student protests blazed around Pepperdine "at Cal Berkeley, at Stanford, at UC Santa Barbara, at UCLA, everywhere. Each interest group demonstrated to draw attention to its list of grievances and its list of demands,"[4] shuddered Henegar and Rushford. But Pepperdine seemed different. Many people pictured Pepperdine as a Christian college that kept its nose clean and stayed out of trouble. They thought Pepperdine ran a tight, bomb-proof ship. They had no idea how many little fires were extinguished before they could flame into conflagration. Republicans and Rotarians, seeing Norvel and me around town, praised Pepperdine administratively, if not academically. Most of our conservative patrons never considered the hostile campus climate in which we lived and worked.

LOVABLE CHARLIE LANE

But actual conditions jeopardized public relations. Some media criticized "the abandonment of the inner city" and salivated to puncture Pepperdine's image. Norvel and I could endure forever the daily campus heat. What we could not endure for a day was some catastrophic problem with widespread negative publicity. The shooting was an unimaginable human tragedy. In addition, if Pepperdine looked out of control like other schools, it could sink the Malibu ship.

"Wait a minute, Charlie! I ain't done nothin'!" headlined a local African-American-owned newspaper. "With those pleading last words, both hands raised up in the air, 15-year-old Larry Donnell Kimmons had his guts blasted out by a gray-haired man he considered his friend," sensationalized the neighborhood *Los Angeles Sentinel.*[5]

For 12 years, from 1957 to 1969, William Charles Lane served as Pepperdine's highly popular security guard. Totally dedicated to the college, he was not some macho Robocop. A convivial and even charismatic campus fixture, he had served in his native England at Scotland Yard and was respected by faculty and students alike. Charlie circulated around the small campus seven days a week, all day long, conversing cheerfully with one and all. Retired administrator James C. (Chip) Moore worked as a student with the man he considered "a personal and professional 60-year-old grandfather figure."[6]

Incredibly, in retrospect, the 60-year-old Charlie was the only full-time security guard on the 1969 Pepperdine security force. By 2009, Pepperdine at Malibu employed a University Public Safety Department of 110, including 35 full-time professional officers, 35 part-time students and 40 volunteer firefighters braced against perennial Santa Ana winds.[7] This public safety team coordinates with the University Emergency Operations Committee. Campus security is a hugely staffed, meticulously prepared professional organization.

"CHARLIE GOT A SHOTGUN?"

But, according to historian Howard A. White, back in Charlie's day it was after "the tranquility of the campus was shattered in August 1965 by the Watts riots" that "the administration announced the hiring of another security guard. There had been only one up to that time."[8]

Charles Lane served long and lonely years in a place that, in the late 1960s, became more menacing by the month. According to subsequent diagnosis, he suffered from "post-traumatic stress disorder."[9] No one sensed he was close to breaking under escalating and unrelenting pressure. No one knew, let alone approved, his decision to start carrying a shotgun. Legally, but surreptitiously, months before the shooting Charlie obtained a permit "to carry a firearm in the performance of his duties." No one had seen the shotgun before he stuck it in Larry Kimmons's face. Then everyone wondered why he secretly resorted to a deadly weapon, recalled Dr. Steven Lemley who, as Norvel and Helen's son-in-law, was in touch with these details at the time.[10]

Catherine Meeks, an African-American undergraduate honor student, answered for the aggrieved. She recorded the tragedy in her 1978 book, *I Want Somebody to Know My Name*, published by Thomas Nelson. "I strongly believe the security guard never intended to kill that child. But it was a big mistake for the college to leave him there as the only security guard for so many years. Lane got a gun because of fear. The security guard had worked on the campus for years. He was there before the community had become more heavily populated with blacks as the whites fled to the suburbs. He was there before the revolt in Watts. Fear! That is why Larry died that night," Meeks concluded.[11]

The shooting occurred at 5:15, Wednesday afternoon, March 12, 1969. Nine neighborhood teenagers had come to the campus to play basketball in the gymnasium as they often did. It was a common practice approved by Pepperdine. The tiny gym was located at the corner of 79th and Budlong, next door to the president's residence. On this day, however, the boys were accosted by Lane. He told them they could not enter the gym because it was in use for another college event. What happened next all depends upon which of the two radically divergent accounts you believe.

"HE SAID" AND "THEY SAID"

Charles Lane told Norvel and me, in the presence of his lawyer, that he informed the boys to leave the campus. He told them that the gym was unavailable and instructed them to go back out through the gate. They refused and resisted, Lane said. They grew aggressively argumentative. "So, just to frighten them, I opened my trunk, lifted out my shotgun and placed it up on the hood of the patrol car," Lane told us.

But the boys refused to budge, Lane said. The dispute quickly grew louder and hotter. "Only to frighten them further, I picked up my shotgun off of the car hood and pointed it in their direction," he continued. Suddenly, Lane said, Kimmons leaped forward, "grabbed the end of the gun barrel and attempted to wrest the weapon away from me." A wild struggle ensued over possession of the gun. It inadvertently discharged, at point blank, into Larry Kimmons's chest, Lane told his lawyer, Norvel and me.

But, in court, sworn eyewitness testimony of five of the eight surviving boys contradicted Lane's account. They denied any kind of a struggle. They testified that Lane threatened Kimmons, as the group's leader, with arrest and Juvenile Hall detention. Lane attempted to handcuff him. Kimmons backed off spreading his arms apart, they said. At that point, testified the five boys, Lane lifted his shotgun off the car. At two feet away he aimed it straight at Kimmons. He pumped it once and fired.[12]

The five boys testified to being "shocked and horrified." One of them, Michael Jones, "thought for a moment that Lane was only kiddin' around and that the shot was only a blank." When he saw his friend "flat on his back with blood gushing out of his chest, I knew it wasn't a joke!"[13]

"The tight-lipped police, tense over three days of campus unrest elsewhere, released only fragmentary information."[14]

But within the hour Pepperdine's great tragedy had hit radio and television news in Los Angeles and across the nation. "News alert! At Pepperdine College in Los Angeles a 15-year-old African-American boy from the nearby campus neighborhood has been shot and killed by a security guard." It was a hard night's news. Thousands held their breath to see what would come next.

THE KIMMONS FAMILY

Racing through heavy afternoon traffic, I got back to the campus in 30 minutes and turned into the 79th and Budlong entrance. Driving past the gym, I was halted by police. After questioning they cleared me into Norvel's driveway. Just across the driveway a dozen squad cars, tops flashing red and blue with spinning lights, swarmed around a jittery mass of anxious students and angry neighbors.

"People were everywhere," Catherine Meeks remembered. "Policemen. Reporters. Adventure seekers. Friends. Enemies. The world of our campus was turned upside down. The people from the Los Angeles Rumor Control Center were there trying to learn the facts. Answers were being demanded because this was the 1960s and black folks were not tolerating the murder of blacks by whites as they had before."[15]

Meeks epitomized the majority of positive Pepperdine black students who remained calm under fire. But her friend, Cookye Williams, epitomized the negative Pepperdine black students who reacted in the opposite direction. Cookye was the hot-headed leader of the Black Students Alliance (BSA), Pepperdine's version of Berkeley's Black Student Union (BSU). Cookye consorted with national leaders of the Black Panther Party. Three Black Panthers flew from Detroit to Los Angeles to stir the Pepperdine pot. "They were bent on revolution and threatening to burn the campus down," Meeks remembered. "Rage and frustration threatened to consume them as Cookye Williams herself vividly recalled thinking, 'Yes, burn the school down!'"[16] As Pepperdine president I interacted daily and in detail with all of these black organizations and their student leaders.

Quaint Pepperdine College became a smoldering battlefield. Charles Lane and the eight survivors were whisked away for interrogation at the neighboring 79th Street Division of the Los Angeles Police Department. Norvel and I were whisked away into his big living room full of cops and Pepperdine brass for another kind of police interrogation.

"Norvel," I instantly insisted upon arrival. "There's a surly mob out there that could mean more violence. The best thing to immediately cool things down would be for us to go over now to the Kimmons's residence and confess our sorrow to the whole grieving family."

"No way!" interrupted a police captain. The police insisted that we not risk a personal trip to the Kimmons residence, three blocks away on 82nd Street, for fear of inciting racial repercussions.[17] Hearing that, Norvel was not inclined to go. The police produced and read a report of outraged family and friends gathered in grief at the residence. They feared it could be explosive.

But Norvel, as usual, came through. "Yes, let's go get on top of this thing," he said. "Let's convey our sympathy to the family. But take Dr. Allen with us to offer medical assistance," Norvel wisely suggested. Dr. William L. Allen, who delivered our two middle sons, was in private practice but also served as the Pepperdine College physician. Dr. Allen, Dr. Young and I walked out as some policemen shook their heads. All agreed policemen should not escort us to the grief stricken home at 1607 W. 81st Street.

Ten minutes later we pulled up in front of the little green house on the corner where Larry lived his whole short life.[18] A crowd of perhaps 30 or 40 scattered across the yard, stood on the porch and filled the living room. Palpable grief flooded the warm March night. In contrast to the loud crowd on campus, this small gathering was silent except for whispered and tearful expressions of grief. The three of us exited the car and were greeted graciously at curbside. We all shook hands and shared business cards. They quietly escorted us across the porch and into the living room. Our three faces were the only white ones for blocks around.

"A SUFFOCATING SADNESS"

As Meeks recounted, "an almost suffocating sadness loomed in the Kimmons home." Larry's mother, a large woman in her 30s, sat in a tan leather lounge chair surrounded by silent family and friends. Two courteous escorts quietly introduced Dr. Young, Dr. Allen and me to her. She spoke to us with a dazed expression on her face.[19]

I leaned down to hold her hand and to say that, as the father of four sons, my heart was breaking for her. "I can't imagine your pain," I recall saying. It was one of the saddest moments of my life. The young son of this devastated mother lay dead. He was needlessly, and perhaps recklessly, slain on our campus by our stalwart security guard. Norvel and I knew it was an inexcusable tragedy. We anguished in guilt and shuddered in suffering over Charlie's concealed shotgun.

Dr. Young, Dr. Allen and I could see that Larry's mother, Clydie Kimmons, and all of the family welcomed our visit. They appreciated our sincere sympathy. We expressed to Mrs. Kimmons our most profound sorrow and asked her forgiveness in the name of Christ. We promised to help her family in every possible way going forward. We cried along with everyone else in the room. Norvel suggested that we bow for prayer. The ten or twelve of us in the living room held hands in a tight circle as Norvel found the perfect pastoral words to seek God's blessing.[20]

After a tearful half hour, the three of us all shook hands and said good-bye. All could see our overwhelming sorrow. Whether they also saw the slight fear we felt walking back to our car I do not know. But our visit helped. Even the police later admitted that it calmed things down that night.

THE KIMMONS FUNERAL

But the next day's near hysterical campus climate, coupled with concern for the Kimmons family, caused Norvel and me to order an unprecedented Pepperdine action. We closed the college for a full week, from Thursday, March 13, through Wednesday, March 19. We simply could not risk more violence.

The morning after the shooting Norvel and I conducted a huge assembly in the college auditorium that attracted one thousand of Pepperdine's 1,600 students. The BSA loudly issued "five non-negotiable demands" at the meeting. Their demands, the usual ethnic studies list for the day, were featured the following morning in the *Los Angeles Times*.[21]

Three days later, Sunday, March 16, with the college completely closed, the annual Pepperdine Bible Lectures began as scheduled, "but were moved to the Inglewood Church of Christ, a safer and less volatile venue."[22] The tense week of school closure climaxed with Larry Kimmons's funeral at 11:00 a.m., Tuesday, March 18, at St. Marks Methodist Church, 1801 East 28th Street. Gay dressed our four sons, ages 11 to 4, in Sunday suits. Two hours before the funeral our family visited again in the Kimmons's home. Our sons will always remember visiting that grieving family and the sad funeral that followed.

"The memory of the funeral is forever burned in my mind by a single incident," Meeks wrote years later. "As is the custom in black funerals, the casket was opened for everybody to see Larry's body for the last time. When this was done, his mother screamed out his name and the sound pierced my heart like an arrow."[23]

Throughout the explosive days ahead, Larry Kimmons's mother led "toward peace and love rather than toward vengeful violence," Meeks reported. "She had survived the faithlessness of her husband, the years of scrubbing floors in white people's houses and the amputation of her leg. Now came the murder of her son. But she continued to have hope until she went home in 1973 to the God she loved," Meeks concluded.[24]

TERRIFYING DEATH THREATS

Shortly after the funeral, a major administrative realignment reshaped Pepperdine's future. Norvel and Helen finally decided to leave the traumatized Los Angeles campus and Gay and I moved with our four sons into the

President's residence to take charge. Norvel was moving up to the newly created position of chancellor and I was elected the fourth president and chief executive officer of George Pepperdine College in Los Angeles. After 12 tough years the Young family left the embattled Los Angeles residence and moved into the magnificent Adamson Beach House at Malibu.

After two happy years of good schools and safe living at Malibu's Sunset Mesa, the Banowskys moved for the next two years to the command position in the president's residence on the Los Angeles campus and scrambled to find a school for the boys. More terrifyingly, the Banowsky family also received several written death threats of sufficient seriousness to attract the attention of the FBI.

Seven months after the Kimmons shooting, and shortly before moving out of our Malibu residence, Gay got a maladroit but ghastly handwritten four-page unsigned letter postmarked in Inglewood, California, on November 12, with the salutation, "Dear White Racist." The letter read in part: "You can not be home 24 hours a day to watch your children but we can! If Pepp. does not meet our demands very bad things will happen to your family. Dig? There will be bombings, burnings, rapes! Dig? We work with the Black Panthers and do not believe in non-violence but in black power. We are armed and ready. Dig?"

The letter listed five non-negotiable demands. "(1.) A Black President (L.A.) when Pepp. Col. moves to Malibu; (2.) Total Black control of Pepp. Col. (L.A.) equal to the distribution of Blacks in the Black community; (3.) We would not dream of Black control in Malibu . . . How can you white racists demand control of a col. in the Black community? Is this Christian? What hypocrasy!; (4.) More Panther control of Black studies and the elimination of Black Uncle Tom Teachers! (5.) Courses in the Black Revolution."

"We have already burned down the Pepp. Bowlin Alley! Your family comes next," the letter closed. "So think Twice! Think of your family! Are they really safe?"[25]

Days later, Gay stood apprehensively at her Sunset Mesa kitchen window. For an hour she had watched a young black man fidget on the sidewalk across the street. Gay decided to go out and see for herself just exactly what was going on. "Can I help you?" she asked. "No ma'am," he politely answered. "I'm here selling candy for Goodwill Industries. I've finished this neighborhood and I'm just waiting now for my boss to come pick me up."

After moving to the Los Angeles campus, the Banowsky family received two more death threat letters. There were almost daily disturbing phone calls. Michael Burton, president of the Young Republicans, telephoned the police and me to warn of an "unstable angry man (Burton produced the man's name, address and telephone number) who intends to harm Dr. Banowsky. In view of the Hearst kidnapping," warned Burton ominously, "I really fear that someone as prominent as Dr. Banowsky could be the next victim."[26] Our sons, living for two years in that fermenting inner city, accumulated a storehouse of real-life experiences, some frenzied, all meaningful.

THE LANE VERDICT

Meanwhile William Charles Lane, after being held in police custody for less than two days, "on suspicion of manslaughter," was released on $5,000 bail.[27] Norvel and I retained a Los Angeles criminal defense attorney and placed Charlie on leave with salary and benefits. Pepperdine paid all his legal expenses and prompted hundreds of supportive letters to the judge from faculty, students and alumni. President Nixon, who debated Pepperdine as a Whittier College student, also sent a letter on Lane's behalf. Norvel and I were advised by our friend Tom Bradley, the first black Los Angeles mayor. Charlie was headed for freedom but only following a year of excruciating legalities.

Charlie's year began when Los Angeles County District Attorney Richard Howard deferred action on the manslaughter charge pending outcome of the coroner's inquest. For the inquest a ten-member jury was impaneled. Five teenagers who were with Kimmons, five Pepperdine students and five police officers comprised the total of fifteen witnesses who testified under oath. On April 16, one month after the shooting, the coroner's inquest jury verdict came down. They, unanimously, found that Charles Lane was guilty on the manslaughter charge.

That sent Lane next to his preliminary hearing on June 4. Following two days of testimony, the judge ordered Lane to stand trial. Lane next appeared on July 1, in Los Angeles County Superior Court before Judge James F. Healy Jr., to enter his plea of "innocent." Lane's attorney then initiated the crucial plea-bargaining process with District Attorney Howard. Meanwhile, the 12-member trial jury was being impaneled.

Suddenly, on October 16, the day his trial was to begin, on advice from his lawyer Charlie changed his plea from "innocent" to "no contest." Now, whatever might come, Charlie would be spared the humiliation of a long public trial—the answer to our fervent prayer. Judge Healy set sentencing for November 28. We "prayed without ceasing."

Somewhat regrettably, District Attorney Howard felt the need for a public press conference to calm things down. "Charles Lane now faces a possible sentence of anywhere from one year to 15 years in prison," Howard announced. "The severity of his sentence will depend upon the degree of

WILLIAM CHARLES LANE
From 1957 to 1969, Charlie Lane
served as the sole, full-time Los
Angeles campus security guard. On
March 12, 1969, he shot and killed a
neighborhood teenager.

the manslaughter, whether it is voluntary or involuntary. That must now be solely determined by Judge Healy."[28]

When the loathsome nine-month legal process ended, William Charles Lane received the lightest possible sentence. Judge Healy ruled the death to be "involuntary manslaughter." He suspended Lane's sentence of "one year in the county jail," and placed him on probation with two conditions. One was a modest $500 fine. The other, a tribute to Charlie's credibility, was "that he not carry a firearm unless required in his work." Judge Healy pronounced the postscript for thousands of Pepperdiners. "Charles Lane has suffered sufficiently from the shooting incident itself and imprisonment would serve no useful purpose."[29]

No one connected with Pepperdine in those days has ever escaped the sense of human loss that came with Larry Kimmons's death. Larry Kimmons is not forgotten. I am told that his name is still mentioned in the brief accounts of Pepperdine history given to incoming freshmen. Nothing that has happened since, nothing that will ever happen, can erase that stain in our story.

"ALL HELL BROKE LOOSE"

In the months following the Kimmons shooting, racial tension surrounded the Pepperdine campus. But when Lane's light sentence came down, "all hell broke loose" and turbulence intensified for a year. Our freshly formed Black Student Association (BSA) branded Lane's sentence "an outrageous whitewash" and staged daily demonstrations up and down the promenade. Off campus, the Black Panthers inflamed community animosity.

Six months after the shooting a terrorist attack hit the campus without warning. On September 7, 1969, arsonists attempted, in a well-practiced procedure, to burn down the college auditorium. After midnight, on the weekend school opened for the fall semester, the terrorists (police reported they were all Pepperdine students) broke into the auditorium. They soaked the heavy purple stage curtains with gasoline and set them ablaze.

Fortunately, some less-combative black students got word through the grapevine of the sneak attack. They talked to Matt Norvel Young III who rushed to the president's residence to tip me off.[30] I called for help. A rapid fire department response extinguished the flames before they engulfed the building. Damage was contained to the stage area. Quick repairs were made before weekly chapel to hide the hideous insult.

But the arsonists soon hit again. This time they burned a building down. Richard Ralphs, a member of our president's board, had given Pepperdine an old Ralphs Food Store building on Vermont Avenue next to the campus. It was a flat, worn building that would require complete renovation for classroom use. Therefore, we quickly converted it into a makeshift bowling alley for student recreation. Days after the aborted attack on the college auditorium, arsonists hit the remote and less-protected bowling alley and burned it down.

A week later Norvel called a news conference at the Los Angeles Biltmore Hotel. He issued a defiant statement of Los Angeles campus commitment. "We are now serving the largest proportion of black students of any independent college in America, with, of course, the exception of the Negro institutions of the South," Norvel said. "We will never forsake our historic mission in the community where we have always been at home," he pledged.[31] Then he called Mrs. George Pepperdine to the microphone. She volunteered her leadership of the campaign to raise funds for the Larry Kimmons Memorial Scholarship Fund.[32]

The center was holding. The Los Angeles campus seemed to be making it. Meanwhile, the glittering Malibu campus was soaring straight up. The time had come to go public. We scheduled the historic "Birth of a College" dinner.

1. Bill Henegar and Jerry Rushford, *Forever Young: The Life and Times of M. Norvel Young and Helen M. Young* (Nashville: 21st Century Christian, 1999), 196.
2. Ibid., 195.
3. Candace Denise Jones, "White Flight? George Pepperdine College's Move to Malibu, 1965–1972" (master's thesis, Pepperdine University, 2003), 45. Many primary media sources cited in this chapter were prompted by Ms. Jones's original research.
4. Henegar and Rushford, *Forever Young*, 195.
5. "Guilty Verdict in Death of Pepperdine Visitor," *Los Angeles Sentinel*, April 17, 1969.
6. Jones, "White Flight," 63.
7. Jerry Derloshon, "Heroes on the Line," *Pepperdine People*, Spring 2008, 14–16. Pepperdine University's Department of Public Safety is led by director Earl Carpenter and deputy director Rob McKelvy. The University's Emergency Operations Committee chairman is Gary Hanson.
8. Jerry Rushford, ed., *Crest of a Golden Wave: Pepperdine University, 1937–1987* (Malibu: Pepperdine University Press, 1987), 108.
9. James Smythe, personal interview with the author, January 25, 2006. The Banowsky Papers.
10. Steven Lemley, personal interview with the author, April 16, 2008. The Banowsky Papers.
11. Catherine Meeks, *I Want Somebody to Know My Name* (New York: Thomas Nelson, 1978), 70. There were contradictory reports "that the college issued Charlie both the shotgun and the pistol." (Bob Andrew, *Long Beach Independent*, April 2, 1969).
12. Jones, "White Flight"; County of Los Angeles, Office of Chief Medical Examiner-Coroner, "Medical Examiner-Coroner's Inquest Held on the Body of Larry Donnell Kimmons," (Los Angeles, April 11, 1969), 95 (Hereafter cited as "Coroner's Inquest").
13. Ibid.
14. "College Guard Held in Shotgun Death of Youth," *Herald Examiner*, March 13, 1969.
15. Meeks, *Know My Name*, 69.
16. Jones, "White Flight," 58.
17. Henegar and Rushford, *Forever Young*, 197. "The two went to the home against the advice of police, who thought there could be racial repercussions."
18. Meeks, *Know My Name*, 45.
19. Ibid., 73.
20. Jones, "White Flight," 56. "Banowsky recalled being 'received graciously by all of the Kimmons family and their friends who had gathered. We expressed our deepest regret and sympathies, prayed together and offered our help.'"
21. Robert Rawitch and Stanley O. Williford, "Pepperdine Security Officer Jailed in Slaying of Student," *Los Angeles Times*, March 14, 1969, 14. The five Black Student Union demands were: "(1) Keep the Los Angeles Police off the 'Christian campus'; (2) Pay the costs of the boy's funeral; (3) Provide financial assistance to allow Kimmons' brother and sister here to obtain a college education; (4) make efforts to postpone the departure of Kimmons' brother James, who is due to leave shortly for Viet Nam; (5) Distribute handbills in the community regarding the youth's death and announcing memorial services for him."
22. Henegar and Rushford, *Forever Young*, 199.
23. Meeks, *Know My Name*, 74.
24. Ibid., 51.
25. Anonymous letter to Gay Banowsky, November 12, 1969. The Banowsky Papers. The letter's reference to the "bowling alley" referred to an arsonist attack, some months earlier, on a Vermont Avenue recreational building.
26. Michael Burton, personal letter to the author, December 1, 1969. The Banowsky Papers.
27. In a bail amount discrepancy, a later news article reported it to be $6,500.
28. "Pepperdine Guard Pleads 'No Contest' in Murder," *Los Angeles Sentinel*, October 16, 1969, 47.
29. "Security Man on Probation after Slaying," *Los Angeles Sentinel*, December 4, 1969.
30. Matt Norvel Young III, personal interview with the author, January 23, 2007. The Banowsky Papers.
31. President M. Norvel Young, Pepperdine College News Release, March 18, 1969.
32. Howard A. White, Pepperdine inner-office communication to Ron Ellerbe, April 9, 1970. The Banowsky Papers.

"I have the unique honor in educational history of designing a new campus in one of the most beautiful places on the planet."

WILLIAM L. PEREIRA
Master Architect
Pepperdine University

THE MIRACLE UNVEILED

After several years of a largely silent campaign, the Malibu miracle went hugely public at the "Birth of a College" dinner on February 9, 1970. The two featured speakers were master architect William L. Pereira and Governor Ronald Reagan. Norvel and Bill stand with them to salute the fabulous original Pereira Malibu campus vision.

CHAPTER 10

THE "BIRTH OF A COLLEGE" DINNER

As the 1960s subsided and the 1970s arrived, many people at Pepperdine began to feel the hope of redemption, to sense the joy of rebirth with the coming of the Malibu campus. Norvel Young and I were emboldened by the accelerating certainty of success. We felt empowered to take the next giant step.

TIME TO GO PUBLIC

"Bill," announced gifted promoter Norvel, with exquisite timing, "now is the time to go public. Now is the time to announce our Malibu plans in the biggest possible way."[1]

Word was out. Pepperdine was on to something big at Malibu. Our architect, William L. Pereira, had completed—in spectacular color schematics—his vision of the Malibu campus buildings and grounds. Thousands of alumni, patrons and potential donors were eager to see and hear details for themselves.

Norvel knew the appropriate setting would be an elegant dinner. So we orchestrated a black-tie gala, at the Century Plaza Hotel in the tony Century City district of West Los Angeles, set for the evening of February 9, 1970. We recruited an elite sponsoring committee for the dinner, with Leonard K. Firestone as chairman. Pat Boone and the Pepperdine College Chorus and Orchestra provided entertainment. Governor Ronald Reagan delivered one of his major addresses on private higher education.

The dramatic highlight of the evening was a ten-minute academic interlude. President Young and Richard Mellon Scaife, in ceremonial cap and gown, conferred on Ronald Reagan the George Pepperdine College honorary doctor of laws degree "with all the rights and privileges thereto appertaining." Pepperdine was ahead of its time to pick the embattled first-term governor to receive its ultimate honor. The Pepperdine doctorate was the second of 27 such honorary degrees Reagan would receive, including one from Oxford University. Only his Eureka College alma mater beat Pepperdine to the punch. At the time of conferral, with Reagan embattled as the devil incarnate on some California campuses, the Pepperdine doctorate made a media splash.[2]

"It was an auspicious beginning," Norvel reminisced in 1998 shortly before his death, almost three decades after the great event.[3]

Years later, in 1987, Pepperdine president and historian Howard A. White emphasized the impact of that historic dinner: "The administration [made] careful plans for the public announcement of Pepperdine's expansion. The event that followed on February 9, 1970, was one of the most memorable occasions in the history of Pepperdine College. In Pepperdine lore it is known as the 'birth of a college.'"[4]

Overwhelming response to the dinner invitations caught Norvel and me by surprise. Reservations filled the grand ballroom of the Century Plaza Hotel. Therefore, in an unprecedented move, we quickly "engaged the grand ballroom of the nearby Beverly Hilton Hotel."

Pulling out all the stops, we had doubled the size of the original target audience. The total of 3,400 people, packed into both ballrooms is, by far, the biggest banquet ever held in Pepperdine history—an inconceivable feat for a school of its size and stature.[5] Reagan and the other participants shuttled by limousine from one ballroom to the next. The debated black-tie requirement did not discourage attendees. Bohemian Club brother Hernando Courtright, who ran the nearby Beverly Wilshire Hotel, wrote: "Bill, your deal was the biggest banquet in the history of Hollywood and West Los Angeles."[6]

One of my contributions to the dinner was lining up the event's three superstars—Firestone, Pereira and Reagan. To tie that trio together at the top of the extravaganza guaranteed its success.

LUCKMAN AND PEREIRA

Public presentation of the Malibu campus architectural design proved to be a highly successful feature at the big banquet. But the actual process of picking the architect had been an agonizing handwringer. The hiring of William L. Pereira engendered a gentlemen's dispute between Norvel and me. In January 1969, when the time came to crown the Malibu master architect, Norvel and I suddenly confronted inimically opposite instincts.

God blessed Pepperdine with the planet's most beautiful blank canvas. An unparalleled opportunity, it demanded an unsurpassed master artist. It was a sacred aesthetic obligation to all who would love Pepperdine past, present and future to pick the perfect campus designer.

In Southern California, bungled architecture abounded. We would be given but one chance with our challenging Malibu canvas. If, on those precariously vulnerable hills, we botched that chance by bungling the basic architecture, the masterpiece would mutate into a surrealistic nightmare.

Months earlier this crucial architectural decision seemed a foregone conclusion. Norvel and I together would have eagerly hired the famous Luckman and Pereira firm. California's hottest architects, Luckman and Pereira designed the Los Angeles International Airport, the Los Angeles County Museum of Art, the Disneyland Hotel and other glamorous public projects.

Our fundraising campaign coveted Luckman and Pereira prestige. Pepperdine labored under a fundraising handicap I dubbed "the prestige gap." People who knew us liked us. But too few knew us. Worse still, many who knew and liked us chose to contribute to Occidental, Pomona and USC for the much greater recognition and prestige.

"Many in the Southern California educational establishment," Norvel's biographers remembered, "had for some time viewed Pepperdine as an upstart and a second- or third-rate school." When Pepperdine proposed building a whole new campus at Malibu, "they added to that epitaph 'grandiose,' 'pretentious' and 'shallow.'"[7] By retaining the Luckman and Pereira firm we would clean up that second-rate image and close the "prestige gap." I could hear the critics cluck, "Oh, Pepperdine hired Luckman and Pereira for the Malibu campus? Maybe Pepperdine's finally getting somewhere!"

What put the blue ribbon on the candidacy of Luckman and Pereira was that Norvel and Charles Luckman were personal friends. Luckman was a generous member of Norvel's Pepperdine president's board. Luckman helped conclude the controversial Malibu site selection. It would have been a piece of cake if Norvel and I could have hired Luckman and Pereira for the Malibu master plan.

LUCKMAN OR PEREIRA

Instead, we found ourselves thrown into a dilemma. We could no longer choose Luckman and Pereira. We would now be forced to choose either Luckman or Pereira. After years of celebrated partnership, in 1959 they had fallen out in bitter business separation. A marriage of opposites, none anticipated their divorce. "Too bad!" I could hear the critics cluck. "Those guys were great. They'll never be the same alone."

People took sides. When the time came to finalize our decision on the master architect for the Malibu campus, Norvel and I took fiercely opposing sides. Norvel fought for Charles Luckman and Associates. I fought for William L. Pereira and Associates.

Norvel supported Luckman for excellent reasons. He and Helen were personal friends of Chuck and Harriet Luckman. A stalwart president's board member, Chuck made modest Pepperdine gifts. He was a leader of our downtown Republican business establishment and a first-rate architect whose executive design style appealed to President Young.

My sharp disagreement put Norvel on the spot. Eschewing confrontation, Norvel bent over backward to ameliorate enemies. He would never offend a friend. To snub Chuck by giving the coveted Malibu campus design to his divorced partner was unthinkable. Neither Norvel nor I was personally close to Pereira. I pled art over friendship. I favored Pereira for strictly professional reasons.

I liked both men. The affable Luckman, a superior executive, delegated to a talented staff. Pereira, managing less business with less staff, worked more hands-on. Handsome, white-haired and perennially tanned, the 50-year-old Italian bachelor was a reclusive loner with few close friends. Businessmen around town who knew both men took Luckman's side.

I spent hours scrutinizing both men and their sharply contrasting visions for the Malibu campus. Luckman unveiled his vision in his spacious Beverly Wilshire headquarters. An institutionally dignified theme, it seemed like a sweepingly streamlined UCLA by the sea. Norvel liked it a lot. It was far from my Malibu campus dreams.

PUSHING FOR PEREIRA

Bill Pereira's creative architectural renderings looked precisely like my Malibu dreams. On a late afternoon in January 1969, Pereira invited me to come to his Beverly Hills home. At the door he handed me a hot cup of black coffee. He took me straight to his bedroom. He showed me where he worked in pajamas through the night under a light hanging brightly over a square table near his bed. He flipped through a large portfolio and talked slowly as he turned its pages. He showed me, for the very first time, his inspirational vision of Pepperdine University at Malibu. Those sketches, shared for the first time that afternoon, presented in sharp detail "the most beautiful campus in the United States."[8]

My spine tingled. I adored Pereira's pictures of a contemporary but traditional, colorful but subtle, strong and straight but soft and sweet seaside Mediterranean village. Later I characterized his distinctive Malibu architecture in the Pepperdine literature as "Spanish revival, El Camino Real, modern Mediterranean but distinctively Southern Californian."

"Bill," Pereira suggested as we finished our three-hour meeting, "Gay's an artist. Take this set of sketches home to see what Gay thinks."

We shook hands on his front porch. I shared with Bill the tension because of Norvel and Chuck. "I'll go have a long talk with Norvel," I reassured Pereira. "He'll come along. Bill, you're the man for this Malibu campus."

Norvel and I spent days wrestling with this dilemma. I hated ever to oppose Norvel. Sometimes a fight's unavoidable.

"Brother," Norvel pled. "I like Pereira's vision, too. But what about Chuck? He'll be mortified. He's a great architect, one of our best friends and the prospect for a big gift."

"Norvel, what's Chuck given so far?" I rebutted, knowing it was modest.

"Well," reasoned Norvel, "Chuck's a long-term friend. He'll give a lot some day."

"Chuck could someday," I pointed to the prestige gap. "He's already given lots to USC where he's done lots of work. But Norvel, this is not about friendship or money. It's about the way our campus will look forever."

Norvel graciously relented.

"President Young," Norvel's biographers recorded, "later gave Banowsky the credit for obtaining the services of world renowned architect Pereira. '[Bill] sold me on [Pereira],' said Norvel. 'But one of the most difficult things was deciding what to do about Pereira's former partner, Charles Luckman. Pereira and Luckman had parted ways and were not very friendly at the time. But Luckman was a friend to Pepperdine and had helped us pick the Malibu site and other things. We had to go tell him that we were going with his former partner. Nobody would go with me, so I had to go see Charles alone with the news. Though it was difficult, he remained our good friend through the following years.'"[9]

Norvel understated his own magic. The master of keeping friends forever, he didn't get that touted Luckman gift for years, but he didn't give up. Chuck eventually endowed the Charles and Harriet Luckman Distinguished Teaching Fellows Award at Pepperdine University for superior classroom instruction.[10] The magnanimous Norvel consented to help me hire Pereira with one hand while he most graciously collected Luckman's gift with the other.

PEREIRA COMES TO CAMPUS

But after Pereira got the job, we butted up against his artistic eccentricity. We understood and liked one another. We worked together closely. He got the Malibu job because of me. But as weeks passed, I grew irritated with Bill's stubborn refusal to make a personal visit to the Malibu site.

From his Wilshire Boulevard office, Pereira argued that a personal on-the-ground Malibu visit by him was unnecessary. He reiterated his long list of personal friends all along the Colony. He insisted he drove by the site frequently. To prove it, he pulled from his desk drawer a stack of eight-by-ten color photographs taken by his staff of every minute detail of the hills, canyons, rocks and rills of the campus site. Nonetheless, I insisted he experience those hills for himself before designing our master plan.

"We've only got this one shot to get it right, Bill." I insisted. "You're the man. You've gotta kick the dirt for yourself!"

"OK, Bill," Pereira finally conceded. "When do you want me to come?"

"Any hour of any day," I replied.

Within a week Pereira came to Malibu. "Hey, Bill!" he called, rolling down the big black Bentley's back window. His chauffeur maneuvered off the highway onto the grass and opened the door for his patrician passenger.

Pereira had requested a 30-minute visit. Flamboyant attire signaled his intention to stay no longer. I was dressed in jeans. He chugged alongside, across the meadow and up the hill, in a vested suit with coat and tie. On top of all that was his trademark black cape draped artfully over his shoulders. I prayed Pereira wouldn't plant his shining Gucci loafers into the middle of a fresh cow patty.

It turned into a terrific visit. Pereira, seduced by the charm of the site, worked creatively with his camera. His 30-minute visit turned into two fascinated hours. The two Bills, from that day on, shared a charmed vision of the world's most beautiful campus.

Taking his orders only from God, our Italian prima donna performed heroically. Every nook and cranny of the Malibu masterpiece bears his distinctive touch. Critics now claim that, in Pereira's vast body of work, the Malibu campus may be his very best.

BIG DINNER COMMITTEE

William L. Pereira was on board. My next assignment was to recruit Leonard K. Firestone, president of the Firestone Tire and Rubber Company, as the dinner committee chairman. My friend Len came through. On Len's letterhead, Norvel and I mailed out 10,000 elegant invitations boasting a sponsoring committee of founding names soon to grace the campus: Seaver,

Scaife, Payson, Adamson, Stauffer, Tyler, Thornton, Elkins, Keck, Rockwell, Appleby, Huntsinger, Murchison, Phillips.

Serving with chairman Firestone on the dinner committee were Edward L. Carter, chairman of the University of California board of regents and chairman of the Broadway Department Stores; Franklin Murphy, former UCLA chancellor and chairman of the board of Times-Mirror Company; J. Leland Atwood, North American Rockwell; Stephen C. Bilheimer, Silverwoods; Robert Coe, ambassador to Denmark; Donald W. Darnell, Fluor Corporation; Wilbur H. Davies, Fleming H. Revell; Robert J. Downey, TRW Systems; Bryant Essick, Essick Investment; Charles R. Fleisman, A. J. Bayer; Patrick J. Frawley, Eversharp; Paul Helms Jr., Helms Bakeries; Jack K. Horton, Southern California Edison; Donald C. Ingram, Ingram Paper; Gerald M. Jennings, Everest and Jennings; Walter Knott, Knott's Berry Farm; Saul Levy, Southland Press; Frederick Llewellyn, Forest Lawn; C. Daniel Martin, Martin Cadillac; Ferdinand Mendenhall, *Van Nuys News*; H. W. Morrison, Morrison-Knudsen; Clint W. Murchison, Murchison Brothers; Edwin W. Pauley, Pauley Petroleum; Richard Ralphs, Ralphs Grocery; Robert O. Reynolds, California Angels; Henry Salvatori, Grant-Oil Tool; and C. W. Smith, Security Pacific National Bank.

From Hollywood came Bob Hope, Jimmy Stewart, Don Defoe, Art Linkletter, Robert Stack, Gene Autry, John Wayne, Danny Thomas, Sammy Davis Jr., Charlton Heston, General Omar Bradley and Will Durant.

Len Firestone was the ideal chairman for such a distinguished committee and Norvel and I drove downtown to book him. We took the elevator to the Arco Tower top floor, sat down and described the dinner. Len agreed to serve.

Norvel and I were prepared to present to Len a much bigger proposition and so we changed the subject. At year-end, December 31, 1970, we were poised to elevate the institution from Pepperdine College to Pepperdine University. That proposal sought to name our two separate colleges. We prepared a proposal to name the Malibu campus, for a gift of $6 million, Frank R. Seaver College. We proposed to name the Los Angeles campus, for a gift of $4 million, Leonard K. Firestone College. Norvel and I prayed that, come January 1, 1971, we would be Pepperdine University with Firestone College at Los Angeles and Seaver College at Malibu. We held our breath.

LEONARD K. FIRESTONE COLLEGE

I was totally committed to the Malibu campus. However, with thousands of others I was increasingly distressed over deterioration in Los Angeles. I lamented the Herculean thought of trying to operate two very different campuses. I sympathized with Norvel's determination to succeed in Los Angeles. Friends J. P. Sanders, Howard White, Frank Pack, Jack Scott, Jennings Davis, Calvin Bowers, Grover Goyne and Zane Reeves reached me with their devotion to serving in the inner city.

A spirit of service was in the air. "Ask not what your country can do for you," challenged President Kennedy. Thousands joined the Peace Corps to serve the underprivileged around the world. The church was affected. Washington Gladden's social gospel anthem, "O Master, let me walk with Thee, in lowly paths of service free," became a favorite Sunday song. Racial justice—"Free at last, Free at last"—was the issue of the age. African-American students were enrolled at Pepperdine from its 1937 founding and welcomed into the dormitories by 1941.[11] For my 1960s generation, with conscience vexed by American history, any thought of abandoning the inner city brought guilt.

Norvel and I brainstormed about the Los Angeles campus future, and came up with the idea of creating the Martin Luther King College. Our model would be Hunter College in the City University of New York system, in Manhattan's Upper East Side. Founded in 1870, Hunter earned an academic reputation for excellence in diversity and minority opportunity.[12] Norvel and I wanted the Leonard K. Firestone College. Len was our only wealthy Republican supporter with liberal social views. Len was our sole prospect. A Nelson Rockefeller crony, Len backed Nixon in 1968 and was appointed Ambassador to Brussels. Gay and I were houseguests there of Len and Nicky. With his heart for minorities, Len shocked Republicans by serving as campaign chairman when Tom Bradley defeated incumbent Sam Yorty to become the only African-American mayor of Los Angeles.

Norvel and I handed Len an attractively bound document titled, "The Case for Firestone College." He flipped quietly though its pages for two or three minutes.

"Len," I said, "as you can see, we've come today to talk to you about creating the Leonard K. Firestone College on our Los Angeles campus. If you'll spread $4 million over a number of years we'll keep Firestone College vital for the inner city."

THE FIRESTONE FIELDHOUSE

"No way," Len politely replied. He reminded us of his USC trustee service. He compared both schools' locational problems. "But USC's big enough, and close enough to the city, to stay put. Pepperdine, or any small college by whatever name, won't succeed way down there where you are," advised the racially sensitive man who ran a tire manufacturing plant near our campus.

"I can't help you in Los Angeles. But I'll be glad to head that dinner committee. And I'll help you in Malibu. You're lucky to get that land. Bill, you're the perfect man to lead its development. Just let me know where you need me."

You could have knocked me over with a feather. Norvel and I had sweated for weeks over how to pay for the Malibu campus gymnasium. It had to be ready when the campus opened. I bit the bullet. "OK, Len. What we need is a gymnasium. It's easy to get people to pay for libraries and chapels but nobody wants to buy a gym. If you'll commit $1 million we will christen the Firestone Fieldhouse." I recalled that the gymnasium at Texas Christian University in Fort Worth when I grew up was called a "fieldhouse." The Firestone Fieldhouse alliteration had an attractive ring.

"Sounds good to me," Len replied. "I'll think it over."

The glowing Norvel added his own twist. "Len, Bill's Firestone Fieldhouse idea brightens both of our reputations. The *Los Angeles Times* parodies us as right-wingers. Some right-wingers resent your political support for Mayor Bradley. Firestone Fieldhouse at Malibu will moderate your image and ours," Norvel chuckled.

Norvel and I silently rode down 50 floors in the crowded Arco Tower elevator feeling sad about Firestone College but glad about Firestone Fieldhouse. We rejoiced that Len so eagerly agreed to serve as the "Birth of a College" dinner chairman.

BOOKING GOVERNOR REAGAN

Pereira and Firestone were on board. My next job was to book Governor Reagan.

"Dr. Banowsky," chirped my administrative assistant, Phyllis Dorman, over the "Tower of Power" intercom. It was Tuesday, December 9, 1969, and Phyllis was flush with excitement. "Governor Reagan is returning your call, Helene's holding for you."[13]

I pushed the button. "Hello, Helene, this is Bill. How are you?"

I knew Helene von Damm from political events and Sacramento trips. Austrian born, Helene was Reagan's gatekeeper. She immigrated to America and trekked across the country to volunteer for Reagan's first gubernatorial campaign. She then served as his personal secretary in Sacramento and at the White House. In 1983 President Reagan sent Helene von Damm back to her homeland, like Cinderella, as the United States Ambassador to Austria.

"Oh, just fine, Dr. Bannovfski," pronouncing it in fine European fashion. "So nice to hear from you. The governor is ready now."

REAGAN RAISING MONEY FOR MALIBU

At the February 9, 1970 "Birth of a College" dinner, Chancellor Young presents to
Governor and Mrs. Reagan three of the early major Malibu campus supporters. The
Reagans focus on George W. Elkins, who gave $2 million for the campus auditorium,
and are flanked by Pat Boone, who gave $3 million for the Boone Center for the
Family, and Charles S. Payson, who gave $4 million for the Payson Library.

For the Malibu miracle backdrop, I had inherited Bill Teague's role of college executive by day and GOP speaker by night. That got me well acquainted with the now-historic five most-famous palace guards—Helene von Damm, Edwin Meese III, Michael Deaver, Judge William P. Clark Jr. and Lyn Nofziger. Lyn and I were "close."

"Bill," the colorful Nofziger instructed during a PSA flight from LAX to Sacramento, "politics is quid pro quo. In the Latin that means 'something for something.'" Pepperdine supported Reagan. In return, he had already addressed the Los Angeles campus chapel, inspected Malibu campus construction, praised Pepperdine's values and supported its bold university expansion. Now we were asking the governor of California for something big in return for our steadfast support.

The "Birth of a College" dinner was Pepperdine's first booking of Reagan for a truly major event. The governor's Sacramento office was run by Meese and Deaver. Judge Clark, an omnipresent force, functioned as Reagan's alter ego and most intimate advisor. Nofziger worked a notch below the power of committing the governor to a schedule. Clark worked a notch above it. To control the schedule—to get firmly booked on Reagan's calendar—meant dealing directly with Meese and Deaver.

Wednesday, November 19, 1969—three weeks before Reagan's confirmation call back to me and three months before the actual February 1970 event—I flew to Sacramento to meet face-to-face with Meese and Deaver. They were a delicately balanced team of truly contrasting personalities. I described to them both the black-tie gala, the prestigious dinner committee, the distinguished crowd. The clincher came in my proposal to confer the doctor of laws degree.

"OK, Bill, you're on," nodded Deaver.

"Looks like the night of Monday, February 9, would be best for the boss," Meese agreed. "Go ahead and book the Century Plaza. Get your invitations in the mail. When you get home give the boss a courtesy call to confirm it."

Tuesday, December 9, Helene called back with the governor on the line. "Hey, Bill, how are ya?" came the huskily warm Hollywood voice. "What's all this about your big dinner? I hear you want me to be your bait," he chuckled.

"Governor," I replied, "with you as the inspirational speaker for this huge event, we will most surely get our Malibu campus built on schedule."

"Bill," he answered, "you've got a beautiful piece of ground there. I drive past it to go ride at the ranch. I see you're moving dirt. I love your big flag!"

The 1968 day the Malibu land closed escrow I erected, high on the central hill where the Brock House would be built, a 100-foot-tall flagpole flying a 20- by 30-foot American flag. Walter Glass, my best friend and first faculty member to move to Malibu, ran it up on the empty campus every morning. He took it down every night. Betty Glass, dubbing herself "the Pepperdine Betsy Ross," sewed its fraying edges. We flew that flag midst construction dust for three years before the campus opened. I loved flags and erected ten flag courts around the campus.

Reagan, elected governor in 1966, was campaigning hard for reelection during our February 1970 dinner. The academic establishment was his archenemy. He was under attack on campuses throughout California. Pepperdine prided in him. In return, he praised Pepperdine up and down the state.

Reagan cut his teeth in the First Christian Church of Tampico, Illinois. Like many at Pepperdine, at age 12 he was baptized into Christ by immersion for the remission of his sins. He attended Eureka College, a Pepperdine-type Disciples of Christ school in Illinois. Eureka emerged, like Pepperdine, out of the energy of the American Restoration Movement. Pepperdine's Restoration wing sometimes called Reagan's wing "liberal," but there was nothing liberal about rural Illinois in the 1920s. Background differences between Pepperdine and Reagan boiled down to the piano at his church and the dances at school. On the dancing subject Reagan shocked me with a phone call. "Bill, I wanna clear something up with Nancy." Mrs. Reagan had returned from a Republican luncheon to report, "Pepperdine prohibits dancing!"

"I told Nancy that's crazy," said Reagan. "You guys aren't extreme." But when Mrs. Reagan persisted, "to straighten it out with Nancy" he dialed me. "I know it's not true," he said mildly. For him, opposition to school dances would be like opposition to card playing or to attending movies or to drinking coffee and tea.

I swallowed hard. The board of regents was engaged in a controversial conversation to relax the longstanding policy prohibiting student dancing off campus. I assumed that's how Nancy must have heard.

"Oh, no, governor. We have strong feelings against drugs and alcohol. We have no strong feelings about dancing," I stammered. "We haven't had any on campus yet. But our board just approved off-campus dances. That's probably how Nancy heard it." My good friend Nancy always enjoyed checking up on me. We connected. She was more candid than her husband.

"Oh, well, OK, Bill. I figured it was something like that. I'll set Nancy straight," he concluded.

For a few days I held my breath. But that's the last I heard from the governor on the subject of dancing.

THE BIGGEST 1960s MILITARY BRASS

The formal February 9, 1970, fellowship dinner of 3,400 included scores of Hollywood celebrities and world luminaries, including General and Mrs. Alexander Haig and General and Mrs. Omar Bradley. General Haig was President Nixon's Secretary of State and General Bradley led the Allied invasion of Normandy. Gay jokes with Mrs. Haig while Generals Haig, Banowsky and Bradley stand at erect black-tie attention. (It was black-tie three times a week.)

THE HISTORIC DINNER

Pereira, Firestone and Reagan were booked. Norvel and I turned to promotion. We mobilized the campus. We stimulated the alumni. We alerted the community. We advertised in the media and worked the phones. "The response was so favorable that soon the grand ballroom of the Century Plaza was completely filled," recorded historian White. We "engaged the grand ballroom of the nearby Beverly Hilton Hotel for the same evening to accommodate those who wished to attend."[14] Much to our ecstasy, it too was soon filled.

Reagan, Pereira and others on the program shuffled between the two hotels in the back of a limousine. Officially christened the "Master Plan Announcement Dinner," George W. Elkins, chairman of the president's board, extended the welcome at the Century Plaza. At the center of the Malibu campus, Mrs. Frank Roger Seaver led the pledge of allegiance. Pat Boone led the national anthem. Richard Mellon Scaife led the degree presentation to Governor Reagan. Kenneth Hahn, Los Angeles County supervisor, offered the invocation. Donald V. Miller, chairman of the board of trustees, delivered the benediction. Former Pepperdine vice president William J. Teague, who lost his 1968 congressional race 15 months earlier and was running again in 1970, returned to make introductions.

At the Beverly Hilton Hotel, seven others participated. Substituting for Teague, "Dr. Jack Alan Scott, the new dean of instruction for the Malibu campus, introduced the new administrative and faculty heads of the Malibu campus and Dr. Howard A. White, who will be administrative vice president of the Los Angeles campus. Dr. White," reported the *Graphic*, "described the vital role of the Los Angeles campus. He emphasized that Pepperdine has a valuable contribution to make in relation to its location in the inner city."[15]

At the Beverly Hilton, "Jeb Magruder, special assistant to President Richard M. Nixon, read a personal letter from the president. 'I remember when, as a student at Whittier College, I debated with Pepperdine students— and lost! I send my congratulations to Pepperdine on your new Malibu campus.'"[16]

At the Century Plaza, President Young bestowed on Reagan an honorary doctor of laws degree. The *Los Angeles Herald-Examiner* quoted Norvel: "'You have exhibited exemplary leadership . . . and served with distinction as governor.' Richard Mellon Scaife, the college board member who presented Reagan the degree, called the governor 'one of the outstanding leaders of our time.'"[17]

"Private Colleges Win Reagan's Praise for Spirit of Freedom," headlined the next morning's *Los Angeles Times.* It celebrated Reagan's major 40-minute address, delivered with high style in both ballrooms.[18] Prepared in his own hand, it is arguably his premier statement on the values of independent higher education.

The *Los Angeles Herald-Examiner* gave Reagan his new title:

> Dr. Ronald Reagan, governor of California, praised Pepperdine and other independent colleges as "the educational whetstone that helps to hone the public education process. Independent colleges educate more than 25 percent of California's undergraduate and graduate students and are absolutely essential to the total educational scheme of this state."
>
> Reagan said he believed "the Federal government should grant tax credits to parents who pay tuition fees for their children attending independent schools. It also should explore the possibility of extending tax credits for contributions to the independent colleges."[19]

"Reagan compared 'disruptive tactics' of militant students on state campuses to those of the Hitler youth movement," reported the *Los Angeles Times*:

> "It is on the smaller private college campus that the spirit of the '70s—the 1770s—will be revived. While some students have legitimate complaints about an education that grinds them through a computer, Pepperdine does not turn out 'don't fold, mutilate or tear' graduates," said Reagan.
>
> Turning his attention to dissidents on state campuses, the governor said he had "recently heard a secret recording made at a meeting of militants planning the disruption of one of our schools. They were plotting to set one of the biggest buildings on fire," he said.[20]

"The private college is the bulwark of freedom," the *Graphic* reported as Reagan's theme for the address. "The governor said the private colleges are responsible for saving the taxpayers of California more than $200 million dollars a year, not counting the physical plants. Reagan feels the private college helps slow down the fast expansion of the state schools."[21]

Following Governor Reagan, "Dr. Young introduced Dr. Banowsky. 'He's the leader we're building this college around,'" reported the *Graphic*.[22] I presented the three crucial Malibu campus building blocks.

First, I addressed the fundraising campaign. Our goal was doubled from $12 million to $24.5 million. "Thanks mostly to Mrs. Frank Roger Seaver," I proclaimed, "we have already passed the halfway point, with $14 million underwritten."

Second, I described the interdisciplinary curriculum being designed for the new campus. I introduced the blue-ribbon faculty committee leading its development.

Third, I introduced the spectacular Malibu campus architecture and its creator, William L. Pereira. We worked together, as a rehearsed team, presenting a colorful slide show to unveil his master plan. Response to this initial viewing of Pereira's vision was highly positive. People were excited by Pereira's warm red-roofed, soft white-sided and dramatically sharp-edged contemporary Mediterranean buildings hugging what he called "those voluptuous Malibu hills."

One of the most excited was Margaret Martin Brock, a brand-new Pepperdine friend. "Often called Mrs. California Republican, Mrs. Brock," Bill Youngs reported, "knew of Pepperdine College only casually until she received an invitation to attend the announcement dinner of February 9, 1970." Mrs. Brock didn't know it but she was destined to build the Brock House, the panoramic residence of Pepperdine presidents dedicated in 1975 by her friend, President Gerald R. Ford.

"'I almost didn't go,' Margaret laughed, 'but the Century Plaza is only two blocks from where I live so I finally decided I would attend. Now I'm sure glad I did.' She had never met Pepperdine's young president, Dr. William S. Banowsky. That night she did!" recorded biographer Bill Youngs, who further quoted Mrs. Brock: "'Two minutes after we met, Dr. Banowsky asked me if I would help get Senator George Murphy to be the speaker for the Malibu campus ground breaking on May 23, 1970. I did! And that flag ceremony at the ground breaking really got to me.'"[23]

The "Birth of a College" dinner sent imaginations racing and tongues wagging. The Malibu vision we dared to dream moved toward reality. A mere three months later came the ground breaking, a chance to give people a taste of salt air and to share with them "A Spirit of Place."

1. M. Norvel Young, memorandum to William S. Banowsky, October 16, 1969. The Banowsky Papers.
2. Myrna Oliver, "State's Private College Praised by Reagan," *Los Angeles Herald-Examiner*, February 10, 1970, 6. "Dr. Ronald Reagan, governor of California has praised Pepperdine College.... Dr. M. Norvel Young, Pepperdine president bestowed on Reagan an honorary doctor of laws degree.... It is the second honorary degree for Reagan."
3. Bill Henegar and Jerry Rushford, *Forever Young: The Life and Times of M. Norvel Young and Helen M. Young* (Nashville: 21st Century Christian, 1999), 211.
4. Jerry Rushford, ed., *Crest of a Golden Wave: Pepperdine University, 1937–1987* (Malibu: Pepperdine University Press, 1987), 111–112.
5. Ibid., 112. By comparison, President Andrew K. Benton announced at the board of regents meeting in June 2008 that, "The recent School of Law dinner which featured Chief Justice John Roberts was the largest university celebration dinner Pepperdine has ever held, with over 1,500 guests in attendance." The "Birth of a College" dinner was, obviously, excluded from routine comparison.

THE MIRACLE AND THE MEDIA

Bill found immeasurable fundraising leverage in his three years of regular weekly exposure on KNBC-TV. He is shown here having a coffee break during the on-location *Sunday Show* and interviewing loyal Pepperdine boosters Bob Hope and Art Linkletter on his own *Now With Banowsky*.

6. Hernando Courtright, letter to the author, February 15, 1970. The Banowsky Papers.
7. Henegar and Rushford, *Forever Young*, 218.
8. *The Best 361 Colleges, 2006 Edition* (The Princeton Review: Random House, 2006).
9. Henegar and Rushford, *Forever Young*, 206.
10. *Pepperdine University Facts, 2002–2003*, 11.
11. Audrey Gardner, "A Brief History of Pepperdine College," (master's thesis: George Pepperdine College, 1968), 16. The first college catalog announced that members of all races could attend Pepperdine but restricted boarding facilities to "members of the Caucasian race because of limited facilities. As soon as growth of the college will permit, an International Hall is planned for the housing of the various groups of other races. In this building provision will be made for each racial group to have its own social functions."
12. http://www.hunter.cuny.edu
13. I was working in the two-office suite Norvel and I shared in our makeshift administration building. Acquired in 1961, and the major expansion of the Los Angeles campus during Norvel's presidency, the old building was a remodeled Von's Market commercial store. Two blocks from the campus, on the northwest corner of Vermont Avenue and 81st Street, it housed central administration. Ascending up past a mezzanine into a narrow pyramid, the third floor had barely enough space on top for Norvel and me and our secretaries, Phyllis and Mabel. Everybody called it the "Tower of Power."
14. Rushford, *Golden Wave*, 112.
15. *Pepperdine Graphic*, February 12, 1970, 1.
16. Ibid.
17. Oliver, "State's Private College," 6.
18. Robert Kistler, "Private Colleges Win Reagan's Praise for Spirit of Freedom," *Los Angeles Times*, February 10, 1970, 10.
19. Oliver, "State's Private College," 6.
20. Kistler, "Private Colleges," 10.
21. *Pepperdine Graphic*, February 12, 1970.
22. Ibid.
23. Bill Youngs, *The House That Brock Built* (Malibu: self-published, n.d.), 9. The Pepperdine University Presidents Home was dedicated by Gerald R. Ford, president of the United States, September 20, 1975.

FRANK R. SEAVER COLLEGE

From the helicopter, it may look like a neatly carved pound cake laid out on the kitchen table. In reality, it's the neatly carved and completely compacted building pad for Seaver College. The white-topped tent in the bottom corner provided the dedication stage for Seaver College, with the big crowd and all of their cars spreading out beyond.

CHAPTER 11

THE MALIBU GROUND BREAKING

Historian Howard A. White enshrined the February 9, 1970, "Birth of a College" dinner as "one of the most memorable occasions in the history of Pepperdine College."[1] But Norvel Young and I calculated a one-two punch. We decompressed for two days and on the third day we launched around-the-clock planning for the next supernal Pepperdine event—three months later.

"Dr. William S. Banowsky will be officially installed as chancellor of the Malibu campus May 23 in an impressive hillside ceremony on the new $24.6 million campus site. The event will also mark the dedication of the Malibu campus which is scheduled to open for classes in 1972," reported the *Pepperdine News*. "David M. Lawrence, editor and publisher of *U.S. News and World Report*, will deliver the keynote speech and other notable dignitaries will speak.

"The installation and dedication will be held at a high point of the campus where the chapel will be constructed. With the appointment of Dr. Banowsky to the chancellor position, Pepperdine has paved the way for eventual university status with its multicampus concept,"[2] the news article continued.

DEDICATING THE CAMPUS

"This is to confirm our conversation relating to the dedication ceremony," Pepperdine vice president Larry Hornbaker wrote Merritt H. Adamson, May 14, 1970. Larry reviewed with the recent donor of the Malibu land a list of eight logistical items that were needed to prepare for the event: "To remove the entrance gate into the Malibu site . . . To dismantle 200 yards of the barbed wire fence . . . To remove all of the cattle from the meadow . . . To hold the big luncheon for David Lawrence in the backyard of the Adamson Beach House." It was a major Malibu miracle moment.[3]

All Pepperdine friends and followers had heard Malibu buzz. Many had seen, at the Century Plaza dinner, the dazzling William L. Pereira pictures. But very few had actually seen with their own eyes Pepperdine's future home. Norvel and I knew that, when they did, they would be blown away. We scheduled a late-May weekend when the Pepperdine "congregation" could again assemble, not in some plush ballroom, but out on the freshly graded Malibu ground itself. They would stroll below the mountain peaks, smell the salt air and chaparral, and exult in the magnificent sweep of the land down to the sea.

At the "Birth of a College" dinner 3,400 people packed two ballrooms. That many and more turned out for the Malibu ground breaking. Except for Bible Lectures, it was the largest audience up to that time in Pepperdine history. The assembly included Pepperdine faculty, staff, students and alumni; members of the board of trustees and the president's board; Church of Christ members from across the country; many new Malibu neighbors; and academic delegates, including presidents and official representatives, from 48 universities and colleges around the country.

The program called for dedication of the Malibu campus, ground breaking for construction and inauguration of the founding chancellor of the Malibu campus. I delivered the "A Spirit of Place" inaugural address that, in the opinion of Henegar and Rushford, "found its way into the folklore of Pepperdine."[4]

FOUR TITLES IN TWO YEARS

Over a period of only two years, President Young motivated me with four successively higher titles. I arrived in June 1968 as the first executive vice president of Pepperdine College. Nine months later, January 15, 1969, Norvel added "director of the Malibu campus."[5] At the May 23, 1970, ceremony I was installed as founding chancellor of the Malibu campus. "This honor," Henegar and Rushford wrote, "acknowledged the important role he would play in the building of the campus that would soon rise literally beneath the feet of the attendees."[6]

News of this third new title had actually surfaced six months earlier, on October 19, 1969, in the *Santa Monica Evening Outlook*:

> Dr. M. Norvel Young announced Dr. Banowsky's appoint-
> ment as the Founding Chancellor of the Malibu Campus
> today. President Young said Dr. Banowsky will coordinate
> all phases of the development of the new Malibu campus.
> "The aim," Dr. Young added, "is to achieve an integrated
> program between the Los Angeles and the Malibu campuses

GENEROUS HARD HATS

The two strongest early financial supporters of the Malibu miracle were Richard
Mellon Scaife of Pittsburgh and Mrs. Frank Roger Seaver of Los Angeles. Good
friends Dick and Blanche survey the magnificent Malibu campus.

THE AFTER IN 1972

This was the Malibu miracle in its first 1972-73 year of operation.
No administration building, no faculty and staff housing, no
law school. But the magical Seaver College was off and running.
The Brock House stands sentinel over the panoramic scene.

and Dr. Banowsky has the responsibility to carry out this multicampus concept." He will direct the recruitment of faculty and staff, refine the interdisciplinary curriculum, lead the capital funds campaign and direct the design and construction of all facilities.[7]

"Pepperdine College's new Malibu campus," elaborated the next day's *Los Angeles Times*, "will offer a curriculum built around the unity of knowledge, rather than academic speculation, according to Dr. William S. Banowsky, whose appointment as chancellor of the new campus was announced Sunday . . . Banowsky, a 33-year-old evangelical Protestant minister with a USC doctorate in communications, will be one of the country's youngest campus chiefs. Banowsky is known for his defense of traditional ethical and religious values in debates with *Playboy* magazine and the Episcopal Bishop of California, James A. Pike," reported the *Los Angeles Times*.[8]

For the fourth title, nine months later on January 1, 1971, I was elected fourth Pepperdine president. This was the first time that the title would be president of Pepperdine University rather than Pepperdine College. Dr. Young moved to the position of chancellor of the university. He also, for a few months, reigned as chairman of the board of trustees and chairman of the executive committee of the board. This unconventional arrangement seemed necessary at the time. We knew it would be temporary. We thought it was justified by the speed of things. Massively consequential decisions were being made in the moment. It was more of a battle than a time for participative deliberation. Norvel exploited every instrument of leadership for this march into new territory.

For the May 23 dedication, Strecker Construction Company graded and leveled the entire central knoll where Seaver College soon would rise. Some faculty argued the ceremonies should be conducted out on the flat meadow rather than up on the knoll. Norvel and I held out for the knoll. Guests parked their cars on the meadow and the flattened knoll. They sat in long rows of white folding chairs. Pepperdine faculty joined visiting delegates for the processional and convocation.

At 10:30 a.m., the color guard from Point Mugu Naval Air Station raised the flag on the hill where Brock House would be built. Their band played the national anthem. It was breathtakingly beautiful. Mrs. Frank Roger Seaver led the pledge of allegiance. Calvin Bowers, Dean of Ethnic Studies, delivered the invocation. Supervisor Burton Chase and United States Senator George Murphy spoke briefly, but inspirationally.

Keynote speaker David M. Lawrence, editor and publisher of *U.S. News & World Report*, delivered his 30-minute address, "The Role of the Private College in Today's World." Lawrence said, "Moral force is the greatest means of achieving peace on earth. Private colleges have a special opportunity to fulfill the inspiration God has given us to love our neighbors and serve mankind."[9]

The program climaxed with my 12-minute address. Of hundreds of Malibu miracle speeches, that inaugural address has been most frequently quoted. Years later, a Pepperdine historian called it "an eloquent statement of strength and spirituality in defining this new campus."[10] Norvel widely circulated it as "a statement of the philosophy of the College."[11] Subsequently, "A Spirit of Place" has been cited countlessly for 40 years. "Sometimes," as my father said on this occasion, "you just get it right." If I were addressing that same occasion today I would say the same thing. "Aside from Mr. Pepperdine's 1937 founder's address," testified eminent Payson Library Archivist Dr. James Smythe for the record, "this is the most famous speech in Pepperdine history."[12]

> Today [I began], we dedicate this campus in the midst of the saddest semester in the history of American higher education. Six college students have been shot to death in the clash of consciences. Campus scenes of tear gas and bayonets are featured on the news. Scores of colleges have closed. As polarization accelerates both sides warn the worst is yet to come.
>
> The boys who die in Vietnam today are grandsons of men who marched off in 1917 to fight the war to end all wars. Why then start another college? Because we have not chosen this time so much as the time has chosen us . . . We are determined to bring together on these hills a community of scholars who hold distinctive spiritual beliefs.
>
> Unlike most church-related colleges, in our era of expansion we will strengthen not loosen our ties to the churches of Christ. But we will resist any sectarian spirit, do nothing to stifle open inquiry and never pose as an institution that knows all God's truth.
>
> What we hope to create here, in these hills, is *a spirit of place*.

OPENING ON SEPTEMBER 5, 1972

As soon as we caught our breath, on Monday, May 25, 1970, Norvel and I caucused confidentially to confront the crucial questions: What should we announce as the certain date to open the Malibu campus for classes? And when should we announce it? We had to get it right! The *Los Angeles Times* had already gleefully exposed a little egg on our faces by our unrealistic references to a possible September 1971 opening.[13] On top of construction, we had to assemble faculty and staff and recruit academically superior students. That demanded precise lead time and commitment to an invariable date. Norvel and I knew we dare not announce an opening date and then fail, for any reason, to make it. Pepperdine's reputation was at stake.

Norvel and I consulted our team of twelve before picking the opening date. After deliberation, all agreed we could open for the fall semester of 1972—barring disaster. Monday, September 4, 1972, was Labor Day. We circled our calendars for the next day, Tuesday, September 5, 1972. That allowed 27 months for every detail to be completed, down to the last library book.

The two-year lead time targeted high-school juniors for Malibu's founding freshman class. But we decided to get a running start by recruiting 150 high-school seniors into the "Malibu Pilot Program." After spending the 1971 school year on the Los Angeles campus, they would transfer as sophomores to Malibu in 1972.[14] Illustrating the quality of those first 1971 students was freshman L. Randolf Lowry, now the president of Lipscomb University.

LOCKOUT IN LOS ANGELES

Sadly, as the Malibu campus developed into a place of perfection, the Los Angeles campus descended into a place of intimidation.

Local newspapers delivered grim facts in 1970. The *Daily Breeze* reported on our campus surroundings in this way:

> As the neighborhood gets older it gets blacker. Today the Southwest Los Angeles area of the Pepperdine campus *has the highest crime rate in the city, higher even than Watts* (emphasis mine). The Black Panthers have headquarters eight blocks from the president's office, a distance shorter than a walk across many campuses. . . . The number of black students has risen at Pepperdine, especially since the Watts Riots of 1965. This term, 22 percent of the 2,400-member student body are black, *the highest ratio for any integrated college in the country* (emphasis mine). A few of these blacks, about 75, staged a demonstration last week when 40 policemen were called to the campus. The students held the main classroom building for more than eight hours but gave up when given a final warning by Malibu Chancellor William S. Banowsky.[15]

A single match ignited this biggest student explosion in Pepperdine history. It was a two-day blast on Wednesday and Thursday, December 9 and

10, 1970. Thursday, the *Los Angeles Times* headlined: "BSU Protests Negro's Firing at Pepperdine."

> About 50 members of the Black Student Union at Pepperdine College marched through school buildings Wednesday, peacefully disrupting classes in protest of the recent firing of Ron Ellerbe, a black public relations representative at the college. . . . Aside from the reinstatement of Ellerbe, the students also demanded: both black and white students not to attend classes; efficient full-time black counselors and tutors; two buildings to be dedicated to Larry Kimmons, a black killed on campus; two mandatory ethnic studies classes for each student; the immediate hiring of a black financial officer who will be more responsive to the financial needs of the black students; more black-oriented books in the library and an enlarged black recruitment program.[16]

Later, the article reported, "An undisclosed number of police were called on campus."[17] But the *Los Angeles Times* report of Wednesday's events was only the beginning. At 2:00 a.m. on Thursday, in the dead of dark, the black students dropped their atom bomb. The BSU launched the ultimate sneak attack to shut down all Pepperdine College operations.

"About 75 black students," according to the *Long Beach Independent Press-Telegram*, "broke into the Academic Life Building, the central classroom facility. From the inside, they padlocked short chains around the metal push-bar handles of the building's four big glass double doors and locked everybody out."[18]

Scores of faculty, staff and students arriving for 8:00 a.m. classes Thursday morning found themselves completely barricaded out of the classroom building. Within an hour, a mob of several hundred shocked and surly Pepperdiners, neighbors, media and police crowded around all four of the building's barricaded doors. For two hours, the locked-out mob looked through the glass doors at the transgressors inside, who stared straight back.

The Black Students Union disgraced the college in a lockdown of the institution. By 10:00 a.m., the mob crowded the main Pepperdine academic entrance for two blocks along 79th Street. Newspaper and television reporters swarmed like flies, jockeyed for position, pushed to get pictures of the perpetrators through the glass doors. The news alert of the lockout was on media everywhere. The African-American students, at long last, had publicly humiliated pristine Pepperdine.

The day before, a small group of policemen came to the campus in response to Wednesday's class disturbances. But now, on Thursday, a virtual battalion of the Los Angeles Police Department arrived. Ominously, they

soon radioed downtown for a SWAT squad backup. The police shouted
warnings through all four glass doors. But the black students, anticipating
and even inviting police reaction, simply shouted back. The more vigorously
the police responded, the more media exposure the black students received.
Pepperdine's BSU knew the game and were sophisticated in playing out the
protest tactics of the day.

At 1:00 p.m., after being stalemated for five hours by defiant black
faces televised through glass doors, we received the students' manifesto.
Through the crack between the chained front double doors, they pushed a
printed leaflet addressed "To the Administration of Pepperdine College." It
proclaimed, "Ten Non-negotiable Demands." On cue, BSU co-conspirators
outside the building circulated hundreds of the leaflets throughout the crowd.
They wanted one and all to follow the escalating drama. The leaflet repeated
Wednesday's demands for black faculty, administrators, trustees and financial
aid personnel. It added a big "cash settlement payment to the family of Larry
Kimmons."

THE EVACUATION THEORY

"But the issue behind the demands, both blacks and whites agree," according
to the *Daily Breeze*, "is whether Pepperdine is abandoning its crime-ridden
Los Angeles campus to once again become a white suburban college in
Malibu . . . If you visited the Southwest Los Angeles campus and then drove
to the new Malibu site, it would not be hard to believe in *the evacuation theory*"
(emphasis mine).[19]

The hours passed. The clock ticked. The media reported. The pressure
built. Mortification mounted. Norvel and I felt unspeakable frustration.
We sequestered ourselves in Norvel's huge living room with Pepperdine
administrative leaders and an equivalent number of police officers. Advising
Norvel and me were Howard White, Oly Tegner, Bill Stivers, Charles
Runnels, Jerry Hudson, Jack Scott, Jim Wilburn and Larry Hornbaker.

The police presence included uniformed officers, business-suited
detectives and five African-American undercover agents disguised in jeans,
tennis shoes, tattoos, earrings and Afros.

Outside more uniformed officers and undercover agents scattered
throughout the crowd. The Los Angeles Police Department assembled near
the gymnasium, its helmeted 20-member SWAT squad at military attention
in two rigid rows of ten. That positioned them squarely in the center of the
action. They were about a half block from the swarming 79th Street crowd
and a half block from the Budlong Avenue high command at the president's
residence.

Everyone in Norvel's living room was anxious and angry. But none knew what to do. How could we gain control? How could we minimize damage? How could we get reporters off campus? How could we get ourselves out of the news? How could we get doors opened, protesting students out and hundreds of students back into class? Above all, how could we guarantee no one would get hurt? Or killed!

How could we do something so smart and so fast that our supporters would praise us for it? I knew Pepperdine's friends were glued to their television sets. I dreaded the disastrous impact this high-handed lawlessness from a bunch of protesters would have on our "law and order" supporters. "We simply must keep the Malibu campus construction on course," I pledged to myself.

THE SWAT SQUAD

Someone said no crisis should ever be wasted. We finally decided to launch a powerful counterattack. We would have to show some strength. All advisors in the living room agreed the activists would never back down until confronted by overpowering force. But there was drastic disagreement over how to deliver such force.

After two hours of heated debate, the disagreement boiled down to two desperate options. All police and most Pepperdine administrators contended that the SWAT squad should execute the armed confrontation for which it was trained. Since the Watts riots, in which several officers were slain, police in the area had been on the defensive, itching to crack some outlaw heads.

A few of us argued to the contrary. I opposed an armed police invasion of the building. I contended that the Pepperdine administration should attempt its own intervention with our own students.

The high command in Norvel's living room had a lot to say. The most intriguing reports came from the brilliantly disguised undercover officers. They returned from ground zero after talking through the glass doors to rebellious students. What did these undercover police agents think we should do?

"Those cats don't plan to move an inch," they admonished. "They're locked in. They're gettin' on TV and newspapers. They got food for days. They got that long demand list just waitin' for your answers. This is where the book calls for our SWAT boys. 'Course, that's the very thing those locked-in dudes expect—and want! They know lots of police power from us means lots of publicity for them. The more police, the more press."

The uniformed officers and business-suited detectives nodded in unison. Then came their dramatic demonstration.

"See this chain cutter?"as a big man with a top badge brandished aloft the tool. "We'll position our guys at all four doors with helmets and vests, though we don't think those kids are armed. We'll shove these cutters through the cracks, cut the chains, storm the building and corner, cuff and arrest every perpetrator. We'll transport them within ten minutes to our lockup. That's our plan. We strongly urge you to approve it. You must authorize our immediate action now before this situation gets completely out of hand and someone gets hurt or killed."

THE HAYAKAWA EFFECT

My stomach grew nauseous.

"No," I protested. "We can't have that. We can't play into their hands by having television scenes of the SWAT squad cracking Pepperdine students with billy clubs. That horrible scene will sink us."

"Well now, Bill," countered Dr. White, "What other option do we have? Let these professionals do their job. This is not an academic but a law enforcement problem."

Under threat of physical peril Howard White and I rose to the occasion. Close friends for a lifetime, we ordinarily agreed on everything. This time, we had opposite gut reactions. I hated to disagree with my senior mentor, who was dean of graduate studies. Though much younger, I outranked him as executive vice president. We both reported to Norvel.

"OK, Howard, I'll tell you what to do," I answered. Howard respected that. "First, we must keep the police out of this. Think of the bloody riots erupting at other places over such situations. We don't want another Kent State here with dead students."

"Second," I persisted, "we must walk out there, in the name of Pepperdine, and read these kids the riot act. We must do just what Dr. S. I. Hayakawa did."

I had suddenly summoned a sanctified source. In December 1968, after two years of strikes and shutdowns at San Francisco State University, semanticist savant Samuel Ichiye Hayakawa became the school's third president in 24 months. He inherited violent confrontations with the Black Panther Party, the Third World Liberation Front, the Black Student Union, the American Federation of Teachers and the Students for a Democratic Society. All these groups, gathered round a sound truck, shouted for an indefinite continuation of the total university strike. Hayakawa shoved through the mob, yanked their electrical plug and silenced the sound truck's loudspeakers. A highly celebrated professor, Dr. Kay Boyle, called him "Hayakawa Eichmann." He shouted back, "Sister, you're fired!" and later did fire her. The media genuflected and California voters sent the Republican Hayakawa to the U. S. Senate in 1976.[20]

"Let's do what Dr. Hayakawa did," I argued. "These kids expect an armed response. They don't expect disastrous damage to their academic records. That might panic them into coming out. There's a chance they'll fold in the face of grave academic retribution from institutional authority."

"Bill, that's your bravado," scoffed Howard. Howard and I were like family and we paid one another the compliment of candor. If Norvel was an older brother to me, Howard was a loving father. But it was the low-key Dr. Olaf F. Tegner who broke this deadlock. Oly played the trump card of all time. Pepperdine's longest-tenured professor, Tegner built the graduate school of education and capped his 60-year career as vice president for educational relations.

"No, Howard! I think Bill's right!" exclaimed the always soft-spoken Oly. The room fell silent. "I agree with Bill. We must give Bill's plan a chance to succeed before we give up and lose control. Come on, Bill," finishing his decisive speech. "I'll go out there with you."

THE MIRACULOUS SHOWDOWN

Helen insisted that Norvel not go, because, "They might kill the president!" Norvel's pacifistic personality did not suit this assignment. When Oly heard Helen he thought: "Well, if they are going to kill Norvel, what makes you think they won't kill me?"[21] But Oly walked out with me, nonetheless.

It was about a block and a half from Norvel's house to the Academic Life Building. At the gym, Oly and I walked ten feet past the bulletproof-jacketed SWAT squad. "Bill," he said, "we've got to keep those guys out of this." But the next day's newspaper reported: "Chancellor Banowsky confronted the students just as the police were arranging themselves into a skirmish line."[22]

We turned left down the 79th Street sidewalk. The huge crowd, seeing us approach in serious blue business suits, cleared an opening all the way down to the big double glass doors at the main entrance. Oly and I inched forward, almost up against the glass. We stood two feet from the enclosed culprits. I glanced down at my blank yellow legal pad. As if reading a carefully prepared document, I extemporized above the crowd noise.

"I hereby command you, in the name of Pepperdine College, to unlock these doors immediately. Pepperdine College has identified every one of you and reported your names to the police." (Although we had identified several, I exaggerated a little.) "If you do not open up these doors," I continued, "within the next five minutes we will turn your names over to the police. The SWAT squad is preparing to enter, apprehend and arrest you. However, as of now, this is no police matter. It still remains a Pepperdine matter. Please be wise! We can still resolve all of this among ourselves."

"If you refuse," Dr. James Smythe stood close enough to hear me shout, "we will file felony charges and prosecute you to the full extent of the law. Even worse, you will be immediately expelled from the college. This felony will be on your scholastic transcripts, on your permanent academic record. Your educational careers will be ruined."

"If you remove these chains, and open these doors now, no disciplinary action will be taken. But if you refuse, within five minutes you will be arrested under grave criminal punishment. And you will face a crippled academic future forever. It's your choice," I said, glancing at my watch. "You have only five minutes to come out. Beginning right now."

A STAR IS BORN

Backing a few feet away from the glass doors, Oly and I edged into the crowd. We heard clicks and saw flashes from dozens of cameras. I took a deep breath, shook Oly's hand for standing with me and said a silent prayer. Everything grew quiet.

"Within seconds—not minutes but seconds—the students began leaving," reported the *Los Angeles Times*.[23] The BSU president approached the glass door and unlocked the chain. With help from others, he shoved both front doors wide open. Simultaneously, black students opened the building's other three doors. With loud cheers and sighs of relief, hundreds of irritated students flooded into the building from all sides. Acquiescing black students blended into the crowd. Classes started in ten minutes. The crisis ended instantly.

Amazed police appeared palpably disappointed, mystified media suspiciously disbelieving. But, within a half hour police and media rushed off to the next hot spot.

For Pepperdine it was, miraculously, the last horrifying Los Angeles campus event. We faced smaller student squabbles. But this campus commandeering was the last major crisis prior to the opening of the Malibu campus two years later. And, as the media reported, it was the coming of the Malibu campus that fueled this crisis.

"Banowsky, always mindful of public perception," charged critic Candace Denise Jones, "neutralized all potential criticism and any threats to the Miracle in Malibu." She accused me of "diffusing student agitation by implementing many of the black students' demands while publicly maintaining a conservative image."[24] But the media reported my contention that the hard-handed measures brought against demonstrators were not done in order to save face or pride.

THE BIG SHOWDOWN (FRIDAY, DECEMBER 10, 1970)

"Dr. William S. Banowsky, Chancellor of Pepperdine College ordering protesting African-American students to halt their demonstration or face suspension."

Los Angeles Times photo by Steve Fontanini

This major crisis created much media praise. That evening, the television news featured the dramatic showdown at Pepperdine's front door. The next day's *Los Angeles Times* pictured my jut-jawed profile on page one of the Metro Section above the fold. I stood in confrontational face-off against an angry line-up of glass-enclosed students with bouffant Afros. For tax-paying Californians fed up with Black Nationalism and campus unrest, it was the picture worth a thousand words. For Pepperdine, it was worth millions of dollars for Malibu construction.

Under the front-page picture, the *Los Angeles Times* quoted my ultimatum: "You've got to disperse within five minutes. Every student who does not will be immediately suspended and the Los Angeles Police Department is standing by to disperse you."[25]

TOUGH STAND

"Toughness today is part of a college president's job and William S. Banowsky appears ready with a toughness of his own," reported the *Graphic*. "In his appearance as regular cast member of the KNBC 'Sunday Show,' Dr. Banowsky called on campus administrators 'to toughen their spines' in dealing with student violence. This included 'full cooperation with the police,' inviting them on campus and helping them procure court proceedings against student law-breakers. Assailing the 'New Left Movement,' Banowsky charged that 'the true test of loyalty is a willingness to help the FBI and CIA to infiltrate the campus and all of its cells of lawlessness,'" reported the *Graphic*.[26]

INAUGURATING THE MALIBU FOUNDING CHANCELLOR

The brand-new golden medallion adorning Bill's chest, he and Norvel celebrate
the Malibu groundbreaking with the California Republican United States Senator
George Murphy and David M. Lawrence, editor and publisher of *U.S. News and
World Report*.

In every miracle there is a moment when the sun comes shining through
and to many of us this was the moment. The confrontation that could so
easily have turned violently tragic was a major Malibu miracle turning point.

A minor overnight celebrity, I was hailed as "the young Pepperdine
Hayakawa." The *Santa Monica Evening Outlook* story, headlined "The Tough-
Talking Chancellor," reported, "Banowsky's edict immediately ended the Los
Angeles campus row."[27] Madison Avenue could not have promoted as much
goodwill as provided by that improvised confrontational stroke of luck—or
providence. With the opinions of police and Pepperdine administrators
running heavily against the intervention, its outcome seems one more in a
ten-year sequence of minor miracles that made the Malibu miracle.

The stock of Pepperdine College soared and small donations poured in.
I was overwhelmed with speech invitations, elected to 12 corporate boards,
given my own weekly newspaper column and half-hour KNBC-TV talk show,
and Governor Reagan named me the Republican National Committeeman
from California. Norvel and I hired a public relations firm to close the
Pepperdine prestige gap with months of positive follow-up press.

"Dr. Banowsky admits that he 'thrives on the sheer toughness of the presidency,'" reported the *Graphic*. "He is now verbally attacked by some while being highly acclaimed by others. 'The tasks are so great that any college president must decide where to succeed and where to fail,' he says. President Banowsky certainly appears to be serene in the controversy and personal attacks," concluded the *Graphic*.[28]

Within days of defeating the Black Student Union, on New Year's Day 1971, Norvel and I proclaimed the college "Pepperdine University." I was elected its first president.

"BANOWSKY NEW PREXY, YOUNG TO HEAD BOARD"

That startling 1971 headline launched Pepperdine University.[29] Norvel and I, along with his wife Helen, were elected to the board of trustees and granted highest administrative and governance offices. For all practical purposes, for better or worse, for the year of 1971 Norvel and I were in charge of things.

Occasionally in life, and this once in mine, the stars align so perfectly you sense invincibility. By God's grace, from 1968 through 1972, Pepperdine lined up four colossal stars in an invincible row: the Malibu land; the Seaver fortune; the county permits; and the board granting to Norvel and me not merely the administration but also the governance control of the institution through the crucial 1971 construction year.

This was a bizarre but dynamic phase of Pepperdine governance. "We're in way over our heads," said Donald V. Miller, the man Mr. Pepperdine picked to replace him as board chairman in 1948. "You and Norvel will have to lead us out."[30] That original George Pepperdine College board of trustees deserves tremendous credit. They got things started and kept them going under dire circumstances. When the time arrived to expand the governance, the trustees themselves brilliantly managed their own merger into the enlarged ecumenical board of regents. But you only lose your leadership when you cease to lead. Twelve aging trustees struggled hopelessly to govern a transformed institution. Credibility cratered with their outrageously unanimous vote to reject the Adamson gift of Malibu land because of its "prohibitive development costs."[31] Norvel and I quickly raised $3 million for development, reversed the trustees and took charge.

With the Malibu land debacle the board deferred and stepped aside for Norvel and me. It was not a board and administration conflict. It was not a takeover. It was a handover. Trustees, a close band of brothers and sisters, believed that Norvel and I were "providentially joined together and lifted up to higher ground for Pepperdine's good," as trustee James L. Lovell said in his church paper.

The board doubled the power for Norvel and me. They elevated us from mere administration and elected us full voting trustees. For a tiny board to fill three seats—including Norvel and me and Helen Young—with employed administrators was highly irregular. The trustees, even more irregularly, also then bestowed upon Norvel and me the two highest offices of not merely the administration but also of the board.

"Dr. M. Norvel Young has been elected chairman of the board of trustees, chancellor of the university and chief policy officer. Dr. William S. Banowsky has been elected Pepperdine's fourth president and chief executive officer," proclaimed the *Graphic* in February 1971. "Last month in San Francisco the California Newspaper Publishers Association," the next sentence added, "called Dr. Banowsky 'a tough young administrator' when he addressed their annual convention as keynote speaker. 'To allow President Banowsky to devote himself to developing and founding the whole multicampus complex, Dr. Howard A. White has been named executive vice president and chief operational officer of the university,' announced longtime board chairman, Donald V. Miller, who has moved to chairman of the executive committee."[32]

The board granted Norvel and me powerful autonomy, provided we could pay for it. For a full year—at the very pinnacle of Malibu risk-taking when the most definitive decisions determining Pepperdine's spiritual, academic and financial future were being made—Pepperdine was blessed by God with the lean leadership of a two-man entrepreneurial team at the top. The Malibu miracle did not happen accidentally in a bureaucratic atmosphere. Norvel and I made it happen by being free, gutsy and fast-acting in an exquisitely balanced partnership. When your life is on the line, two heads are better than one and they are infinitely better than 21.

But, as time passed, normalcy returned. After but 12 months of two-man rule, Norvel surrendered the highest office of board chairman back to long-time trustee Robert P. Jones. The full board resumed control.

"YOU WILL CHEAT OBLIVION"

Norvel and Helen were peerless correspondents. About twice a quarter Gay and I opened long, meticulously typed missives. For 25 years my executive assistant Phyllis A. Dorman opened all my mail except for Norvel's and Helen's letters. After this roller coaster ride of promotions and titles, Norvel wrote on March 1, 1971: "Dear Bill and Gay, Before beginning a busy day, I want to tell you again how thrilled Helen and I are with your ever increasing share of the close partnership we prize at Pepperdine. You will leave a lasting legacy. You will cheat oblivion."[33]

I've long loved that "cheat oblivion" phrase. Nearing the end now, it feels like Norvel could have been correct.

1. Jerry Rushford, ed., *Crest of a Golden Wave: Pepperdine University, 1937–1987* (Malibu: Pepperdine University Press, 1987), 111–112.
2. Kenny Waters, "Dr. Banowsky Installed: Malibu Hilltop Ceremony Marks Chancellorization," *Pepperdine News*, May 1970, 1.
3. Larry Hornbaker, personal letter to Merritt H. Adamson, May 14, 1970. The Banowsky Papers.
4. Bill Henegar and Jerry Rushford, *Forever Young: The Life and Times of M. Norvel Young and Helen M. Young* (Nashville: 21st Century Christian, 1999), 212.
5. "Campus Director Named: For Malibu College," *Santa Monica Evening Outlook*, October 17, 1969, 1.
6. Henegar and Rushford, *Forever Young*, 212.
7. "Banowsky Named Founding Malibu Chancellor," *Santa Monica Evening Outlook*, January 15, 1970, 3; "Malibu Chancellor Banowsky," Pepperdine College news release, September 29, 1969.
8. William Trombley, "New Campus to Stress 'Unity of Knowledge': Pepperdine's Malibu Branch, *Los Angeles Times*, Monday, October 20, 1969, 12.
9. Ronald Ellerbe, "The Birth of a College," *Pepperdine College Alumni Voice*, Volume 33, Number 3, Fall 1970, 19.
10. Patricia Yomantas, in Rushford, *Golden Wave*, 178.
11. William S. Banowsky, "A Spirit of Place" (Malibu: Pepperdine College Press, June 1, 1970), 1. "These remarks, delivered on May 23, 1970, at the dedication ceremony for the new campus of Pepperdine College at Malibu, are published as a statement of the philosophy of the College."
12. James Smythe, personal interview with the author, January 25, 2006. The Banowsky Papers.
13. See note 8 above.
14. "Malibu Campus 1971 Freshman Pilot Class Planned," *Santa Monica Evening Outlook*, May 20, 1970, 8.
15. John Crowe, "Pepperdine: A Changing Scene," *Daily Breeze*, December 20, 1970, 1.
16. "BSU Protests Negro's Firing at Pepperdine," *Los Angeles Times*, December 10, 1970, 22.
17. Ibid.
18. "75 Students Face Suspension for Blockade at Pepperdine," *Independent Press-Telegram*, December 11, 1970, 1.
19. See note 15 above.
20. http://www.library.sfsu.edu/strike/chronology.html.
21. Henegar and Rushford, *Forever Young*, 198.
22. See note 15 above.
23. Eric Malnic, "Black Students' Strike Forces Pepperdine College Shutdown," *Los Angeles Times*, December 11, 1970, 6.
24. Candace Denise Jones, "White Flight? George Pepperdine College's Move to Malibu, 1965–1972" (master's thesis, Pepperdine University, 2003), 89-90.
25. See note 23 above.
26. Chuck Wright, "Banowsky Thrives on Challenges of Post," *Pepperdine Graphic*, May 6, 1971, 1.
27. "The Tough-Talking Chancellor," *Santa Monica Evening Outlook*, December 11, 1970, 6.
28. See note 26 above.
29. "Banowsky New Prexy; Young to Head Board," *Pepperdine Graphic*, February 25, 1971, 1.
30. Donald V. Miller, personal interview with the author, March 15, 1969. The Banowsky Papers.
31. Ibid.
32. See note 29 above.
33. M. Norvel Young, personal letter to the author, March 1, 1971. The Banowsky Papers.

"In American higher education during the last third of the twentieth century Pepperdine was among those universities achieving the greatest growth in the fastest time."

R. GERALD TURNER

President
Southern Methodist University
Former Chancellor
The University of Mississippi

PART III

THE GROWTH OF
PEPPERDINE UNIVERSITY

THE FATHER OF PEPPERDINE UNIVERSITY

"M. Norvel Young was the leader who guided Pepperdine from a small college with
950 students in Los Angeles to full-fledged Pepperdine University at Malibu with an
enrollment of 9,500." —*New York Times*, February 23, 1998

CHAPTER 12

THE COLLEGE BECOMES A UNIVERSITY

This 1971 declaration debuted, not in an academic monograph, but in the *Oil World Journal.* A profile of Fritz Huntsinger and his 1970 gift of $2.5 million for Huntsinger Academic Center celebrated Pepperdine's university status.[1]

FATHER OF THE UNIVERSITY

Of the 12 publicly traded New York Stock Exchange corporations I served as a director, one was the company Fritz Huntsinger founded—Vetco Offshore Industries.[2] Vetco, based in Ventura, California, supplied equipment for ocean drilling worldwide. Pepperdine's major source of financial support, the Hydril Company, also supplied worldwide drilling equipment.

Mrs. Frank R. Seaver's Hydril stock gifts largely built and endowed the Malibu campus. Pepperdine's other "petroleum friends" included Richard Mellon Scaife, Clint W. Murchison, Edwin W. Pauley, Lew O. Ward and Henry Salvatori. The Pepperdine ascendancy so awed these men that one called Pepperdine, "the oilman's academic darling."[3] These patriotic oil tycoons hung out together and gave the Malibu miracle its biggest boost.

Even with such support, how did "little Pepperdine College" become a university? What was the process? Was accreditation required? Were faculty involved? How was this quantum leap so swiftly and smoothly orchestrated? How did the struggling college transform itself into a full-fledged major university?

These questions spotlight the leadership of M. Norvel Young—the father of Pepperdine University. Norvel may have been the only one who never doubted Pepperdine's ultimate triumph. When bitter years brought the survival fight, others seemed content to persevere as a college. Without Dr. Young's progenitive powers there would be no Pepperdine University.

The futuristic Norvel grew up in Nashville, three blocks from the campus of Vanderbilt University. He was inspired early and joined Pepperdine in 1938 with a Vanderbilt master's in history. He had been to the big league. He dreamed of making Pepperdine a university.

Norvel got his doctorate at George Peabody College but he never liked its name. Calling himself a "wordsmith," he grew impatient with "George" as part of Pepperdine College's name. "Nobody says 'Elihu Yale University' just 'Yale University,'" he reasoned. "We should look less like a Bible college, sound less parochial. First names on schools create second-rate clutter." In 1957, when Norvel became president, he preferred "Pepperdine College."

In the 1960s, when Norvel campaigned for me to return to Pepperdine, achieving university status was not part of our deal. I returned, not to help Pepperdine become a university, but to build the Malibu campus. Norvel's incessant university talk sounded impractical, if not a bit silly.

It sounded a lot less silly when Norvel telephoned at 7:00 a.m. on the morning of Tuesday, February 10, 1970. The night before, for the "Birth of a College" dinner, we filled the two biggest ballrooms in West Los Angeles with 3,400 supporters. "Bill," Norvel said, cutting to the chase after mutual congratulations, "now we must do two things. We must set a date for the Malibu ground breaking. And, Bill, it's time to proclaim Pepperdine University!"

The stunning dinner victory cleared my vision. "Norvel," I replied, "I couldn't agree more." Confidence aglow, Norvel and I felt bullish, if not a bit bulletproof. Allowing three months preparation, we picked Saturday, May 23, 1970, to dedicate the Malibu campus. Then we turned our attention to attaining university status.

NO ACCREDITATION PROCESS

Tutored by Pepperdine lawyers, Norvel and I studied how to qualify as a university. We learned California public education defined institutions systematically, but private education operated them unilaterally. No criteria controlled names. If a private college declared itself a university, an indifferent academic establishment left it free to name itself as it pleased. We confronted, not an accreditation process, but a public-relations procedure. That's all we needed to know.

If Norvel and I could muster the nerve, academic process would permit us to proclaim the college Pepperdine University. Since we did not want to look ridiculous, we spent several months mustering the nerve, making a convincing case with Pepperdine's boards, faculty, patrons and alumni, and with California's academic, political and media establishments. We worked throughout 1970, won unanimous support and proclaimed Pepperdine University on January 1, 1971. Without much change in the ingredients we dramatically enlarged the size of the container. Norvel and I also doubled the positions at the top. He became the first chancellor and I became the first president of the university.

Over the months, we petitioned the advice and consent of academic and political powers. We created public leverage by letting the word seep out slowly. After a decade as Pepperdine president, Norvel Young enjoyed statewide respect as chairman of the 15-member Independent Colleges of Southern California. Governor Reagan also appointed friend and neighbor Norvel to the California Coordinating Counsel on Higher Education in 1968.[4] His biographers pictured the Reagan-Young friendship in 1970, as Norvel took his turn as chairman of that powerful nine-member board: "One day at the Adamson Beach House, Ronald and Nancy Reagan came to lunch while he was governor of California. The next day, the governor showed up at the front door with a small tree in a tub to express his appreciation for the Youngs' hospitality."[5]

Matt Young recalled, "Reagan came to the beach house in his jodhpurs spontaneously and unannounced, by himself with neither security nor fanfare. My sister Marilyn answered the door and he gave her a tree."[6]

FRIENDS IN HIGH PLACES

Guiding Norvel and me through this passage were three California public higher education comrades: Glenn Dumke, Edward Carter and Franklin Murphy. Leading statewide lights, they were our Bohemian Club brothers, Pepperdine honorary doctorate recipients and high profile guests at the recent "Birth of a College" dinner.

Dr. Glenn Dumke revered Pepperdine's faith and learning mission. We already knew Glenn's career at Occidental College, so when Governor Reagan appointed him chancellor of the California State University System we had a friend in high places. Later, when President S. I. Hayakawa resigned in 1972 to run for the United States Senate, Glenn would make major media waves urging me to become president of San Francisco State University.[7]

Chancellor Dumke promoted Pepperdine within the state universities. Ed Carter handled the senior universities. Norvel and I knew Ed as chairman of Broadway Department Stores. When Governor Edmund G. (Pat) Brown appointed him chairman of the University of California board of regents we had another friend in high places.

Norvel first knew Dr. Franklin Murphy as chancellor of the University of Kansas. The three of us were confidants during Franklin's tenure as

UCLA chancellor. When publishing magnate Otis Chandler anointed him chairman of the Times Mirror Company we had another friend in high places. Franklin prepared the *Los Angeles Times* to treat our university announcement positively.

Norvel insisted on breaking the university announcement and breaking the Malibu ground simultaneously. He scheduled two meetings. Monday, May 4, the Pepperdine College board of trustees voted to become Pepperdine University. Tuesday, May 5, the Pepperdine faculty voted to support the advance. Norvel then let the cat out of the bag publicly at the May 23 dedication. "In six months," he proclaimed, "Pepperdine College will officially become Pepperdine University." He christened it "a multicampus concept."[8]

I followed Norvel with my inaugural address as founding chancellor of the Malibu campus and hailed "expansion of the Pepperdine dream to university status."[9] Details came days later in the published "A Spirit of Place" pamphlet. Norvel mailed out 40,000 copies. Its back cover published this first description of the new Pepperdine University: "Pepperdine College at Malibu is the newest member of the multicampus concept which, together with the original college in Los Angeles, the Pepperdine School of Law in Santa Ana, and the campus in Heidelberg, West Germany, will be the basis for the move to Pepperdine University status on January 1, 1971."[10]

ART OF IMPROVISATION

Pepperdine took the university leap of faith without any master plan. The nearest thing the Malibu miracle ever saw to a master plan was a 25-page document I drafted in 1968. Upon returning as executive vice president, I worked two months on "The Case Statement for a New Campus" that our fundraising consultant, Robert Johnson Company, insisted we produce prior to the public campaign. Norvel assigned the task to me. I retained Abilene, Texas, publicist Walter Burch to assist and we authored the legendary "Pepperdine Affirms."[11] Except for that enduring affirmation the case statement was forgotten. It held no hint of becoming a university because in 1968 that seemed as far away as the moon.

Norvel, the best-read man I knew, always had a book in hand. He read in bed and everywhere else he could sneak a peek. Mention it, and Norvel had already read it. "Bill," he exhorted one 1971 day, "you must read Carey McWilliams's new book on the 1880s founding of USC. It sounds just like us."

"USC was never really 'founded.' Like Topsy, it just grew," wrote McWilliams, editor of *The Nation* magazine. "In fact, the needs were so numerous and urgent that there was really no time to plan; the institution had to act first and plan later; in a word, it had to improvise. Improvisation, in fact, became a way of life."[12]

"That's what we've been doing, Bill." exulted Norvel. "Like USC, Pepperdine University is being born in creative chaos." Does USC's story paint Pepperdine's chaos into bright colors of unfolding providence? Or did Pepperdine just get lucky? Norvel and I decided most issues on the spur of the moment. We had no time to huddle. We called audibles at the line of scrimmage. We hung on to go with the flow. We composed on the spot. We shot from the hip. We extemporized as we went. By whatever metaphor, "improvisation became a way of life."

FUMBLING FOR A FOUNDER

It was improvisation that led us to Mrs. Seaver. On November 1, 1968, Norvel and I started with no plan to finance the campus. We were flying, as aviators say, by the seat of our pants. With no endowment, Pepperdine lived hand to mouth. While Norvel raised money for operations, he had not raised a dollar for expansion or endowment. The 1968-69 Pepperdine College Financial Statement reported total expenditures of $5,285,655, with total revenue of $5,583,305, and gifts and grants totaling only $820,904.[13] With a minuscule operating surplus, we sailed into uncharted waters without a compass.

Raw improvisation, aided by divine guidance, financed the Malibu miracle. Norvel and I intuited that the only way to do it was the way universities had always done it. We must find one donor to contribute most of the money and name the campus in his or her honor. But how much money? Recalling that Mr. Pepperdine's gifts totaled $3 million, Norvel and I settled arbitrarily on $6 million. Among Pepperdine prospects, who could, and would, give that much?

We sifted through names like Huntsinger, Tyler, Stauffer, Ralphs, Straus, Thornton, Elkins and others that would later grace campus buildings. We searched for a campus founder to pay for site development, utilities, roads, parking lots, sewers, sidewalks, lighting, landscaping and much more. By January 1, 1969, we narrowed the list to Richard Mellon Scaife, Charles S. Payson and Mrs. Frank Roger Seaver. The Scaife and Payson families were two of the wealthiest in America; the Seavers were one of the wealthiest in the west. All three families loved Pepperdine dearly and would eventually rank among its biggest donors.

Norvel and I, with no notion of the outcome, prepared three formal proposals. The trial and error of fundraising requires rough-hewn readiness to endure rejection in pursuit of success. We had no idea who might say yes and who might say no. Call it a fishing expedition. We followed the dictum of Christ: "Keep on asking and it will be given you."[14] In October 1969 Norvel and I booked appointments back east with Dick Scaife and Charlie Payson.

SCAIFE AND PAYSON

We flew first to Pittsburgh for lunch in Scaife's offices high atop the Alcoa headquarters. Dick and I were close, but he loved Norvel as an older brother. Two top lieutenants, Charles Ford and Richard Larry, joined us. When Norvel and I finished our one-hour presentation Ford and Larry responded positively. They loved the idea of Scaife College at Malibu. Scaife demurred. "No way, guys," he graciously responded. "Of course, I'll help. I love Pepperdine. But I'm already high profile enough. Please, just keep my name off things."

Prompted by his conservative convictions, Scaife's gifts—totaling $12 million from 1968 through 1978—helped propel the Malibu miracle. His disdain for personal attention inspired my benefactors' inverse recognition rule: "The richer they are, the less publicity they want." After all of his generosity through the years, there is no Scaife building at Malibu.

The inverse publicity rule also undermined our Payson case. The Payson money was multi-generational. Charles married Joan Whitney, daughter of legendary New York billionaire Payne Whitney. Joan owned the New York Mets. When their son, John M. Payson, had a difficult freshman year at Bowdoin College, the family pursued his transfer to Pepperdine. Mr. Payson contacted his California business companion, Fred Llewellyn. Charles knew that Fred was a member of Pepperdine's president's board. Charles had not yet met President Young. But Charles did know that Norvel was a member of Fred's Forest Lawn board. When Charles called Fred, and Fred called Norvel, the ducks lined up. Norvel harmoniously spun many magic circles in fulfillment of his goals.

"Why, of course," Norvel assured Fred. "We can enroll John Payson. But tell his dad and mother I look forward to meeting them."

Professor James Smythe recalls some sticky transfer details. "Because of his Bowdoin College record, the Pepperdine entrance and credits committee ruled unanimously against the admission of John Payson. President Young overruled them. It's great that he did!"[15] Norvel's positive relationship with the faculty permitted him to sometimes ignore, and occasionally even countermand, faculty preferences.

John Payson got married and came to Pepperdine in 1967. He majored in English under department chairman Smythe and graduated with honors in 1970. The Paysons, proud Pepperdine loyalists, gave more than $5 million to the Malibu miracle while avoiding most of the publicity.

"No thanks, Norvel," Charles Payson replied after our dinner with him, Joan and John in their New York home. "We're not interested in Payson College. But we're grateful for what you've done for Johnny and will help you in every way." Payson Library stands as a monument to the family's generosity, which continues to this day. John Payson delivered the April 2005 Seaver College commencement address.

THIRD TIME CHARM

The third time was the charm. Providentially prepared, Blanche Seaver answered emphatically, "Yes!" The cause-centered Mrs. Seaver, pursuing no personal glory, sought only to serve God and country. Her first-generation money was all hers. Mr. Seaver was gone and they had no children. Blanche determined to contribute her fortune to promote Christian education and Americanism "in memory of my beloved Frank."

Norvel and I unveiled the proposal for Seaver College at a 1969 Thanksgiving dinner for six. Blanche and nephew Richard joined Norvel and Helen and Gay and me for turkey and dressing in the Los Angeles campus president's home. Two years earlier, October 11, 1967, Norvel and Bill Teague proposed to Blanche and Richard "to name a new campus somewhere for $4 million." They were turned down flat. This time they committed to contribute $6 million over six years. Norvel and I committed to name the whole Malibu campus—yes, the entire 138-acre campus—"Frank R. Seaver College." Soaring meteorically without a flight plan, Norvel and I miscalculated strategically. Our shortsightedness would later disappoint the Seaver family.

Disappointment emerged from Pepperdine's improvisation. As Norvel and I presented proposals to three different prospective founders we also experimented with three Pepperdine prototypes. For five roller-coaster years, from 1967 to 1972, Norvel and I wandered through three institutional models in a trial-and-error effort to get it right. We were saved in the end by the Malibu miracle. But there's no way to appreciate the redemption apart from the wilderness wandering.

The three irreconcilable institutional models, as Norvel and I envisioned and exhausted them, were: Pepperdine College Multicampus Concept in 1967; Pepperdine University at Los Angeles in 1970; and, finally, Pepperdine University at Malibu, with Seaver College at its center, in 1972. Let's look at all three.

PEPPERDINE COLLEGE
MULTICAMPUS CONCEPT

Our wilderness wandering began with the Pepperdine College Multicampus Concept. Howard White recorded, "On January 25, 1967, Vice President William Teague announced that the college was considering additional locations. *He emphasized that the Los Angeles campus would not be abandoned, but that the institution was moving toward a multicampus concept*" (emphasis mine).[16]

Our commitment to dedicate the Malibu campus to the Seaver family was predicated on the permanence of the Los Angeles campus. Today, Teague's artful announcement may sound like the first subtle hint of evacuation. But back then most heard Teague's emphasis as expansion. "The college, he announced, was moving toward a 'multi-campus concept' . . . *And the Los Angeles campus, he emphasized, would not be sold*" (emphasis mine).[17]

Emphasis on the permanence of Los Angeles sounds, today, propagandistic. But back then it was echoed by Vice President Teague, Dean J. P. Sanders, dean of graduate studies Howard A. White, Religion Department chairman Frank Pack, dean of students Jennings Davis and others. "The Los Angeles campus will never be sold or abandoned," all promised. "Pepperdine has a moral obligation to stay in this community," heralded longtime Department of Education leader Olaf H. Tegner in 1969, "*until the end of time!*" (emphasis mine).[18]

Oly often told me how he most reluctantly changed his mind when the Watts riots delivered the deathblow. It was an agonizingly slow, five-year, breath-by-breath death of George Pepperdine's vision. Publicly, there was never a discouraging word. But, privately, I expressed grave doubts to Norvel. His commitment was to keep the Los Angeles campus alive during the inexorable move of most undergraduate work to Malibu.

PEPPERDINE UNIVERSITY AT LOS ANGELES

The hope of permanence led to model two, Pepperdine University at Los Angeles. In February 1970, Norvel and I privately decided to move toward university status. The multicampus concept was all the rage. It would provide organizational energy for a four-campus university. "*We will be emphasizing the advantages of smallness in each location with Los Angeles at its center as the administrative hub*," said Dr. Young (emphasis mine).[19] Refinements of the university concept appeared in a bulletin issued in October 1971. Now a nostalgic snapshot in time, it presented details of the vaunted four-campus system. The Los Angeles campus still reigned as the principal "hub of the new university, serving increasing thousands of commuter and graduate students."[20] Thanks to Norvel Young's entrepreneurial leadership, it did.

Enrollments in business and education soared in rented off-campus commercial centers. In 1969, the business department became the Graduate School of Business and Management. In 1970, the education department reorganized into a professional school of education and, soon thereafter, the Graduate School of Education and Psychology. "These two strong schools," Norvel proclaimed, "anchor the Los Angeles campus as the solid university foundation."[21] Privately I warned Norvel that the Los Angeles campus had no longstanding future. He would have none of it. His commitment kept the lid on things during the move of university headquarters and administration from Los Angeles to Malibu.

"The first of Pepperdine's campuses-away-from-Los Angeles," declared the 1969-1970 President's Report, was the Year-in-Europe program at Heidelberg, Germany. Launched in 1963, it had already achieved a decade of success. In the twenty-first century, it remains one of Pepperdine's best programs, having served more than two thousand students. In 1969, as the multicampus concept was rolled out, it provided evidence for the reality of multiple campuses. Moore Haus (a historic home named in honor of Pepperdine's pioneering comptroller, J. C. Moore) was adjacent to the world-famous Heidelberg Castle and the University of Heidelberg, founded in 1386. But if calling Moore Haus a "campus" was a bit of a stretch, returning students, singing "*Ich hab'mein herz in Heidelberg verloren*" didn't care.

THE LAW SCHOOL

"Buoyed by the youthful support of Bill Banowsky," wrote Pepperdine biographers, "Norvel Young launched out in a number of entrepreneurial ways. He was approached by Edward Di Loreto and others about becoming affiliated with a small, evening law school in Orange County."[22] We completed Pepperdine's multicampus university by acquiring the law school.

"We see by the papers that Pepperdine College has acquired a law school," Texas church editor Reuel Lemmons's October 1969 *Firm Foundation* reported. "It all makes us wonder if we are about to experience our first multicampus university (among Church of Christ-related colleges). Could be! It seems obvious that plans point in that direction."[23] Norvel primed his friend Reuel, who soon joined Pepperdine's board of trustees.

An ardent believer in legal education (Gay and I have four lawyer sons and two lawyer grandchildren), I was ambivalent about Orange University. Floundering from its 1964 founding, it saddled us with an unaccredited night school, part-time faculty and marginal students meeting in a rented commercial building with virtually no library. I sensed we might succeed sooner by building our own Malibu law school, which we soon did. Norvel, who never looked a gift horse in the mouth, was not the least bit ambivalent.

Pepperdine announced its new law school at a May 27, 1969, Disneyland Hotel luncheon. My job was to recruit a dean of the Wilburn, Scott, Hudson, Hornbaker, Runnels caliber. The new dean would have to raise money, build a full-time faculty, recruit students, assemble a library, mobilize into daytime operation and earn academic accreditation from the California Bar Association, the American Bar Association and the Association of American Law Schools.

I called John Allen Chalk, a talented preacher. As I left the Texas pulpit for Pepperdine, John left for the University of Texas law school. Graduating to a prestigious law firm, he was perfect for our job. The bad news was he didn't want it. The good news was he recommended Ronald F. Phillips.

"My heart fell," Phillips confessed, "when Dr. Banowsky took me to Orange County and showed me our quarters. But I decided to take the job anyway."[24] Dean Phillips took command in September 1970, put Pepperdine's law school on the map and became a 40-year Pepperdine personality. His genius was consistent excellence, attention to detail and insistence on a moral view of legal education and practice. He passed the baton to leaders who would advance the law school into the upper tiers. Succeeded as dean in 1995 by Richardson R. Lynn, Ron served for many years as vice chancellor. In 2004, Kenneth W. Starr, a historically revered legal scholar with humble Church of Christ roots, became dean. "In the last five years," reported President Andrew K. Benton, "judged against 184 ABA-accredited law schools, Pepperdine jumped from 99th to 55th, a faster and greater ascent than any other law school by a wide margin."[25] Dean Starr's sights are set on the most elite law school circle.

MALIBU: CAMPUS NUMBER FOUR

Malibu became campus number four. But Malibu was never envisioned as the university center, much less its whole. For ideological and financial reasons, Malibu was seen as subordinate to the principal Los Angeles campus. Vice President Teague's 1967 announcement of the "multicampus college concept" called only for a *second campus undergraduate extension* (emphasis mine). That description stuck to the emerging Malibu campus, through thick and thin, for the following five years. Throughout its conception and construction, the Malibu campus was seen as an exotic subsidiary.

Therefore, on that fateful Thanksgiving night of Wednesday, November 26, 1969, we made the Seaver College commitment assuming Pepperdine

TWO FOUNDING FRIENDS

Ronald F. Phillips, founding dean, points out to President Banowsky the ever-
growing excellence of the new Pepperdine University School of Law. Dean Phillips
and Dr. Banowsky share deep Texas roots.

RDINE
RSITY
OF LAW

THE REAGAN CONNECTION

Governor Ronald Reagan, frequent Malibu campus
visitor and promoter, also traveled to Orange
County for an address to the Pepperdine University
School of Law in its original rented location.

would be in Los Angeles forever. Operating at that time under the 1967 "multicampus college concept," we planned two campuses. Seaver College at Malibu would be a subordinate companion for the principal Pepperdine College at Los Angeles. With every good intention, and in good conscience, Norvel and I promised Blanche and Richard that the Seaver flag would fly at the top of the Malibu mast. We signed the 1969 contract to fly it. Furthermore, in February 1970, even as Norvel and I graduated to the "Pepperdine University at Los Angeles" model, we continued to assume a university headquartered forever in Los Angeles. We also continued to assure the Seaver family that Malibu was all theirs. Therefore, the Seaver family was devoted to the separate and independent Seaver College identity.

PEPPERDINE UNIVERSITY AT MALIBU

By January 1972, I was envisioning a third model: Pepperdine University at Malibu. Both Norvel and I failed to see the inevitability of the Malibu miracle. Norvel remained unwilling to give up on Los Angeles even as I shared with him my sense that Pepperdine's only future was at Malibu.

Pepperdine had become many things to many people. Norvel and I scrambled to put the scattering parts and pieces under one big tent. How else could our disparate constituencies—trustees and president's boards; faculty and alumni; undergraduate and graduate students; residents and commuters; whites and blacks; Los Angeles loyalists and Malibu enthusiasts; urbanites and suburbanites; Church of Christ members and zealous ecumenists; Orange County lawyers and Heidelberg lovers; liberal Democratic media and conservative Republican patrons—be satisfactorily served? As with the Israelites of old, perhaps Pepperdine's "wilderness wandering" was preliminary to winning the "promised land."

Meanwhile, Norvel and I wasted a lot of time and energy running from pillar to post. My wife, Gay, observed: "Nobody could call the Malibu miracle a flash of lightning. It just oozed out, over several years, by dribs and drabs!"

MALIBU PARADIGM SHIFT

Then, one fair day, we woke up to the brilliant sunshine of the Malibu miracle paradigm shift. Trouble was, we didn't all wake up at the same time. Charles Runnels, Jerry Hudson, Larry Hornbaker and I saw the sunshine on the day the new campus opened. Jack Scott and Jim Wilburn, who, like colonial governors, took turns as caretaker provosts of the fading Los Angeles campus, also found its future untenable.

PEPPERDINE PRESIDENTS' RESIDENCE

The Brock House, built in 1972, was dedicated

in 1975 by President Gerald R. Ford.

Howard White was among the last to see it. Howard was not a man who changed his mind easily. Since 1958, he had been a superior academic leader with an idealistic devotion to Pepperdine's Christian mission in the heart of the city. By 1971, I had elevated him to executive vice president of the university. Following the dramatic defeat of radical students in the lockdown of our main building, Howard received death threats (along with others of us). In the highest administrative role, and the most visible person in campus operations, Norvel and I felt Howard should have a security guard assigned to him permanently. Howard now personally felt the effects of campus instability. He began an intellectual pilgrimage away from what he called "my most naive position."

In mid-summer, 1971, I called a meeting that consisted of Howard White, J. P. Sanders (who was on his way to join Columbia Christian College as president), Silas Shotwell, Carl Mitchell, Norvel and Helen Young. We gathered on the back patio of the Youngs' Adamson Beach House to talk through the future of the Los Angeles campus. Howard suddenly startled us with a moment of levity. "Bill, I have finally concluded this with regard to the Los Angeles campus: We should just scuttle the ship!" "Well," I replied to the laughter of others in the group, "remember, Howard, that we're still *on* the ship." Soon after, in more measured tones, he advised me: "I have come to the decision that whatever we care about must be moved to Malibu." He and Maxine and their teenage sons, Ashley and Elliot, moved from their Los Angeles home to Malibu. More than a decade later the process was concluded under Howard's own presidential watch. In Pepperdine's 50th anniversary pictorial history, Howard put the paradigm shift on record:

> The first students who entered school at Pepperdine University's new Malibu location on September 6, 1972, called it the "dream campus." ... The *Los Angeles Times* later wrote that "Pepperdine University is in a class by itself. ... Its main campus has become a glittering diamond set on 650 acres at Malibu. The sparkle runs deep, and to many observers it symbolizes the university's academic progress." ... Its dramatic development caused the whole process to be known among Pepperdine's supporters as the Malibu miracle.[26]

However, the paradigm shift also became the great divide. Faculty assured of security in Malibu were on board. But a larger number felt bitterly marooned in Los Angeles. They began to interpret all of our language as a cover-up for conspiratorial evacuation. Norvel, maneuvering in the middle, finally realized that survival of the Pepperdine legacy demanded moving the cornerstone of the Christian mission to Malibu. If I could convince the

Seaver family to move over and take second place in Malibu, Norvel agreed to save the Pepperdine name by moving it to Malibu. The Seaver family agreed to be part of a larger Malibu university rather than the freestanding college in Malibu first proposed to them.

The unpredictably creative art of fundraising causes some name changes. Norvel and I proposed various donors' names for the same Malibu buildings, bridges, benches, boulders, streets, rooms, plazas, fountains, athletic facilities and, as we have seen, for the college itself. Several names on Malibu buildings were not the first proposed. The Murchison name defined the science center for 30 years before fading over funding in favor of Keck Science Center. Just as Trinity College became Duke University when it received the tobacco fortune, private institutions often alter names to honor donors.

Pepperdine was vulnerable. Lawyers advised Norvel and me that if the Seaver family litigated, in contractual obligation, we would become Seaver University at Malibu with Pepperdine College at its center. The magnitude of the Seaver contributions alone would justify it.

Propelled by Los Angeles failure and Malibu success, the paradigm shift hit with hurricane force followed by the surge of a tsunami. Nothing was ever the same. The size, shape and mission of the Malibu campus expanded exponentially. Designed to be secondary, it suddenly became primary. Serving at first only a few, it grew to serve many and perhaps ultimately all. In a quantum leap, Malibu moved from Pepperdine's circumference to its epicenter. No human made the movement or caused the shift or drove the transformation. Malibu drove itself. Launched as a subservient satellite, Malibu transfigured into Pepperdine's permanent home and only hope.

MRS. SEAVER'S CONFUSION

With the Malibu miracle paradigm shift came institutional model number three: Pepperdine University at Malibu. It turned Pepperdine's Seaver agreement upside down. Seaver College, no longer enveloping the whole Malibu campus, would become a subordinate part. Blanche Seaver, who created the campus, must slide back to second seat and abdicate the lion's share of Malibu glory to George Pepperdine—who never even laid eyes on the campus. Norvel and I feared that the disappointed Seavers could abro gate the contract.

Richard Seaver held the power. On Saturday afternoon, March 20, 1971, Richard and I met alone at his Bristol Street residence in Brentwood, a few doors down from Charles and Amy Jo Runnels. Anxious and fatigued, I reclined on the living-room carpet, a pillow beneath my head. Richard relaxed on the couch above. After hearing me out, he spoke.

CONGRATULATIONS FROM REAGAN

Pepperdine Patron Saint Ronald Reagan congratulates
Chancellor Young and founding Dean Phillips and his wife,
Jamie, on the Orange County law school acquisition.

THE DURANTS

This picture, featured in the brand-new
People magazine, shows Dr. Banowsky
conferring matching honorary
doctorates from the new Pepperdine
University school of law on the famous
twentieth-century historians and
philosophers Will and Ariel Durant,
who loved Pepperdine.

"Bill, I sympathize. The Los Angeles campus is dying. Pepperdine's legacy is really on the line. The only thing to do is move Pepperdine to Malibu. We'll help build Seaver College at its center. Aunt Blanche is intransigent. She never changes her mind. She won't understand. But I can handle Aunt Blanche. Just soft-pedal Pepperdine around her and praise Seaver College. She'll support you forever. You're doing the right thing, Bill."

History pivots on pinpoints. Had barrister Richard Carlton Seaver been small-minded enough to sic on us a team of tough attorneys to fulfill contractual compliance it would have been Seaver University at Malibu with Pepperdine College its undergraduate jewel. Richard saved the Pepperdine name and legacy. "God bless you, Richard," I gratefully exclaimed, reaching up from the floor for his hand. "No wonder Norvel always calls you 'God's gentleman'!"

The naming crisis was concluded—just like that! All who love Pepperdine should remember that Richard Seaver once held the complete power to call it the other way.

For a time Richard's 80-year-old aunt openly contested his decision. Within days, Charles Runnels met with Norvel and me. "Boys," he exclaimed, "we've got big trouble! Last night, I sat with Blanche at the Century Plaza head table for her annual Hollywood Bowl board dinner. When the MC introduced me, as 'vice chancellor of Pepperdine University at Malibu,' Blanche erupted loud enough to be heard back in the kitchen: 'No!' she shouted. 'Pepperdine is down in Los Angeles! Seaver College is out in Malibu!'" George Hill, Larry Hornbaker and several other Seaver escorts reported identically awkward experiences. Gay and I experienced it a dozen times.

Associate Vice President Bill Henegar reported his own awkward moment. "In the early days of Seaver College, Religion Division chair Carl Mitchell made the mistake of writing Mrs. Seaver on a regular Pepperdine letterhead," explained Henegar. "Though it was a very complimentary and respectful letter, she was most unhappy because of the Pepperdine nameplate! I quickly arranged for the production of some brand-new stationery. Now we've got an official Seaver College letterhead to use."

Mrs. Seaver was not assuaged. She persisted. She even sent me three letters on this subject after I became president of the University of Oklahoma. On March 23, 1979, she wrote: "Bill, in return for all that you constantly thank me for, why can't you just get it named Seaver University, which is truth and honesty? I have been asking you that for several years. I am very embarrassed and that is your one and only failure!" On June 20, 1979, she wrote: "Why don't they voluntarily say Seaver University and Pepperdine College. Charles Runnels tells me he is working on it. How long must I wait?" Blanche also complained constantly around town to many others. On January 1, 1980, the famous Roger Wagner, director of the Roger Wagner Chorale, wrote: "My Dear Blanche, it was revealing to learn from you how the Malibu campus continues to be advertised as Pepperdine. Considering your enormous generosity you must insist on the name change or cancel all future pledges."[27] The disappointment to Mrs. Seaver was a sad shadow lingering over the Malibu miracle success.

NORVEL YOUNG AND BLANCHE SEAVER

A quarter century later in 1996, at the age 102, Mrs. Seaver "graduated into the larger life," as she unfailingly put it. She had found total peace with Pepperdine University at Malibu and profound fulfillment in Seaver College. "Mrs. Frank Roger Seaver," the *Los Angeles Times* quoted Pepperdine president David Davenport, "made our Malibu campus possible."[28]

Did she really? Look at the facts! Pepperdine agreed, for $6 million, to memorialize the Seaver family exclusively with the entire Malibu campus. As Pepperdine University began its long Los Angeles death, the Seaver family graciously accepted second place. Meanwhile, they magnanimously escalated their gifts from the original commitment of $6 million to actual gifts of $300 million. That was the heart of the Malibu miracle, pure and simple, end of story, period. That Mrs. Seaver's salvation of Pepperdine goes largely unappreciated is somehow at the heart of the story's spirituality. She doesn't mind. Like most heroines, she found complete satisfaction in hard earthly realities and went on joyfully to her heavenly reward.

Mrs. Seaver is the Malibu miracle heroine. Dr. Young is its hero. I wrote this book so that all who love Pepperdine could know and love Blanche and Norvel. They live on in a class by themselves.

The *New York Times* saluted Dr. Young as the father of Pepperdine University. Within hours of his 1998 death, the newspaper that prints "all the news that's fit to print" enshrined him: "M. Norvel Young was the leader who guided Pepperdine from a small college with 950 students in Los Angeles to full-fledged Pepperdine University at Malibu with an enrollment of 9,500."[29] That time the *Times* got it right.

1. *Oil World Journal*, September 8, 1971, 29.
2. The other 11 were the Coca Cola Bottling Company of Los Angeles, Litton Industries, the Thrifty Corporation, Tenet Healthcare Company, the Fleming Companies, Oklahoma Gas and Electric Company, Oklahoma Publishing Company, the Texas Rangers, Fidelity Union Life Insurance Company and Lomas and Nettleton Mortgage Investors.
3. Fritz Huntsinger Jr., personal letter to the author, October 15, 1971. The Banowsky Papers. Fritz Huntsinger Jr. was a key offshore industries executive and Pepperdine financial supporter. He

bestowed the honorary doctor of laws degree hood on President Gerald R. Ford at the September 20, 1975, ceremony.

4. Bill Youngs, "The Young Years," *Pepperdine Alumni Voice*, Fall 1969, 16.

5. Bill Henegar and Jerry Rushford, *Forever Young: The Life and Times of M. Norvel Young and Helen M. Young* (Nashville: 21st Century Christian, 1999), 272.

6. Matt Young, personal interview with the author, January 12, 2008. The Banowsky Papers.

7. William Trombley, "Banowsky Offered San Francisco Presidency," *Los Angeles Times*, February 14, 1972, 12.

8. "Pepperdine Dedicates New Malibu Campus," *Santa Monica Evening Outlook*, May 24, 1970, 1.

9. William S. Banowsky, "A Spirit of Place," (Malibu: Pepperdine College Press, June 1, 1970), 4.

10. Ibid., 9.

11. Here is the final Walter Burch draft. The Banowsky Papers.

"Pepperdine College Affirms"

- That God Is.
- That His eternal purpose in Jesus Christ is being worked out in human history.
- That the educational process cannot with impunity be divorced from the divine process.
- That a liberal arts education grounded in the eternal scheme has ultimate significance by offering students a theme for living, a purpose for being, and a faith that can perceive beyond the frontier of human experience.
- That knowledge makes a claim on mankind—presenting itself, as a sacred trust, for recognition and understanding.
- That the cultivation of disciplined minds is the primary function of education; therefore intellectual growth, in range and powers of thought, must be given priority in the academic process.
- That the central aim of creative teaching is to recognize the individuality of persons.
- That the highest purpose in education is realized when the sensitive teacher, through word and example, is able to create within each student a desire to become free and fully human by accepting a sense of personal responsibility for his own destiny.
- That the quality of student conduct, both public and personal, on and off campus, is a valid concern of the educational institution.
- That a complete education will liberate man from mere existence by fusing eternal hope into his spirit.

12. Carey McWilliams, "Foreword," in Manuel P. Servin and Iris Higbie Wilson, *Southern California and Its University: A History of USC, 1880-1964* (Los Angeles: The Ward Ritchie Press, 1969), xiv.

13. "1968–69 Pepperdine College Financial Statement," *Pepperdine College President's Report: 1969–1970*, 12.

14. Matthew 7:7 (Amplified Bible).

15. Dr. James Smythe, personal interview with the author, October 10, 2006. The Banowsky Papers. John M. Payson took three courses with Dr. Smythe.

16. Jerry Rushford, ed., *Crest of a Golden Wave: Pepperdine University, 1937–1987* (Malibu: Pepperdine University Press, 1987), 111.

17. Henegar and Rushford, *Forever Young*, 189.

18. Audrey Gardner, "A Brief History of Pepperdine College," (master's thesis, Pepperdine College, 1968), 77.

19. M. Norvel Young, *Pepperdine College President's Report: 1969–1970*, 3.

20. Ibid.

21. Ibid., 2.

22. Henegar and Rushford, *Forever Young*, 208.

23. Reuel Lemmons, "Pepperdine's New Law School," *Firm Foundation*, October 15, 1969, 1,

24. Ronald F. Phillips, personal interview with the author, October 2, 2002. The Banowsky Papers.

25. Andrew K. Benton, personal letter to the author, October 15, 2009. The Banowsky Papers.

26. Howard A. White, in Rushford, *Golden Wave*, 163.

27. Mrs. Frank Roger Seaver, personal letter to the author, March, 23, 1979; Mrs. Frank Roger Seaver, personal letter to the author, June 20, 1979; Roger Wagner, personal letter to Mrs. Frank Roger Seaver, January 1, 1980. The Banowsky Papers.

28. Myrna Oliver, "Blanche E. Seaver, Major Donor to Colleges, Dies" *Los Angeles Times*, April 14, 1994.

29. Obituary of M. Norvel Young, *New York Times*, February 23, 1998, New York edition.

"This Malibu campus achieves absolute perfection and the man who pulled it all together is Bill Banowsky."

GERALD R. FORD
38th President of the United States
September 20, 1975

FUNDRAISING

On a typical Malibu morning, President Banowsky visits amid construction with donor Clint Murchison. In the background, Vice President Larry Hornbaker discusses with Mrs. Seaver, Mrs. Brock and Gay the construction of the Brock House.

CHAPTER 13

CONSTRUCTION OF THE MALIBU CAMPUS

At last came the great day—Monday, January 13, 1969. Pepperdine College launched phase one of site preparation for its Malibu campus. "Dr. Banowsky," recorded President M. Norvel Young, "was challenged to take the lead in constructing a truly innovative master plan that would directly influence the shape of brick and mortar."[1] On that first day who could have dreamed it was destined, one day, to be voted "the most beautiful campus in America"?

PROVOST JERRY E. HUDSON

As president, I committed to leadership by delegation. By February 1, 1969, I had organized the construction leadership team, commonly called "the team of twelve." It included two Pepperdine executives and ten construction professionals. "In the discharge of the duties of office there is one rule of action more important than all the others," advised Ronald Reagan. "Never do anything that someone else could do for you. Delegate!"[2]

Dr. Jerry E. Hudson joined me at the Pepperdine pinnacle. A protegé of Dr. Howard A. White, Dr. Hudson earned his PhD at Tulane University and joined the Pepperdine history faculty in 1962. He rose through the ranks to become dean of the Los Angeles liberal arts college in 1970. Deep roots of the Hudson and Banowsky friendship ran back to idyllic undergraduate days at David Lipscomb College in 1950s Nashville. Jerry wooed Ann around campus while I wooed Gay. Twenty years later, both families landed all alone high atop the brand-new Malibu campus. The Banowskys and their four sons lived in the Brock House. The Hudsons and their four daughters lived next door in the Mallman House. Jerry and I, working intimately together, built the campus and felt on top of the world. For us it was Camelot!

While organizing the construction team of twelve, I also formed the Malibu faculty interdisciplinary committee to redesign the undergraduate liberal arts curriculum.[3] I first appointed Dr. Hudson chairman of the committee's humanities division. Then, I promoted him to the powerful position of Malibu provost and dean. In that dual role, recorded his mentor Dr. White, "he had immediate oversight of the construction of the physical facilities and the planning of the academic program."[4]

The founding student newspaper reported in 1972 that Dr. Hudson "headed the administration of the new campus." The students got it right. Jerry Hudson played an indispensable Malibu miracle role. He capped his career with distinguished presidencies at Hamline University in Minnesota and Willamette University in Oregon and of the Collins Foundation. Dr. Hudson continues in 2010 as a life member of the Pepperdine board of regents.

Together, Dr. Hudson and I hired three key companies to head the design and construction. Industry parlance labeled them "design contractor," "project contractor" and "project coordinator."

For design contractor—the master plan architect—we hired William L. Pereira and Associates. Bill Pereira augmented his personal leadership with two top architects who worked full time for two years as members of the team of twelve. Serving under Pereira, Ron Baldwinson and Bud Wilson were the hands-on designers of the campus.

TOPODYNAMICS AND MORAN

When it came to hiring the project coordinator, a pair of hard-nosed CPAs anchoring Pepperdine's board of trustees called the shot. George A. Evans and Robert P. Jones insisted on Topodynamics, Inc. They knew the firm's two principals, Andrew K. Rawn and Robert Wood. Rawn, a six-foot-five, construction-hardened leader, would control major contractors. Wood, his young burr-headed architect partner with a gift for working with people, pulled together loose ends.

Pereira and Topodynamics helped Pepperdine pick the project contractor. We sought a major Southern California company specializing in institutional construction. Rawn and Wood nominated Moran Construction Company, a century-old firm headquartered in Alhambra for which both had worked. Pereira seconded the motion. In January 1969, Pepperdine hired Moran as Malibu campus contractor.

Norvel and I also favored Moran because of our admiration for its chairman, Jack Bernard. He was a Rotarian brother from Los Angeles Club Number Five. Jack and I were also members of an elite business group called

Norvel, Gay and Bill congratulate donor Fritz Huntsinger.

Vice President Hornbaker talks with his good
friend Frances Smothers, the benefactor of the
beautiful Smothers Theater.

Bill congratulates donors Morris B. and
Gladys Pendleton on the Pendleton
Learning Center.

the 100 Club. A mutual admiration society, the club met for cocktails every Tuesday at 5:00 p.m. in the Fireside Room of the California Club to pat one another on the back and exchange war stories. We kept a low profile and printed no membership roster. Our sole stated purpose was social but our 100 meticulously vetted members, including only one academician, quietly helped run the city of Los Angeles.

Pereira respected Moran's record in institutional concrete construction. The two firms worked together to create the campus of the University of California at Irvine. At Malibu, Pereira's fortress-like fireproof buildings demanded the most expensive steel-reinforced concrete, poured in place. All agreed Moran was the company to build them. Bernard delegated the Pepperdine job to Jack Eiden. He moved to Malibu full-time as construction manager. Robert Eldridge led from Alhambra as general director. Ronald Lerg served as project engineer.

Site development came first. That meant moving Malibu mountains! With millions of cubic yards of earth to move, our first down-to-earth decision was selecting earthwork professionals. For two sensitive jobs, we retained James L. Slosson as project geologist and Olen Murray as geological engineer. On January 3, 1969, from among six bidders, Pepperdine awarded the phase one grading contract to Strecker Construction Company. Strecker brought to the team of twelve Superintendent Allen and grading foreman Ace.

All hands on deck, the Malibu campus construction team of twelve was: Banowsky and Hudson for Pepperdine; Rawn and Wood for Topodynamics; Baldwinson and Wilson for Pereira; Slosson and Murray for geology; Allen and Ace for Strecker; and Eiden and Lerg for Moran. The team arranged three construction trailers into a U-shaped command center on the central hilltop. For three years, it met in this "war room" at 7:00 a.m. every Monday morning, rain or shine, to settle fusses and plan the "most beautiful campus in America."

LOCATING SEAVER COLLEGE

Moran's appointment of Jack Eiden was providential. This lean, taciturn leader really built the Malibu campus. Hundreds of hard hats, from scores of companies, helped make the miracle. But as quarterback of the team of twelve, Eiden called the signals. He ran every detail.

He went to work at Pepperdine on January 1, 1969, and committed five years of his life to creating the campus. For three years he worked for Moran. When the campus opened, I put him on Pepperdine's payroll for two more years as director of construction, maintenance, the physical plant, landscaping and security. He knew the campus like the back of his hand. He built it! Jack

Eiden may never receive a Pepperdine honorary doctorate but he deserves one.[5]

However, Eiden's unrelieved headache began when Pepperdine launched earthwork before Pereira could finish his master plan. Loose ends dangled on all sides. The biggest one demanded to be nailed down: precisely where, on the 138 acres, should Seaver College be built? Say what? Yes, looking back over 40 years, the Seaver site seems God ordained—as if it has descended from heaven. But back in the uncharted beginning it was very much up in the air! The untouched land was breathtaking, but it was also a blank canvas.

Many Pepperdiners are probably surprised to learn that most of the team of twelve automatically assumed Seaver College would be built out on the open meadow bordering Pacific Coast Highway. There was ample room. The meadow held 40 of the original 138 acres, larger than the 34-acre Los Angeles campus.

Building in the meadow would have been highly cost effective. Millions of dollars could have been saved by avoiding any attack on the hills and staying out on the existing grade of flat compacted ground. Most people felt it best for Seaver College to nestle down under the hills in the middle of the meadow, displayed gracefully along the highway.

Three of us thought otherwise. The team of twelve split into two camps, one concerned with cost and the other with design. Pereira, Hudson and I opposed Moran, Topodynamics, Strecker, Slosson and Murray. We insisted that Seaver College sit, not down under the hill, but high up on top of it. Our nine colleagues felt pressure to control costs and complete the project on time. But Pereira, Hudson and I felt a different pressure—to produce the most beautiful possible campus regardless of time or costs. Sensing the miraculous moment, we were focused not on costs for the moment but on results for the ages. To lift Seaver College and splay it grandly across the magnificent hills was a daunting and expensive challenge. But Pereira, Hudson and I knew it was right. We won that battle.

LOCATING THE MAIN ENTRANCE

The next big design debate was determining the location of the main campus entrance. Surprisingly, Seaver College earthwork began *before* the main entry site was settled. Like the Seaver College site, the Malibu campus gateway seems today ordained by God. But back in the uncharted beginning the main campus entry was very much up in the air.

The nine leaders who wanted to build in the meadow assumed the location of the entry to be a foregone conclusion. They all agreed it should, of course, be at the new corner intersection connecting Pacific Coast Highway and

Helen Pepperdine, Dean Ronald F. Phillips, Architect William L. Pereira, President Banowsky, Moran Company Chairman Jack Bernard, Blanche Seaver, Supreme Court Justice Blackman and donor Odell McConnell break ground for the law school.

Chancellor M. Norvel Young imprints his signature forever in the Payson Library cornerstone along with Charles S. Payson and his son, John, a distinguished Pepperdine alumnus.

John C. Tyler, Bill, Blanche, Norvel, George W. Elkins, William L. Pereira,
Dr. Michael DeBakey and Alice Tyler break ground for Tyler Campus Center.

Mrs. Pepperdine, Morris Pendleton, Blanche, Flora Thornton, Odell McConnell and Bill break
ground for the Pendleton Learning Center.

Malibu Canyon Road. It took a century to create the corner. Most of the team assumed Pepperdine should seize it for its main campus entry.

When Pepperdine acquired its land in 1968 there was no corner intersection. The isolated center of Malibu enjoyed no connection of its two major thoroughfares. Malibu Canyon Road terminated a half mile east of Pacific Coast Highway. It turned sharply south and dumped all traffic into Malibu Civic Center Way. Pepperdine quickly convinced the county to complete this long overdue traffic improvement. Winning praise from Malibu and San Fernando Valley commuters, we also created, at public expense, the campus southern border and major front intersection.[6] People assumed Pepperdine also created its campus gateway, complete with traffic lights and turning lanes. Stately corner gates, with maximum visibility and easiest accessibility, could open onto the campus as a four-lane divided boulevard rising graciously under the Cross Theme Tower up to Seaver College. Highly cost effective, it would utilize the existing grade of compacted soil. The idea of a grand intersection entrance excited Norvel. Most of the team of twelve pushed hard for it.

Once again, Pereira, Hudson and I disagreed. We fought to protect the front meadow, free of traffic and clutter, as an unobstructed panorama. We envisioned a subtle side entrance at a new, smaller intersection a half mile up Malibu Canyon Road. Traffic would funnel, virtually unseen, into the campus through the quiet of Winter Canyon. But there was a big cost downside. Winter Canyon cut-and-fill earthwork demanded an extra $300,000.

We turned again to Mrs. Seaver. Blanche adored erudite bachelor Bill Pereira. The three of us met atop what was becoming the Cross Theme Tower hill. We imagined the campus gateway opening off Malibu Canyon Road and winding up through exotic Winter Canyon. As we confronted the cost problem, Blanche quoted American writer and naturalist Henry David Thoreau: "I am monarch of all I survey!" Her aesthetic eye saw the strength and beauty of the subtle side entrance. She called Richard Seaver. They immediately contributed a special block of Hydril Company stock for the extra site work. Protecting the integrity of the intersection and the beauty of the meadow, we christened the new entrance Seaver Drive.

The Seaver College and main entrance location victories directed me to two other dissentient resolutions. I resolved to forever protect the meadow. It glorified our front yard and harbored us high above the highway and busy beach. Savoring the sweetness of Malibu, I also elevated the acquisition of more land above all else. Sensing the miracle was essentially tied to this mystical place called Malibu, I pushed to get just as much of it as possible while the getting was good. During my tenure, Pepperdine acquired adjoining land, by gift or purchase, until the original 138 acres mushroomed into 632. Within another decade, Dr. White added 187 acres. Gifts had brought another 11 acres for today's 830-acre campus.

MOVING MALIBU MOUNTAINS

"Site development" is code for the ugly, essential and often controversial preparation of the ground for construction. On January 13, 1969, Strecker Construction Company moved its fleet of dozers and scrapers to Malibu on flatbed trucks. Huge yellow machines cranked up, crawled off the flatbeds and up the 200-foot central hill. Strecker's challenge was to chop the hill in half, to cut across its wide top where Brock House now stands. To slice straight down to create the Seaver College site. Before the dust would settle, three years later, Pepperdine moved an incredible three-and-one-half million cubic yards of earth.

Timing is everything. The Malibu campus could never be developed today. The massive movement of that much rock and dirt required dynamiting, bulldozing, excavating, scraping, trucking, grading, leveling, compacting and draining ancient ocean mountains untouched by the hand of time. There is no conceivable way, today, that Pepperdine could obtain environmental approvals and state, county and city permits to move that much earth. Back then there was no city of Malibu to monitor us, no California Coastal Commission to stop us. There was only Los Angeles County, and Pepperdine enjoyed aggressive support from the board of supervisors and building department. "Their continuing cooperation," recorded Jack Eiden, "made it all possible."[7] Without a single denial or significant delay, we moved Malibu mountains in a rare window of historic opportunity rapidly being slammed shut forever. Much of the freedom was made possible by the influence of alumnus Kenneth H. Hahn, powerful Los Angeles County supervisor.

The Seaver College site demanded the deepest draconian cut. First came a 70-foot cut to create the finished elevation of Seaver Drive as it rises around the central hill. Next came a 40-foot cut on down to Seaver College. During that first year, just to create the Seaver College site, Strecker moved one million cubic yards from the central hill down into Marie Canyon. Such messy and massive earthwork generated high costs and controversy. Prophets of doom predicted the cost-and-controversy combination would kill the embryonic campus. Pepperdine proved them wrong only by winning an all-out, three-year, touch-and-go dirt war.

President Banowsky and Vice Chancellor Charles B. Runnels go over design plans with architects William L. Pereira and associates.

STAUFFER CHAPEL

University board member Peter Ratican assists Mrs. Pepperdine, and Board of Trustees Chairman
Donald V. Miller, Chancellor Young and Vice President Larry Hornbaker assists Mrs. Seaver in
the ground breaking.

For the 1972 Stauffer Chapel dedication, distinguished Seaver College
religion professors Dr. Frank Pack and Dr. Tony Ash share the front row
with Blanche Seaver, Gay Banowsky and guests.

GRADING BY IMPROVISATION

Earthwork began on January 13, 1969, only a year after land acquisition. There was no time for a grading master plan. We delegated and improvised.

We daily charted our course while bulldozing at full speed, one cut ahead of the ecological police. With no overall plan, Eiden led the frenzied scramble to stay one legal scoop ahead of Strecker's onrushing machines. As the machines dug deeper into the mountains, Eiden pushed harder for geologist Slosson and engineer Murray to produce faster piecemeal plans. Then, the ink barely dry, Eiden pushed them through the permitting process with the help of his building department friends. On a few days, we produced a partial grading plan and rushed it to the county for approval as we were making the cut it approved.

"Those maddening Pepperdine machines," complained one official Eiden friend, "are chewing out ahead of our permits!"[8] Adam Smith, the eighteenth-century Scottish economist, popularized the term "invisible hand" to illustrate the impact of self-interest on free enterprise. We watched the "invisible hand" at work every day as the campus contours took voluptuous shape. We thought God was directing our daily decisions. With the perspective of 40 years, the probability of divine presence seems to me more intriguing than ever.

With daily improvisation, the cubic yardage of moving earth increased exponentially. Some of us on the team of twelve pushed to escalate volume. Most urged restraint to avoid going broke, getting sued or starting a landslide. Our aggressive side, driving to make all of the hay we could while the sun shone, won the dirt fights.

Pepperdine quickly acquired, in additional acreage, all of the Marie Canyon drainage from the mountains to the coast highway. This enabled Strecker to move the million cubic yards from the Seaver College site and compact it down into Marie Canyon. To accomplish this, Eiden built an earthen dam at the top of Marie Canyon. Dubbed the "upper debris basin," it served during construction as a glittering mountain drainage lake. Later, it provided a stable for campus horses. Currently, it serves as a parking lot for trucks and buses. But President Andrew K. Benton has drawn plans for its ultimate incarnation as a world-class intercollegiate soccer stadium.

Eiden buried a ten-foot-diameter drain pipe deep under Marie Canyon. Rainwater ran easily off the mountains, into the upper debris basin and down to the ocean. The drainage system transformed Marie Canyon into a massive dry receptacle for dirt from the Seaver College site. Hundreds of tons of earth, compacted according to code, were pushed and trucked less than 200 yards into Marie Canyon, deep beneath the eventual athletics, housing and other facilities. We minimized Malibu opposition by prohibiting dusty dump trucks loaded with dirt from wobbling off campus onto the sacrosanct Pacific Coast Highway. The orderly operation to cut the hills and fill the canyons kept all dirt on site. Pepperdine developed the Malibu campus without hauling a single shovel of dirt away from the site.

Master builder Eiden was an aspiring novelist taking night courses in creative writing at UCLA. His personal diary is a rich source of Malibu miracle minutia and construction detail. He wrote that I pushed unmercifully to create the Seaver College site. "For weeks, Dr. Banowsky daily donned boots and jeans to take his command position atop the central hill." Eiden didn't appreciate "the intrusion and contradictory signals to my men. Dr. Banowsky creates tension pressing Strecker to go faster. At our second Monday leadership meeting he contradicted my weekly progress report in front of the whole team. He said he talked with Allen and Ace a day earlier. They informed him fewer men and machines were working than I officially reported. On days Dr. Banowsky shows up," Eiden ordered Allen and Ace, "give me a meticulous count of men and machines. I intend to hand him unassailable numbers."[9]

Eiden's diary also reported "ridiculous demands about ecology. Dr. Banowsky warned Strecker to protect the natural beauty, above all else. That was a bit much! Those scrapers scoop 20 cubic yards per swipe at hundreds of swipes per day. Here's Dr. Banowsky making speeches to environmentalists and promising to build the campus without disturbing a blade of grass. He pushes me to level every mountain while promising ecologists we're preserving the native flora and fauna. My respect for Dr. Banowsky kept me from saying that the whole site is sagebrush, not trees or grass, and I can't dig a footing, or pour a sidewalk, without destroying all of it!"[10]

Despite his complaints, Eiden and I bonded through years of creative achievement. Jack's job was to lead. Mine was to push. I pushed Slosson and Murray for grading plans; Pereira for building plans; the county for permits; the graders to stay ahead of construction crews; the concrete pours to come on the day after steel installation. I pushed for a sewer solution. I pinned a time-flow chart to my bathroom wall and car dashboard to calculate where we were in comparison to where we ought to be, in order to finish by September 6, 1972.

SLOSSON'S LANDSLIDE FEARS

As the more aggressive dirt moving got underway, project geologist Slosson caught a bad case of bureaucratic cold feet. His caution in preparing and permitting grading plans created costly delays. Slosson specifically feared that the giant cut through the central hill, with massive excavation of unstable alluvial soil, would trigger a major landslide. Slosson feared he could be blamed and perhaps sued.

Slosson, to my utter shock, surreptitiously wrote this to the building department: "A soft soapstone strata, deep beneath the surface of the central ridge, consisting of talc, chlorite and magnetite, renders the entire slope unstable. Any further excavation would be extremely unwise."[11] For the first time, panicked county officials momentarily quit cooperating. Pereira, Eiden, Rawn, Wood and Murray screamed in chorus at Dr. Hudson and me, "Your geologist quit certifying permits! Now what do we do?"

What I did was fire Slosson on the spot. His timidity threatened to maroon the Seaver Drive surface 40-feet higher than today's finished elevation. Landslide or not, we had to cut the mountain down. On August 1, 1970, I hired Beach Leighton to replace Slosson. The team of twelve rejoiced in Leighton's arrival, with one reservation. "Leighton has no landslide fears but he's slow as molasses," said Eiden's diary. "How can we accelerate Leighton?"[12]

On a providential tip from Andy Rawn, I discovered the unorthodox, Malibu-based, Mexican-American earthwork genius, Luis Manzano. A charismatic University of Guadalajara-trained geologist, Manzano could look at a mountain and, intuitively, know what to do. A local legend, in the 1960s he designed Malibu West at Trancas where the White, Stivers and Glass families resided. Betty and Walter Glass lived on Manzano Drive for 40 years.

To maintain continuity, Leighton and Murray signed off on county paperwork. But they followed the on-site leadership of maestro Manzano. The earthwork wizard designed, scraped and shaped the entire Malibu campus. Somewhere on campus there should be a sign, "Made by Manzano."

LUIS MANZANO TO THE RESCUE

On Wednesday, June 2, 1971, Pepperdine launched, under Luis Manzano, the second-phase site preparation. Without breaking stride, Manzano cut the controversial central mountain from the spot of Slosson's panic to today's finished perfection. That's not the only mountain Manzano moved. His mightiest volume of earth came from the big upper mountain that Norvel Young christened "the offending ridge." As we stood at the Seaver College site, looking northeast to the top of Marie Canyon, Norvel teased, "Bill, you just hate that offending ridge, don't you?"

I did! The trajectory of the ridge gorged its mass from the peak of the mountain to the bottom of Marie Canyon. It ruined the sweetest mountain views from every perspective on the campus. Worse still, it buried beneath its boulders the entire eventual location of the law school. It eliminated any other construction over its 200-acre expanse.

Worst of all, the offending ridge chopped the crucial campus circular drive into two isolated streets. Manzano had graded Seaver Drive to the east and John Tyler Drive to the west. But he had absolutely no way of connecting them. Both drives dead-ended up against the base of the offending ridge. Manzano moved the ridge to create Huntsinger Circle and join the two drives.

Thus legends emerge. "The president squinted his eyes, scrutinizing the terrain . . . 'Now that's an offensive mountain,' said William S. Banowsky . . . Not a week later, the 'mountain' was gone," chronicled Pepperdine's Patricia Yomantas years later. "He clearly is a man who moved mountains."[13]

Luis Manzano moved the mountain. I merely raised the money to pay for it. The offending ridge created one and one-half million cubic yards of dirt that cost a million dollars to move. I raised the cash and Manzano cut it down.

For a year I worked directly with Manzano, and his two Mexican aides, in his residential three-car-garage office at Big Rock, in Malibu. We squinted at complicated geological survey maps spread out across brightly lit drafting tables. Almost like priests at an altar, Luis and I bowed together over squiggly county maps as he deciphered their complicated codes for me.

In phase one, Strecker moved a million cubic yards to create the Seaver College site. In phase two, Manzano and Kirst moved two and one-half million more to create every other campus nook and cranny: both entrances; streets and parking lots; student, faculty and administrative housing sites; athletics facilities; and finished landscaping. Without Manzano, Pepperdine could not possibly have developed so many Malibu acres or completed the project on time. Without Manzano the campus could not conceivably look as it does today. Three construction professionals contributed most to the finished product of the Malibu miracle: William L. Pereira in design, Luis Manzano in site development and Jack Eiden in brick and mortar.

"If You Have Faith as Small as a Mustard Seed," Norvel headlined the words of Jesus across the *Alumni Voice*. "You can say to this mountain," he quoted further, "'Move from here to there' and it will move. Nothing will be impossible for you."[14]

KIRST CONSTRUCTION COMPANY

Despite biblical inspiration, when Luis Manzano came on board, the Strecker Construction Company quickly became a problem. Manzano moved so fast to produce plans that Strecker could not keep up the grading pace. The new campus fell dangerously behind the earthwork schedule. With Strecker's

12-month contract expiring, I decided to make a major site development change.

On January 4, 1970, the team of twelve met privately as a team of ten at Moran's Alhambra headquarters. Excluding Strecker's men, Allen and Ace, we opened phase two grading bids from seven other companies. Stunningly, Kirst Construction Company came in $1 million under the other six. Our leadership team split again, along different lines. Pereira's men now joined Topodynamics and Moran to oppose Kirst. Fearing Kirst's bid was way too low, and that he would go broke, they cited HUD rules for rejecting financially questionable bids.

"Dr. Banowsky," reported Jack Eiden, "You may not have noticed, but Kirst just lost millions on that failed professional basketball team. With a negative net worth, Kirst could go bankrupt and we'll never finish on time."

"Yes, I did notice, Jack," I answered. "But did you notice Kirst is bonded by a big insurance company?" Walking around the table, I put my hand on Jack's shoulder. "For a million dollars I'm willing to take the risk. That's lots of money, Jack! It's like turning down a huge donation. I want you to save the million but make Kirst perform." Kirst proved to be a wise risk. He more than doubled the total volume of Strecker's earthwork. In 12 months, Strecker moved a million cubic yards. In 18 months, Kirst moved two and one-half million.

CONSTRUCTING THE BUILDINGS

In March 1971, Pereira produced final working plans for the founding circle of Seaver College buildings: Huntsinger Academic Center, Pendleton Learning Center, Payson Library, Tyler Campus Center, Murchison Science Center and Elkins Auditorium. Pereira's contract also included 16 residence buildings for 800 students, but those plans were not yet ready for bidding.

The government indemnified local banks to loan interim cash for construction provided Pepperdine adhered to HUD regulations. Accordingly, Pepperdine delivered Pereira's working drawings to a dozen union trade rooms throughout Southern California. An astonishing total of 200 bids arrived from framing, concrete, electrical, plumbing, air conditioning, glazing, flooring, finishing and other companies. On March 1, 1971, a crowd of construction managers met at Moran's Alhambra plan room to open and read the bids. HUD rules required awarding to lowest bidders, without negotiation, so contractors and subs took their best shots.

For the first six big buildings, our team predetermined a budget limit of $6 million. If bids exceeded that, Pereira would have to redesign. We held our breath. Lost time for redesign would jeopardize the deadline. Happily, those first buildings came in 5 percent below our limit. Construction commenced

POURED CONCRETE AND STEEL

In 1971, helicopters were employed to deliver material and equipment to the construction site. Below, the beautiful Scaife Bridge is under construction just beneath the Mullin Town Square.

on Monday, April 12, 1971, with a ground breaking ceremony featuring famed space scientist Wernher von Braun. I announced that "the Phase I construction will cost approximately $26,600,000."[15]

As construction continued, the landslide ghosts of terminated geologist James Slosson returned to haunt us. In addition to landslide concerns, California is earthquake country and a major fault runs offshore along Malibu. Ordinary earthquake anxieties, combined with Slosson's landslide predictions, spooked our structural engineer, Dick Snyder, of Brandow and Johnson Company. To reassure the building department, Snyder dictated that buildings around Seaver College be constructed on 40-foot-deep, steel-reinforced concrete piles, far deeper than customary foundations. Snyder's overkill added time and expense. But he got the county on our case and we had no choice.

As luck would have it, the drilling hit hard rock in the first ten feet. The bits jammed. Explosive experts were then lowered in buckets and set dynamite charges to clear the blockages. But their explosions only fractured big boulders into wedging pieces, creating greater drill problems. Eventually, boulders as big as dump trucks were pulverized and removed. But that left huge holes requiring tons of concrete refill.

"Those first big buildings surrounding Seaver College," predicted Eiden's diary, "will remain unmoved even when the big one comes. Centuries from now, when the buildings are long gone, archeologists will still decipher their size and shape from that deep underground acropolis of pile columns."[16]

MORLEY CONSTRUCTION COMPANY

The enormous concrete volume made Morley Construction Company's work critical. For that first circle of six buildings, Morley pumped and poured 350,000 cubic yards of concrete. But Morley's young foreman was a mixed blessing. Happily, he drove men and machines for maximum daily pours. Sadly, he ignored warnings and created two serious concrete blowouts.

The blowouts came because the foreman installed his concrete forms with too few walers. The walers were long bolts connected horizontally through flat plywood panels to opposing panels. That created the force for holding everything in place against the mounting pressure of rising concrete. The higher the walls—and some of ours were very high—the greater the pressure against the plywood forms at the bottom. The daring young foreman bolted in too few walers. Two massive concrete blowouts splintered forms and splattered concrete everywhere.

The second blowout prompted a rare job-site visit by William L. Pereira. "He arrived royally in his limousine," wrote Eiden, "and swept into the

In 1972, with school in Malibu already open, Firestone Fieldhouse sprints toward its 1973 completion. In the foreground dust, the Raleigh Runnels Memorial Pool has not yet begun.

trailer, black cape flowing, lecturing everybody in sight. He warned me that, as master architect, he would not be associated with shoddy construction and demanded a personal inspection of both shattered walls. Pereira seemed satisfied with our blowout repair."[17]

In its third month, construction moved into high gear. "At its zenith, 1,500 men and women worked on Pepperdine's project. In addition to 1,000 job site personnel, another 400 worked in off-site material assembly and supply and 100 more in design and engineering," calculated Eiden.[18]

The complexity of the tight timetable led me to retain Mark Johnson of Management Consultants in San Diego as a "critical path scheduler." Johnson conducted weekly campus exercises with the team of twelve to detect bottlenecks and blockages. Like cars on a crowded freeway, if one sub-contractor slowed, others backed up. If one broke down, all stopped. Any delay jeopardized the schedule. Johnson criticized Pepperdine's contracts for failing to mandate automatic penalties for slowdowns and breakdowns. Eiden, Hudson and I compensated by preaching to the contractors that, if Pepperdine failed to occupy on schedule, default suits for tuition refund, faculty reimbursement and other damages would follow. Our preaching, and Johnson's professional expertise, kept the schedule.

"GREATEST CAMPUS FIRESTORM"

Slosson's dreaded landslide never came. But what did come was a truly historic episode in Malibu's seemingly annually reoccurring natural disasters. On Friday, September 25, 1970, the "greatest of twentieth-century Southern California firestorms" blazed toward our campus in "perfect fire weather (drought conditions, 100-degree heat, three percent humidity and an 85-mile-per-hour Santa Ana wind)."[19] The Eagles 1970s rock band memorialized the winds blowing "down across the desert through the canyons of the coast to the Malibu."[20]

. The fire, coalescing with several blazes in the San Fernando Valley, "ultimately took ten lives and charred 403 homes, including a ranch owned by Governor Ronald Reagan. Firefighters said the cedar-shake roofs 'popped like popcorn' as a 20-mile wall of flames roared across the ridge line of the Santa Monicas [and across our campus] toward the sea. With the asphalt on [Pacific Coast Highway] ablaze and all escape routes cut off, terrified residents . . . took refuge in the nearby lagoon."[21]

Fortunately, there was little on the campus to be burned. But evacuating workers worried about Kirst's equipment. With no time to load it onto flatbeds, what would keep raging flames from igniting the vulnerable fuel-loaded machines?

Beverly Stauffer speaks inspirationally at the 1972 dedication of Stauffer Chapel, which she christened "the little chapel on the hill."

The 1964 Republican candidate for president of the United States, Senator Barry Goldwater, assists Bill, Blanche and Lawrence Welk in the Tyler Campus Center dedication.

The fire department urged Kirst's men to drive their machines into what they hoped would be a safe haven in the meadow. For 12 sweltering hours, the workers cleared the meadow brush into a wide circle and shoved an earthen berm around it. Eiden colorfully described the "caravan of scrapers crawling down from the central hill into the meadow's safe circle [like] a parade of steel dinosaurs replicating a race from some prehistoric lava flow."[22] The circular barricade worked. The voracious fires roared through, scorching every foot of the empty campus, but no fuel tanks ignited.

But then came the flood. With the arrival of rainy season, for five days and nights a torrent pounded Pepperdine's blackened hills. And with the rains came the mud slides. Entire mountain walls collapsed, where they annually fail, along Pacific Coast Highway and the Malibu Canyon Road. Those of us driving to the campus encountered days of detours and hours of delay.

Most terrifyingly, the torrential rains threatened the denuded campus with massive flooding and mud slides because of the potential failure of the freshly formed earthen dam. It now held back an engorged lake of rainwater overflowing the new Marie Canyon upper debris basin. The unstable dirt wall of the hurriedly erected dam was under severe pressure. If it failed, Marie Canyon would be devastatingly flooded. All of the summer's site work of countless compacted slopes and pads would be swept away to the ocean.

The makeshift basin, designed to control normal rainfall, accommodated the gradual release of moderate amounts of water. Water routinely percolated through a round standpipe down through the ten-foot Marie Canyon drain to the ocean. But the standpipe, not designed to withstand a deluge, had multiple drainage holes clogged with trashy debris and brush. Tremendous water pressure pushed against the back of the dirt dam, and overflowed its top.

Working around the clock, Jack Eiden loaded three workers into a rubber raft to clear the drainage and clean lake debris. Their inflatable boat was intermittently rocked by strong suction as the cleared standpipe drains pulled the water out beneath them. Meanwhile, dozers and trucks evacuated tons of silt and muck from the lake's swollen banks. For a full week it was touch and go. Like the fire fortress in the meadow, the shaky Marie Canyon dam also held.

THE STUDENT HOUSING HEADACHE

A last big headache developed over construction costs for student housing. Pepperdine did not desire a cozy Malibu Mediterranean village dominated by institutionalized dormitories. Watching the failure of the Los Angeles campus as a residential college, I personally challenged Pereira to produce "innovative and intimate family residences irresistibly attractive to young people."[23] We provided prime space under the hillside adjacent to Seaver College, facing west toward the Point Dume sunset, for Pereira to put 20 houses of 50 occupants each. The Malibu campus would be anchored with a thousand happy residential students.[24]

Pereira designed world-class student housing, but the bids came in at twice the budgeted maximum. Heading into the home stretch, we were completely broke and had totally exhausted our government-guaranteed borrowing options. We fixed a desperate limit of $200,000 per house, $4 million total. But the bids came back at $400,000 per house, $8 million total.

HUD rules permitted bid rejection for financial exigency. We alerted the government and rejected the bids. For the first time, we also rejected Pereira's plans. Pereira had insisted upon duplication in the housing of his academic building plans, with institutional-grade concrete and steel construction. When Pepperdine demanded redesign, Pereira reluctantly compromised from institutional to commercial quality. When Pereira's revised plans still exceeded budget, Andy Rawn and Bob Wood delivered us from despondence. Their recommendations demonstrated the Topodynamics Malibu miracle contribution.

Vetoing not only institutional but also commercial construction, Topodynamics insisted on common residential housing quality. This meant ordinary wooden-platform frame apartment buildings with minimum concrete foundations and no window eyebrows, double-paned glass, oversized openings, solid-core doors or institutional hardware. Topodynamics next insisted Pereira be ordered to redesign for ordinary housing and, if he hesitated, be replaced. Then Topodynamics pushed for Norwood and DeLong, a construction firm specializing in ordinary housing, to be the contractor. They concluded that Moran, without housing experience, could not meet budget. Finally, Topodynamics urged private financing to permit Pepperdine to avoid bid risks while handing the job to Norwood and DeLong.

Grudgingly, Pereira redesigned the student residences. Norwood and DeLong constructed on time and within budget. Aside from a few student fists punched through hollow-core doors, and buddies being shoved through Masonite wardrobes, the housing has served honorably through the years.

RALEIGH RUNNELS MEMORIAL POOL

If we were broke, and couldn't borrow, where did we find $4 million for housing? Once again, we found it in Mrs. Frank R. Seaver's Hydril stock portfolio.

In addition to permanently endowing the campus, Mrs. Seaver also totally subsidized its construction. She funded the crucial infrastructure such as the Winter Canyon entrance, major roads, minor walkways, bridges, courtyards, parking lots and fountains. Together, Blanche Seaver and Dick Scaife paid for virtually all site development.

Mrs. Seaver also fully, or partially, matched named donors of several buildings. When Mr. Murchison defaulted on his commitment, Mrs. Seaver gave $2 million for the science center. When Mr. Tyler's pledge was deferred for 27 years, Mrs. Seaver built the campus center. (In 1971, Mr. Tyler executed a charitable remainder trust of Farmer's Insurance Company stock. When he died in 1973, Mrs. Tyler challenged his will to exclude Pepperdine. She lost in court. Subsequently, when she died in 1998, Pepperdine finally received $35 million. But, back in 1971, it was Mrs. Seaver's $3 million that built Tyler Campus Center.) Ultimately, Blanche Seaver contributed to Elkins Auditorium, Stauffer Chapel, the Brock House, Firestone Fieldhouse and the Raleigh Runnels Memorial Pool.

The unsurpassed Olympic-sized swimming pool honored the late son of Charles and Amy Jo Runnels. Raleigh Neal Runnels was a tenth-grade honor student at Palisades High School, excelling in football, baseball, cross country and track, just as the Malibu campus was breaking ground. He enrolled as the first founding 1972 freshman and counted the days for school to start. Sadly, he was never able to realize his Malibu campus dream. On July 1, 1972, eight weeks before school began, he lost his valiant two-year fight against cancer. It was shattering.

Norvel and I conducted the memorial service. Three days later, we walked beside the Firestone Fieldhouse, in construction dust, with Charles and Amy Jo and Blanche and Richard Seaver. Blanche adored Raleigh. To insure his memory, she committed $650,000 on the spot while Morris B. Pendleton and others added $300,000 more. It became "the only Malibu facility to be paid for before it got built," as Charlie Runnels occasionally brags. The Raleigh Runnels Memorial Pool was eventually seen and experienced by hundreds of millions around the world as the water polo venue for the 1984 Olympics. Scores of names grace the campus with a beautiful story behind each one. But I take joy in remembering this one and only Malibu miracle use of the word "memorial."

Raleigh Runnels didn't make it for the Malibu opening. But 860 other students did report for duty to the founding faculty for the first classes on Wednesday, September 6, 1972.

1. M. Norvel Young, "The Malibu Campus," *Pepperdine University Bulletin*, October 1971, 6.
2. Richard Reeves, "My Years with Ronald Reagan," *American Heritage*, February/March 2006, 54.
3. Bill Henegar and Jerry Rushford, *Forever Young: The Life and Times of M. Norvel Young and Helen M. Young* (Nashville: 21st Century Christian, 1999), 206.
4. Howard A. White in Jerry Rushford, ed., *Crest of a Golden Wave: Pepperdine University, 1937– 1987* (Malibu: Pepperdine University Press, 1987), 165.
5. Jack Eiden, "The Eiden Document," August 2005. The Banowsky Papers. Many details in this chapter were recalled, and recorded, in a document written by Jack Eiden at age 82.
6. *Malibu Times*, January 26, 1971.
7. Eiden, "The Eiden Document," 83. Olen Murray to Jack Eiden, "Site Development Memorandum," May 10 1969. "Everybody is swamped and we simply can't obtain the necessary permits in time for the grading. Therefore, we just must begin the grading without the permits. I suggest that you blow a little smoke to L. A. County."; Jack Eiden to Olen Murray, "L. A. County," May 16, 1969. "Yesterday, I met with the L. A. County district engineer and told him we could not wait for his plan check. He agreed to let me proceed with the grading and I had agreed to make any changes they felt necessary later on." With Eiden's direction, we did from day to day whatever was neccessary to keep the big grading machines working.
8. Eiden, "The Eiden Document," 122.
9. Ibid., 141.
10. Ibid., 144.
11. Ibid., 156.
12. Ibid., 181.
13. Patricia Yomantas in Rushford, *Golden Wave*, 177.
14. Bill Youngs, "The Young Years," *Pepperdine Alumni Voice*, Fall 1971, 4.
15. Mike Pollock, "Von Braun Lauds Science in Pepperdine Ceremonies: 500 Attend Ground Breaking at Malibu; Honor Paid to Principal Donors," *Van Nuys (California) News*, April 15, 1971, 1.
16. Eiden, "The Eiden Document," 67.
17. Ibid., 91.
18. Ibid., 97.
19. Mike Davis, "Let Malibu Burn: A Political History of the Fire Coast," from *LA Weekly*, 1996, reposted at http://la.indymedia.org/news/2007/10/208946.php (accessed September 18, 2009).
20. Don Henley and Glenn Frey, "The Last Resort" (Hollywood, California: Cass County Music, 1971).
21. See note 20 above.
22. Eiden, "The Eiden Document," 67.
23. William S. Banowsky, memorandum to William L. Pereira, "Student Housing," April 16, 1971. The Banowsky Papers.
24. "It Happened in 1972," *Pepperdine Graphic*, March 4, 1976, 1.

FOUNDING CHANCELLOR OF THE MALIBU CAMPUS
Pepperdine Physician Dr. William L. Allen, Malibu campus Dean Dr. Jack Alan Scott
and Seaver College Professor Morris Womack congratulate Bill on his installation as
Founding Chancellor of the Malibu campus.

CHAPTER 14

THE MALIBU FACULTY AND STUDENTS

The Malibu campus opened Wednesday, September 6, 1972. But before that, the time arrived in 1970 to appoint the founding faculty.

What should have been a time of excitement turned into controversy. The process of cherry-picking the few faculty deemed appropriate for Malibu exacerbated the perennial Los Angeles division. Archivist James Smythe lamented: "Some faculty were headed happily to Malibu. But most of us, including me, felt marooned in Los Angeles." Dr. Smythe, who served Pepperdine 60 years, ended up at Malibu.[1]

The Malibu miracle was born in struggle. While the Malibu campus flourished, Pepperdine in Los Angeles foundered.

"GRIM FACULTY CRISIS"

"There was a grim faculty crisis over the move to Malibu," wrote Candace Denise Jones. Some believed that leaving the Vermont Avenue campus conflicted with the college's Christian mission. "The excluded faculty and those who opposed the move to Malibu found themselves alienated from the administration. A bitter divide within the faculty ensued."[2]

The Malibu miracle, like the miracle of birth itself, was accompanied by pain. The pain of a demoralizing faculty division shadowed the miracle's first three years. Back then that divisive shadow seemed unavoidable. Today it seems to have been unnecessary. Norvel and I underestimated the magnitude of the Malibu miracle. From the perspective of history, it now seems inevitable that the Malibu campus would draw thousands of students. But in those tenuous days there were only 138 raw acres, no money and no track record of miraculous success. Norvel and I shunned failure by setting our first Malibu sights abysmally low. To eke out a safe start, we designed a campus with a few small buildings and an avant-garde curriculum for 400 students and 30 teachers. The process of handpicking "the chosen Malibu thirty" was, for some faculty, the last straw.

"Bill," Norvel joked, "Malibu's like Noah's Ark! Only so many can board the boat!" We underestimated by 700 percent how many faculty and students Seaver College would soon accommodate. We paid a price for planning to leave half the faculty off the boat.

"All faculty wishing to teach at Malibu," I announced on April 15, 1971, "should apply now to be assured of an appropriate position." The air cleared, the cleavage continued.[3]

"There was, indeed, tension among many faculty," conceded Dr. Jerry Hudson. As Malibu provost, Dr. Hudson witnessed an inconceivable enrollment explosion. "Some of the tension was on philosophical grounds for appearing to be fleeing the inner city," he said, "and some on practical grounds because initially so few faculty were selected to move to Malibu."[4]

Provost Hudson understated. Tension ran high enough for superior faculty to flee. Richard T. Hughes, youngest 1972 faculty member and first recruited for Malibu, retreated to Texas in 1976. Sickened by the split, he "left conflicted and frustrated by the polarized setting. Those were extremely difficult years," Hughes confessed in 1998. "A vast ideological chasm now ran through the heart of the faculty, dividing it down the middle."[5] With the maturing Malibu miracle, Hughes returned for many years of distinguished service.

Other professors were lost to the cause. "It makes me feel kind of sad thinking back to those days," grimaced Professor Stephen Sale in 2002. "It wasn't all just good times. It was very hard." After determining to stay with what he called "the campus that was truly Pepperdine," Dr. Sale softened and joined the Malibu faculty from the first and helped design the history curriculum.[6]

"Early in the planning," recalled Archivist Smythe, "Malibu was rolled out as an experimental program for a limited number of undergraduates and faculty. No Los Angeles faculty were believed appropriate for Malibu. Specialized faculty with an innovative spirit were being recruited. Most were depressed and feared being left out altogether if the Los Angeles campus failed." Dr. Smythe's sense of rejection was shared by many.

Suddenly came the Malibu miracle paradigm shift. "Miraculously," reported Dr. Smythe, "when the administration took the Malibu lid off, enrollment exploded. Faculty positions were available to all who chose to go and most faculty ended up at Malibu. But for so many to have felt left out for so long caused damage."[7]

FACULTY FRUSTRATION

The faculty was deeply divided. Norvel and I took heat from both sides. Frustration festered for several reasons. One was inadequate facilities. In 1958 Norvel recruited chemistry professor Loyd Frashier from the University of Georgia with the promise of a new Los Angeles campus science building. By 1968 Norvel broke ground twice, but built nothing. For ground breaking three, Norvel believed Clint Murchison, owner of the Dallas Cowboys NFL team, would give $1 million. "Trustee James L. Lovell supplied DuPont dynamite and Clint pushed the lever to blast a hole and lay the cornerstone. But the building never began," chuckled Dr. Frashier in 2005.

In 1971, Clint moved to the top of the prospect list for the Malibu science center. Gay and I hosted Saturday lunch for him with Governor and Mrs. Reagan and the Youngs. Reagan, dreaming of the presidency, focused on the Texas millionaire whose Cowboys were playing the Rams the next day in the Los Angeles Coliseum. This luncheon stands as the one time Ronald Reagan solicited a Pepperdine gift. Norvel and I cornered the governor, requesting that he "suggest $1 million to Clint." He did. Clint agreed. Pepperdine hailed Murchison Science Center. Thirty years later, Dr. Frashier still cherished the joke about the curious Los Angeles campus visitor. "Say, what's that empty space between the business building and gym used for?" the visitor queried. "Oh," joked the guide. "That's where we practice our science building ground breakings."[8]

Quite naturally, the faculty felt some frustration as the time neared for the campus opening. During years of Los Angeles campus atrophy some faculty may have also atrophied. There were many fine teachers, but few scholars publishing academic work in refereed journals. The faculty argued that they were "victims of the demands made of them as teachers. All of them were required to teach 14 to 15 units in the first two trimesters and 10 to 12 units in the third trimester."[9] Dr. White systematically weeded out the weakest. He instructed the strongest to pray for Pepperdine and wait for their ship to come in.

Frustration also festered over my political speech making and media appearances. "Television is the instrument of Satan," warned theologian Elton Trueblood. Like a moth I couldn't stay away from the flame. Things I said that sounded good off campus sounded crazy on campus and left me open to constant counterattack. Media attention, excellent for building the campus, was problematic for faculty relationships.

Sunday, February 28, 1971, I appeared on *Firing Line*, William F. Buckley's nationally syndicated PBS show. "The Buckley-Banowsky discussion," cautioned the *Graphic*, "will focus on major cases of student unrest and differences between black and white students' demands."[10]

My Bohemian Club of San Francisco brother Bill Buckley and I were candid enough on camera that Richard H. Peairs, Western Regional Director of the American Association of University Professors, fired off a letter to English Professor Grover Goyne, president of the Pepperdine AAUP chapter, with a copy to me. "President Banowsky's 'Firing Line' views were deeply disturbing to faculty," Peairs notified Goyne. "Banowsky's description of the AAUP as 'an academic union' was most unfortunate. His praise for the Malibu program plan not to offer tenure to its faculty was disgusting."[11]

I wrote a quick note to my good friend Grover. "As you know, our original Malibu plan was experimental. It required a small number of secure young faculty with no interest in tenure. Since taping Buckley's show more than a month ago that plan has changed. I've changed my mind on tenure. But, Grover, I haven't yet changed my mind about calling AAUP 'a faculty union.'"[12]

I wasted little time attempting to earn artificial faculty approbation. We were all in the same boat. We were destined to win or lose together. If we made it to Malibu we all would win. If we missed Malibu we would all lose. I ignored boos and hisses. I endured one faculty strike.

February 1, 1974, the Seaver College faculty struck for a day. They were protesting over low salaries. "Dr. Banowsky meets brick and mortar cash flow scrimping on our bread and butter," protested Dr. John Nicks. His faculty senate compatriot, Dr. Ken Perrin, laughed years later about "those lean Banowsky years when the academic mission of the university got put on hold in pursuit of campus construction."[13] Faculty friends knew me well but few knew the life-and-death struggle to finance and operate one campus exploding in Malibu and a second one dying in the ghetto.

LEADERSHIP BY DELEGATION

Norvel and I edged forward, one might say under combat conditions, to make vital administrative appointments. The secret to successful leadership, in my experience, was to appoint the strongest possible administrators and to delegate to them the greatest possible power. Pepperdine sought the perfect team of leaders to produce two results. First, we sought total detailed supervision of the two-campus operation. Second, we sought freedom for me from administration in order to devote myself full-time to fundraising. I authorized accessible surrogates to act on my behalf, without bureaucratic delay, in the interest of faculty and students.

Director of university publications Bill Henegar remembered Vice President Larry Hornbaker's instructions: "President Banowsky insists that all Pepperdine publications be the very finest. My orders are to spare no expense in producing only the very highest quality printed pieces." Henegar thought to himself at the time, "It's most unusual for an executive to give his designers such carte blanche." Today Henegar thinks this tradition of delegated freedom from the top down led to Pepperdine's reputation for excellence. Henegar also heard prominent printers say that Pepperdine produced better color printing than the larger universities. Donors received, gratefully, the high quality invitations, the programs of dedication, the bountiful brochures and other printed pieces, and saw in all of them Pepperdine's commitment to excellence.[14]

Some surrogates were so ingenious they had me working for them. "The Conversation Day Committee," created by Seaver College Dean Norman Hughes, lasted for a few maddening months. This conduit encouraged students to bring complaints personally to me at Brock House. "President Banowsky expressed a willingness to overcome communication barriers by increased contact with students," rejoiced the *Graphic*. "Now we will be carefully watching to gauge the sincerity of President Banowsky's commitment."[15]

Every trailblazer hears his own call. In Pepperdine's expansion epoch I heard the call to build the campus. Had I divided my energies, attempting also to act as the chief campus administrator, I would have failed in both callings. High success exacts laser focus. As Pepperdine's 1960s dean of students, I focused on students. Now, a decade later, gifted colleagues served students' needs tactically and logistically. My job was to serve strategically by building the campus. I fulfilled those conversation days with students at the cost of fewer conversation days with donors.

Administrative appointments, made with faculty in mind, were praised by faculty. The Malibu miracle leaders included Jerry Hudson, James Wilburn, Norman Hughes, Robert Thomas, Charles Runnels, Bill Henegar, Jack Scott, Gerald Turner, Helen Young, George Hill, Larry Hornbaker, Jere Yates, Steven Lemley, Frank Pack, Tony Ash, Calvin Bowers, William Stivers, James Smythe, Bob Gilliam, Norman Hughes, Richard Hughes, John Nicks, Carl Mitchell, Ron Phillips. Bob Fraley, Israel Rodriguez, Shirley Roper, Claudia Arnold, Warren Dillard, James Penrod, Ed Rockey, John McClung, James Greer, James Atkinson, Sam Jackson, Jon Johnson, Loyd Frashier, JoAnn Carlson and Neva Hash.

In tribute to Pepperdine's leadership tradition, many of these administrators graduated to prestigious presidencies. Through the Malibu miracle years the list included Howard A. White, Pepperdine University; Jerry E. Hudson, Hamline University and Willamette University; Jack Alan Scott,

Orange Coast College and Pasadena City College; J. P. Sanders, Columbia Christian College; William J. Teague, Abilene Christian University; Robert Gerald Turner, the University of Mississippi and Southern Methodist University; Michael Amour, Columbia Christian College; Steven Lemley, Lubbock Christian University; Robert Thomas, the University of Montana; William S. Banowsky, the University of Oklahoma; Rex Johnston, Columbia Christian College; David Davenport, Pepperdine University; Michael Adams, the University of Georgia; Mike E. O'Neal, Oklahoma Christian University; Andrew K. Benton, Pepperdine University; James Kossler, Pasadena City College; and L. Randolph Lowry, David Lipscomb University.

Other presidencies have been filled by former Pepperdine students, including Thomas D. Gillespie, Princeton Theological Seminary; Laura Skandera, Pitzer College; J. Richard Chase, Wheaton College; L. D. Webb, Columbia Christian College; Otis Gatewood, Michigan Christian College; Ruth Johnson, Apple Valley (California) Community College. Current Pepperdine president Andrew K. Benton correctly believes that "the one most defining denominator in the Pepperdine backgrounds of these presidents was the influence of M. Norvel Young."[16]

EXECUTIVE VICE PRESIDENT

By late 1970, the time had arrived to name my own replacement as chief operating officer of the university. All eyes focused on four strong men: Howard Ashley White, Jack Alan Scott, Jerry E. Hudson and James R. Wilburn. These were four superstars of the Malibu miracle management team, as their subsequent stellar careers conclusively proved.

In 1968, Norvel crafted for me the position of executive vice president. I exercised its powers for Pepperdine College. Now my own executive vice president must manage day-to-day details of a multicampus university in four scattered locations. He must raise morale while I raised money. He must build the faculty while I built the campus. On the day I appointed Dr. White, some faculty dubbed him "the inside president."

If Norvel and I made music like Rodgers and Hammerstein, Howard and I did business like Sears and Roebuck. For ten Malibu miracle years, Howard solved all problems and caused none. He kept me advised while I raised money. "Bill," he phoned twice a day, "here's why I'm calling." In three or four minutes he said good-bye. Twice a week he arrived at Brock House to execute two hours of sensitive business in 20-minute meetings. Deftly disposing of agenda, he knew preferred outcomes. He usually reported them as accomplished. Our meetings always included a few good laughs.

Sometimes a brief prayer. But no small talk. I was humbled by Howard's high loyalty. A brilliant Southern gentleman with incorruptible personal integrity and childlike faith in the promises of God, Howard White gave all he had to Pepperdine until the day he died in 1991.

SCOTT AND HUDSON AND WILBURN

The three younger Malibu administrative stars were plucked out of the Los Angeles faculty. I lifted Jack Scott out of the religion department and made him Malibu dean, Jerry Hudson out of the history department and made him Los Angeles dean and Jim Wilburn out of the political science department and made him assistant to the president.

That was round one. Perfect-appointment obsessions soon forced me to switch Jack and Jerry completely around. As the Malibu miracle paradigm shift had earlier forced an awkward reordering of the Seaver and Pepperdine names, it now forced an awkward flip-flop in the top administrative spots. On June 1, 1969, I had put Jack in the highest position as chairman of the Malibu Campus Interdisciplinary Committee. Six months later, I promoted him to dean of the Malibu campus. The seven division chairs managing the new curriculum were to report to him. "Jack's branded with the 'Malibu brand,'" lamented his left-wing confederate, Zane Reeves.[17]

Simultaneously, to the counterbalancing position of dean of the Los Angeles college, I appointed another close friend, Jerry Hudson. Suddenly, the Malibu miracle paradigm shift turned the Scott and Hudson appointments upside down.

It took awhile, but by the fall of 1971 I conceded how it had to be. On September 1, 1971, I inaugurated the two new top positions to lead the new two-campus university structure. For the two new positions I selected the new title of "provost." When the meteoric paradigm shifted Malibu up and Los Angeles down, I knew Jack and Jerry would have to be shifted too. I brought Jack back to Los Angeles and moved Jerry out to Malibu.

"Jack, I want to promote you to provost," I said to Dr. Scott in my Tower of Power office. "But hang on. I have in mind provost of the Los Angeles campus. By administrative necessity I must name Jerry Hudson Malibu provost. You know how close Jerry is to Howard White." Jack's face blanched white. He walked out of my office in shock, speechless.

Why did I trade Jack for Jerry, a move that mattered in both men's superlative careers? Jack Scott from Sweetwater, Texas, ideally suited the inner city. In the Los Angeles community he led African-American students and preached for a local black church. His moderately Democratic but deeply held political convictions would not keep time with Pepperdine Republican priorities. Jack had a lot of integrity.

Meanwhile, I knew in my soul that maximizing Pepperdine's potential would demand, for the foreseeable future, doctrinal commitment to conservatism in religion and politics. That meant both the Church of Christ and the Republican Party. Scott cautiously aligned with the first. He openly fought the second. Hudson, on the other hand, was Howard White's non-partisan protegé, soon to serve alongside his tutor in the Malibu Church of Christ eldership. Therefore Dr. White and Dr. Hudson were tied together at the hip and ran everything. Jerry also directed campus construction for five years and contributed mightily.

Destiny awaited Scott. After two years as founding provost of the Los Angeles campus, he shifted to the public sector. After two college presidencies, and 12 years in both chambers of the California state legislature, he capped his career as chancellor of the California Community Colleges. Today three million students, on 110 campuses, make Pepperdine-honed Jack Alan Scott from Sweetwater, Texas, chancellor of the largest system of higher education on the planet.

Dr. James R. Wilburn was a third Malibu miracle leader who could have succeeded to the Pepperdine presidency. From assistant to the president, Wilburn rose through the ranks to replace Scott as second, and longest-serving, provost of the Los Angeles campus. Wilburn served as vice president for university affairs, dean of the school of business and management, and dean of the school of public policy. He also performed sensitive assignments such as answering directly to Governor Reagan in leading CREEP, the 1972 "Campaign to Re-elect President Nixon." Pepperdine's most durable and versatile leader, Dr. Wilburn served for more than 40 years in a greater variety of key posts than any other person.

With Pepperdine producing a college-president bumper crop, it occurred to me one of these men could replace me. It didn't occur, due to his age, that it might be Dr. White. But Dr. Scott, Dr. Wilburn and Dr. Hudson seemed preordained to the presidency.

INTERDISCIPLINARY CURRICULUM

The first Malibu job, for all three of these men, was to design and construct an innovative new curriculum. "We saw the move to Malibu as a wonderful opportunity to develop a new curriculum and a new campus," said Provost Hudson. "Those kinds of chances have not come along in higher education very much in the last hundred years."[18] Scott, Wilburn and Hudson, joined by James Smythe (humanities), John Nicks (social sciences), Loyd

President Banowsky, Provost Hudson and Seaver
College interdisciplinary curriculum leader Dr.
Jere Yates meet with Mr. Huntsinger.

PRESIDENT FORD ON BOARD

In 1974, Bill and Gay visited the White
House to book President Gerald R. Ford
for the historic 1975 campus visit.

Frashier (natural sciences), Larry McCommas (fine arts), Edward Rocky (communications), Jere Yates (business), Tony Ash (religion), Norman Hughes, Pence Dacus and Bob Gilliam, formed the Malibu Campus Interdisciplinary Committee.[19] It was commissioned to consolidate 16 segregated disciplines of the traditional liberal arts curriculum into six divisions. Over the months, the committee creatively instituted seven divisions: religion, social science, natural science, fine arts, humanities, communication and business. Astonishingly, with only occasional tweaking, this design has endured through all of these years, and disciplined the meteoric Seaver College flight to academic prestige.

Along with administrators, the Malibu miracle produced a crop of presciently distinguished faculty. I single out Dr. Stephen D. Davis, not as exception, but as exemplification. Distinguished professor of biology Davis came from Texas A&M University in 1974. Over the next quarter century he earned national distinction and, in 2002, was awarded Pepperdine's largest National Science Foundation grant of $300,000. His scholarly task was "to document drought tolerance in the native chaparral scrub covering the Malibu hills surrounding the campus."[20] In 2008 Dr. Davis also received the $200,000 Baylor University Robert Foster Cherry Award for Great Teaching. It is the only national award for exceptional teaching presented by a college or university.

The Malibu miracle also produced a new catalog for the new Pepperdine University. After changing the campuses, revising the curricula and moving from a college to university, the time arrived to revise the *Pepperdine College Catalog*. Its 1970 version, originally composed in 1937, had never seen a thorough revision and regurgitated outworn phrases of founding verbiage. It cried out for updating. I answered the cry. In 1972, at my Brock House desk, I composed the first ten pages of the catalog in modern Malibu language that remains largely intact today.[21] Meanwhile, Hollywood's famous Bob Hope delivered the first Malibu commencement address. The *Los Angeles Times* reported: "President Banowsky conferred an honorary doctorate on Bob Hope along with six undergraduate and 79 graduate degrees."[22]

COMPLAINTS AND CRITICISM

The Lord may have used Norvel and me for the Malibu miracle, but not all Pepperdiners cheered the performance. "With the roses you get the brickbats," Norvel always said. For brevity I will illustrate with but one of a schoolbag full of brickbats. This one was thrown at my Sunday, April 5, 1970, *Los Angeles Times* op-ed piece, "Score One for Tolerance." The newspaper solicited my rebuttal to a free-speech assault by the free-speech radical, Dr. Herbert Marcuse. "The 71-year-old enfant terrible of the New Left," editorialized the *Los Angeles Times*, "has protested the forthcoming appearance of Dr. Fred Schwarz, leader of the Christian Anti-Communism Crusade . . . Marcuse's own right to teach at UC San Diego has been nobly defended by the university yet he would deny to a conservative the privilege he himself, as a liberal, has been afforded."[23]

The *Los Angeles Times* invited me to call out the visionary for violating his own vision. My rebuttal turned the tables by arguing the classic free-speech case as created by guru Marcuse himself.

Associate professor Maurice Ethridge had initially objected, only two weeks earlier, to my veto of a proposed Pepperdine speech by left-wing campus goddess Angela Davis. After I rejected Davis, Ethridge called my attack on Marcuse for rejecting Schwarz "exploitative and hypocritical. Your excellent article in Sunday's paper was the last straw. It made me sick at heart. It is an exemplary case of hypocrisy. I came to Pepperdine in 1968 with great confidence in you and respect for you. After your hypocritical Marcuse article I have neither. This article proves that truth is of no importance to you except where it can be of exploitable advantage. Whatever integrity you ever had has been sold for a mess of political pottage."[24]

Ethridge wrote, simultaneously, to the *Los Angeles Times*. "Banowsky chides Marcuse for 'a dogmatism that prefers uniformity to diversity.' Yet I can think of no better definition of the Pepperdine policy on dissent. We do not even allow those who are not members of the Church of Christ to conduct the devotional in our chapel's services. I object to Dr. Banowsky's comments on freedom of speech not because I disagree with Dr. Banowsky's excellent article but because Dr. Banowsky's article does not agree with his own behavior."[25]

The high-profile Ethridge attack brought Pepperdine greater financial support than ever. Vice President White, certainly no right-winger, wrote: "Bill, you did a terrific job debating Marcuse. Your incisive *L.A. Times* editorial will expand your base of support."[26]

BIGGEST AND BRIGHTEST

Despite divided faculty, Pepperdine opened its Malibu campus on schedule at 8:00 a.m., Wednesday, September 6, 1972. The founding class numbered 475 freshmen. They were joined by 120 sophomores who had been recruited as 1971 freshmen. In their first year they had studied the Malibu curriculum in the Seaver Learning Center, the last building to be constructed on the Los Angeles campus—yes, with a $500,000 cash gift from Mrs. Seaver! The advanced transfer students pushed the number of Malibu undergraduate founders to a grand total of 867. They came with the highest Scholastic Aptitude Test scores in Pepperdine history to that point, 20 percent of them above the 93rd percentile. In a ten-year 1976 to 1986 Seaver College academic miracle, the SAT scores soared another 160 points.[27]

The rising tide lifts all ships. The Church of Christ relationship soared. However, church undergraduate enrollment on the Los Angeles campus plummeted to an all-time low of 5 percent. Therefore, in 1970 Pepperdine commissioned a two-year campaign, led by the legendary four horsemen—George Hill, Bob Fraley, Silas Shotwell and Don Williams—to recruit the 1972 Malibu students from church congregations. Malibu opened with a precipitous leap in church students, reaching one-third of the 1972 freshman class. That remains the all-time Pepperdine record for Church of Christ student enrollment. One of the founding freshmen was Paul Long from Tarzana. Long was destined to follow Fraley and Hill in the admissions high trinity. Their combined service inspired more than 50 Pepperdine years. Recruiters maximized the government's "co-religionist category," legalizing admission and financial favoritism for Church of Christ students and faculty.

MAESTRO JERRY RUSHFORD

At a time when the world was falling in love with the Malibu campus, steps were taken to ensure that Church of Christ members would love it most. The annual Bible Lectures became the vehicle to ensure the deep church relationship. Having written my USC doctoral dissertation on the influence of the Abilene Christian College lectureship from 1906 to 1960, I knew how much the lectures meant to Pepperdine's church relationship. But the lectures were dying in Los Angeles and the 1957 series had been completely cancelled. They revived in Malibu under the historic direction of Dr. Jerry Rushford.

"When Pepperdine moved to Malibu in 1972," reported Dr. Rushford, "there was a renewal of interest in the Bible Lectures and they have grown in attendance every year since." Some people once saw Pepperdine as a worldly college that had moved far beyond its affiliation with Churches of Christ in corrupt California.[28] Some people now can scarcely believe that the world's largest annual assembly of Church of Christ members now occurs in California every spring with the Pepperdine Bible Lectures audience exceeding 5,000. This is tribute to 30 years of historic leadership by Dr. Jerry Rushford, the greatest lectureship director in the history of the American Restoration Movement.

For the first three Malibu miracle years, financial fear kept the faculty on the back burner with the flame turned low. If I replayed all Malibu miracle

Dr. Jerry Rushford has directed the Pepperdine Bible Lectures for nearly 30 years. Under his leadership this annual forum has earned a reputation as one of the finest lecture series in the nation.

During the Pepperdine Bible Lectures, the largest sessions are held in Firestone Fieldhouse. This photo shows an evening lecture in 1995.

miscalculations, that would rank high. In the replay, faculty would be featured with super salaries to match their super campus. But all is well that ends well. In 1974, I repented and launched the salary turnaround with a 25 percent pay increase. Salaries increased sharply thereafter throughout the balance of my presidency.[29]

1. James Smythe, personal interview with the author, January 16, 2004. The Banowsky Papers.
2. Candace Denise Jones, "White Flight? George Pepperdine College's Move to Malibu, 1965–1972" (master's thesis, Pepperdine University, 2003), 83.
3. William S. Banowsky, memorandum to Pepperdine Faculty, April 15, 1971. The Banowsky Papers.
4. Jones, *White Flight*, 84.
5. Richard T. Hughes, "Getting it Together: The Role of Cultural Diversity in a Christian University," in Steve Moore, ed., *The University Through the Eyes of Faith*, (Indianapolis: Light and Life Communications, 1998), 132.
6. Jones, *White Flight*, 84–85.
7. James Smythe, personal letter to the author, February 10, 2003. The Banowsky Papers.
8. Loyd Frashier, personal interview with the author, June 10, 2005. The Banowsky Papers.
9. James Smythe personal letter to the author, March 19, 2009. The Banowsky Papers. "We were expected to read the many latest seminal books and articles that had recently appeared for these courses. We were expected to provide private, individualized counseling for all students in upper or lower division, prepare texts, read and evaluate five or six term papers for all courses. Freshman English required evaluating 8 to 10 compositions per trimester for each student, including a major term paper for the second course. Most faculty had to have a second job to adequately support their families. When I received my PhD in 1955, I was eager to do serious research and publication. But teaching four freshman English Composition courses on top of two upper division courses made publishing impossible. What was true of me was true of the other teachers also. Any shortage of published scholarship resulted from the immeasurable demands to teach. Any atrophy in publication was compensated for by muscular growth in classroom instruction. We might have atrophied but it was the system that caused it."
10. *Pepperdine Graphic*, February 25, 1971, 1.
11. Richard H. Peairs, personal letter to Grover Goyne, March 25, 1971. The Banowsky Papers; "Program Features Banowsky," *Pepperdine Graphic*, February 25, 1971. This letter arrived on January 12, 1971: "You did a brilliant job on Firing Line and I want to thank you for it. How lucky Pepperdine is to have you! Yours faithfully, William F. Buckley Jr.—Bill." Mr. Buckley passed away in 2008.
12. William S. Banowsky, personal letter to Grover Goyne, May 10, 1971. The Banowsky Papers.
13. James Smythe, personal interview with the author, June 10, 2005. The Banowsky Papers.
14. Bill Henegar, personal memorandum to the author, April 16, 2009. The Banowsky Papers.
15. "Unfinished Business," *Pepperdine Graphic*, October 23, 1971, 1.
16. Andrew K. Benton, personal letter to the author, March 4, 2007. The Banowsky Papers.
17. Jones, *White Flight*, 87.
18. Ibid, 83.
19. James Smythe, personal memorandum to the author, March 4, 2009. The Banowsky Papers. "McCommas was a superior musician but, for purposes of stronger administration, President Banowsky asked me to add the Fine Arts to Humanities."
20. Dr. Davis is the acknowledged chaparral expert throughout the state of California.
21. "General Information: An Introduction," *Seaver College of Arts and Sciences Academic Catalog: 2008–09* (Malibu: Pepperdine University), 11–15. Except for the number of schools and students, the opening section, "History of the University," remains largely as written in 1972: "Pepperdine University is an independent, medium-sized university enrolling approximately 8,000 students in five colleges and schools . . . Pepperdine University maintains a relationship with the Churches of Christ, of which Mr. Pepperdine was a lifelong member. It was the founder's plan for the school to be nonsectarian and independent of ecclesiastical controls. Accordingly, faculty, administrators and members of the Board of Regents represent many religious backgrounds, and students of all races

and faiths are welcomed. It is the purpose of Pepperdine University to pursue the very highest academic standards within a context that celebrates and extends the Christian faith."

22. "Pepperdine Students Graduate, *Los Angeles Times*, December 5, 1972, 16. My close friend William French Smith, soon to become President Reagan's Attorney General, wrote me this January 3, 1973, note: "An extra copy of your *LA Times* editorial. But I hope you never leave Pepperdine. We need you here in the Republican Party."

23. "Sauce for Marcuse Is Sauce for ...," *Los Angeles Times*, March 30, 1970; William S. Banowsky, "Score One for Tolerance," *Los Angeles Times*, April 5, 1970. The Banowsky Papers.

24. Maurice Ethridge, personal letter to the author, April 7, 1970. The Banowsky Papers.

25. Maurice Ethridge, letter to the editor, *Los Angeles Times*, April 7, 1970, 16. The Banowsky Papers.

26. Howard A. White, personal letter to the author, April 6, 1970. The Banowsky Papers.

27. Jerry Rushford, ed., *Crest of a Golden Wave: Pepperdine University, 1937–1987* (Malibu: Pepperdine University Press, 1987), 163, 214.

28. Bill Henegar and Jerry Rushford, *Forever Young: The Life and Times of M. Norvel Young and Helen M. Young* (Nashville: 21st Century Christian, 1999), 138-139.

29. "Trustees Approve Faculty Pay Hike," *Pepperdine News*, February 1974, 10. "According to Dr. Howard A. White, executive vice president, full-time faculty on the Los Angeles and Malibu campuses will receive 25 percent salary increase during the fall and winter trimesters."

"Pepperdine's plans for a 125-foot tower, atop its most prominent mountain 350 feet above sea level, with a lighted 50-foot-high indention of the cross of Christ, will offend many Malibu residents."

ALVIN S. KAUFER
Malibu Homeowners' Association, 1972

"IT'S NO OIL DERRICK!"

The steel fabrication for the Cross Theme Tower that defines Pepperdine University architecturally was erected over one frantic weekend in late May 1972, only one-half step ahead of Malibu protestors.

CHAPTER 15

THE THEME TOWER CONTROVERSY

The Bible calls the cross "an offensive stumbling block" and that's the way it seemed to some Malibu neighbors when Pepperdine built its Cross Theme Tower.[1]

This is the story of the Malibu miracle's 40-year fight to build and defend the Theme Tower that defines Pepperdine architecturally. All battles of my presidency, but this one, ended decades ago. This one won't go away. Four decades later irate e-mails come from students, unborn at the time of the original controversy, but disgusted with me for "turning off the cross lights— forever." I plead innocent to the "forever" charge.

Master architect William L. Pereira completed the working drawings for the Theme Tower in March 1972. A tough two years later, May 7, 1974, the completed tower was dedicated. Through the years, just as one chief opponent, Alvin S. Kaufer, predicted, it has offended many Malibu residents. But it has thrilled many more and the good fight keeps on fighting.

"LET YOUR LIGHT SHINE"

The battle broke out in 1972 when shocked neighbors living in the celebrity Malibu Colony beachfront community below the campus saw Pereira's tower plans. Their response was, "It will be an intrusive sectarian symbol, a brightly lit ecological offense towering over our homes at night."[2] After figuratively, and perhaps sometimes literally, choking in three years of silence on Pepperdine construction dust, the big cross was the last straw for some neighbors. April 1, 1972, the Malibu Homeowners' Association filed for a temporary restraining order in California state court. If successful, it would delay or even derail the Theme Tower.

Sensing imminent danger, I cut a quick deal with the Malibu Homeowners' Association to get the tower built. The purely personal, one-sentence verbal statement empowered Pepperdine to build the tower without hindrance. In the bitter pill for Pepperdine generations to swallow, I agreed "not to light the cross at night *during my presidency*."[3]

I proposed a temporary "during my presidency" gesture to get the tower built. Somehow, that statement was transmuted into permanent Pepperdine policy. The truth about the tower got garbled. Some students suspected me of making an outer darkness deal with the devil, citing as sad proof decades of darkness since my presidency. "To get the tower built, Banowsky turned off the lights forever,"[4] they said. Occasionally at Pepperdine, all heaven breaks loose as some disheartened students march forth chanting: "'You are the light of the world. A city on a hill cannot be hidden. Neither do people light a lamp and put it under a bowl. Instead they put it on its stand, and it gives light to everyone in the house. In the same way, let your light shine before men, that they may see your good deeds and praise your Father in heaven.'"[5]

OBELISK VERSUS CROSS

Winding the clock back a bit, the Theme Tower controversy didn't begin among our neighbors. A preliminary bout broke out between the architect, Bill Pereira, and me; it was the only design dispute our close partnership permitted. Pereira and I were in such close agreement on design that our colleagues deferred to "the two Bills." But what happens when the two Bills can't decide? Pereira and I were irreconcilably committed to incompatibly different visions for the tower. The conflict was simple. I wanted the traditional cross. Pereira wanted the classical obelisk.

We agreed on other details. As for location, it must indeed "rise from atop the most prominent mountain, anchoring the central Seaver Drive entrance and commanding the coastline for miles around." We agreed on its 125-foot height. "The famous cross soaring over Rio is 125 feet tall and that's the perfect height for us," said Pereira matter of factly.[6] But at that point, our gentleman's agreement ended.

Pereira owed his Pepperdine job to my intervention. Norvel Young pushed hard for Pereira's ex-partner, Charles Luckman, to be the campus master architect.[7] Pereira appreciated my total support. We grew close. The beauty of the Malibu campus reflects the chemistry of our companionship. We had only one design disagreement. It was this architectural doozy, this head-on collision between the obelisk and the cross, two anciently revered religious symbols.

THREE BANOWSKY BOYS

At the 1972 ground breaking for the Cross Theme Tower, three Banowsky boys led the way. Bill Jr. directs on the left. On the right, Britton and David hold aloft the Pereira tower rendering.

Since the 1968 Malibu land gift I had dreamed of anchoring Pepperdine to the cross of Christ as the symbol of Pepperdine's core mission commitment. There was never a cross of any kind on the old campus. But now we were perfecting everything. With several crosses already adorning the hills around Los Angeles, I dreamed of lifting up in the Malibu hills the tallest Southern California cross of all. I envisioned, of course, the traditional cross of Christ with a rigid upright beam traversed by a perfectly matching horizontal bar.

But Pereira dreamed of building the more innocuous religious symbol that soared above Egyptian, Greek and Roman cities of antiquity. Fabled architects usually arrive for work with artistic visions already ensconced in their minds, and Pereira arrived at Pepperdine loving the obelisk so much he felt foreordained to build one on our campus. A simple monolithic pillar tapering into a sharp pyramid at the top, it was the Washington Monument all over again. Pepperdine University would enshrine the cross of Christ as its timeless symbol only by first defeating Pereira's hallowed obelisk.

Pereira yearned to build his Pepperdine obelisk before I knew what one was. He praised it as the vertical complement to his horizontal buildings. He praised its shape and height and glorious history. I answered that the cross complemented his buildings in ideal verticality and height with a more glorious history.

Pereira loved the cross, too. He resisted its architectural exploitation. A practicing Italian Catholic who wore a gold cross dangling round his neck, Pereira said, "Bill, I hate this commercialization."

With the cross and obelisk locked into a collision course, I leveled with Pereira. "Bill, everybody's voted. Nobody wants the Washington Monument on our campus."

The head-shaking Pereira countered, "Bill, I took my own vote. I don't want a huge literal cross of Christ on my professional reputation."

"Bill," I said, "an obelisk is too trite for a theme."

"Bill," Pereira said, "nothing's more trite than the cross."

SOMETHING SYMBOLIC

Pereira, a big man in spirit, astonished me by magnanimously terminating the Theme Tower debate. Deferring to my love for the cross he unconditionally surrendered his obelisk—almost.

"OK, Bill," he concluded. "I'm going to design a cross. But I'm not sure yet what it ought to look like. Let me play with it a few days. There's hostility to a literal cross. I'd like to soften it up around the edges. If I can't come up with something symbolic, my friends in the Colony may go berserk!"

"Symbolic" sounded "New Age" to me, and I shuddered. I wanted the literal cross, not some fuzzed-up version. Reassuring me, Pereira went to work doing what he did best.

The triumphant call came at 5:30 a.m. on April Fool's Day—Saturday, April 1, 1972. "Bill, I've found it!" Pereira's call woke Gay and me. He had worked for three days in his bathrobe to create the now-celebrated Pereira compromise. In inspirational simplicity, Pereira produced a tapering tower with neither pyramidic top nor crossing horizontal bar. It was actually two towers joined by the cross. Each tower, vertical on the inside, tapered on the outside to a soaring pyramidic top. It was a stylized obelisk split down the center and connected by the cross of Christ. The 125-foot tower featured a 50-foot indention of the cross subtly highlighted with tiles and lights. A masterful merging of the classic symbol with the Christian cross, Pereira's design quickly became Pepperdine's global signature.

In postlogue, Pereira acquiesced to my love of the cross without forsaking his obelisk. He kept on searching for the perfect place to put it. He soon found it. Within months William L. Pereira and Associates designed the world-famous Transamerica Tower, its pyramidic obelisk jutting out high above the city of San Francisco skyline.

Today, jutting out high above the Malibu skyline, is Pereira's obelisk-like Cross Theme Tower. You'd think, after four decades, the ruckus it caused going up would have died down, maybe even reached a statute of limitations. But, conceived in conflict and born in pain, the fight lives on. It episodically flares. The *Los Angeles Times* headlined a recent flare-up, "Support for Lighted Cross Rekindles an Old Debate."[8] It's an old debate filled with hogwash.

"THE CROSS WILL NEVER SHINE"

"In 1973, when the tower was completed," the *Los Angeles Times* printed, without proof, "then Pepperdine president William S. Banowsky promised Malibu residents that the cross would never shine as originally planned. It now stands, not as a beacon, but as a landmark with only the sound of electric bells chiming every half hour."[9] Hogwash.

The *Los Angeles Times* account missed, by a full year, the date of the community showdown that cut the deal to build the tower. The showdown did not come "in 1973 when the tower was completed," as the *Los Angeles Times* said. The showdown came in March 1972, so that tower construction could begin. The newspaper produced no evidence of me ever saying, "the cross will never shine as originally planned." I never said it. Some said, most

WIRED FOR LIGHTS!!!

Forty years after its construction came incontrovertible proof that the Cross Theme Tower was originally wired to be lit. In 2009, Pepperdine student Paul Volcheff took these actual photographs of the wiring from inside the tower itself.

lately, that the deal I cut left all wiring for lights out of the tower construction. These very recent images prove them wrong.

Idealistic students have now come to believe that I agreed to turn the lights off forever. They counterattack against the darkness. They flash the Pepperdine seal—its brightly lit beams of heavenly light emanating from the cross—on their computer websites, their coffee mugs and their T-shirts. In 1972 I commissioned Bill Henegar to create the official university seal. "The radiating lines from the Theme Tower," explained Henegar, "were not intended to symbolize the spirituality of the physical tower itself but the spiritual influence of the Pepperdine people."[10] The Pepperdine people now prick the press to produce tower hogwash. "In fact," said President Andrew K. Benton, "student efforts to light the cross pop up about every three months."[11]

After 40 years of marriage, the Malibu community accords its university high respect. It was not always so. Pepperdine was not invited to town by boosters building a bigger Malibu. Pepperdine certainly enjoyed, from the earliest hour, the brilliant support of Malibu pioneers Judge John J. Merrick, Frank Morgan Sr., Pierce Sherman, Jack Carrodi, Reverend Walter Gerber, James Praino, Dr. Herbert Snow and others. But, except for one exclusive family's land gift, Pepperdine arrived uninvited and under widespread suspicion. "The values and character of the campus do not mesh that well with those of the community," concluded the academic observers of the day. Since the days of silent movies, Malibu meant serenity, privacy, no more cars on the highway, and no more construction in the hills. Malibuites threw no Pepperdine welcoming party. When they saw what we were up to, suspicion turned to resistance. They saw bulldozing of coastal land, decapitation of ocean hills, dynamiting of rock and soil, obliteration of trails for hiking and riding. They saw, where mountains stood sentinel for centuries, sudden open spaces being filled with man-made things. The final offense was the asphalt flowing to cover the ugly cuts so cars could claim the hills.

For ecologically traumatized Malibuites, the tower added to the environmental war a battle of "political correctness." Since 1954 the San Diego city council has been in and out of federal court to save the 43-foot cross atop Mt. Soledad. In 2004 the Los Angeles County board of supervisors abandoned the gold cross that adorned the county's seal for a half century. In 2006 the president of William and Mary College caught holy hades for diminishing the place of the chapel cross "out of respect for our many students who are Jews, Hindus, Muslims or Buddhists." The Christian students and alumni told him "to put it back where it belongs." So it goes for the emblem of suffering and shame.[12]

Pereira did, indeed, come up "with something softer, something symbolic," as he said. But it failed to placate his "friends in the Colony." They first understood its full size, shape and symbolism on March 4, 1972, when Pepperdine had to first go public before the Regional Planning Commission in Long Beach. We did our homework and, on an 11–0 favorable vote, we proceeded on to the county supervisors' Friday public meeting to pick up the permit. We anticipated, of course, the usual Pepperdine 3–2 vote. That's when some of Pereira's Colony friends did, indeed, finally "go berserk."

ALVIN KAUFER AND MARCA HELFRICK

It was a messy early-1970s open neighborhood fight. "Rumors still persist," the *Graphic* awkwardly speculated, "that Barbra Streisand is to blame for complaining about the lights."[13] Finally, in 2006, the *Los Angeles Times* got on track. It correctly commemorated Alvin S. Kaufer as "the prominent Malibu attorney who spearheaded the original fight against the theme tower in the 1970s."

Kaufer took up the fight "because of the offense to a substantial number of Malibu residents of a big cross looking out over the coastline." Kaufer candidly confessed to the *Graphic*: "I don't object to the cross symbol itself. I don't mind the small cross on the hill across the street between Webster School and Our Lady of Malibu church. But this large cross out on the campus hill on the big tower will be a real serious imposition for some people."[14]

Kaufer strengthened his hand by recruiting community leader Marca Helfrick to serve as co-chair of the organization to defeat the tower. Marca, president of the Malibu Homeowners' Association, had been my personal friend. "Helfrick's homeowners' group," reported the *Graphic*, "had worked closely as Dr. Banowsky's advisory council."[15]

For the tower fight Marca defected to Kaufer. The separate reasons these two leaders listed for opposing the tower mirrored the two community complaints. For Kaufer, a Jewish Democrat, it was the cross, as we have seen. For Helfrick, a Protestant Republican, it was aesthetic. "The tower was out of context with the surrounding countryside," she grumbled to the *Graphic*. "The tower was supposed to be 'nestled in the hills,' not jutting out from them!"[16]

MALIBU LEADER ZIFFREN

Paul Ziffren of Ziffren and Ziffren, a downtown Los Angeles firm, was another unique community leader. Paul, my Malibu-Colony Jewish friend, kept me informed on community activities and attitudes. Prior to the incorporation of the city of Malibu, the Malibu Chamber of Commerce was the highest civic authority. Paul and I were fellow directors. We bonded locally but also filled similar political positions nationally. Paul was the Democratic National Committeeman from California. I was the Republican National Committeeman from California.

Paul's wife, Mickey, and Gay were close friends. All four of us traveled together as guests of Israel for ten days in the Holy Land. When Republican patron Asa Call died, Democrat patron Paul served as a pallbearer. "Dear Paul," I scribbled in a note, "Seeing you as Asa's pallbearer reminded me again how much you constantly do to break down religious and political barriers. Sincerely, Bill."[17]

On weekends, Paul and I walked and talked along the Colony beach. "Bill," he warned me with every huffing, sandy step, "there's a growing group going public against the tower. They're searching for some sympathetic state judge to hear their case and grant a temporary restraining order to halt construction." Thanks to Paul Ziffren's covert coaching, Pepperdine eased quietly out ahead of the restraining order, quickly secured the permit and immediately constructed the tower.

But that begs the question as to how Pepperdine achieved such political development dominance. How did Pepperdine so readily prevail against such formidable odds? How did Pepperdine surf through 36 months of unfettered regulatory freedom to build its Malibu campus without any denial or delay? The short answer is that for a miraculous four-year window of opportunity— 1969 through 1972—Pepperdine formed a dynamic partnership with the building department of Los Angeles County. We had the law on our side.

MALIBU POLITICAL MAGIC

Pepperdine built its campus in a Malibu power vacuum. The coastal area had not yet been incorporated into a city. The "non-city" of Malibu was almost like an exciting taste of the old Wild West. Malibu had been "an unincorporated area of Los Angeles County" forever. Cityhood did not come until 1990; therefore, Pepperdine faced no municipal construction politics but, instead, looked only to Los Angeles County for essential approvals.

In addition to the local vacuum, Pepperdine's political fortunes doubled with the second California vacuum, created by the absence of any statewide coastline control. The newly created California Coastal Commission assumed environmental regulatory control of the campus a mere 60 days after the campus opened in 1972. Pepperdine built its campus in a governing gap without any interference from either the non-city-of-Malibu or the nonexistent California Coastal Commission. Built at the far edge of the county, above local but below state power, there were no municipal watchdogs

BEAUTIFUL AND BRIGHTLY LIT

The Cross Theme Tower holds the commanding position above the world-famous Malibu Movie
Colony. The twinkling lights of the Colony Beach are seen on the right side of the tower.

and no California cops. The Malibu miracle was a miracle of unfettered construction freedom.

In the unincorporated Malibu area, construction of any kind was supervised by "the County of Los Angeles, Department of Building and Safety, Coleman W. Jenkins, Superintendent." Mr. Jenkins and his people facilitated Pepperdine's project, from start to finish, by approving permits and executing inspections without the advice or consent of anybody but their supervisorial superiors. Construction codes in those pro-growth days tended to enable rather than restrict. "These county codes are enforced," as Jack Eiden put it, "by good-ole-boy-bureaucrats with little interest in preserving possums and none in protecting tree huggers."[18] Hard-hat conservative Democrats who ran construction in the county loved Pepperdine, and Pepperdine loved them. For 36 months, in a heavenly marriage, the county approved hundreds of separate Pepperdine permits one at a time and denied none.

The building department reported straight up to the powerful board of five elected Los Angeles County supervisors. Any construction controversy unsettled at the departmental level was simply bounced forward for resolution at the regular Friday public meeting of the supervisors. Approval of any contested issue required but three supervisorial votes. During the months of Malibu campus construction, the building department officials had disagreed among themselves on but three minor construction issues. Those little issues were quickly approved by three-to-two supervisorial votes. For all practical purposes, from 1968 through 1972, Pepperdine could build whatever it pleased, whenever it pleased.

SUPERVISOR KENNY HAHN

Pepperdine controlled the construction of its Malibu campus because of its unique influence with the Los Angeles County board of supervisors. A win took three votes and there was absolutely nothing nefarious about it. Three supervisors loved Pepperdine with passionate support. Warren Dorn, of the First Supervisorial District, was a Reagan Republican and Norvel Young's good friend for 40 years. My friend, Burton Chase, was a Reagan Republican who represented the Fourth District, including "the unincorporated area of Malibu."

The third guarantor of Pepperdine's Los Angeles County political power was a partisan Democrat. He automatically lined up with his two Democrat colleagues, Supervisor Bonelli and Supervisor Debs, to defeat beleaguered Republicans Chase and Dorn. He automatically lined up, that is, unless it was a Pepperdine vote. This moderate Democrat was the dear and faithful Pepperdine alumnus, Supervisor Kenneth H. Hahn. He always voted with

Chase and Dorn when it came to a concern for Pepperdine.[19] As Kenny's charismatic daughter Janice put it, "Daddy's the Pepperdine poster boy!"

Kenny Hahn grew up in the First Christian Church near Pepperdine's Los Angeles campus. His widowed mother, with seven sons, couldn't afford tuition. Kenny paid his way through Pepperdine raking leaves and cleaning toilets. After 1944 graduation and naval officer service, he returned to teach at Pepperdine. He was soon elected youngest city councilman in Los Angeles history. Then he was elected youngest supervisor in Los Angeles County history and served his mostly African-American Second Supervisorial District for 40 years. His brother, Gordon, and daughter, Janice, also served on the city council. His son, James K. Hahn, with undergraduate and law degrees from Pepperdine, served from 2000 to 2005 as the mayor of Los Angeles. The whole Hahn family, always at the heart of Los Angeles public service, was also at the heart of the Malibu miracle.

Interestingly, Pepperdine's fortuitous partnership with Los Angeles County was forged in the friendship of two of the miracle's main men— Kenneth H. Hahn and Frank Roger Seaver. Astonishingly, Mr. Seaver preceded Mr. Hahn as an elected Los Angeles County supervisor by half a century. At the age of 29 in 1912, Frank was elected to the county office Kenny now held. Frank Seaver was now Kenny Hahn's most fabled constituent and the two former naval officers grew close.

"Back at Pomona College," reminisced Frank in 1960, "the great Theodore Roosevelt spoke on campus. He inspired me to try for a career in politics. Well, I tried. I ran for the state legislature. I was defeated. Then I ran for the Board of Freeholders of Los Angeles County, what we now call the supervisors. I was elected. We drafted the county charter. It's still in use today and amended very little."[20]

In 1958 Kenny appointed Frank Seaver, the lone surviving Los Angeles County founder, to lead the Citizens' Charter Revision Committee. After meeting eight months with no charter changes, the committee commended Frank's founding authorship and adjourned. Four years later in 1962, on the county's fiftieth anniversary, Hahn honored Mr. and Mrs. Seaver with a caravan of vintage 1912 open cars touring from the Seaver home at Chester Place to the Los Angeles County Hall of Administration. Kenny soon encouraged Frank to make his first modest Pepperdine gift. "Kenny's responsible for Mr. Seaver's early interest," reported Archivist Smythe. "Kenny influenced him to remember Pepperdine modestly in his 1964 will. That later helped to inspire Mrs. Seaver to give her entire fortune."[21] At the Malibu ceremony to commence construction in April of 1971, Supervisor Hahn, along with pioneering space scientist Wernher von Braun, was a principal speaker.

Even with Kenny in Pepperdine's corner, the Cross Theme Tower fight turned ugly. On those three previously contested building permits Pepperdine played the Hahn trump card three straight times, three biting defections from his Democrat duty that angered many Malibuites. "This time," warned friend Ziffren, "they'll make Hahn eat his trump card. They plan to bypass Hahn and the county board altogether and go into state court for a temporary restraining order. They want to halt construction and buy precious time to beat the tower permanently."[22]

A temporary restraining order was the silver bullet Pepperdine dreaded. Relatively easy to obtain, it halted work while lawyers scrambled for a permanent injunction. An injunction would require Pepperdine to spend months, if not years, overcoming an avalanche of brand-new environmental laws.

It was time for political diplomacy. On Monday, May 15, 1972, Norvel Young and I picked up Pepperdine Spanish professor Bill Stivers. The three of us drove to downtown Los Angeles for a meeting in Supervisor Hahn's office. Bill Stivers, Kenny's best friend, served from 1952 to 1962 as Kenny's chief deputy. Bill knew where the bodies were buried. If Norvel and I expected a difficult meeting with Kenny we took Bill with us. Harry Marlow, another proud Pepperdine product, who replaced Stivers as Hahn's chief deputy, escorted us into the inner office. Ever-ebullient Supervisor Hahn sat all us old Pepperdiners down around his conference table to plan Theme Tower strategy.

"Kenny, we've got to get our tower built before our opponents can talk some friendly judge into giving them a restraining order," I opened. "And we're down now to a few days."

"Well, Bill, I can call Warren and Burton today and nail down three votes for the tower on Friday's agenda," replied Kenny. "But obviously, that would be a big tactical mistake. When we approve it the Malibu people will see it and shoot and kill it before you guys can get it built. You say it's a fast job? Great. This is one of the very fastest jobs when we must both simultaneously approve it while also building it. So just how soon can you boys start?"

"Kenny, we're building it right now!" I blurted. "At this very moment, the total prefabrication is being finished out at the Riverside Steel Company. Next week we're trucking all of the parts and pieces to Malibu after midnight. The prefabrication will be screened from passers-by. It will be stowed on Seaver Drive as it bends through Winter Canyon behind the tower hill. The parts and pieces will be assembled on the ground into 12 sections. The sections will go up fast, in one day, one section bolted on top of another all the way to the very top. In five days it'll be covered with a thick masonry finish and look just like all of Pereira's other buildings only be hollow inside."

"You don't mean it!" Kenny said, shaking his head admiringly.

"Yeah, we do mean it, Kenny!" affirmed Norvel. "It's Pereira's ingeniously lightweight design, real strong, maintenance free and absolutely beautiful. Most crucially, it'll go up real fast."

"Well then," enthused Kenny, "let's get it up!"

"To get out ahead of the restraining order," I revealed, "we've got to go next weekend. Kenny, can you put the Theme Tower on the supervisors' agenda a week from Friday? If so, at midnight on that very same Friday we'll truck the prefabrication from Riverside to Malibu and work all weekend under floodlights to send it up 125 feet. Once the frame's up we'll perfect the tile, the masonry and the lighting at leisure."

"OK, boys," concluded Kenny with a broad smile and slap of the conference table. "It's a done deal!"

NO LIGHTS OR LITIGATION

As Norvel Young and Bill Stivers headed for the door, I lingered for a final favor. "Kenny, I'm sorry but I have a shocker for you. We can't erect the tower until we can first excavate and pour several tons of concrete to install the underground foundation. It must go down 20 feet deep before we can move the steel on top of it. But, Kenny," I said, gulping hard, "we've got no foundation permit. We didn't want to start a war by advertising a request for the foundation permit on your public agenda. The foundation permit is now set for your agenda a week from Friday, right alongside the tower permit itself. But, obviously, we can't wait that long to lay the foundation. Kenny, we've got to start digging it today."

"No problem, Bill," Kenny replied. "Go right ahead. The supervisors often initiate big projects with 'foundation only' permits when the building itself must yet be permitted. I'll file the paperwork and nobody'll notice 'til the tower goes up. By then you'll have in hand both of your legal permits that the board will approve a week from Friday, one for the foundation and one for the tower."

The foundation went down quickly on Wednesday. On Friday, May 26, 1972, by two separate three-to-two votes, the supervisors approved both the foundation installation and the tower construction. Assembly and erection of the fabrication went without a hitch. Climaxing a tranquil Malibu weekend, Monday's sun rose over the Santa Monica Mountains at 6:47 a.m., illuminating the prefabricated steel. Standing in stark 125-foot-tall nakedness, as Pereira predicted, it did roughly resemble a poor man's Eiffel Tower.

MALIBU COMMUNITY SHOWDOWN

The phone woke Gay and me at 5:00 a.m. Monday morning. Paul Ziffren was up early to warn us that our neighbors, with steel in their faces, plotted maximum revenge. "Bill, they'll be filing the first lawsuit against you today," he said. "They're demanding the dismantling of the steel fabrication, charging it was bootlegged into Malibu illegally over the weekend to evade appropriate governmental jurisdiction. This is Monday, Bill. It's possible they'll have a temporary restraining order by Friday. You'll countersue, of course, but it'll take six months to get your campus back on track, if ever."

Paul paused. The phone fell silent. I felt sick. I could picture on Pepperdine's main hill an ugly unfinished frame, rusting for months—or years—in shameful remembrance of bitter defeat. "OK, Paul, you've got my attention. Tell me what to do," I answered.

"Meet with them, Bill," Paul shot back. "Some of these people may not like you, but they respect you. There's nothing like talking. Get together with the whole group, face-to-face, as soon as possible."

"Paul," I pushed back. "When can 'as soon as possible' be?"

"Three days," he replied. "I'll get a big crowd together for a community meeting at the Malibu Civic Center at 7:30 Wednesday evening. You and I can meet Wednesday afternoon to prepare."

When Wednesday came, Paul and I talked for two hours. His promotion and organization of the meeting had gone well and he expected a big crowd. He described some key personalities expected to attend and anticipated for me some of their key questions. It was then, for the first time, that the question of lights on the cross was put forth. Paul spent ten minutes telling me to get ready to make a quick deal with the community to keep the lights turned off in the cross at night, "for a while." It didn't sound like a big deal. "OK, Paul," I agreed as we walked together across the Brock House bridge. "I'll see you down below at the Civic Center in a couple hours."

With neither notes nor aides, I went alone to the meeting. A hundred people filled the room, for two hours of sometimes harsh criticism and many questions. Mostly, I just listened. Finally, from the far-right corner came the quintessential question for which Paul had prepared me.

"President Banowsky, if we were willing to drop litigation would you be willing not to light the cross at night?"

I paused. I looked around. There were no reporters or tape recorders. No recording secretary compiled any minutes or notes of the meeting. I put nothing in writing before, during or after the meeting. All discussion was purely extemporaneous, off-the-cuff, no notes, nothing. No media stories were ever filed about anything with respect to that meeting.

So there I stood in front of our community, thinking: "He who hesitates is lost." I stood there knowing that if we slowed construction we would be stopped. If we were stopped we might never get started again. On the other hand, we could build the tower with my personal decision "not to light it at night during my presidency." I felt called to get the tower built—not to get it lit. I didn't have the authority to create long-term policy and I didn't consult the board. I called no faculty meeting. "My successors," I naively imagined, "could freely light the cross later."

"Yes!" I answered loudly. "I agree not to light the cross at night *during my presidency*."

The meeting was instantly over; it was a wise and safe way to conclude bitter community controversy and construct the tower. "Banowsky's promise," the *Graphic* reported, "satisfied the surrounding property owners who had complained that the cross was a religious imposition to the people who live here."[23] The property owners were satisfied. The lights were not lit. Both armies retreated from the battlefield. All guns fell silent except for occasional potshots exchanged with Pepperdine students. As mute evidence that the lights were not forever extinguished, Pepperdine built its tower with the Pereira-designed lighting system intact. The Morrow Meadows Corporation won the electrical bid and installed the lights.

According to the university's public information office, the tower lights have been turned on from time to time at the pleasure of the administration. "Some years after the building of the tower," said Lyric Hassler, Pepperdine senior public relations advisor, "and after senior administration of the university had changed around a bit, and new individuals took on new posts, the university began to light the tower."[24] If so, it soon went dark again but Hassler insists it has been lit.

ALVIN AND MARCA EVER AFTER

"The enthusiasm of students is sweet, it is thoughtful and it reflects the great joy of my work. But should we light the tower?" President Benton probes with consummate balance. "I still don't know. Is our message conveyed clearer? I don't think it takes a neon-lit cross to strengthen our outreach."[25]

Frankly, President Benton, I don't think so either. Sensitivities in our neighborhood matter more than lights on our campus. After all these years I argue not that the cross *should* be lit, only that it *could* be lit.

Do you remember Alvin Kaufer and Marca Helfrick, who met in 1972 when they partnered to oppose the tower? Well, guess what? They married at the ocean a year later in 1973, and lived in Malibu bliss for 30 years, until

Alvin's 2005 death. About the fight, the classy Marca conceded to the campus newspaper, "I don't think I'd do all that over again."

I'm tempted to answer, "Yes, Marca. I don't think I'd do all that over again either." But then, again, "I really wanted it there at the time," as I told the *Los Angeles Times* in 1976. "I wanted people to know the kind of place this is."[26]

1. Matthew 11:6; Luke 7:23; Romans 9:33; I Corinthians 1:23; Galatians 5:11.
2. Paul Ziffren, personal letter to the author, June 16, 1972. The Banowsky Papers.
3. No media or other authorities have called once to question me about the veracity of that statement that has stood unchallenged. My promise was limited to my presidency, period.
4. Kaitlin Flynn, personal interview with the author, January 6, 2008. The Banowsky Papers.
5. Matthew 5:14–16 (NIV).
6. William L. Pereira, personal memorandum to the author, March 14, 1971. The Banowsky Papers.
7. Bill Henegar and Jerry Rushford, *Forever Young: The Life and Times of M. Norvel Young and Helen M. Young* (Nashville: 21st Century Christian, 1999), 206.
8. Lynn Doan, *Los Angeles Times*, July 1, 2006, 12.
9. Ibid.
10. Bill Henegar, personal letter to the author, February 1, 2009. The Banowsky Papers.
11. Lynn Doan, *Los Angeles Times*, July 1, 2006, 12.
12. George S. Gibson, *National Review*, October 24, 2006, 21.
13. Kaitlin Flynn, "Tower Remains Dark; Debate Persists," *Pepperdine Graphic*, April 2, 1973, 1.
14. Chris Parker, "Theme Tower Controversy Cools," *Pepperdine Graphic*, April 2, 1973, 1.
15. Ibid.
16. Ibid.
17. William S. Banowsky, personal letter to Paul Ziffren, July 19, 1978. The Banowsky Papers.
18. Jack Eiden, The Eiden Papers, March 20, 1973. The Banowsky Papers.
19. Pepperdine conferred an honorary doctor of laws degree on Hahn on October 1, 1971. Kenneth Hahn served as a Los Angeles County supervisor for 40 years, from 1952 until 1992. He died October 12, 1997. Burton W. Chase served from 1953 until 1973 and Warren M. Dorn served from 1956 until 1973. Chase was replaced by James A. Heaps and Dorn by Baxter Ward. "Los Angeles Board of Supervisors," Wikipedia Web site, http://en.wikipedia.org/wiki/Los_Angeles_County_Board_of_Supervisors (accessed September 20, 2009).
20. Jane Werner Watson, *The Seaver Story*, (Claremont, CA: Pomona College Press, 1960), 21–22.
21. James Smythe, personal interview with the author, August 5, 2005. The Banowsky Papers.
22. See note 2 above.
23. See note 15 above.
24. Lyric Hassler, e-mail to Kaitlin Flynn, March 4, 2007.
25. See note 8 above.
26. Bill Trombley, "Pepperdine Torn by Dissension," *Los Angeles Times*, April 18, 1976, 12.

SOUNDS OF SILENCE

Surveying Seaver College, from the Brock House deck, Blanche and Bill enjoy a quiet
Malibu sunset. They may also be saying a little prayer that the sewage disposal crisis
will not close the campus.

CHAPTER 16

THE MALIBU SEWER WARS

After the Cross Theme Tower controversy, Pepperdine faced one final Malibu campus construction fight. But it was a big one.

Campus completion got caught in the crossfire of the 100-year war to keep a public sewer system of any kind whatsoever out of Malibu forever!

"NO SEWER HERE!"

Today, Malibu is probably the most sophisticated place left on the planet without any public sewage disposal system, and that's no accident. A century of vigilance guaranteed it. Malibuites were among America's earliest environmentalists. Fifty years before ecologists became ubiquitous, Malibuites were national no-growth leaders. The 1950s popularized handwritten Pacific Coast Highway signs from Santa Monica to Oxnard proclaiming: Small is Beautiful! Less is More! Not in My Backyard! No Sewer Here![1]

By the late 1960s, when Pepperdine built its campus, "prohibition of a Malibu public sewer had become a left-coast extreme but highly effective anti-development strategy."[2] The entrenched antidevelopment policy required residences and businesses along the 27-mile Malibu coast-line to install private cesspools or septic tanks. It was a desperate strategy. Septic tanks clogged, cesspools overflowed, smelly trucks pumping thousands of toilets hindered highway traffic. Nonetheless, Malibuites preferred the disadvantages of no public sewer to the disasters of population growth, construction dust or highway traffic. The sewer wars continue today. In 2009, the California Coastal Commission filed suit to coerce the city of Malibu to construct a public sewer. This will be a ten-year battle. But, way back in the late 1960s, what would Pepperdine possibly do to install a campus sewer system by September 6, 1972?

We have seen, in 1968, the site-selection fight that broke out over the exorbitant cost of Malibu development, with Norvel and me on one side and the board of trustees on the other. The monumental site-preparation costs panicked the trustees into voting unanimously to reject the Adamson offer of Malibu land. "The 15 members of the board of trustees finally met to decide the future direction of undergraduate study at Pepperdine. After much discussion," recorded Henegar and Rushford, "they decided to decline the offer of the Malibu property." In addition to the absence of any sewer, trustees believed that "the College simply did not have the money to invest in moving the thousands of tons of earth to build on the hillsides."[3]

Norvel and I worked with the board to raise $3 million. We captured the Malibu land and readily connected the emerging campus to gas, water and electricity. Fresh water, for instance, went in wonderfully. William L. Pereira designed, and Chicago Bridge and Iron Company built, a two-million-gallon reservoir atop the highest campus mountain. Fresh water was continuously pumped up from the coast highway. It kept the reservoir full and it flowed down, under perfect pressure, to serve the entire campus. The water solution proved perfect. Any sewer solution seemed hopeless.

KENNY TO THE RESCUE

In May 1971, Norvel and I sought sewer counsel from Los Angeles County supervisor Kenneth H. Hahn. As earlier stated, for all sensitive meetings Norvel and I included Kenny's best friend and former chief deputy, Bill Stivers.

"Kenny," I opened, as the four of us settled in around his conference table. "After all our Malibu progress we've run into an insurmountable problem. We have no sewer and no way to get one. School opens in less than a year. We'll never get a certificate of occupancy. We can't flush our commodes. Kenny, tell us what to do."

"OK, boys," Kenny consoled. "The county's way ahead of you. We're announcing our modern Malibu sewer system next month. Congratulations, your timing's perfect!" Norvel, Bill Stivers and I floated out of Kenny's office on sewer cloud number nine. But within weeks came the official public announcement: "To solve the sewer problem Los Angeles County will construct a modern sewage disposal system throughout all of Malibu. The bonds to authorize funds for sewer construction will require a majority vote of Malibu residents on election day, November 4, 1971."[4]

Pepperdine was ecstatic. The public sewer, perfectly timed to solve the last problem, was the answer to Pepperdine prayers. Then came the election-day shock. The Malibu voters, in no mood to answer Pepperdine's prayers, buried the sewer referendum in a landslide. That was only shock number one. "No Sewer Here" had triumphed once again.

Pepperdine turned, desperately, to plan two.

TRUCKING TO TAPIA

Prior to pinning all its hope on the public referendum, Pepperdine agreed to joint-venture, if necessary, a shared private sewer system with the adjacent housing developer, Alcoa. The Alcoa option suddenly accelerated as Pepperdine shifted its sewer hopes from politics to free enterprise. Then came shock number two. Three weeks following the failed public referendum Alcoa horrified Pepperdine by abruptly withdrawing from the joint-venture sewer agreement. Alcoa's planned custom houses, also facing fierce community opposition, were selling slowly. "We have decided to wait a little longer on our shared sewer system," tersely wrote Alcoa's lawyer.[5] But Pepperdine couldn't wait and, therefore, turned to plan three.

Diving deeply into Malibu's hallowed tradition, for two months we wrestled with the draconian solution of constructing 26 scattered septic tanks to serve separate campus bathrooms and kitchens. The more we examined that option the more bizarre it grew. We couldn't build and pump and truck sewage from 26 scattered septic tanks in constant need of repair. What, then, *could* we do? We turned to plan four.

Robert Wood, the young Topodynamics architect and engineer on our construction team of twelve, came up with the sewer solution. If Pepperdine couldn't build its own system, Wood shrewdly sensed, it could rent some space on some existing Los Angeles County system. Wood surveyed the vicinity. He quickly found his answer. It was a large public facility only five miles away at Tapia Park.

The Tapia Treatment Plant of Las Virgenes Water District was situated near the top of the Santa Monica Mountains sloping eastward. It served, principally, the Conejo Valley cities of Agoura and Calabasas. This location positioned Tapia Treatment Plant to be fed and fueled by a large lake formed from five converging creeks. The ultra-modern plant was designed to transform all raw sewage into "virtually pure reclaimed effluent water."[6]

Guided by Supervisor Hahn, with assistance from Supervisor Burton Chase whose district included Tapia Plant, Bob Wood and I began serious sessions with county sewer chiefs and the Tapia plant manager. We ended up with an expensive public-private deal enabled only by the personal leadership of Supervisor Chase and Supervisor Hahn.

The Tapia Plant agreed to receive by truck, and to treat by the ton, all Malibu campus sewage. Pepperdine agreed to pay a pricy monthly tonnage fee; we also agreed to return all of the reclaimed effluent back down to the campus. "For every one gallon of sewage trucked from Pepperdine to Tapia one gallon of treated effluent will be trucked from Tapia to Pepperdine," read the agreement.[7] The county stringently rationed the amount of effluent allowed to flow from the Tapia Plant down Malibu Creek past Pepperdine into the Pacific Ocean at the Malibu Lagoon and Surfrider Beach.

RECLAIMED EFFLUENT

The political issue had little to do with treating raw sewage and everything to do with disposing of wastewater. Although Tapia's reclaimed water was touted as "virtually pure," at the end of its short ride down the mountain were the precious beaches of the Pacific. Agoura and Calabasas already generated the maximum amount of reclaimed water permitted by the county to flow down Malibu Creek. Where else could Pepperdine's treated tertiary go?

When the Pepperdine to Tapia sewer deal went public, it drew fire from the Colony big guns. Detractors attacked the desperate solution at its weakest point. They blasted, not the amount of sewage to be treated, but the amount of wastewater to be generated. "You're sure not going to send your wastewater down Malibu Creek," cried the Colony. "So, just where else do you guys plan to put it?" The only possible Pepperdine solution to the effluent quandary boiled down to trucking every drop of reclaimed water back down to campus.

We struggled with the idea of a two-way, ten-mile round-trip trucking solution. Trucks transporting sewage five miles up would be cleaned, refilled and turned around to carry effluent five miles back down. That mandated acquisition of a fleet of sewer trucks and construction of a high-tech collection and pumping station. After three months, Pepperdine abandoned the sewer trucking option as unsanitary, if not insane. But from frustration sprang salvation. Once again, Pepperdine's savior was burr-headed Bob Wood. The Topodynamics leader showed us plan five.

"DON'T TRUCK! PUMP!"

"Bill," Bob joyfully phoned. "I've got great news. I've been talking to the Tapia people. They say we were wise to abandon the trucking plan. But you know what they said we should do?" I could almost see Bob's eyes lighting up. But I had no idea what the Tapia people said we should do.

"Well," Bob enlightened me, "they said we should build our own pipeline. They said that we could just pump all of our sewage up to Tapia!"

To make a long story short, that's what Pepperdine did. But if trucking was a nightmare, pumping was no piece of cake. Pushing and twisting raw sewage 24 hours a day, seven days a week, five winding miles uphill along a rugged, heavily traveled and environmentally scrutinized public road produced unimagined headaches.

Headache number one was the expensive installation of two six-inch-diameter pipelines, side by side in the ditch along five miles of Malibu Canyon Road. Kirst Construction Company won the bid and built the pipelines. Initiating down at the campus, the outgoing delivery pipeline pushed sewage up to Tapia. The incoming return pipeline flushed it back down to campus, in the form of reclaimed effluent.

The Kirst crews crawled on their bellies for two months, in narrow ditches only inches from endless Malibu Canyon traffic. They cut through rock, excavated the ditch and installed the pipelines. They backfilled and landscaped the trenches according to county code. Kirst connected Pepperdine to Tapia and commodes could finally be flushed.

Headache number two pounded down on the campus end of the line. Pepperdine was required to install an expensive high-tech comminutor. Ugly, smelly and loud, it was a collection tank and pumping station boasting a 100,000 gallons-per-day capacity. McKeand Mechanical Company erected it at the bottom of the campus, near the highway. Campus waste drained down, mostly by gravity flow, into the high-intensity comminutor. It came out pulverized into a slurry of watery particles.

Pumping raw sewage through fragile pipelines in public places produced problems. Blockages, leakages and breakdowns occurred all around the circular system. That triggered the emergency alarm. The emergency alarm system diverted sewage out of the pipeline into the campus emergency holding tank to be hauled to Tapia by a half dozen emergency trucks. It was a tedious business with many emergencies. Sewer officials cautioned constantly against "a drop escaping the pipeline and leaking down through Malibu canyon into the ocean."[9]

Headache number three was that the trucking solution demanded the construction of a large campus holding lake. Jack Eiden, the Moran Company construction foreman, considered the daily effluent a daily burden. "During the heavy fall rains," Eiden wrote, "we simply could not absorb Tapia's daily water delivery back down to the campus. Sometimes our effluent deficit reached one million gallons. Tapia had the draconian option of shutting off the sewage valve at their end of the line if we didn't keep the effluent valve open at our end of the line. It was touch and go."[8]

Right on most things, Eiden was wrong about the wastewater. That daily volume of reclaimed water forever filled the sparkling lake with Malibu miracle landscape blessings. We were planting scores of trees and irrigating hundreds of acres of flowers, plants and grass. We solved Eiden's overflow problem by creating, out in the meadow, a beautiful lake to manage emergency rain collection along with enough water for seasonal firefighting and unlimited irrigation.

THE RESTRAINING ORDER

Kirst Construction Company launched pipeline construction April 15, 1972, and finished, four months later, August 15, 1972. On August 16, days before the first fall classes started, the Malibu sheriff served Pepperdine with a lawsuit. Filed in state court by the Malibu Homeowners' Association, it condemned "the slapdash Pepperdine sewer connection to Tapia as illegal, unsanitary and contrary to Los Angeles County public health codes." It called for "a temporary restraining order" to halt construction. It named as co-defendants Pepperdine, the Los Angeles County departments of building and sanitation and the five elected county supervisors in "a conspiracy to circumvent the forthcoming California Coastal Commission."[10]

The November 3, 1972, Proposition 20 vote to empower the new commission was only 60 days away. If the state court anticipated that victory, and deferred any action on the restraining order, county supervisors would transfer final action on the legality of the Tapia sewer connection over to the new state commission.

The day for school to open, Wednesday, September 6, 1972, neared. Pepperdine was on pins and needles.[11] We held our breath, hired top lawyers and "prayed without ceasing" that the county supervisors, the state court and the California Coastal Commission would keep the Tapia sewer connection and Pepperdine classes open.

During these tense hours, Pepperdine raced toward final inspection and receipt of the certificate of occupancy. The big day fell on Labor Day, Monday, September 4, 1972. The makeshift sewer was the toughest but certainly not the only test. During the countdown Pepperdine and the county cross-checked a list of 50 problematic items, large and small. In the final days, finishing touches were applied to the Cross Theme Tower and to student housing. In the final hours the campus infrastructure of paved roads, walkways and parking lots was barely completed.

Sully Miller Company won the infrastructure contract to finish grade and pave the roads, sidewalks and parking lots. Unfortunately, an unrealistic bid put the Sully Miller men under intense time pressure and their frenzied reaction provoked others. Two additional companies labored alongside to complete underground gas and electric connections. In the last days our aggressive workers above interfered with those immobilized below. During the last week Sully Miller machines spewed concrete and asphalt 24 hours a day, up and down the new mountain streets and out over the parking lots.[12] Throughout the long last night Provost Hudson rode herd on men and machines to assure completion of the central parking lot mere minutes before final inspection.[13]

THE FINAL INSPECTION

At 8:00 a. m., five of us who worked together for three years met as a group for the last time. Jerry Hudson, Jack Eiden and I represented Pepperdine. Donald McAdams and Edward Thompson represented the upper echelon of Los Angeles County public professionalism that had given Pepperdine unstinting support. McAdams supervised the Malibu branch of the Los Angeles County Department of Building and Safety. Thompson was fire marshal of the Los Angeles County Fire Department in Malibu. Both agencies had to approve Pepperdine's certificate of occupancy. For two casual hours, the five of us walked every floor of every building. We enjoyed another hour in a van touring paved streets and lots. All construction trailers banished, we sat in final summit around a polished conference table in Tyler Campus Center. Don McAdams laid out on the table the official Los Angeles County document. He ceremoniously signed and dated it, 11:45 a. m., September 4, 1972.

"Congratulations gentlemen, here's your certificate of occupancy!" beamed McAdams, handing it to me. I passed it to Jerry. He handed it to Jack and Jack put it in his briefcase. It was over and we were in.

"Based on my say-so," expanded McAdams, "Ed Thompson's fire department has also signed off. Congratulations, boys, you're in and you're legal."

The five of us strolled from Tyler Center onto the central plaza of Seaver College. We slowly ascended the broad concrete stairs leading up to the sparkling circular fountain adorning what is now the Mullin Town Square. In the parking lot scores of students scurried with suitcases to new dorm rooms. Surveying the hectic parking lot, I sensed failure to build a high-rise parking structure to serve the whole central area would eventually be a master-plan mistake.

Around the fountain frolicked a dozen magnetic young freshmen in the soft morning sun. All of them ignored five old suits in front of Elkins Auditorium, huddled together under the big coral tree transplanted ten days earlier.

"These kids think you guys are their new teachers," said Hudson with a grin.

"Well, they're sure bright-looking kids," Eiden observed admiringly.

"Yeah, but they look like high-school kids," McAdams said.

"Well, that's what they were 'til today," responded Hudson.

"But boys with short haircuts and girls in skirts? Sure not what you see around Malibu," pondered Thompson.

"Well," I said gratefully, "from here on out Pepperdine kids and Malibu will seem synonymous."

"HARMONIC CONVERGENCE"

"A harmonic convergence created the Malibu campus," concluded Norman Cousins.[14] Was the *Saturday Review* editor correct? If so, the convergence included the divine harmony of Norvel and me; of the George Evans-inspired Adamson gift; of Blanche and Richard giving together the Seaver fortune; of Pereira's majestic design; of Los Angeles County construction jurisdiction; of the Kenny Hahn trump card; and of the teamwork of academicians and builders. But none of that would have mattered without the miraculous environmental timing.

Pepperdine, less than a half step ahead of California's ecological movement, barely escaped an avalanche of antidevelopment regulation that would have killed the campus. The Malibu campus opened 60 days before the California Coastal Commission was empowered to prohibit it forever. With less red tape than is now required to plant a tree, Pepperdine opened its Malibu campus without filing any California environmental document.

"Over the centuries," I often perorated, "all will see that no better use could have been made of these acres than to become the home of a private university." It is gratifying to know that, over and over, Pepperdine's Malibu campus has been voted most beautiful in America by students in both formal and informal polls.

But just when one thinks it's over, it's only begun. Pepperdine opened its campus, but it had not gotten out of the sewer woods. The tenuous Tapia connection continued under intense litigation. The state court could conceivably condemn it as illegal and close down the campus.

"Don," I said, putting the question to the county's McAdams. "We're worried about that restraining order. We're also worried that with the California Coastal Commission sure to win, they could just come in, condemn our sewer and close the campus."

"That'll all sort itself out," McAdams reassured. "It was positive sign that the judge deferred action on the restraining order until after the passage of Proposition 20. Then the court will certainly transfer jurisdiction over Malibu construction from the county to the coastal commission."

Without waiting for Proposition 20, Pepperdine dodged another unanticipated statewide bullet. On September 18, 1972, the 13th day after campus opening and in preparation for the Proposition 20 victory, the California Supreme Court ruled preemptively to prohibit any developer from initiating any new coastal project before election day.[15]

"UNTIMELY AND VOID"

Just as anticipated, on November 6, 1972, the voters empowered the California Coastal Commission. The state court immediately transferred jurisdiction over the legality of the makeshift Pepperdine sewer solution to the new agency. The nine new commissioners held the power to close the campus as a health hazard. Providentially all nine commissioners were Republican friends of ours. They were freshly appointed by Governor Reagan. Mike Deaver, Ed Meese and Lyn Nofziger in the governor's office were especially helpful during the hearing process.

It was a two-round California Coastal Commission process. Round one was November 19, 1972. Pepperdine appeared in Long Beach before the commission's 11-member southern regional division. We won easy approval for the Tapia sewer connection on a ten-to-one vote.

Round two came ten days later, November 29, 1972, in Sacramento, this time before the full commission. Our opponents sent tough lawyers. But it was, ironically, on a legal technicality that Pepperdine prevailed. "The opponent's appeal," recorded historian White, "arrived at the state office fifteen minutes after the deadline and was declared '*Untimely and Void*.'"[16]

"Untimely and Void" became the postscript for all efforts to defeat the Malibu miracle. After flushing uphill to Tapia for three years, Pepperdine and Alcoa finally joint-ventured, in 1975. We built an ultra-modern sewage disposal facility. The plant is situated on Malibu Country Estates at John Tyler Drive. But its big holding lake sits in the Pepperdine meadow, containing sufficient effluent to serve forever the 830 beautiful but thirsty Malibu acres.

1. *Small is Beautiful: Economics as if People Mattered*, was written by E. F. Schumacher and published in 1973 by Harper and Row. Economist Schumacher borrowed the ecological phrase as the title for his philosophical book.
2. Jack Eiden, The Eiden Papers, April 22, 1971. The Banowsky Papers.
3. Bill Henegar and Jerry Rushford, *Forever Young: The Life and Times of M. Norvel Young and Helen M. Young* (Nashville: 21st Century Christian, 1999), 193.
4. *Los Angeles County Bulletin*, July 2, 1971, 3. The Banowsky Papers.
5. Tobin T. Smithson, personal letter to Joseph L. Bentley, December 15, 1971. The Banowsky Papers.
6. *Los Angeles County Bulletin*, April 16, 1969, 2. The Banowsky Papers.

7. Eiden, The Eiden Papers, May 20, 1971. The Banowsky Papers.
8. Ibid., July 22, 1971.
9. Ibid., August 16, 1971.
10. Joseph L. Bentley, personal letter to the author, August 17, 1971. The Banowsky Papers.
11. Classes opened 8:00 a.m., Wednesday, September 6, 1972. At 8:30 a.m., the first faculty meeting was held in Tyler Campus Center fireside room. On Thursday, at 10:00 a.m., the first required chapel was conducted for all students in Elkins Auditorium.
12. Eiden, The Eiden Papers, August 26, 1971. "Sully Miller's comeuppance came when the late August Santa Ana winds lifted their headquarters trailer like a huge box kite, flipped it over, and pancaked it top down in the central parking lot. Dr. Banowsky had called them that arrogant company with a testicular hold on our campus completion. Dr. Banowsky was delighted." The Banowsky Papers.
13. Jerry Rushford, ed., *Crest of a Golden Wave: Pepperdine University, 1937–1987* (Malibu: Pepperdine University Press, 1987), 163.
14. Norman Cousins, personal letter to M. Norvel Young, January 24, 1975. The Banowsky Papers.
15. *Malibu Times*, September 25, 1972, 1.
16. Rushford, *Golden Wave*, 163. "The school was barely open when a series of legal developments occurred which, had they happened earlier, would have prevented, or at least seriously injured, the project. Only two weeks after operations began, the California Supreme Court issued a decision that could have delayed all building pending the preparation of lengthy environmental reports. The Los Angeles County General Plan adopted in 1973, could have adversely affected the building of the school if it had been adopted a few months earlier before the permits were issued. Certainly Proposition 20 creating the California Coastal Commission, exactly sixty days after the campus opened, would have halted all plans for the new campus had it come any earlier."

"What is being dedicated here today was made possible by the genius, work, thrift and unselfishness of a man who called himself 'just a plain old duffer.' Some duffer!"

RONALD REAGAN
40th President of the United States
April 20, 1975

THREE CLOSE COLLEAGUES

California Governor Ronald Reagan, Seaver College Founder Blanche Seaver and Pepperdine President William S. Banowsky at the dedication of Frank R. Seaver College, May 25, 1975.

CHAPTER 17

THE DEDICATION OF SEAVER COLLEGE

Surveying Pepperdine University's first seven decades, no year looms larger than 1975. The year of 1975 was large for sorrow and for joy.

Great 1975 joy emanated from the Malibu campus appearances of two contemporary world leaders who were among Pepperdine's closest friends. Ronald Reagan, the two-term California governor who was at that moment preparing to run for president of the United States, came to dedicate Frank R. Seaver College on April 20, 1975. Five months later, on September 20, 1975, Reagan's 1976 Republican-primary opponent, incumbent President Gerald R. Ford, came to dedicate both the Brock House and the Firestone Fieldhouse.

Between those two historic highs came the lowest of lows. On September 16, 1975, a scant four days before President Ford's appearance, Chancellor M. Norvel Young suffered his tragic and nationally publicized automobile accident. The next chapter will present crucial details of that Pepperdine catastrophe. This chapter describes the 1975 days of pageantry with President Ford and Governor Reagan.

A YEAR LIKE NO OTHER

What, then, was the precise date of the Malibu miracle? Who knows? Only a fool would attempt to fix material markers around an apparent miracle. To bracket the supernatural with calendared dates is a contradiction in terms. When did the Malibu miracle begin? When did it end? Caution, the speculation sign is out.

With that reservation, for many of us the Malibu miracle certainly seemed to fully encircle the dramatic decade from 1968 through 1978. And most of us comfortably concluded that it began publicly at 10:00 a.m., Wednesday, October 2, 1968, with the Adamson gift of 138 Malibu acres. The supernatural events seemed to subside a bit ten years later. Pepperdine, without any loss of forward momentum, seemed to settle down into a more normal rate of ascendancy. For many of us, the Malibu miracle seemed to have climaxed on August 15, 1978, in the seamless transfer of power to the fifth president, Howard Ashley White.

Two-thirds of the way through that dramatic decade, after the miraculous 1968 take-off but before President White's smooth 1978 landing, the Malibu miracle seemed to have peaked. Perhaps the peak day was April 20, 1975. Ronald Reagan, "the patron saint of Pepperdine," was now running for president of the United States. To celebrate the dedication of Seaver College, he delivered his classic address on the values of independent higher education. In a Malibu miracle moment, the two first ladies, Mrs. George Pepperdine and Mrs. Frank R. Seaver, embraced on stage. Seaver College was official. In 1975, Pepperdine University, with an annual operating budget of $25 million, enrolled seven thousand students in all of its programs. Of that total, Seaver College enrolled three thousand highly qualified undergraduates.

But if 1975 was a year of incomparable joy, it was also a year of unfathomable sorrow. Sorrow and joy flowed together in that third incredible week of September. Within five fateful days, Tuesday through Saturday, came the thrill of victory and the agony of defeat. The defeat came first. At noon, Tuesday, September 16, Chancellor Young suffered his tragic accident. Victory came days later, at noon, Saturday, September 20, when President Gerald R. Ford came to campus.

COURTING MRS. SEAVER

Five months earlier, the euphoric April celebration had focused solely on Mrs. Seaver. Just as the institution will forever honor Mr. George Pepperdine, it will forever honor the founder of the Malibu campus. "Without [Mrs. Frank Roger Seaver's] rare generosity," emphasized Pepperdine historian White, "the 'Malibu Miracle' would have been impossible."[1]

By 1975, Mrs. Seaver's historic gifts had been widely publicized. That made the official christening of "Frank R. Seaver College" something of an open secret. I had first announced it publicly only four months earlier at the Malibu commencement ceremonies on December 15, 1974. Until that moment everything at Malibu was known as Pepperdine University. But as

Pepperdine soared to the highest Malibu heavens, people knew Mrs. Seaver's generosity had fueled the whole flight, and they dearly loved her for it.

Five years earlier, in 1969, Pepperdine had committed to the Seaver family to name the college in honor of Frank R. Seaver. The agreement called for naming it at the earliest appropriate moment after it was built and paid for. To continue raising money from others, everyone agreed to delay the christening of Seaver College until all construction bills were paid. "When the last brick is laid," Blanche recited midst construction dust, "the last dollar will be paid." By 1975, Blanche and her sparkling college were out of debt. The construction dust settled. Anxiety receded. Academic quality accelerated. Enrollment skyrocketed. Operations stabilized. Joyfully, thanks exclusively to $300 million in irrevocable trusts executed by Blanche and her nephew, Richard Seaver, for the first time Pepperdine had begun to accumulate a large permanent endowment.

Seaver College was made possible because, when she discovered the Malibu campus, Mrs. Seaver simply stopped giving to anything else. "When [Frank] left us," she explained, "he had completed seven of eleven great buildings he wanted to build. I completed the other four. When I saw that I was free to complete a building on my own, I gave one to Freedoms Foundation at Valley Forge in memory of our Number One American, General of the Army Douglas McArthur, who had been Frank's idol through the years."[2] Blanche and I traveled together across the Pennsylvania countryside to christen her McArthur building in the presence of many Washington luminaries. I delivered the 30-minute dedication address. Days later, the *Dallas Morning News* turned it into its lead editorial titled, "Liberty is Limited."

"'Never have men and women been more free to think, to read, to speak out, to organize, to question authority, to write, to stage, to film what even a few years ago would not have been permissible,' said Dr. William S. Banowsky, president of Pepperdine University. 'We now face a chilly truth: Having flung off one restraint after another we have not learned to restrain ourselves. Without restraint, life tends toward self-indulgence, social disorder and the destruction of freedom itself.'"[3]

Unsurprisingly, that speech won a Freedoms Foundation Award. More importantly, it may have helped to win the whole heart of Mrs. Seaver. Prior to that patriotic Pennsylvania day, the Seavers may have already contributed to many causes as much as $100 million. But following that day, and for the remainder of her very long life, Mrs. Seaver made no major gift to any cause other than Seaver College and Pepperdine University.

BAPTIZING MRS. SEAVER

But how did Pepperdine ever earn such total loyalty? To begin with, we were always carefully counseled by the family consigliere, Richard Seaver. "Take warning, Bill," chuckled good friend Richard. "Aunt Blanche can be very fickle. She gets excited by some new cause, gives money, gets turned off and goes on to the next handsome, conservative suitor."

Pepperdine, though duly warned, was never really anxious about Mrs. Seaver's total loyalty and devotion. Our fellowship with her was unfathomably deep and spiritually grounded. By 1975, she had become the adopted member of both the Banowsky and Runnels families. Charles and Amy Jo, and Gay and I, had already shared seven years of our lives with Blanche—all of the birthdays, Thanksgivings, Christmases, New Years and endless public events. Administrator George Hill, also a Church of Christ minister, lifted our load. He became Mrs. Seaver's constant escort around town, with assistance from Larry and Carol Hornbaker, Suzanne and Warren Dillard, Bob and Peggy Bales and others who pitched in, night after night.

Meanwhile Mrs. Seaver, nondoctrinal in her conservative Christian commitment and Congregational in her denomination, was primed for the nondenominational Churches of Christ. She thrilled in the simple worship centering on the Lord's Supper, Bible preaching and a cappella singing. Blanche worshiped faithfully with the Inglewood congregation from 1970 until her death in 1996.

Dr. Runnels, an elder of the Inglewood congregation, and Amy Jo escorted Blanche to church every Sunday, followed by lunch at their favorite Los Angeles Country Club table. English professor James Smythe was her Inglewood minister and confidant. In 1978, when Mrs. Seaver expressed an interest in baptism, all of us read the Bible together. On April 30, 1978, at the age of 86, Blanche, with the humble faith of a child, was buried with Christ in baptism for the remission of her sins. Pepperdine trustee James L. Lovell rejoiced nationwide in his respected church newspaper: "Many of you know, or have heard of, Mrs. Frank Roger Seaver. She is the one that has given so many, many millions of dollars to Pepperdine University to establish Seaver College and to build the whole Malibu campus. In fact, Mrs. Seaver had just recently become the first nonmember of the Church of Christ ever to be elected to the new Pepperdine board of regents.

"This lovely lady is very deeply spiritual," continued Lovell. "She always has been. For many years she has attended worship at the Inglewood Church of Christ with Charles and Amy Jo Runnels where she has heard our best teachers and preachers. On April 30, 1978, Brother Bill Banowsky baptized this wonderful lady, age 86, into Christ. Thanks be to God and to our Lord and Savior. Mighty is the power that worketh in us."[4]

Richard Seaver, Blanche's high-church Episcopalian nephew, responded with his trademark wry smile: "Bill," he pronounced, in imitation of a commencement recitation, "thanks to you Saint Blanche is now Sister Seaver with all Church of Christ rights, privileges and duties thereto appertaining." The wise Richard, a conscientious Christian with a roguish sense of humor, always promoted Pepperdine come what may. He and trustee Lovell joined thousands of others to rejoice that the founder of Seaver College—and the endower of Pepperdine University—had united with Mr. George Pepperdine's beloved Church of Christ. It was a fitting 1978 Malibu miracle climax.

THE BLOSSOMING UNIVERSITY

The coming out of Seaver College certified the coming of age for Pepperdine University. The academic momentum of the prestigious liberal arts college inspired the four underdeveloped graduate schools to also flex their competitive academic muscles to the fullest. A mere month after the dedication of Seaver College, the fledging school of law—acquired on the run in 1969—announced its migration from a rented Orange County facility to its sanctum sanctorum high above the Pacific. The move to Malibu launched the law school's drive for national academic distinction. Dean Kenneth W. Starr has moved the ratings from the 90th toward the 50th position. Ken aims for "a top ten slot even if it takes awhile."[5]

By 1978 the school of law was completely consolidated at Malibu. In close concert with the surge of Seaver College, this bold move signaled the seriousness of Pepperdine as an emerging university. The energizing Malibu momentum then brought from executive vice president White the boldest 1975 decision of them all.

"It's time to bring everything else in Los Angeles that we really care about out to Malibu as soon as we can," he officially recommended to me on October 12, 1975.[6] The school of education and psychology, the school of public policy and the school of business and management, fully integrating into a maturing university and all headquartered in Malibu, now pursue both national academic distinction and sacred Christian mission.

CLASS BY ITSELF

In 1975, Pepperdine rocketed toward distinction and praise rang from far corners. The *Los Angeles Times*, Pepperdine's predictable nemesis, at long last ladled out the very highest praise. "Pepperdine University is in a class by itself. Its Malibu campus has become a glittering diamond set on 650 acres. The sparkle runs deep, and to many observers *it symbolizes the university's academic progress.* The man most responsible for all of this progress is the Pepperdine president Dr. William S. Banowsky."[7] Barry M. Richman of UCLA and Richard N. Farmer of the University of Indiana also praised Pepperdine. Their book, *Leadership, Goals, and Power in Higher Education: A Contingency and Open-System Approach to Effective Management,* was published as a volume in the Jossey-Bass Higher Education Series. Its concluding chapter, "Policy Implications and Institutional Change," crowned Pepperdine as "the example of how to make profound institutional change smoothly and quickly."[8]

Richman and Farmer compared the progress of Pepperdine with that of Harvard, Yale, Michigan, Pennsylvania, Wisconsin, Berkeley and Stanford. "Pepperdine University seems to be successful in large part because it has a very able and dynamic chief executive, William S. Banowsky, who has worked his way up the Pepperdine system since 1959. Only 38, Banowsky has been seriously mentioned as a Republican candidate for California governor. He is host of *Inquiry,* his own NBC television show. He is a director of numerous major corporations (including Coca-Cola) and of nonprofit organizations (including KCET-TV). He played the central role in raising funds for the expensive Malibu campus. He did this in three years, from 1969 to 1972, during a period of serious economic recession. He also played the key role in raising funds for scholarships, loans and other kinds of financial aid for a sizeable proportion of students from minority and poor families. There is a good fit between this university and its goal system and the type of chief executive it has," propounded Richman and Farmer.[9]

DEDICATING SEAVER COLLEGE

In 1975, to determine the ideal Seaver College dedication date, I dialed the Reagans' private number at 16695 San Onofre, Pacific Palisades. Governor Reagan was the only candidate to deliver the Seaver College dedicatory address. "The patron saint of Pepperdine" was also Mrs. Seaver's close friend. He was now warming up to run for president of the United States and the Pepperdine people were avid Reagan fans. With no graduation ceremony or other attraction for the Seaver College dedication, Reagan's presence alone would guarantee a big crowd.

"Governor," I said on the phone. "As you know, we can offer you any Sunday afternoon in March, April or May."

"Boy, Bill," Reagan warmly responded. "I still remember that first big night we had five years ago at the Century Plaza." My recent letter of invitation had reminded Reagan of the 1970 "Birth of a College" dinner, where he took the Malibu miracle public with a masterful address to 3,400 Pepperdine supporters packed into two big ballrooms.

TELLER AND REAGAN ROBE UP

Governor Ronald Reagan was the popular favorite to deliver the Seaver
College dedicatory address. But Dr. Edward Teller, one of the creators of the
hydrogen bomb, was also a featured speaker.

"Of course, Nancy and I are good to go again. We'll be your bait one more time," chuckled the man destined to also be one of the great twentieth-century leaders. "Bill, how does Sunday, April 20, look to you?"

"It looks good," I said.

"It's a deal," he said.

That was it. At 2:00 p.m., Sunday, April 20, 1975, the ceremony to dedicate Frank R. Seaver College was orchestrated in the outdoor amphitheater above Stauffer Chapel, with panoramic skies and endless ocean. The standing-room-only crowd, monarchs of the vista from Palos Verdes to Santa Catalina Island, bathed in the soft afternoon sunshine. Governor Reagan was introduced by Richard Seaver.

"If Frank were here," Governor Reagan opened, "he'd be embarrassed. He was modest, unassuming, a gentleman who shunned the spotlight. Frank's interest was not in collecting accolades but in making it possible for others to grow and expand and thus extend the cycle of benefits of this American dream.

"The Seaver gifts were given with no strings attached," Governor Reagan continued. "Once Frank and Blanche determined a project merited their support, they also determined that it was of sufficient integrity to seek its own course."

Governor Reagan then launched into his masterful address praising the virtues of independent higher education. This speech matched, in depth and luster, his "Birth of a College" address of five years before.

"Independent colleges are our greatest guarantee of academic freedom," Reagan declared that beautiful day. "In a world of so much turmoil, when old and valued traditions are being challenged, there is special joy in seeing this new Seaver College come into being here at Pepperdine. Seaver College will certainly be a place where the values that have been tested by time will be passed along to the generations yet unborn," prophesied Reagan.

A SPIRIT OF PURPOSE

Following Governor Reagan, I delivered a Seaver College dedicatory address to spotlight the miracle-making Mrs. Seaver. Titled "A Spirit of Purpose," the speech was the companion to "A Spirit of Place," delivered five years earlier for the Malibu ground breaking. In tribute to Mrs. Seaver a few paragraphs are briefly recalled here.

"Five years ago, on May 23, 1970, we first broke this hallowed ground to build Seaver College. We pledged then to bring together on these hills a community of scholars holding distinctive spiritual beliefs.

"Mr. George Pepperdine was a lifelong member of the Church of Christ. In 1970, we pledged to keep Christian values at the heart of the educational process, to resist any sectarian spirit, to encourage full and open academic inquiry. We affirmed that while our vision of truth is limited, ultimate truth exists. The universe is undergirded by an objective moral order. While keeping pace with change, we affirmed our main purpose in this place will be to discover what is not changing. Our central conviction will always be that Jesus Christ is the same yesterday, today and forever.

"Therefore, what we do here today, in the dedication of Seaver College, is for the ages. No other institution of human creation is of such enduring quality as the institution of higher learning. Nations and civilizations rise and fall while universities and colleges survive and thrive. Among the oldest continuing human creations are the great universities at Paris, Oxford and Cambridge. They stretch back across the centuries to the 1100s. Harvard University was established in 1636, 140 years before the founding of the United States. During World War II, when Germany was leveled by Allied artillery, not one bomb was dropped on the university city of Heidelberg.

REAGANESQUE

Ronald Reagan dedicates the campus while Seaver College Professor Warren Kilday,

Dr. Edward Teller, Vice Chancellor Runnels, Senator Murphy, Richard Seaver and

Chancellor Young listen approvingly.

God willing, Frank R. Seaver College of Pepperdine University is destined to serve young people in this place for centuries to come. The very thought sends a chill down our spines.

"In 1937, Mr. George Pepperdine chose as the motto for his college this verse of scripture from the book of John: 'Freely ye received, freely give.' No person has more powerfully lived that truth, in the presence of us all, than Blanche Ellen Theodora Ebert Seaver. Theodora, her middle name of five, is my favorite. Of Greek derivation, it means 'the gift of God.' The providence of God brought Mrs. Seaver into our lives."

LITTLE GLASS CUTTER

"Some lives can be best characterized by stunning biographical detail. Blanche Seaver's is not one of those. Her biography is, of course, impressive. But high-flown factual rhetoric about an important public personality is not the same as knowing the person herself. One of the private family stories I know is that long ago, as a little girl, Blanche was allowed to assist in her father's popular Chicago paint and supply store. What she relished most was tailor-cutting exquisite pieces of glass ordered by her father's customers. She is most proud of never having broken even one piece of her father's expensive glass. Blanche was so dependable she was permitted to use her father's special diamond-point glass cutter. 'Bill,' she said only weeks ago, 'please don't let them call me a philanthropist! I'm no philanthropist. I'm just a little glass cutter.'

"'Blessed are the pure in heart for they shall see God.' It is Blanche Seaver's purity of heart, not these external credentials, that makes her character so wonderfully worthy of emulation. She embodies those qualities of spirit and mind to which young people in Seaver College will always be pointed. Given the circumstances of great wealth and ceremony surrounding her life, it is a tribute to Blanche Seaver that she has remained such a natural and unaffected person.

"Mrs. Seaver has a tremendous capacity for love. She has a great appreciation for beauty. She is capable of natural joy. She is devoted to standards of dignity and decency in the highest tradition of Western civilization. She is a tireless worker for endless causes with a voracious zest for life. She is a person of transparent sincerity.

"And, as we all know, Blanche is no shrinking violet who leaves us in doubt about her convictions. What is most important, she has the complete courage of her convictions. She not only stands up and speaks out when popular to do so. She is just as militant as a minority of one. Long ago she adopted for her life's motto these stirring words from her friend, the famous Father James Keller: 'What one person can do!'"

THE PEPPERDINE
PATRON SAINT

A relaxed and gratified Ronald Reagan
completes his address and carries away
the inspirational speech he personally
wrote for the dedication of Seaver
College.

BLANCHE REJECTS NIXON

"And Governor Reagan, our distinguished speaker today, will forgive me for sharing with you a true and precious story known only to him and me. On a sunny Sunday afternoon, in the winter of 1972, I drove Blanche to the governor's Pacific Palisades residence to get his rescue on a big political and public relations problem.

"For reasons of both conscience and obstinacy, Blanche had chosen for the first time ever to bolt the political party she and Mr. Seaver had supported all their lives. Her big problem with the Republican Party was her 'dear old friend,' Richard M. Nixon. Most of her Republican friends were signing up, if reluctantly, to serve as honorary delegates to the 1972 Republican National Convention in Miami to renominate Nixon. Only Blanche and a few others were boycotting Nixon. My only concern was that it could prove awkward for Mrs. Seaver to isolate herself from the GOP in this way. I had failed to make any headway whatsoever. I sought reinforcement from Governor Reagan. He warmly welcomed Blanche and me into his Pacific Palisades living room and went right to work on Blanche.

"I can only say that after two hours of the most persuasive arguments imaginable, from two guys she liked a lot, Blanche replied to the governor: 'Ron, I know I may be the only one who feels this way. But I must live with my own conscience.' When the honorary delegates for the historic 1972 Republican National Convention were chosen they included all of the highly distinguished Republican leaders in California except Mrs. Frank Roger Seaver. Her name was conspicuous by its absence. Retrospectively, Mrs. Seaver's conscientious objection to her old friend Nixon may not be so much an embarrassment as a compliment to her character.[10]

"I must add a final word about Mrs. Seaver's capacity for loyalty. So fierce is her loyalty that Richard Seaver once wryly observed, 'Aunt Blanche's enemies may have no virtues but her friends also have no vices.' Mrs. Seaver's profound patriotism is part and parcel of this profound loyalty. So is undying devotion to her beloved Frank. He died in October of 1964. For more than a decade, Mrs. Seaver has executed her monumental work in his name. At 2:00 p.m., every Sunday afternoon, week after week and year after year, she arrives at his graceful tomb in the Forest Lawn Memorial Park."

SPIRITUAL SECURITY

"For Mrs. Seaver, underlying all these qualities is a fundamental spirituality. It is not the power shakers of politics but the beloved leaders of religion—Dr. James W. Fifield, Rabbi Arthur Magnum, Cardinal James McIntyre—who are, hands down, the most intimate friends at the heart of Blanche Seaver's life.[11]

"An incredibly non-materialistic philosophy of life has been the basis for Mrs. Seaver's matchless generosity. Blanche knows that life does not consist in the abundance of the things possessed. She possesses neither a cottage in Carmel nor a home in Palm Springs. She and Mr. Seaver have never even owned their own personal family residence. She still rents, 'from my very dear friend Cardinal McIntyre,' the mellow old house at 20 Chester Place in Central Los Angeles. She wears no jewelry, neglects her wardrobe and, as we all know, appears for the same annual banquets, year after year, in the same familiar gowns.

"Her joy is not in getting but in giving and I have never met a person who gets more joy out of giving. Not just big buildings but a bouquet of roses for a wedding anniversary, a candy-gram at Christmastime, vitamin-C tablets to her friends with the sniffles, a bottle of wheat germ for those who look anemic—always, the same simple and contagious joy of giving and giving and giving and giving.

"It has taken great faith and boldness for Blanche to give away these hundreds of millions of dollars. We can name many others who have been as materially blessed. But none has been less materialistic than Blanche. Most of us just simply lack the courage to give away those material things that we suppose define our very lives. It is profoundly inspirational that Blanche Seaver never once defined her security in material terms. For that reason Blanche Seaver has always been profoundly secure.

"Mrs. Seaver, therefore, knowing clearly the difference between this brick and mortar and the soul of her college, leads us today in this dedication. Governor and Mrs. Reagan, ladies and gentlemen, from this day forward her Malibu college shall always be known to men and women everywhere as the Frank R. Seaver College."[12]

"I AM ONLY ONE"

I concluded by introducing Mrs. Seaver.

The huge audience rose in a swelling ovation. Blanche stepped to the center of the stage. We bear hugged. She took over by tearfully, and graciously, acknowledging "this highest of all honors bestowed on me and my late beloved husband, Frank. To live in the hearts of the loved ones we leave behind is not to die. My dearly beloved husband—Frank Roger Seaver—has lived in my heart, constantly, since the day he graduated into the larger life more than a decade ago. He was a profound Christian and patriotic American who believed that the youth of America constituted the future of America. He wanted to strengthen the American young people in order to strengthen

the American future. Frank R. Seaver College in Malibu is the culmination of his vision. It is the labor of his love. It is the crowning tribute of his life.

"I can remember, as though it were yesterday, when there was nothing here on these sacred acres but those beautiful hills high in the sky. I can vividly recall experiencing personally, with President Banowsky, every step along the path of development, especially cutting down all the lumps and bumps and moving and leveling so much earth.

"My heart was deeply touched when I was asked that this beautiful school be named Frank R. Seaver College, in honor of my beloved husband.

"Governor Reagan and I obviously share the deepest possible interests in assuring that independent higher education is kept strong and free from government control. Our pure American heritage is love of liberty and faith in God. But our nation must be kept strong within if we are to remain strong without, the land of the free and the home of the brave. Never before in American history have we been so much in need of responsible leadership. Today, the searching eyes of the nation have come to rest upon us. We must carry forward with us the highest hopes and confidence of our parents, of our teachers and of our Lord. We must be prepared for the crucial role of leadership that lies just ahead.

"Seaver College certainly offers hope for the future. Here, in this place, you have been given this wonderful opportunity to find the knowledge, the faith and the courage for the work you have been called upon to do. When confronted with any challenges you will say: I am only one. But I am one. I can't do everything. But I can do something. What I can do, that I ought to do. What I ought to do by the grace of God, I shall do.

"My warmest thanks and heartfelt appreciation to Pepperdine University for this greatest of all honors bestowed upon me this day. May God richly bless each and every one of you throughout all of your lives," Mrs. Seaver tearfully concluded.[13]

TWO FIRST LADIES

The big crowd rose once again for a standing ovation. Mrs. George Pepperdine, wife of the university founder, stepped forward to embrace Mrs. Frank Roger Seaver, the founder of the college. It was a marriage made in heaven, the merger of two immortal names in American higher education. It was official. It was Seaver College of Pepperdine University.

Mrs. Pepperdine and Mrs. Seaver, clutching one another's hands, stepped back. They waved arms together to embrace the crowd. Mrs. Pepperdine presented to Mrs. Seaver an autographed copy of Mr. Pepperdine's 1959 biography, *Faith Is My Fortune*. Two women at the heart of Pepperdine history stood on stage for an inspirational interlude, accepting appreciation. If a single moment could have certified the Malibu miracle that would have been it: 3:30 p.m., Sunday, April 20, 1975.

1. Jerry Rushford, ed., *Crest of a Golden Wave: Pepperdine University, 1937–1987* (Malibu: Pepperdine University Press, 1987), 167.
2. Bill Youngs, *The Legacy of Frank Roger Seaver* (Malibu: Pepperdine University Press, 1976), 113.
3. "Liberty is Limited," *Dallas Morning News*, September 27, 1971, 18. At almost the same moment, the *Arizona Republic* issued its lead editorial, "Warning for Lenient Parents," based on another of my speeches: "'At a time when leadership is so desperately needed we capitulated to our own children,' said President Banowsky. 'Thousands of teenagers, wet behind the ears and without benefit of having lived long enough to acquire either judgment or wisdom, become the sages of our time. Little wonder ours is called "the age of alienation" and that young people, especially, feel cut adrift and deeply depressed by a sense of impermanence, a trivial rootlessness.'" (*Arizona Republic*, November 30, 1971, 16). Also about that time, the *Pepperdine News* reported that I had been retained as a regular commentator on the new KNDC (Channel 4) weekly television program. The *Sunday Show* premiered February 21, 1971; it was broadcast live from various locations each Sunday and featured events and issues of local interest.
4. James L. Lovell, "Pepperdine University," *Action*, June 15, 1978, 2.
5. Kenneth W. Starr, personal interview with the author, 2007. The Banowsky Papers.
6. Howard A. White, personal letter to the author, October 12, 1975. The Banowsky Papers.
7. Marshall Berges, *Los Angeles Times Home* magazine, August 1, 1978, 12.
8. Barry M. Richman and Richard N. Farmer, *Leadership, Goals, and Power in Higher Education: A Contingency and Open Systems Approach to Effective Management* (San Francisco: Jossey-Bass, 1974), 309–311.

9. Ibid., 310.
10. Mrs. Seaver lost faith in Nixon because of what she saw as liberal social and economic policies. She seemed prescient within months, when the Watergate scandals ended the Nixon presidency.
11. Rabbi Edgar F. Magnin, DD, was also my close friend. On January 23, 1973, he wrote to me. "Dear Bill: I read in the paper today that you are not taking any bigger job but are going to stay here with us. That's wonderful. We need you. Cordially, Edgar."
12. William S. Banowsky, "A Spirit of Purpose" (address, Seaver College dedication, Pepperdine University, Malibu, CA, April 20, 1975).
13. Blanche Seaver (address, Seaver College dedication, Pepperdine University, Malibu, CA, April 20, 1975).

"Pepperdine University Chancellor M. Norvel Young was jailed on suspicion of manslaughter and felony drunk driving for a traffic accident in which one person was killed and two critically injured."

CALIFORNIA HIGHWAY PATROL
Tuesday, September 16, 1975, 12:30 p.m.

"MOST HISTORIC EVENT"

The student newspaper, the *Graphic*, proclaimed President Ford's September 1975 Malibu campus visit "the single most historic event in Pepperdine's 38-year existence." It still is. The President of the United States arrived on *Marine One* from Point Mugu Naval Air Station.

CHAPTER 18

DR. YOUNG'S TRAGIC ACCIDENT

"Saturday, September 20, 1975, was the single most historic event in Pepperdine's 38-year existence," proclaimed the student newspaper, the *Graphic*. Gerald R. Ford, the 38th president of the United States of America, had come to the Malibu campus.

But President Ford's spectacular visit had been eclipsed, four days earlier, by Pepperdine's great tragedy. On the Tuesday before the President Ford Saturday, Dr. M. Norvel Young caused an automobile accident near the campus that took two innocent lives.

BROCK AND FIRESTONE

Pepperdine welcomed, through the years, several former and future presidents. But this September 1975 day marked the only Pepperdine appearance of a sitting president of the United States. The crowd of 18,000, the largest ever not only in Pepperdine history but also in the history of Malibu, assembled in temporary bleachers spread across the Firestone Fieldhouse parking lots. President Ford, friend of Margaret Brock and Leonard K. Firestone, was coming to Pepperdine to honor both. At a 10:30 reception for 400 insiders, President Ford would dedicate the Brock House, the new residence for Pepperdine presidents. At 11:30 he would dedicate Pepperdine's athletics arena, the Firestone Fieldhouse, and address the audience of 18,000.

For the media it was a field day. President Ford was gearing up for his 1976 campaign against Democratic challenger Jimmy Carter. Ford's three-hour Pepperdine stay was covered by the three national television networks, all local stations, 50 members of the Washington press corps and a hundred other reporters from Southern California.

These 1975 times were especially tense. Months earlier the Watergate scandal had forced President Nixon's resignation. Furthermore, President Ford's Malibu appearance fell in between two terrifying California assassination attempts. In Sacramento, September 5, 1975, Lynette "Squeaky" Fromme stumblingly stuck a gun in Ford's face but was unable to fire. In San Francisco, September 22, 1975, two days after Ford's Pepperdine visit, Sarah Jane Moore fired but missed.[1]

DR. YOUNG AND PRESIDENT FORD

Meanwhile, incomparable campus tension lingered over the tragedy four days earlier. At 12:05 Tuesday afternoon, September 16, 1975, an alcoholically impaired Norvel ignited a Pacific Coast Highway blaze seen around the country. With this event coming only days after the Fromme assassination attempt, a spooked White House considered canceling Ford's Saturday appearance. Some aides advised him to abort the California campaign schedule and remain in Washington. Wednesday, after the accident, I called President Ford at the White House. "Bill, don't worry about it," he warmly reassured. "Betty and I will be there with bells on. But we're heartbroken for Norvel and Helen."

It was an official three-hour presidential visit. Marine One, the presidential helicopter, arrived on campus Saturday morning at 10:30 and departed at 1:30. Before the arrival, a dozen Pepperdine administrators rose at 5:30 a.m. to rehearse security measures with the Secret Service. Half a dozen sharpshooters took positions along the Santa Monica Mountains that encircled the campus. Undercover agents, dressed and looking like students, mixed and milled in the crowd. Electronic specialists commandeered the Brock House and installed extensive equipment in the guest bedroom behind the kitchen.

Alongside the Secret Service, the Banowsky family scurried to prepare for 400 brunch guests, including our four boys' hero, John Wayne. In those days nearby Hollywood boasted a bevy of Reagan Republicans; James Stewart, Robert Stack, Pat Boone, Gene Autry, Ralph Edwards, Danny Thomas, Zsa Zsa Gabor, Robert Young and other luminaries brightened the Brock House dedication.

WELCOMING PRESIDENT FORD

Marine One flew to Malibu from nearby Naval Air Station Point Mugu. At 10:15, I drove down from the Brock House to the baseball field. Stunningly, a thousand Ford fans already encircled the outfield fence, some arriving three hours early. I went through college on a baseball scholarship. Standing all alone in the dreamy reverie of center field, I was thrilled over the recently transplanted 90-foot palm trees surrounding the ballpark. But, as an old cleanup hitter, I lamented our field design. It put the stiff ocean wind at the pitcher's back but in the batter's face, a mild Malibu miracle mistake.

Center-field solitude was shattered by the sight and sound of three choppers churning in off the coast. President Ford's helicopter crossed over the beach, circled the campus and eased down onto the lush outfield grass. I edged in under whirring blades. The door swung open. The steps swung down. A smartly decorated Marine appeared in stiff salute. President Ford appeared in the doorway, smiling and waving. He danced down athletically and grasped both of my hands in his. "Hey, Bill, how're ya doin'?" shouted the world's most powerful leader.

President and Mrs. Ford loved Pepperdine. When he left the White House he joined our governing board. He made financial gifts and served as a Pepperdine University Life Regent until his death in 2006.[2]

"Bill," confided President Ford during our four-minute limousine ride up to the Brock House. "Betty and I were devastated to hear about Norvel."

LARGEST IN MALIBU HISTORY

The crowd of 18,000 assembled on temporary bleachers in the Firestone Fieldhouse parking lot. This remains the largest gathering of any kind in the entire history of Malibu.

POMP AND CIRCUMSTANCE

President Ford and President Banowsky, marching before the
crowd of 18,000, became close personal friends who golfed
together at Beaver Creek, Colorado, where they enjoyed
neighboring residences.

"THE OVAL OFFICE"

Within months of the major Malibu meeting, President Ford summoned Bill to the Oval Office and urged him to join his cabinet as the Secretary of the Interior.

HOLLYWOOD FOR FORD

Renowned twentieth-century movie star John Wayne enjoys a jovial moment with friends Blanche Seaver and Fritz Huntsinger. Los Angeles Mayor Tom Bradley sits at the left table.

FANS AND FOLLOWERS

Flanked by Secret Service agents, and followed by a mob of media and admirers, President and Mrs. Ford are escorted by Bill and Gay across the bridge into the Brock House.

Leonard K. Firestone, a Pepperdine regent and major donor, was President Ford's friend and the United States Ambassador to Brussels.

Richard Mellon Scaife of Pittsburgh, a Pepperdine regent and major donor, was Governor Reagan's personal friend. Dick, Norvel and Bill pose in front of the Reagan residence fireplace.

Governor Reagan was also the good friend of Clint Murchison, who owned the Dallas Cowboys NFL team. The governor enjoys a relaxed Malibu campus lunch with Clint, Blanche, Norvel, Gay and others.

"Mr. President, it's been a nightmare," I replied. "But Norvel's facing up like a man. He will definitely recover. The wondrous Helen joins us onstage today. Some, of course, call for his head. But Pepperdine people love Norvel. We're circling the wagons. You'll see, Mr. President. Rather than damage today's turnout, Norvel's accident has pulled us together."

President Ford's visit fulfilled expectations. A highlight was the first official unfolding of the new Pepperdine flag with its orange and blue waves.[3]

NORVEL'S HIGHWAY HORROR

Halfway up to the Brock House, the limousine rounded Huntsinger Circle. Towering over the busy motorcade were the tranquil Santa Monica Mountains. I recalled a boyhood memory verse: "I will lift up mine eyes unto the hills, from whence cometh my help."[4] I shivered in recall of Tuesday's phone call from my esteemed executive assistant, Phyllis Dorman.

"Dr. Banowsky!" she shouted, and Phyllis never shouted. "It's Helen! She's crying! Dr. Young's had an accident!"

"OK, Phyllis," I said, pressing the button. "Helen?" I heard only sobs. "Helen, is that you?"

"Bill, Norvel's been in a car wreck!" she exclaimed. "The sheriff just called. I'm leaving the Beach House now to go help."

"Where, Helen? Where's the accident? Is Norvel hurt?"

"I don't know about Norvel. I only know it's out on the Pacific Coast Highway at the J. Paul Getty Museum."

"Hang on, Helen," I tried to encourage her, hoping for the best. "These things often don't turn out to be so bad." But this one turned out to be much worse than anyone could have imagined.

"Helen, I'm coming, too. I'll see you at the Getty in 15 minutes. Let's stay in touch with Phyllis. Call her when you learn something." In 1975, before the Thornton Administrative Center, my office was in the Brock House, with Phyllis and her two assistants on the opposite side of the house in the refurbished three-car garage. I buzzed her to call the sheriff. "But, Phyllis, I'll come take it around there. I'm headed to my car now." I dashed through the living room and around the kitchen into the garage. Phyllis handed me the phone with one hand while waving the other in the air.

"Dr. Banowsky, it's the sheriff," she whispered.

"This is President Banowsky at Pepperdine. We just got a call about a coast highway wreck possibly involving our Chancellor Young. I wonder if you know anything about that."

"I can't release details," the female voice replied stiffly. "I can confirm there's been a two-car wreck. It was a rear-ender with serious injuries and perhaps a fatality."

I was stunned. "What about Dr. Young? Is he the fatality?" I held my breath.

"Oh, no," she blurted. "That car crashed from behind. The front car got destroyed. But I won't say another word until the police report."

"Thanks," I said. "Please keep us posted." I handed the phone back to Phyllis, who stood, staring, with her top assistants, Jan Turner and Sherri Keyser.

"Ladies, I don't know a thing. But it feels really bad. I'll call when I learn something. Batten down the hatches for a tsunami of calls," I warned and walked out the door. Ten steps from the garage-office was the family carport. I glanced at the dashboard clock. The police report would put the accident at 12:05 p.m. The dashboard clock now put Norvel in the bottomless pit for an hour. It was 1:05.

With mid-day traffic, I arrived at the coast highway accident scene in 20 minutes. The celebrated Getty Museum intersection was being cleared of the wreckage. Police and firemen swarmed about. Traffic flowed slowly. Both cars were being removed. Norvel's 1972 Ford LTD, its front bashed and burned, was hooked up to a tow truck. The 1967 Falcon, a still-smoldering pile of unrecognizable rubble, was strewn across the top of a flatbed trailer truck. I pulled over and got out to ask the nearest policeman about Norvel.

"THERE WAS NO ESCAPE"

"The driver of the LTD," answered the policeman, "did not seem to be seriously injured. He was definitely not burned and did not lose consciousness. Thirty minutes ago the ambulance took him to the Santa Monica emergency room." What the policeman next said is the saddest thing I ever heard. "Sir, the Ford at about 50 miles an hour plowed into the back of the Falcon with its three trapped passengers. Everything burst into flames." Consumer advocates had targeted the vulnerable Falcon gas tank and this particular Falcon was equipped with a trailer hitch. Norvel's Ford drove the trailer hitch straight through the Falcon's gas tank. Everything exploded. "There was no escape," lamented Norvel's biographers.[5]

The 62-year-old driver of the Falcon, Alice Fritsche, had buckled her 81-year-old mother, Christine Dahlquist, next to her. She had buckled her 78-year-old aunt, Beulah Harrison, into the back seat of the tiny two-door car, on top of the gas tank. Mrs. Harrison died instantly from blunt force trauma and severe burns. From the front seat, mortally wounded Christine

Dahlquist was airlifted to the Sherman Oaks Burn Center, where she also died hours later. The driver, Alice Fritsche, was also airlifted to the Sherman Oaks Burn Center with burns to her face and hands. Transferred two days later to Kaiser Hospital, she fully recovered.

Before leaving the intersection I called the hospital from the corner pay phone to confirm Norvel's condition. The report was positive. I sped back to campus. Phones were ringing. This was Tuesday. President Ford arrived Saturday. We were trapped for the next four days in an Orwellian nightmare of media misery.

DON RUMSFELD'S ANXIETY

My hottest call came from White House Chief of Staff Donald H. Rumsfeld.[6] "Bill, for goodness sake! What's going on out there?" Rumsfeld demanded. "Where does this mess leave us for Saturday?"

"In good shape, Rummy." Back in that day that's what we called him. "Dr. Young's personal tragedy will have no effect on Saturday's attendance or crowd control," I said, hoping and praying silently.

Rumsfeld could be ruthless and he was weary. Norvel's accident, on top of reelection headaches and "Squeaky" Fromme's assassination attempt, fueled speculation that he might move Ford's presidential campaign out of California altogether. I pled with the young Marine Corps aviator, Chicago congressman and Nixon NATO ambassador not to pull the plug. If, for national security reasons, he kept President Ford in Washington, Pepperdine would be devastated but no one else would blame him.

"And by the way, Bill," Rumsfeld pushed. "What about your chancellor? We don't need any pictures of President Ford with your chancellor." Rumsfeld made Norvel's absence a condition of Ford's presence.

"Rummy, Dr. Young will be in the hospital." I shot back. "But twenty thousand other Ford friends will be here. Don't let them down."

"OK, I'll call tomorrow. If we're gonna cancel," Rumsfeld calculated, "we'll have to do it tomorrow. Just keep the lid on, Bill, and I'll see you Saturday in Malibu." To hear all of that on Tuesday afternoon was bad enough, but the devastating national publicity hit Wednesday morning.

NATIONAL MEDIA MISERY

"Pepperdine's Chancellor Held in Fatal Crash," headlined the *Los Angeles Times*, delivering details of death and injury, of a half-empty vodka bottle, of a .23 blood alcohol level.

"Beneath the seemingly glamorous life of the Youngs in a paradise setting, something terribly troubling was stirring." Henegar and Rushford outlined an array of "mitigating circumstances," including Norvel's prescription use of Valium; depression over the on-campus death of a young Pepperdine professor in a motorcycle accident; anxiety over President Ford's visit; and 20 years of financial pressure. On the day of the accident, Pepperdine faced a $5 million accounts receivable cash flow shortfall, and accounts payable was about $3 million. "The stress of knowing that raising the funds for the new campus was primarily on his and Bill Banowsky's shoulders was taking a heavy toll on Norvel," the biographers understated.[7]

"For more than fifty years, Norvel never touched a drop of alcohol," according to his biographers, "but now he convinced himself that taking 'a little wine for thy stomach's sake,' . . . might be helpful. Maybe a cocktail now and then would ease the stress and bring back his optimist spirit.

"Months went by and the drinking became regular. But somehow, Norvel was able to keep his new habit hidden. Only a few people saw the telltale signs," revealed Henegar and Rushford.[8]

A SHOCKED MRS. SEAVER

One of the people who had never seen any sign was the shocked Mrs. Seaver. An hour after the accident came the dreaded call from an outraged Blanche. She had just spent 20 minutes on the phone interrogating her close friend, Edward M. Davis, chief of the Los Angeles Police Department. "Chief Davis!" she shouted at him. "How dare you call Dr. Young drunk and say he caused a wreck! Like my beloved Frank, Norvel Young doesn't even drink!"

"Bill!" minutes later Blanche shouted at me. "Chief Davis said his police force has 'secret, silent drinkers' and that's what Norvel is. I've never been so shocked and ashamed." Forgiveness came hard for Blanche. She committed as a Chicago teenager to the women's temperance movement. She loved socializing but hated alcohol. The waiters at the chic hotel charity balls automatically turned all of the wineglasses at her front and center table upside down. Twenty upside-down glasses—her table for ten with a wineglass and champagne glass at each place—was Blanche Seaver's social signature. "Helen had to know that Norvel was a secret, silent drinker," suffered Mrs. Seaver for several years.

When and how and why did Norvel get started? Who knows for sure? Perhaps one weary evening, out serving Pepperdine, he felt trapped once again inside the small talk of yet another two-hour cocktail party. When the waiter passed with a silvery tray of sparkling glasses, perhaps he, impulsively, took one. Or, perhaps, when the stewardess on a wearying cross-country flight asked, "Sir, what would you like to drink?" he impulsively ordered an adult beverage. However it may have started, his biographers concluded: "[Norvel] found a new friend."[9]

In 1970 Norvel confided, "Bill, I've learned to enjoy an occasional glass of red wine during relaxed California Club dinners with Dr. Arthur Coons." Dr. Coons was the president of Occidental College and the chairman of the board of the Independent Colleges of Southern California. Dr. Coons sensed Norvel's brilliance and took him under his wing. "Bill," continued Norvel, "that fine wine Arthur orders tastes like communion and makes my feet feel warm."

The record reveals that Norvel started quite late and drank relatively little. I believe his naïve, high-risk style of late-life indulgence was more a matter of intolerance than intemperance. One drink was one too many. And, with evidence of depression and fatigue, Norvel was self-medicating.

DEPRESSION AND FATIGUE

"Norvel Young," reported the *Los Angeles Times* in 1975, "said that he drank out of depression."[10] Legal and medical documents diagnosed it as "severe depression and fatigue." Donald V. Miller, chairman of the Pepperdine board, issued this explanation: "While it has not been generally known, Dr. Young has been under a physician's care for more than three years for a serious heart condition. It has required him to take special medication regularly for three years."[11] One of his medications was Valium, about which, Henegar and Rushford noted, "Though the tranquilizer quieted his nerves, it also took away his upbeat attitude and made him depressed."[12] An incorrigible optimist, Norvel was not naturally depressive.

"Just what was Dad's genius?" mused his only son, Matt Norvel Young III, MD. "Dad's optimistic self-confidence tempted him to be a fearless risk taker. Dad was not self-conscious but self-confident to the point of euphemism and vulnerability. He worked at good relationships but didn't worry, down deep, about how others saw him. If he got cold during church he would twill the corners of his handkerchief and drape it over his bald head. He wore his old tractor-tread shoes proudly, never thinking they might look odd to others. That was dad's charming genius. But these positive traits came with a dark side. Dad was sentimental to the point of tearful sadness. He often cited Sir Winston Churchill's 'black dog of depression.' It was the birth of wonder drugs. The anti-anxiety drugs Dad was given caused sedation and brought increased depression."[13]

Not until 1999 did his biographers first expose Norvel's 1969 prior arrest for "driving under the influence." Los Angeles County supervisor Kenneth

F. Hahn managed that messy matter with complete confidentiality. "It may have been better," Henegar and Rushford observed, "for Norvel to 'take his lumps' at that point."[14]

Incontrovertible "depression and fatigue" evidence flowed from an official 25-page document: "Superior Court of California, County of Los Angeles, Probation Officer's Report." This sympathetic but scathing report probably saved Norvel from prison. Norvel was anything but naturally depressive. Court officers and doctors, analyzing his strange depression, speculated about suicidal ideation. "For weeks following the accident we were afraid to leave Dad alone," said Dr. Matt Young. Henegar and Rushford added: "As [family members] observed his mental state, they wondered if he might try to take his own life."[15] Norvel himself confessed: "I indulged in enough self-pity to wish that I had also died in the accident."[16] Norvel, like Abraham Lincoln and others, was "a man of sorrows acquainted with grief."

But the 1970s medical diagnoses merely beg the question: how long? How long had Dr. Young suffered severe depression and fatigue? Had I heard his cry for help in 1973 from Cody, Wyoming? Norvel loved to go to Cody. He cultivated the former United States Ambassador to Denmark, Robert Douglas Coe, at his mountain mansion near the Buffalo Bill Historical Museum. Norvel called me from Cody early one morning. His voice quivering, he described the convivial dinner the night before at Coe's mountain mansion and the difficult drive back down the dangerous road to the Cody motel. Norvel was never consciously reckless. But Helen and I compared notes about his naive and childlike vulnerability. This failure to go about with his guard up had caused his near-catastrophic catamaran accident that was nationally chronicled in a 1975 *Guideposts* magazine article.[17]

"Bill," he hoarsely whispered during the call from Cody. "I must have passed out or something. I don't remember driving back down or how I got here." That very afternoon I met Norvel's flight back to LAX. Over the next months I watched him like a hawk and we talked a lot, until the Cody scare faded into an aberration. Truthfully, I was blind to the sudden depth of Norvel's depression. The policeman at the accident scene had said: "Sir, the Ford hit the Falcon like a suicide bomber." I now shuddered in horrible reprisal of the Wyoming warning. I soon learned that for some who drink such blackouts become common. Seaver College professor of communications Morris Womack visited after Norvel returned home from the hospital. "Morris," Norvel confessed to his good friend, "I don't even remember getting in my car that day."[18]

"THE SLOUGH OF DESPOND"

As Pepperdine president, I heard gossip. But the only alarming negative I ever got on Norvel came hours before the accident. It was at Mrs. Seaver's 85th birthday celebration, on September 15, 1975. Her grand Paisano Party was covered annually by the newspaper society pages and the Los Angeles Latino community. The Paisano Party commemorated the years the Seavers lived in Mexico during the 1920s, complete with mariachis and frozen margaritas—the sole exception to Blanche's ban on alcohol.[19] Gay and I drove from Malibu to the Chester Place party with Norvel and Helen. There we toasted Blanche alongside Pepperdiners Charles and Amy Jo Runnels, Larry and Carol Hornbaker, Bob and Peggy Bales, Warren and Suzanne Dillard, George Hill, John McCarty, Jim Wilburn, Claudia Arnold and 50 other close Seaver friends. One of the very closest was Dr. Richard Call, physician son of community leader Asa Call, and, most crucially, Richard Seaver's closest personal friend.

"Bill, how's Norvel feeling?" Dr. Call asked, oddly I thought.

"Well, Dick, just fine, I think," I replied, sensing he would shortly say more.

"When Norvel and I sat together last week at the museum board dinner he was not fine," he said. Dr. Call and Dr. Young were fellow directors of the prestigious Los Angeles Museum of Natural History. "Norvel was sick and in bad shape," Dr. Call sharply warned. I drove us all home, feeling shocked by Dr. Call's candor, but said nothing that night. The next day disaster struck. Had something as simple as Mrs. Seaver's margaritas caught Norvel off guard? Neither Gay nor I thought so. We compared notes with others who saw Norvel's customary diet soda, but no alcohol. He seemed fine when we said good night but 12 hours later, I wondered whether Norvel had taken that Paisano Party home with him. But I certainly never mentioned that possibility to Blanche.

I knew little about alcoholism and less about suicidal ideation. But a survey of twentieth-century personalities revealed that some famous ones like Frank Sinatra, Mike Wallace and Walt Disney considered, or attempted, suicide. Why? Depression and fatigue.[20] I heard a hint of Norvel's covert depression at La Costa Beach, in San Diego County, on September 10, 1970. We relaxed in the resort house, on the first green of La Costa Country Club, donated by the famous founder of Knott's Berry Farm, Walter Knott. We packed lunch and headed for the beach a mile away. After frolicking a half hour in "luscious San Diego County water two degrees warmer than Malibu," as Norvel described it, we kicked back on big towels in soft sand under the warm sun.

"Bill, you ever wonder what it might be like to walk out under those waves and not come back up?" Norvel asked. One shocking sentence. No more. It sounded like a crude attempt at dark humor. I mocked, "No way, Norvel."

Six months later I heard that same sound again. This time it was on the TWA flight to Pittsburgh to visit, as we often did, both Mrs. B. D. Phillips and Richard Mellon Scaife. We sat on the front row. I was on the aisle. Norvel, sitting by the window, broke the silence.

"Bill, do you ever enter 'the Slough of Despond'?" The well-read Norvel loved obscure literary allusions and had uncorked a new one.

"Whad'ya mean, Norvel?"

"Oh, you know, Bunyan's *Pilgrim's Progress*. Christian, on his way from the City of Destruction, falls into the Slough of Despond. Only Good Help can save him." Staring out the window, Norvel softly added, "Sometimes I think it'd be easier for Helen if Good Help would come take this big bird straight down." One shocking sentence. No more. I shrugged it off as the casual musings of a complicated man and forgot about it until the accident three years later.

NO JAIL TIME!

Norvel would never acknowledge such a role, but for 20 years, he had served as the nearest thing independent Churches of Christ would acknowledge as their worldwide leader. Understandably, he wearied occasionally of such a role. By the early 1970s, after Malibu success but before the accident, Norvel savored a brief taste of freedom. He wanted a bit of breathing room. After all, the church had delivered his first Pepperdine defeat when his calls for money went unmet. As much as he gave, there was little the church could give in return. Brotherly adoration was nice, but Norvel really needed money and the church sometimes seemed a demanding distraction. He hinted at that one day in 1974, during lunch at our favorite Chinese place. Fortune cookies were followed with this riddle: "Bill, they'll never squeeze me back inside that bottle."

"What?" I asked. Though I was usually able to decipher Norvel's code, this time I drew a blank. "What bottle, Norvel?"

"Oh, you know, Bill. Those big round bottles people use to build beautiful model boats inside of. It's Ron Reagan's hobby. Our brotherhood sometimes seems like a beautiful boat inside a bottle. I don't want to get squeezed back inside." *Newsweek* magazine reported the depth of Norvel's religious discomfort to the nation: "Even before the tragedy, Young was having doubts about his religion and his role as a spiritual leader. 'For years,' he told the judge, 'it has been increasingly difficult for me to accept the simplistic assumptions of the hell-fire and brimstone fundamentalism which most preachers in this church teach.'"

Gay and I visited Norvel and Helen at the hospital Wednesday and Thursday. "Bill," Helen said, as we left on Thursday, "tomorrow we must have a little business meeting."

Gay and I crawled out of bed Friday and I vented. "Honey, I've got to go have a serious talk with Norvel and Helen. To save Norvel's life we must preserve him in his position as chancellor. If he loses Pepperdine he loses everything."

"But, honey," answered one of the world's great listeners. "How can we save Norvel's job when he may go to jail?"

"Norvel must never go to jail," I said. "His survival will depend upon both the board and the court. The board must keep him in his job. The court must keep him out of jail. Any sentence other than jail will be survivable. But Norvel must never go to jail. Douglas Dalton, Norvel's lawyer, told me that 25 percent of those who get convicted of vehicular manslaughter serve no jail time. That's our goal. No jail time!" I drove into Santa Monica with a lot on my mind and, when I got there, Norvel and Helen gave me a whole lot more.

THREE BIG RESIGNATIONS

Some church leaders urged Norvel to resign for the good of the school. The same pressure also came from some business leaders. Franklin Murphy, chairman of the Times Mirror Company, and Edward W. Carter, chairman of Broadway Department Stores, spoke the sentiment of some: "Dr. Banowsky, you must go ahead and retire Norvel now in the best interests of Pepperdine." I would have none of it. A decade later Norvel wrote: "Dear Bill, You know how I love you and will always be deeply grateful for your sticking by me at the most critical period of my life."[21]

Norvel and Helen had heard enough criticism over three days to prepare three letters of resignation. Helen welcomed me into the hospital room. She handed me a manila folder containing carbon copies of two resignation letters already mailed and the original signed letter for a third resignation not yet sent.

Norvel resigned as editor of the *20th Century Christian*. In 1937 he and his friends founded the national magazine in his Nashville home. In the accident's wake, the *20th Century Christian* board of directors met in emergency session in Abilene, Texas, to accept his resignation and staunch the brotherhood bleeding. He was replaced by Joe R. Barnett. Norvel also resigned as an elder of the Malibu Church of Christ. On Sunday following the Tuesday accident, Norvel's lifetime friend and fellow elder, Pepperdine University executive vice president Howard A. White, read the letter of resignation.

The third letter, the one as yet unsent, was Norvel's resignation as chancellor of Pepperdine University. Addressed to the board of trustees, signed by Norvel, this letter was never sent. I carried it in my briefcase for many days before I threw it in the trash.

"Norvel and Helen," I told them, "it's heartbreaking to see you forced out of the eldership and *20th Century Christian.* As long as I am president you'll never be forced out at Pepperdine. Don't say another word about resigning. If pressure builds we'll put you on a long sabbatical as chancellor-on-leave. You're not on trial at Pepperdine. I've been working with Bob Jones and we've got the total support of the board."

TRUSTEES SUPPORT NORVEL

Robert P. Jones, chairman of the board of trustees during this dramatic passage, was central to Norvel's survival. A member of the small board that originally hired Norvel back in 1957, Bob Jones was an Arthur Young CPA, a Sierra Madre Church of Christ elder and the sternest critic of Pepperdine's perilous balance sheet. Tall and lean, Bob played basketball for the University of San Francisco and married ardent Pepperdiner, Jane. Their son, Wallace, became a major Pepperdine financial supporter.

After Tuesday's tragedy Chairman Jones conducted a Wednesday conference call with all 12 trustees. On Thursday, I drove downtown to confer in his 40th floor Arco Tower office. "Let's let this cool," Bob said. "Norvel faces a terrible road. But Pepperdine's probably through the worst. It's been three days and we're already off the front page. We'll be OK. But Norvel needs our help. After Saturday's event with President Ford, I'll call a board meeting for Tuesday at Malibu. We'll let everybody talk and settle down. Norvel's been around a long time. It'd be a mistake to take any action until things clear up."

"I agree, Bob," I replied. "Are you aware Norvel and Helen hired prominent criminal defense attorney Douglas Dalton?"

"Yes, I'd heard that," Bob said.

"Well, Dalton called yesterday with more bad news. He found that Norvel had a prior DWI near LAX after a flight in 1969. Norvel called Kenny and there was no publicity. But it'll all come out now and this second offense deals Dalton a difficult case."

"I'm sad to hear that," Bob said, staring far out the window through the hazy L.A. morning sky. "When it rains it pours. Let's take it a day at a time.

We can hold the board together. But Norvel's fate will be up to the court. When does Dalton take Norvel to court?"

"Dalton's stalling too," I replied. "He's delayed the preliminary hearing three or four weeks."

"Good," said Bob as we stood to say goodbye. "We've got some time. Let's divide the work. I'll take the five executive committee members. You take Mrs. Pepperdine. We're gonna need her help."

"I'll meet with her today," I said.[22]

JUDGE PIERCE YOUNG

Dr. Young and his attorney, the distinguished Douglas Dalton, waived the preliminary hearing. The case was remanded for trial to the Los Angeles County Superior Court in Santa Monica. It was at that moment that the trial judge, who seemed providentially assigned to Norvel's case, began to guide it toward positive resolution.

I had feared Norvel might draw a hard-nosed judge noted for maximum sentencing. Instead, Norvel Young drew Pierce Young, the Santa Monica Court's most liberal jurist. Norvel and Pierce had much more in common than the same last name. They were shrewd, 60-year-old, highly educated religious intellectuals. Pierce Young, a 1960s California liberal appointed by Governor Edmund G. "Pat" Brown, was criticized for unpredictable leniency in sentencing. But Norvel's life depended on getting enough leniency to escape incarceration. Judge Young, a nonconformist bachelor, had both the capacity to grasp Norvel's greatness and the courage to rule unconventionally.

On October 30, 1975, Chancellor Young appeared before Judge Young to plead guilty on two charges: Count I, 192. 3A PC (Vehicular Manslaughter with Gross Negligence) and Count II, 23101 VC (Drunk Driving with Bodily Injury). An anticipated sentence for such felonies could be five years in prison. In Norvel's case the victims' family was not vindictive. After suing both Pepperdine and Dr. Young, they agreed to the $300,000 insurance settlement without any civil litigation.

Norvel's fate hung on the sentence to be determined solely by Judge Young, who fixed judgment day for 10:00 a.m., Thursday, December 4, 1975. The day before the scheduled sentencing came one of life's happy calls. "Dr. Banowsky," buzzed Phyllis. "It's Judge Pierce Young on line one for you." Puzzled, I picked it up.

"Dr. Banowsky," came the soft baritone. "I appreciated your letter outlining why you think Dr. Young deserves consideration. I've received more than a hundred positive letters, including one from President Ford, but also some very negative ones. Naturally, Dr. Banowsky, I'm a little confused. I want to do the right thing and would appreciate your counsel."

"Judge Young," I said, dumbstruck. "I'll be of service in any way I can."

"Would you mind coming here to my chambers?" the judge asked. "We can talk here confidentially."

I was stunned. "Thank you, Judge Young. That's most gracious and I'll be there when you say."

"The sentencing is scheduled for tomorrow. But I've already decided to grant Mr. Dalton's petition for postponement for a couple of more months. The worst publicity is over. There's no need for a rush to judgment. Could you come Tuesday at 1:30?"

"I'll be there, Judge Young."

The following day, Thursday, December 4, 1975, Judge Young did, indeed, delay Norvel Young's sentencing until January 27, 1976. Over the following weeks, Judge Young and I met three times in his chambers. The Judge wanted only to know Norvel, his character, his soul. I revealed to him Norvel's godly unselfishness, his natural brilliance, his powerful call to service, his weariness and innocent naiveté. What most impressed Judge Young was the probability that Norvel, born again, would have much more to give. Norvel's most productive years could be ahead. Optimistic about human potential, Pierce Young came to believe that Norvel Young could bless many thousands more for many years to come. Therefore, he saved his calling as well as his life.

THE VICTORIOUS NORVEL

Pierce Young pronounced Norvel Young guilty as charged and sentenced him to one year in custody. But he immediately suspended the sentence and assigned Norvel to six months of public service, fined him $2,000, suspended his driver's license for four years and prohibited him from consuming alcohol. During his public service, Norvel shared his experience with thousands of problem drinkers, published a scholarly paper on stress and alcohol and conducted special courses for drivers who drink. He humbly confessed and sought prayerful forgiveness in 30 church pulpits and a Firestone Fieldhouse assembly of 1,500 students.

This was not the end but the beginning. After a well-earned sabbatical, Norvel settled back into university development and his life of service. In an irony of adversity he raised more millions for Pepperdine after the accident than before, including $35 million from his friend George Graziadio to name the school of business and management. In 1985, he was elected chancellor emeritus. He presided, regally, as the senior officer on the Malibu campus until the day he died, running on his treadmill, at the age of 83. Two thousand admirers attended his 1998 Firestone Fieldhouse funeral. The *New York Times* obituary called him, "the builder of Pepperdine University."[23]

Those who think the Malibu miracle came cheap will never penetrate its wonder. All who owe a debt to Pepperdine owe it to Norvel Young. The modern institution, created under his leadership, was made possible by his pain. Hagiographers will never capture the nuanced magnitude of this servant-leader. But as the semesters roll by he will grow larger. One of these September Founder's Days we should dedicate the life-sized M. Norvel Young bronze.

Meanwhile, some positives spun out of adversity. One of the most positive was the transformation of Pepperdine's governance from an insular board of trustees into a powerful board of regents.

1. Sarah Jane Moore strapped, under her dress, a .45-caliber semi-automatic to her leg. As she scrambled to pull it out and shoot, it misfired. "Squeaky" Fromme, after serving a 30-year prison term, was released on August 14, 2009, at the age of 60.
2. President Ford and I were friends. That day he paid me high compliments. "Dr. Bill Banowsky's great capacity for leadership has been a guiding force in Pepperdine's phenomenal progress and pursuit of excellence. He is the man most responsible for this 'Malibu miracle.' It represents a testament to his skill and diligence. I congratulate you, Bill." President and Mrs. Ford convinced Gay and me to build a vacation residence across the fairway from theirs on the golf course in the new Colorado ski resort, Beaver Creek.
3. Jim Ruebsamen, "Flag Protocol Stated," *Pepperdine Graphic*, September 29, 1975, 1.
4. Psalm 121:1 (KJV).
5. Bill Henegar and Jerry Rushford, *Forever Young: The Life and Times of M. Norvel Young and Helen M. Young* (Nashville: 21st Century Christian, 1999), 228.
6. In Republican politics, I was personally closest to young men near my own age, including Donald Rumsfeld, Edwin Meese, Michael Deaver and Lyn Nofziger. Rumsfeld and I had spent private time together. In May 1972, when Rumsfeld headed President Nixon's Cost of Living Council, I brought him to Los Angeles as featured speaker in the Pepperdine University Great Issues Series. In 1974 we were honored as two of "America's 200 Rising Leaders for the Future" in *Time* magazine's July 15 cover story. All 200 under 45 years old, most continued to rank among America's great leaders for the next 40 years.
7. Henegar and Rushford, *Forever Young*, 226–228.
8. Ibid., 226–227.
9. Ibid., 226.
10. William Trombley, "Pepperdine Torn by Tragedy," *Los Angeles Times*, April 10, 1976, 8.
11. Doug Drigot, "Young Faces Charges," *Pepperdine Graphic*, September 19, 1975, 1.
12. Henegar and Rushford, *Forever Young*, 226.
13. Matt Norvel Young III, personal interview with the author, June 23, 2006. The Banowsky Papers.
14. Henegar and Rushford, *Forever Young*, 227. The date of Young's first DUI arrest was November 14, 1969.
15. Ibid., 231.
16. Ibid., 243.
17. M. Norvel Young, "Ordeal at Sunset," *Guideposts*, August 1975, 17.
18. Henegar and Rushford, *Forever Young*, 238.
19. Chapter 7, "The Miracle-Making Mrs. Seaver," details the seven years Mr. and Mrs. Frank R. Seaver lived and worked in Mexico City in the 1920s.
20. Defamer, "The Big List of Celebrity Suicide Attempts, http://organizedwisdom.com/helpbar/ index .html?return=http://organizewisdom.com/Hollywood_Suicide_Scandals&url=defamer.

com/hollywood/killing-yourself/the-big-list-of-celebrity-suicide-attempts-297235.php (accessed September 22, 2009).

21. M. Norvel Young, personal letter to the author, March 28, 1986. The Banowsky Papers.

22. At 7:00 on Sunday morning, after President Ford's visit, I drove to Santa Monica to tell Norvel all about it. In the hospital lobby I saw the stuffed Sunday news rack featuring the *Los Angeles Times* front page, me in cap and gown and color, standing between President Ford and John Wayne. It produced no consolation. I took the elevator up to Norvel's room on the sixth floor without a newspaper.

23. "M. Norvel Young, 82, Head of Pepperdine University," *New York Times* obituary, February 23, 1998.

"In 1976 we began to elect business leaders from all denominations to transform insular trustees into powerful ecumenical regents."

HELEN PEPPERDINE
Co-founder, 1937
George Pepperdine College

TWO POWERFUL NEW REGENTS
When President Gerald R. Ford left office in 1976, he soon joined the new Pepperdine University Board of Regents. He is pictured above, signing in for the Seaver Board Room meeting, with his good friend and regential colleague Margaret Martin Brock.

CHAPTER 19

THE EXPANDED ECUMENICAL BOARD

It's an ill wind that does not some good blow.

M. Norvel Young's accident sparked the bold decision, after three quiet years of intrepid planning, to proceed immediately with the revolutionary revision of the Pepperdine governing board. Three days after the September 16, 1975, accident, Norvel gave his full blessing to open up the board to include highly qualified non–Church of Christ members. "It's an idea whose time has come," Norvel said. It was a long time coming.

The entirely new board of regents was created on January 17, 1976, to deepen and broaden the foundation of Pepperdine University.

MR. PEPPERDINE'S TRUSTEES

For his 1937 college, Mr. George Pepperdine fashioned a religiously-limited form of governance typical for its time. Christian colleges everywhere, of all stripes and colors, originated under closed governing boards restricted to members of their own denominations. It was customary. Mr. Pepperdine's particular bylaws enshrined the founding restriction in 18 words: "All members of the Board of Trustees shall be members in good standing of the Church of Christ."[1]

For the first decade that governance model worked well enough. Operating his college under a paternal system of financial control, professionally labeled "founder's syndrome," Mr. Pepperdine paid for everything, from the light bill to faculty salaries. Trustees certified his transactions but were not responsible for any money or for any management of their own. Operating like a family business, or perhaps the leadership of a local church, Mr. Pepperdine's board met about once a month, without systematic agenda or much paperwork, often in his own living room.

Mr. Pepperdine kept his board small. For the founding he included only four fellow trustees. They were Donald V. Miller, Clarence A. Shattuck, A. J. Drumm and Hugh M. Tiner. For the fifth trustee he soon added his own wife, Helen. Neither rich nor famous, these early church trustees were honest fiduciaries facing increasingly heavy responsibilities. By 1949 "founder's syndrome" faded and things fell apart financially. In 1951 Mr. Pepperdine declared bankruptcy. The whole weight of the college now crushed down on the beleaguered trustees. In desperation they called M. Norvel Young to the rescue.[2] When Norvel arrived as president in 1957, the board had nine members. Serving alongside Mr. and Mrs. Pepperdine, Mr. Miller and Mr. Shattuck, were Robert P. Jones, James L. Lovell, Orbin V. Melton, Leland P. Derrick and Kenneth Davidson. All nine trustees were traumatized by the extended financial emergency.

"The banks were coming after the college and the trustees to pay Mr. Pepperdine's bankruptcy debts and we had to hire defense lawyers," reflected trustee Lovell.[3] "The financial pressure was unbearable," said the understated Jones. "We were all really very frightened." Through all the years Pepperdine never had a bad trustee. "They were bravely beleaguered," eulogized Norvel. "They did a good job governing an underfunded, racially explosive and religiously divided college. The job simply outgrew them."[4] Five early trustees—Donald V. Miller, Hugh M. Tiner, Helen Pepperdine, Robert P. Jones and James L. Lovell—perhaps earned places in Pepperdine's pantheon of its top 20 leaders.

ONE FOUNDING LAW

By 1971, when the college became a university, the insular board seemed to shrink. By 1977, academic observers, wowed by Pepperdine's progress, questioned its governance. How could such an anachronistic model support a rising university? "All board members must be of this particular denomination," puzzled Barry M. Richman of UCLA and Richard N. Farmer of the University of Indiana, "yet the Church of Christ does not even support the university financially."[5] Mr. Pepperdine's model proved to be inadequate because of the limited number of California Church of Christ members who could qualify as strong board candidates. California was no Church of Christ stronghold. The denominational limitation, on top of California's small Church of Christ population, rendered strong California candidates for board service few and far between.

If the shortage of qualified California Church of Christ board candidates made the board expansion necessary it also made it possible. Why has no other Church of Christ-related institution ever even attempted to add non–

Church of Christ board members? The geographic strength of the church precludes any possibility of such a radical theological departure.

For 20 years, the strength of the church, in the profoundly loyal mind of Norvel Young, inhibited Pepperdine from proceeding with any board change to include non-Church of Christ members. Norvel's hesitation was not superficial. His George Peabody College doctoral dissertation, "A History of Colleges Established and Controlled by Members of the Churches of Christ," made him an expert on board governance of church-related institutions. It left him leery. "Schools who opened their boards to outsiders lost their church relationship," Norvel wrote. "I fear an avalanche of church criticism if the brethren ever believe we've abrogated Mr. Pepperdine's charter by compromising the composition of the board."[6]

For three years I hoped and prayed for my passive-aggressive colleague to join me in this change. He acknowledged its need. But he always wanted to do it later. I bided my time, knowing it would have to be done but dreading being on record as the one having done it. Norvel produced three strong arguments for the status quo.

Argument number one: "Bill, the board composition is not only the founder's law. *It's the founder's one and only law!*" The fascinating feature of Mr. Pepperdine's charter was what it did not say. It gave no religious qualifications for administration, faculty, staff or students. It said nothing about chapel, curriculum or campus life. It completely separated the college from the church with the exception of the board composition. Who was I to petition some pedestrian court to change Mr. Pepperdine's last will and testament on *his one and only law*?

THE SLIPPERY SLOPE

Argument number two: "Bill, I fear your compulsion for board change could push Pepperdine down the slippery slope." Born near one Christian college and educated at another, I had heard tales of academic apostasy all my life. I had heard that Harvard's seal still bears the words "In Christ We Glory," precisely as the Puritans put them there in 1636. I had no compulsion to challenge the lessons of history.

Argument number three: "Bill, many oppose board change but you seem to be the only one pushing it." If none proposed it, and many opposed it, why was I compelled to do it? It was the right and necessary thing to do. A larger, more complicated institution demanded a stronger, more independent board. The advance was essential for the board to keep pace with brilliant and diverse faculty and students. Bottom line, it was the only way to assure Pepperdine's financial future without relaxing its Christian mission. I felt, sincerely, that Christian ecumenism was part of that mission.

I felt alone. Many watched the university outgrow its sectarian board. None called for change. How could such an inexorable issue be so utterly ignored? Just as much else that is inexorable gets ignored. The board composition was the founder's sole prerogative. The sectarian model was sacrosanct.

Norvel hesitated and I vacillated. One month the change seemed inevitable. The next month it seemed irresponsible. I, too, hated church criticism but made peace with it on this issue as the price to be paid for Pepperdine's future. If I had been more daring, I could have found comfort by discussing it with others. But this was one of those subjects nobody ever discussed.

THE ATTORNEY GENERAL

As Pepperdine grew bigger, the trustees' burden grew greater. They gave it all they had. After a decade of sliding downhill, they crashed and burned in 1968. How? They voted, unanimously, 15 to 0, to reject the Adamson offer of Malibu land "because the College simply did not have the money to invest in moving the thousands of tons of earth to build on the hillsides."[7]

Dr. Young and I stepped up. We raised $3 million in cash, accepted the Malibu land gift and took charge. Norvel and Helen Young and I were elected trustees on the small board. At the beginning of 1971, I became university president and chief executive officer. Norvel became chancellor and chairman of the board of trustees. For one critical Malibu miracle year we could have conducted board meetings in a phone booth.

That level of hauteur, along with a covert covey of right-wing critics, attracted the attention of the Charitable Trust Division of the California Attorney General's office. "Due to some unfounded criticism and political harassment," announced Chairman Miller in February 1975, "the board has asked the Attorney General to perform a thorough study of the university and make recommendations for improvement." Miller added: "We are now in the process of enlarging the size of the board."[8] The Attorney General, finding nothing amiss financially, targeted the insularity of the board. The investigation ruled that Dr. Young, as a university employee, should not serve as board chairman and that both he and Mrs. Young should not serve as trustees contemporaneously. Suddenly, to strengthen and diversify the board was merely to comply with California law.

Margaret Martin Brock leads the cheers of the whole business community for the election of charismatic Jewish financial leader Leonard K. Straus as vice chairman of the new ecumenical board of regents..

Bill and Norvel show new regent Richard Mellon Scaife what his $6 million Malibu miracle contribution has created, wind and all.

POWER OF DECISION

There is power in the simple act of deciding. I decided long before the Attorney General's 1975 pressure. The turning point came in 1972, on Gay's September 22 birthday. After a Tyler Center party in Gay's honor with trustees and wives, we prepared for bed at the Brock House. Gay and I compared notes on the subdued trustees. "Yes," divined the equanimous Gay, "they know they're in over their heads. The shame," she said, turning out the light, "is that even Mrs. Seaver is not qualified to serve on our board." That did it. I woke up the next day believing Pepperdine could open its governance to devout leaders without any loss of Christian commitment or Church of Christ character.[9]

I came to believe that Pepperdine, at the most opportune moment, should amend its bylaws to add non–Church of Christ board members. The fashionable word "ecumenical," benignly defined as "the unity for which Christ prayed," was eschewed by some as unscriptural compromise in pursuit of superficial unity. But if the saintly Mrs. Seaver, saving Pepperdine with $300 million while worshiping with the Inglewood Church of Christ where she would soon be baptized, was blackballed because of her immigrant birth into the Congregational Church, the Pepperdine policy was wrong.

I worked out the details in my mind. To avoid tinkering with Mr. Pepperdine's trustees, the revised board would be the board of regents. Distinctive Church of Christ character would be retained through church control of a majority of board seats. The board size must be large to generate the largest number of outside seats. A board of 40 regents would produce 19 new non-Church of Christ regents—a bonanza. The plan would not be fulfilled for four more years but the details were formed in 1972.

THE ADVISORY TRADITION

In the idyllic 1930s Los Angeles was a center of world trade. Pepperdine College compensated for its shortage of church financial leaders by turning to top Los Angeles business leaders. The college venerated the free market economy and promoted American business of every size and shape. Mr. Pepperdine, the unpretentious entrepreneur-in-chief, invented the Western Auto Supply Company as a mail-order automobile shopping mall.

In the Pepperdine DNA, dependence on business traces back to the beginning. On September 21, 1937, Californians by the thousands assembled at the city's southern edge to celebrate their latest entrepreneurial victory, their newest private college. Republican Governor Frank Finley Merriam delivered the business-friendly dedicatory address, adulating the school's free-enterprising founder.[10]

The birth of Pepperdine College was a tribute to higher education and American free enterprise. Those two forces, for Mr. Pepperdine, were two sides of the same coin. He saw little difference between the education that enlightened and the enterprise that enabled. He remained confident in the future when financial pressures forced his college to turn to Los Angeles business leaders. The "development board" tradition runs three generations deep in Pepperdine's ancestry.

THE PRESIDENT'S COUNCIL

Mr. Pepperdine gave all he could. Then President Tiner came up with a stroke of genius. He replaced the support of the founder with support of the founder's friends. In February 1955 he involved Los Angeles business leaders by creating an advisory board that he called the President's Council. Founding members included J. Leland Atwood, chairman, North American Rockwell Company; Donald Darnell, vice chairman, the Fluor Corporation; Bryant Essick, chairman, Essick Investment Company; Stephen C. Bilheimer, chairman, the Silverwoods Company; and Charles R. Fleishman, president, the A. J. Bayer Company.

Dr. Tiner could not generate enough support to solve the college's financial problems. But his 1955 President's Council was the 1975 board of regents in waiting. The seed was planted. For another 20 years the advisory tree matured. In 1976 Dr. Tiner was elected as a founding member of the board of regents he had helped to fashion. He paused to bless those earliest business roots. "The formation of the President's Council . . . *was 'the most significant forward step in Pepperdine College since its establishment in Southwest Los Angeles in 1937'*" (emphasis mine).[11] How could President Tiner have made it any plainer?

THE PRESIDENT'S BOARD

When President Young arrived in 1957, under extreme financial duress, he embraced the President's Council as his best hope for survival. Reared in a Tennessee business family, Norvel knew the ropes. A natural leader, he had built the world's largest Church of Christ congregation, established two national publications and led in the founding of Lubbock Christian University. A director of corporate business boards, Norvel needed no coaching. His major job, said Chairman Miller, "was to relate the college closely to the California . . . business community."[12]

"Bill," chuckled Norvel, "when I got here the President's Council was a bird's nest on the ground"; in Texas quail-hunting lingo, "a big covey waiting to be flushed." Two years later Norvel called me out to help him flush it. He brightened its name from President's Council to President's Board. "Our business friends," he smiled elfishly, "had rather be on a board than a council."

Norvel built the President's Board into an elite list of 50 leading businessmen including Leonard K. Firestone of Firestone Tire and Rubber Company; Walter Knott of Knott's Berry Farm; Edgar F. Kaiser of Kaiser Industries; Paul Helms of Helms Bakeries; J. H. Smith of the Seven-Up Bottling Company; Donald Douglas of Douglas Aircraft Company; Carl P. Miller of the *Wall Street Journal*; and Charles W. Smith of Security First National Bank.

THE UNIVERSITY BOARD

The third generation of business support emerged in 1971. When the college became a university an enlarged title was required for the board of advisors. "Bill, let's name it the University Board," urged Norvel.

I worried. "That sounds pretty prestigious. Won't people think that's the governing board and confuse it with the board of trustees?"

"Don't worry. It'll work out. Our business friends had rather be on a university board than a president's board." The next day Norvel ordered his new letterhead.

Norvel was always eager to include outsider advisors. But when I pushed to open up the governing board to them he resisted. He pushed back for some form of bicameral governance. He liked the idea of two boards. "Like having elders and deacons. It's safer than bringing outsiders straight up into the eldership," he said.

Since Norvel and I communicated daily through inter-office memoranda, the Payson Library Archives document the path to board expansion. I first formally proposed it in a "Confidential Memorandum" of four tightly typed, single-spaced pages dated June 16, 1972.

> Pepperdine can multiply its potential without diminishing its Christian mission. But at our present size, we are already bigger than our official philosophy, and our church base, can support. We can't compete with USC when we can't involve people like my friend, Ambassador Annenberg, on our legal board. Pepperdine's size and operation are now big enough, and complicated enough, to jeopardize the spiritual philosophy of the school. Sheer financial necessity now demands that we go out and get the money anywhere we possibly can. We must now open up the board to these

Charles B. "Tex" Thornton and Flora Thornton, who made possible the Thornton Administrative Center, enjoy the 1978 Pepperdine Associates Dinner with their very tall and famous friend, John Kenneth Galbraith.

Bill congratulates George Elkins upon his election to the board of regents as Mr. Elkins's daughter approves.

faithful, powerful and wealthy outsiders. We can soften our sectarianism without weakening our Christian mission.[13]

The next day Norvel answered in rebuttal. After much back and forth, I launched this January 6, 1973, four-page missive:

> The fundamental decision concerns the question of governance. Will Pepperdine University remain forever under exclusive Church of Christ control? Or will we broaden, and deepen, our governance base to include others who deeply share our core beliefs? It is clearly in the best interests of the university to broaden and deepen the base of legal control. Norvel, we must take this complicated step now, with careful planning. Otherwise, the complicated step will one day overtake us. We must either give birth to this board change under controlled conditions now or, later, in the back seat of some taxi cab. Our objective is to protect the Pepperdine church relationship and to guarantee the board's financial control. We can do both.[14]

TWO GOVERNING BOARDS?

On January 12, 1973, Norvel unveiled his first clear statement on the subject of opening up the board. "I favor two boards," he said. "I favor setting up a Board of Governors of 15 members to share legal authority with the Board of Trustees of 15 members."[15] We soon learned from lawyers that it was illegal for a California nonprofit institution to operate under two governing boards. This set the stage for a single board.

By 1973 Norvel began to soften. But a board of 40 regents would require a majority of 21 Church of Christ members. There were currently but 11 church trustees. We launched a campaign to beef up the board's Church of Christ base to the legally required minimum of 21 members. Norvel extended carte blanche. "The Board must not add any new member who is objectionable to you, either for philosophical or personal reasons," he wrote.[16] Trustees at the time of the 1976 transformation transition were Thomas G. Bost, Joe R. Barnett, Evelyn Clark, G. L. Crothers, Hubert G. Derrick, W. Austin Elmore, George A. Evans, Robert P. Jones, John D. Katch, Reuel Lemmons, James L. Lovell, Orbin V. Melton, Donald V. Miller, D. Loyd Nelson, Ira L. North, Helen Pepperdine, T. A. Rogers, Kenneth A. Ross Jr., Jack Alan Scott, Earl Warford, M. Norvel Young, Helen M. Young, Nile E. Yearwood and I. Of those original trustees, only John D. Katch and I remain as regents in 2010.

THE TRAGIC STIMULUS

Pepperdine's governance drama played silently along. Suddenly, in September 1975, it came to a head out on the Pacific Coast Highway. Dr. Young's accident provided the stimulus. Within hours, I knew that the time had come. The trustees, facing lawsuits for "failed fiduciary performance," retained counsel and conceded that the time had come to ask for help. So did Norvel and Helen when I visited them at the Santa Monica Hospital.

"Norvel," I said. "Your strongest support comes from your business friends who say, 'There but for the grace of God go I!' It'll help me to help you if we move ahead now to put the men who most strongly support you on a brand new board of regents."

"OK, brother," he agreed. "It's an idea whose time has come." Helen nodded her assent. After five years of debate, in keeping with our long partnership, we cut the expanded board deal in five minutes. "But Bill," Norvel added from his hospital bed. "You better go see Mrs. Pepperdine. Her opinion on something like this could make all the difference."

HELEN PEPPERDINE

Helen Louise Davis married into the middle of George Pepperdine's philanthropic life in 1934. The virtual cofounder of Pepperdine College, she held the power to bless or curse any charter change. As a young professional social worker she assisted George in his generosity. They worked together throughout 1937 to build the college. Given George's struggle over whether Christian higher education was consistent with Scripture, it is doubtful that he could have built it without Helen's partnership. In 1941 she joined George on the board of trustees and became its longest-serving member. Popular with faculty and students, she hosted decades of dinners in her home for graduating seniors and parents.

"On religion, Helen delighted in being a bit less doctrinaire than George," said Dr. James Smythe.[17] Helen came from the Restoration Movement's more moderate wing and actually met George at the Arlington Christian Church, where she sang in the choir. She was known for her candor. Helen Young learned "that the founder's wife would not hesitate to tell you when you were wrong."[18] Gay learned that in 1959, at her first monthly luncheon for administrators' wives in Mrs. Pepperdine's home. Gay innocuously misspoke to her friend, Gloria Sanders, wife of Dean J. P. Sanders. "Gloria, Bill and I were honored last Sunday to have Brother Sanders preach at South Gate."

"Please, Gay," interjected Mrs. Pepperdine. "In California we don't call the men at church 'Brother.'" Neither Gay nor I called anybody else "Brother" until we got back to Texas in 1963.

Thirty years later, after Norvel's 1975 accident, Mrs. Pepperdine and I met four or five times at her West Los Angeles residence. With each meeting she grew more enthusiastic. "Bill, this stronger board will ensure George's legacy," she believed. Mrs. Pepperdine encouraged other trustees to support the change and volunteered to make the motion at the board's final meeting.

FIVE CHURCH PROTECTIONS

In October 1975, the board of trustees assigned trustee Thomas G. Bost to coordinate the revision of Second Amended and Restated Bylaws. Bost, with the Los Angeles law firm of Latham and Watkins, brought expert legal guidance and his own charismatic leadership. It was a glorious success.

Whereas at the college's founding Mr. Pepperdine established one Church of Christ protection, in an abundance of caution we now established five. The first required a majority of regents to be Church of Christ members. The next three protected, exclusively for Church of Christ members, the top three positions of president, chairman of the board and chairman of the executive committee of the board. The fifth protection instituted an autonomous Religious Standards Committee, comprised exclusively of Church of Christ members, with great authority.

> The Religious Standards Committee shall be delegated the absolute authority to establish and maintain those policies and practices of religion and spiritual life considered by the committee to be appropriate to ensure a continuing and meaningful relationship between the University and the Church of Christ. This includes, but shall not be limited to, the conduct of chapel assemblies, supervision of the religious curriculum, setting of standards for religion courses required to be taken by students, selection of members of the religion faculty and staff and setting of guidelines and standards concerning religious and moral practices and beliefs to be used in the selection and retention of students and members of the administration, faculty and staff of the University. The Religious Standards Committee shall meet at least quarterly and be empowered to establish and maintain standards for campus life and conduct including dormitory regulations, campus social functions, university social functions and extracurricular activities, and to conduct and sponsor special

convocations, Bible lectureships, campus ministry and evangelism.[19]

On March 14 , 2006, President Richard I. Ingram of the Association of Governing Boards of Universities and Colleges met in a two-day retreat with Pepperdine regents at the Biltmore Hotel in Los Angeles. "Your bylaws," he observed, "contain more detail with respect to religion than any I have seen."[20] Nevertheless, it was a fair exchange. Along with the five ecclesiastical restrictions came the 19 new regents.

THE FOUNDING MEETING

The meeting to dissolve trustees and create regents occurred at the Brock House on Saturday, January 17, 1976. Chairman Miller summarized the situation and opened the floor for questions. There were none. In the final analysis the charter change came smoothly with the support of faculty, alumni and academy. It arrived with the approval of the maturing church brotherhood and the envy of some Bible Belt colleges incapable of emulation. Chairman Miller called for the motion.

"Mr. Chairman," Mrs. Pepperdine rose from her straight-backed chair. "I move that the board approve all of the bylaw revisions as recommended by the executive committee."

Texas church leader Reuel Lemmons stood up beside her. "Mr. Chairman, I second Mrs. Pepperdine's motion."

Chairman Miller called for the vote. He quickly announced that it was unanimous and called on the new trustee from Tennessee, Dr. Ira L. North, for the benediction. Heads bowed, eyes moist, the Pepperdine board of trustees adjourned its last meeting midst a roomful of hearty "amens."

In 20 minutes the same group of 21 reconvened in the Tyler Campus Center with their 19 new colleagues for the maiden meeting of the board of regents. "M. Norvel Young said the change had been considered for a long time," wrote Howard A. White for the official record, "and that the requirement that the majority of the board be members of the church constituency would preserve the character of the institution."[21]

The next day Richard Seaver telephoned from China, praising the trustees' action after seeing the *Los Angeles Times* headline: "Pepperdine Adds 19 New Regents." They were Robert R. Dockson, chairman, California Federal Savings and Loan Association; Mrs. George C. Brock, vice chairman, Republican National Finance Committee; George W. Elkins, president, George Elkins Company; Bryant Essick, chairman, Essick Investment Company; Leonard K. Firestone, president, Firestone Tire and Rubber Company; Miles Flint, vice president, Crocker Citizens National Bank; Fred L. Hartley,

FOUNDING REGENTS MEETING, JANUARY 17, 1976

FRONT ROW (left to right): Earl Warford, Leonard K. Firestone, John V. Vaughn,
Chairman Lloyd D. Nelson, Blanche Seaver, Helen Pepperdine, President Banowsky

SECOND ROW: Donald V. Miller, Hubert G. Derrick, Orbin V. Melton, Evelyn Clark,
Miles Flint, Nile E Yearwood, Reuel Lemmons, Robert R. Dockson

THIRD ROW: Leonard H. Straus, Richard Ralphs, Hulsey Lokey, Chancellor Young,
Hugh M. Tiner, Bryant Essick, T. A. Rogers, George A. Evans, Frederick Llewellyn, Morris
B. Pendleton, Kenneth A. Ross, Jr., W. Austin Elmore, John D. Katch, Vice Chancellor
Runnels and Thomas G. Bost.

chairman and president, Union Oil Company of California; Fritz Huntsinger, president, Vetco Offshore Industries; Frederick Llewellyn, president, Forest Lawn Company; Clint W. Murchison Jr., chairman, Dallas Cowboys, Inc.; Charles S. Payson, chairman, Automation Industries; Morris B. Pendleton, chairman, Pendleton Tool Industries; Richard Ralphs, chairman, Ralphs Grocery Company; Hulsey Lokey, chairman, Host International; Richard Mellon Scaife, vice president, T. Mellon and Sons; Mrs. Frank Roger Seaver, chair, The Seaver Institute; Leonard H. Straus, chairman, The Thrifty Corporation; Alton C. Watson, president, The Adamson Companies; John V. Vaughn, vice chairman, Crocker National Bank.

Longtime trustee Lovell was one of my dearest friends. A George Pepperdine intimate and top DuPont executive, everybody loved church leader Jimmie. Here's what he wrote three months after the historic change: "It is the truth that the greatest contribution the old board ever made to Pepperdine is the fact that we didn't get in the way. When you think about it long enough you appreciate this simple fact all the more."[22] What Jimmie called "the old board"—Mr. George Pepperdine's trustees—fulfilled their duties gloriously.

1. The Articles of Incorporation and Bylaws of George Pepperdine College, July 15, 1937.
2. See Chapter 3, "The Impending Financial Failure," for a fuller discussion of "founder's syndrome" as it affected the early fate of George Pepperdine College.
3. James L. Lovell, personal letter to the author, January 15, 1974. The Lovell Papers.
4. M. Norvel Young, personal letter to the author, June 15, 1974. The Banowsky Papers.
5. Barry M. Richman and Richard N. Farmer, *Leadership, Goals and Power in Higher Education: A Contingency and Open-Systems Approach to Effective Management*, (San Francisco: Josey-Bass, 1977), 309.
6. M. Norvel Young, personal letter to the author, January 12, 1973. The Banowsky Papers.
7. Bill Henegar and Jerry Rushford, *Forever Young: The Life and Times of M. Norvel Young and Helen M. Young*, (Nashville: 21st Century Christian, 1999), 193.
8. Donald V. Miller, *Action*, February 15, 1975, 2.
9. I was not alone. Later, President Davenport e-mailed, "I spoke to the faculty last week on our mission statement, on how my own life and faith are moving, and on how I hoped the university might move. I am soon scheduled to fill the Sunday pulpits of three different Malibu denominations. As Paul Tillich put it, I am learning to embrace, but also to break through, my own particularity. Slowly, but surely, I am trying to stretch." (David Davenport, e-mail to the author, November 3, 1999. The Banowsky Papers.) So was President Benton. "Pepperdine views diversity as one facet of the prism formed by our mission," he emphasized in 2004 (Andrew K. Benton, "On Diversity," Pepperdine University brochure, 2004, 2. The Banowsky Papers.).
10. Frank Finley Merriam was the governor of California from June 2, 1934, to January 2, 1939.
11. Jerry Rushford, ed., *Crest of a Golden Wave: Pepperdine University, 1937–1987* (Malibu: Pepperdine University Press, 1987), 106. President Tiner and I were very much alike in our off-campus public power base. During much of the 1970s, if a faculty or staff member mentioned the name Pepperdine University in the Southern California area, the response was likely to be, "Oh Pepperdine! I heard Bill Banowsky speak a while back. He's fantastic." Hugh Tiner was just as publicly popular and the same was said about him in the 1940s and 1950s.
12. Ibid., 72.

13. William S. Banowsky, confidential memorandum to M. Norvel Young, June 16, 1972. The Banowsky Papers.
14. William S. Banowsky, personal letter to M. Norvel Young, January 6, 1973. The Banowsky Papers.
15. M. Norvel Young, confidential memorandum to the author, January 12, 1973. The Banowsky Papers.
16. M. Norvel Young, personal letter to the author, November 5, 1973. The Banowsky Papers.
17. James Smythe, personal interview with William S. Banowsky, February 15, 2007. The Banowsky Papers.
18. Henegar and Jerry Rushford, *Forever Young: The Life and Times of M. Norvel Young and Helen M. Young* (Nashville: 21st Century Christian, 1999), 85.
19. The Second Amended and Restated Bylaws of Pepperdine University, 14.
20. Richard I. Ingram, "The Funding of Private Higher Education," an address to the Pepperdine University Board of Regents, June 2005.
21. Rushford, *Golden Wave*, 170. In three decades there has been but one little religious spat. "Are we Brigham Young University?" asked irritated regent William H. Ahmanson in 2007. "Are we Mormons?" His irritation stemmed from the announcement that a priceless Drescher Campus site was being given to the University Church of Christ along with a $10 million campaign for a church building. Ahmanson, chairman of Home Savings and Loan of America, did not stand for reelection as regent and President Benton poetically described the proposed church building as "a bridge too far."
22. James L. Lovell, personal letter to the author, March 16, 1976. The Banowsky Papers. Lovell reported to me two years later the only authoritative word of criticism that the governance change seemed to attract: "The church in the East has about given up on Pepperdine. President Cliff Ganus at Harding is riding me for allowing Pepperdine to go worldly by bringing persons on the board not in the Church of Christ."

"It's a miracle each of our seven presidents, from Batsell Baxter
to Andy Benton, was perfect for his time."

HELEN MATTOX YOUNG
1937 Pepperdine Student Founder
July 9, 2006

DYNAMIC PRESIDENTS AND REALLY GOOD FRIENDS

Key to the stunning success of Pepperdine University has been the treasured tradition
of strong presidential leadership. "Lose the presidency and lose the mission," the
Pepperdine board always believed. Pictured are Fourth President Banowsky, Sixth
President Davenport and Seventh President Benton radiating the conviviality of shared
dreams and close fellowship.

CHAPTER 20

THE MISSION OF SEVEN PRESIDENTS

"Although there had been many rumors through the years that President Banowsky would enter politics or take another post," wrote historian Howard A. White, "the university community was somewhat shocked when he called the regents together on August 16, 1978, and tendered his resignation in order to accept the presidency of the University of Oklahoma."[1]

If the university community was somewhat shocked by my resignation, I was astonished by the instant appointment of Dr. White as my replacement. Dr. White's election, as well as that of the other six Pepperdine presidents, came about primarily because of the board's commitment to the Christian mission.

WHY PRESIDENT WHITE?

Explaining the Oklahoma side of the 1978 transition, the *Los Angeles Times* quoted me: "The time had simply come for me to be repotted."[2] But who could explain the Pepperdine side of the 1978 transition? Who could explain how 65-year-old Dr. White, already moving into retirement, could instantly replace me as president in one month without any search process or faculty involvement?

The first unsolicited Oklahoma call came on March 15, 1978. It lit a fuse that burned six months until Dr. White and I assumed respective new offices on September 15, 1978. Gratefully, for the first four months there was no publicity. On July 15, out of 55 OU presidential candidates, the five finalists were announced. My name was among them. That made the month of August a roller-coaster ride on both campuses.

On August 15, 1978, I was elected tenth president of the University of Oklahoma, effective in 30 days.[3] The next day Pepperdine regents assembled, alongside 200 friends and media, in the Los Angeles Hilton Hotel ballroom to accept my resignation. They also named Dr. White interim president until a formal search for the permanent president could be conducted. Dr. White, pledging to do his best, left the next day for a three-week vacation in Dublin, Ireland. He would never serve an interim hour.

With positive reaction to his temporary appointment, and the summer heat waning, on August 31, 1978, the regents unanimously elected Dr. White the fifth Pepperdine president, in absentia. The awed Dr. White got the news when Dr. Nelson dialed his Dublin hotel room. During the dog days of August with summer school ending, faculty scattering and campus emptying, Pepperdine drafted to its highest office its strongest inside man, who had not sought it. In fine Pepperdine tradition the presidential transition was professionally resolved in the quietest two weeks of the year.

According to Dr. White's subsequent reflections, the moment of truth came days earlier in London. Richard Seaver was in London and he invited Howard White to come down from Ireland for dinner. Dr. White perceived the evening as "a personal interview for president." Richard asked Howard to order the wine. Howard danced skillfully down the long wine list, identifying brands and best years. Richard was most impressed. Howard reported to Dr. Jerry Rushford at Pepperdine: "That's when I sensed that I was, indeed, the next president."

HE CAN'T RAISE MONEY!

At first glance Howard White seemed the least likely candidate for president. Turning 65, days before the Oklahoma call he handed me a January 14, 1978, letter tendering his resignation as executive vice president, effective December 31, 1978. He requested five more years of teaching and writing. I promised distinguished professor status, with high salary and low load. "But Howard, I don't want you to go. You've lots of time to think about this. For now I'll stick this letter in my drawer." That's where it stayed until I returned it, three months later, when things got hot in Oklahoma.

Some regents believed Howard was too old for the job. What hurt his case most among the board's businessmen was the absence of any fund-raising experience. A Depression-era Alabama Democrat with few wealthy Republican friends, Howard seemed to some a creature of campus and church, sort of like a high cardinal. "He couldn't find his way to the California Club without a map," a new regent nervously joked.

On the other hand, at second glance, Howard White seemed the perfect choice. He was presidential. A polished academic Civil War historian, his definitive book on the underground slave movement, *The Freedman's Bureau,*

PRESIDENTIAL CONTINUITY

Pictured together for the graduation ceremonies at Malibu in June 1980 were four lifelong friends: Second President Tiner, Third President, Young, Fourth President Banowsky and Fifth President White.

anchored forever his scholastic reputation. Devoted husband, the father of two fine sons and a bishop of the local church, Howard A. White was the "Mr. Chips of Pepperdine." Moreover, he was, hands down, the most elegantly authoritative administrator with whom I had worked. At his prime Howard could have run the entire government.

FAITH AND LEARNING

Transcendental faith, not meticulous management, won Dr. White the job. He overcame his fundraising deficit by bringing the most valued Pepperdine virtue. Howard was a profound Christian who was called to the presidency in the board's pursuit of the Christian mission. The Christian mission is in the Pepperdine DNA. George Pepperdine, a man of very few words, spoke volumes in this 1937 sentence: "I want [to build] a college academically sound, based on Christian faith."[4]

Sixty-two years later the first Pepperdine University Mission Statement, presented by President David Davenport for official adoption on May 19, 1999, echoed Mr. Pepperdine: "Pepperdine is a Christian university committed to the highest standards of academic excellence and Christian values, where students are strengthened for lives of purpose, service and leadership."[5]

Today's president, Andrew K. Benton, issues vigilant Christian caution. "We face great pressures to abandon or dilute our mission every day. Many forces work against the idea that we can be both academically excellent and faith based. We soundly reject that cynical notion but must be prepared to defend our position."[6]

THE HELEN YOUNG THEORY

The way to defend our position, believed the board, was meticulous presidential selection. "Providence," said Helen Mattox Young, "guided the board's selection of all seven presidents." A member of Pepperdine's 1937 founding student body, Helen married her history professor. They formed Pepperdine's powerful leadership team.[7] For 50 years, Helen lived and led on both campuses. Her work with all seven presidents anchored the "perfect presidents" folklore. "Each president," Helen said, "was perfect for his tenure. He was the right man, at the right time, for the right job. That's no accident. Providence protected Pepperdine's mission by providing perfect presidential leadership."[8]

Helen may be biased. But results, as highlighted in President Benton's 2000 inaugural address, bolster her theory. "President Batsell Baxter, enabling Mr. Pepperdine's dreams to become reality . . . President Hugh M. Tiner, building the community from infancy to maturity . . . President M. Norvel Young, leading a period of rededication and faithfulness . . . President William S. Banowsky, creating a period of bold enthusiasm and attainment, shaping the dreams we live today . . . President Howard A. White, guiding the wave of excellence with confidence in God, and with pride in us that made us proud of ourselves . . . President David Davenport, under whose enabling and ennobling leadership we came of age, with ageless convictions intact."[9]

If Helen is right, the agency Providence provided to protect the presidency was the board. "If we lose the presidency we lose the mission," the board always believed. The board never once delegated its power to pick a president to a committee.[10] All Pepperdine presidents, from Baxter to Benton, came into power through tightly controlled inside appointments. All entered the presidency, not by outside searching but by inside promotion. Since 1937, the Pepperdine board established the unbroken tradition of electing to the highest office its most proven inside men.

CONTINUITY AND CONTROL

Pepperdine valued continuity and control. Public institutions valuing transparency and diversity frowned on such privacy. Simultaneous presidential searches during the late 1970s at the University of Oklahoma and Pepperdine University contrasted opposite styles. The six-month public OU search featured a faculty-led committee, national advertising and recruitment of the largest, most diverse candidate field. The six-week private Pepperdine process focused on a candidate field of one and was resolved in one month without any committee or open process.

In May 1978, when the Oklahoma process pushed toward me, I alerted Howard. There was a chance I could be gone. For weeks we breathed in and out together. Micromanaging the transition, Chancellor Young, Vice Chancellor Charles B. Runnels and I formed an informal committee. We soon included all regents and Richard Seaver. Not a regent, but presiding over monumental Seaver gifts, Richard was invited to the transition meetings as a courtesy. He was aghast at my resignation.

On August 2, 1978, I was assured by all seven University of Oklahoma regents that I was their next president. Norvel, Charles and I huddled with Howard. "Howard, we believe God has called you to be the next Pepperdine president," Norvel proclaimed.

Howard pushed up stiffly in his chair. His neck twitched in a manner familiar to those who had seen him agitated. Intrigued, he was also stunned and slow to go along. "You men are getting out ahead of yourselves," he said. Howard knew the negatives he carried in the eyes of some.

DEAR FRIENDS, CLOSE COLLEAGUES . . .

President Banowsky, leaving for the University of Oklahoma in September 1978, presented to his Pepperdine successor the official "Waves 1" California license plate. Lifelong friends, Dr. White had been Dr. Banowsky's undergraduate professor in Tennessee during the 1950s and his Pepperdine executive vice president.

. . . AND SWEET, SORROWFUL PARTING

As the Banowskys departed in September 1978 for the presidency of the University of Oklahoma, Gay was especially honored by the Pepperdine faculty. Professor James Smythe presents the radiantly tearful Gay highest recognition as Richard Seaver and Bill look on.

Chairman D. Lloyd Nelson called the August 13, 1978, executive committee meeting to discuss the election of Dr. White. Two of the men, Dr. Nelson and Mr. Seaver, were shocked by the absence of a customary search process. Dr. Nelson's career as a distinguished USC professor of education had sensitized him to faculty prerogatives. "I fear a terrible reaction if we ordain Howard without so much as a faculty meeting," he worried.

Mr. Seaver's indoctrination as a lawyer and longtime Pomona College trustee sensitized him to academic process. "I second Lloyd's motion," worried Richard. "Howard's a top manager. But he's no candidate for this job. He has no business profile. He has no fundraising skills. We must involve the faculty. We must launch a legitimate national search."

"Richard," Charles Runnels chimed in, "a national search won't produce a longer candidate list. Remember, our new bylaws require our president to be a Church of Christ member." Episcopalian Richard shook his head, but the others of us would have fought for a church leader under any circumstance. The new bylaw finessed forever any religious quarreling over the Pepperdine presidency.

THE INTERIM OPTION

"OK," surrendered Richard. "Then who's out there in your church who can handle this job?"

"Richard," I jumped in. "It's tempting to imagine a world of candidates. That's not the world we live in. Most church leaders who succeed in Bible Belt institutions can't succeed at Pepperdine. We are unique. The men who can handle this job are already here." Joining Howard as viable candidates were James R. Wilburn, Jack Alan Scott, Jerry E. Hudson, Larry H. Hornbaker, R. Gerald Turner and Robert Thomas.[11] Dr. Scott and Dr. Hudson had recently moved into their own presidencies, and Dr. Turner and Dr. Thomas would soon follow. Dr. Wilburn and Dr. Hornbaker neglected presidential opportunities to serve Pepperdine.

I rested the case for Howard by appeal to the financial security of the Christian mission. "Richard, without your Aunt Blanche's $300 million in trust we would, no doubt, turn now to one of these younger stars to raise the necessary money. But the Seaver endowment empowers us to elect Dr. White to provide superior campus management and give highest reassurance to the church."

Despite compelling arguments, Dr. Nelson and Mr. Seaver remained opposed to the immediate appointment of Dr. White as president. Anticipating the impasse, Norvel rehearsed the rebuttal. "Very well then, gentlemen," he said. "But when Bill's resignation goes public next week, our phones will ring off the hook. We could lose control and have the faculty, media and church telling us what to do about the presidency." You could have heard a pin drop on the hardwood Brock House floor.

"Dr. Nelson," said Norvel, "I propose that Dr. White be designated interim president until such time as a search can be conducted and a permanent president selected."

"Interim president! That's the perfect solution!" rejoiced Chairman Nelson. "Everybody will support that while we put together a search committee." Richard concurred. It was a done deal. But if Lloyd and Richard were buying interim time, Norvel, Charles and I were pursuing the permanent solution. As the interim dust settled Howard got stronger. He was more easily elevated to the presidency.

EXECUTIVE VICE PRESIDENT

As continuity and control produced predictability, the path to the Pepperdine presidency grew clear. All Pepperdine presidents, except Baxter and Tiner, were replaced by their second in command. The title "executive vice president" was the magic carpet to the top. Every person in Pepperdine history but two who attained that title stepped into the presidency.[12] I was President Young's executive vice president. Dr. White was mine. Dr. Davenport was President White's. And Dr. Benton was President Davenport's. No other leadership system could have more smoothly produced such dynamic succession. "That's no accident!" Helen Young exclaimed.

The Pepperdine presidential transitions were managed by the outgoing president and a few board members. All presidents except Dr. Benton were hired without benefit of a formal search committee. All presidents were hired at the highest level, by the smallest number, in the quietest way. In this crowded twenty-first-century chase there is much to be said for the privileges of privacy.

The election of President White was anything but odd. It was par for the Pepperdine course, the latest in an unbroken line of handpicked presidents. The first three—President Baxter, President Tiner and President Young— were handpicked by Mr. Pepperdine. With Mr. Pepperdine's passing, the power to pick presidents passed to the incumbent president. Beginning with President Young, the outgoing president was always the key influence in the selection of his successor. "Bill," Norvel said to me one day on the Harbor Freeway in late 1970, "I've been talking to the trustees. Everybody thinks it's time for you to be president. I'll move out of administration to the new fundraising role of chancellor. You'll take over operations." Days later the board elected me fourth Pepperdine president, effective January 1, 1971, as the college became a university.

The baton got passed to Dr. White in the same way. For 20 years Howard and I made a perfect marriage of professional opposites. "Bill, you opened up for me all of the doors," he wrote days before his 1991 death, "that enabled me to experience the greatest leadership opportunities of my life."[13] When I left for Oklahoma, historian Patricia Yomantas characterized the colorful transition: "The Pepperdine board, rather than attempting to find a clone of the youthful president who almost single-handedly built the Malibu campus with an uncanny charisma that won donors and influenced multitudes, instead sought his alter ego. White's election was unanimous."[14]

Dr. White, and subsequently Dr. Davenport, passed the presidential baton along in much the same way. When President White retired in 1985, he ordained President Davenport. When President Davenport retired in 2000, he recommended Dr. Benton as his strongest inside administrator.

Despite academic pressure to be transparent and politically correct, Pepperdine perseveres oppositionally. The board instituted during my presidency the 1976 bylaw that required the president to be a Church of Christ member. The bylaw was narrowed in 2005: "The president must be a member in good standing of a local Church of Christ congregation." Well enough. It may also be wise for Pepperdine to continue to cultivate its presidents from within its own ranks.

Dr. White's stunning election raised questions. Chairman Nelson, seasoned by his USC career, answered. "The board's executive committee had considered conducting a nationwide search for a new president" but concluded that Dr. White "is here and he's our man, an extremely capable man."[15] There were resignations. Dr. Donald Sime, dean of the school of business and management, resigned because he did not want to report to Howard. Most painful was the defection of Richard Mellon Scaife, who was shocked that I would leave Pepperdine to go to a big public institution. Scaife eventually returned. Everyone at Pepperdine made happy peace with President White.

PRESIDENT WHITE: 1978–1985

The student newspaper expressed approval. "Banowsky's former teacher, Dr. Howard A. White, has been chosen by the Board of Regents to succeed him as Pepperdine's president. The *Graphic* supports the selection of White, a man commanding steadfast respect at all levels of the university community."[16] The *Santa Monica Evening Outlook* predicted the academic advance. "If William Slater Banowsky brought badly needed cash and stability to Pepperdine

DOCTOR NANCY DAVIS REAGAN!

In 1981, President Howard A. White erected a mammoth white celebration
tent on the Malibu campus and before a huge crowd conferred an honorary
degree on the reigning First Lady of the United States.

University, Howard Ashley White may be the president who will improve
the university's academic reputation."[17] Indeed!

President White's September 13, 1978, inaugural address, praising the
Seaver $300 million endowment, focused on academic excellence. "This
institution is so strongly established, its friends and supporters are so numerous
and so dedicated, its human and financial resources are so great, . . . that its
future with the help of God is bound to be one of glorious achievement."

Over seven years President White raised faculty salaries from the lowest
national quartile where, because of campus construction, I had allowed them
to linger, to the top 10 percent nationally. He elevated admission standards.
He hired 33 credentialed Seaver College faculty. He shoved SAT scores up
159 points, putting Seaver College in the most elite selective schools category.
"Such an academic advance was anticipated. But Dr. White shocked us by also
becoming a master fundraiser," chuckled Vice President Wilburn. "The more
money he raised, the more Republican he got." President White famously
informed the *Los Angeles Times* that "Republicans either have more money
or they are more willing to give it away." He brought to the Malibu campus

global conservative luminaries such as Richard M. Nixon, William Rehnquist and Nancy Reagan. In regal ceremony, he conferred an honorary doctorate on the sitting First Lady of the United States.

Dr. White's dynamic vice president for development was Dr. Michael F. Adams, destined to become president of Centre College in Kentucky and the University of Georgia. President White "was the primary catalyst for our $100 million 'Wave of Excellence' campaign," emphasized President Adams.[18] The Malibu buildings dedicated during the White administration include Smothers Theatre, the Eddy D. Field Baseball Stadium, Helen Field Heritage Hall, Faculty Housing Phase One, the Music Building and the Odell McConnell Law Center. In the new millennium the faculty ordained that the university's highest honor for excellence in classroom teaching would be known as "The Howard A. White Award." For many Howard was, no doubt, the most popular Pepperdine president.

PRESIDENT DAVENPORT: 1985–2000

Unlike my abrupt departure, President White announced his resignation almost a full year before stepping down. He notified regents on June 12, 1984, of his April 15, 1985, departure. He had been working for more than a year with a committee of regents to compile a list of prospects for president and on the same day that President White informed regents of his decision to retire, "the board unanimously voted to name David Davenport as the sixth president of Pepperdine University."[19] Howard was a man who took no chances.

"Pepperdine has a long tradition of making room for its rising stars," Patricia Yomantas elaborated. When he moved up to become executive vice president in 1983, Dr. Davenport "was a president-in-training and few people at Pepperdine were surprised—or disappointed—when the board of regents, one year later, announced its unanimous selection of David Davenport as the sixth president."[20] Of course, things are always more complicated than they seem. In 1980, Dr. Davenport arrived at Pepperdine from a sterling career in the law and ministry, with success written all over him. A natural leader, he could have done whatever he determined. After several key Pepperdine jobs, President White appointed him executive vice president. Smart money bet then on Dr. Davenport as the sixth Pepperdine president. "He has a great ability to communicate his vision for the future," Chairman Bost enthused, calling Davenport "an obvious choice." His transition to the presidency "proceeded in a very smooth and orderly manner . . . [with] no loss of momentum."[21] The charismatic President Davenport assumed office April 16, 1985.

"What I delight in more than anything else," he rejoiced, "is making a speech about the university. The joy of trying to tell our story in such a way that people want to be a part of the Pepperdine family is what gives me the most energy for my work."[22] Indeed! David Davenport is on my short list—with John F. Kennedy, Ronald Reagan and Barack Obama—of gifted speakers.

Malibu campus buildings dedicated during the Davenport administration include the Thornton Administrative Center, Ralphs-Straus Tennis Center, the Cultural Arts Center, the School of Law Phase Two, the Howard A. White Center, Rockwell Tower Residence Hall, the Payson Library Second Floor, Raitt Recital Hall, Lindhurst Theatre and the Frederick R. Weisman Museum of Art. Most crucially today, Dr. Davenport founded in 1996 the contemporaneously and politically vital School of Public Policy. In 2000, the cutting-edge Davenport Institute of Public Policy was named in his honor.

Dr. Davenport served longer in the Pepperdine presidency than any predecessor but Dr. Tiner. In 2000, after 15 years of meteoric leadership, he stepped aside in Pepperdine decorum for his top inside man.

PRESIDENT BENTON: 2000–PRESENT

Andrew Benton made a name for himself, recalled Lawrence, Kansas, high-school friend Kevin Heck, because "he always did the right thing. He always had goals, good friends and a purpose in life."[23] We could close the book there on President Benton.

Attorney and Oklahoma Christian College administrator Andrew K. Benton came to Pepperdine in 1984 as President White's assistant vice president for regulatory and community relations. He satisfied several levels of government and mollified most Malibu citizens in enabling historic campus development. President Davenport named Dr. Benton vice president and chief of staff in 1985, vice president for administration in 1987 and vice president for university affairs in 1989. After serving as chief executive officer during two Davenport sabbaticals, Andy Benton was elevated in 1991 to the office of executive vice president. Bang!

Dr. Benton became the seventh Pepperdine president on June 16, 2000. Following his predecessors' time-honored tradition, in his inaugural address he acknowledged: "I could not have found a better friend and guide than David Davenport."[24]

Presidents Davenport and Benton partnered to create the towering 50.4 acre Drescher Graduate Campus. It provides the spectacular home for the School of Education and Psychology, the School of Public Policy and the

Graziadio School of Business and Management, alongside other Camelot-like facilities.

President Benton, of all Pepperdine presidents, has been elected by his presidential colleagues to the most distinguished national office. Aside from the president of the University of Notre Dame, Dr. Benton is the only president of a private, religiously affiliated institution ever to be elected the Chairman of the Board of the American Council on Education, the largest professional organization supporting higher education.

A soldier's son, born on a Reno, Nevada, military base, Dr. Benton carries an erect military bearing of his own. A professional, hands-on manager, he devotes time to faculty and students and always teaches a class. He is a music and poetry devotee, and he ministers to underdogs with a pastor's heart.

Some of the Malibu facilities dedicated during the Benton administration include the Center for Communications and Business, Harilela International Tennis Stadium, the Firestone Fieldhouse Expansion, Keck Science Center, Graziadio Executive Center, the Braun Center for Public Policy, the Young Center for Education and Psychology, the Beckman Center for Business and Management, the Heroes Garden commemorating September 11, 2001 and the Mullin Town Square.

"LIGHTS ALONG THE SHORE"

In 1937 Pepperdine's landlocked athletic teams were presciently christened the Waves and, 30 years later, Walter Burch and I together wrote the Waves' Affirmation:

> Pepperdine Affirms
> That God is
> That God is revealed uniquely in Christ
> That the educational process may not, with impunity, be divorced from the divine process
> That the student, as a person of infinite dignity, is the heart of the educational enterprise
> That the quality of student life is a valid concern of the college
> That truth, having nothing to fear from investigation, should be pursued relentlessly in every discipline
> That spiritual commitment, tolerating no excuse for mediocrity, demands the highest standards of academic excellence
> That freedom, whether spiritual, intellectual, or economic, is indivisible
> That knowledge calls, ultimately, for a life of service.[25]

With affirmation and mission perhaps the Waves also need a song. Mr. Pepperdine probably prefers the Phillip Bliss hymn featured at his funeral.

> Brightly beams our Father's mercy,
> From His Lighthouse evermore.
> But to us He gives the keeping
> Of the lights along the shore.
>
> Let the lower lights be burning!
> Send a gleam across the wave!
> Some poor fainting, struggling seaman,
> You may rescue, you may save.[26]

1. Jerry Rushford, ed., *Crest of a Golden Wave: Pepperdine University, 1937–1987* (Malibu: Pepperdine University Press, 1987), 174–175. "[Dr. White] was dean of the undergraduate program when President Banowsky asked him to serve as executive vice president," wrote Patricia Yomantas, "a post he held from 1970 until Banowsky's 1978 resignation. Scholarship, leadership, and strong professional integrity were qualities that commended him to each administrative position."(Ibid., 231).
2. "I have been with one institution for 15 years and am 42 years old. This is a matter of growth both for me and for Pepperdine and the time had simply come for me to be repotted" (*Los Angeles Times,* August 16,1978). Vice President James Wilburn, a fellow Texan sharing my love of country music, chimed in with a Willie Nelson metaphor: "If you don't understand him, and he don't die young, he'll probably just ride away."
3. *Daily Oklahoman*, August 16, 1978. Here was the huge headline: "OU HIRES REAGAN MAN!"
4. Bill Youngs, *Faith Was His Fortune: The Life Story of George Pepperdine* (Malibu: Pepperdine University Press, 1976), 202.
5. Minutes of the Pepperdine University Board of Regents meeting, May 19, 1999. The Banowsky Papers.
6. Andrew K. Benton, personal letter to the author, July 17, 2000. The Banowsky Papers.
7. "Associated Women for Pepperdine: Celebrating 50 Years of Service to Pepperdine Students," *Pepperdine People*, Spring 2008, 18–19. On June 5, 1958, Helen M. Young met with six other women, including Helen Pepperdine, to found the Associated Women for Pepperdine. In 2009, it had a membership of 3,000 women supporting Pepperdine in many ways, including "contributing five million over the years in scholarships to students from Churches of Christ."
8. Helen M. Young, personal letter to the author, July 9, 2006. The Banowsky Papers.
9. Andrew K. Benton, "Promises to Keep: Reaching Deep and Reaching Far," inauguration address, Pepperdine University, September 23, 2000. The Banowsky Papers.
10. See note 8 above.
11. President Harold Hazelip of David Lipscomb University and President Terry Bradshaw of Oklahoma Christian College both reported that Dr. White had sounded them out about the Pepperdine presidency. Both told me, in one way or another, that they were not prepared to deal with life and leadership in California. The Banowsky Papers.
12. The two exceptions were William B. Adrian and Herbert Luft.
13. Howard A. White, personal letter to the author, July 26, 1986. The Banowsky Papers. "If [Pepperdine University] and Seaver College were to last a thousand years—and I pray God they will—the name of William S. Banowsky will be illustrious in all of those years for the magnificent work he has done" (Rushford, *Golden Wave*, 182.).
14. Rushford, *Golden Wave*, 228.

15. "Editorial," the *Graphic*, August 30, 1978, 2.

16. Rushford, *Golden Wave*, 176.

17. Larry Curtains, "White to Be Installed," *Santa Monica Evening Outlook*, September 12, 1978, 3.

18. Rushford, *Golden Wave*, 231.

19. Ibid., 224.

20. Ibid., 239.

21. Ibid, 224.

22. Ibid, 241.

23. Mike Belt, "Ceremony Celebrates Chesty Lion Graduates," *Lawrence (Kansas) Journal-World* September 20, 2004.

24. Andrew K. Benton, "Promises to Keep: Reaching Deep and Reaching Far," inauguration address, Pepperdine University, September 23, 2000. The Banowsky Papers.

25. Walter E. Burch, an Abilene, Texas, consultant, was hired by Dr. Young in 1967 to write the first draft of a fundraising brochure. On November 7, 1967, Burch created draft one of "Pepperdine College Affirms." Five days later, he mailed draft two to Norvel as follows:

    Pepperdine College Affirms
    That God Is.
    That His eternal purpose in Jesus Christ is being worked out in human history.
    That the educational process cannot with impunity be divorced from the divine process.
    That a liberal arts education grounded in the eternal scheme has ultimate significance by offering students a theme for living, a purpose for being, and a faith that can perceive beyond the frontier of human experience.
    That knowledge makes a claim on mankind—presenting itself, as a sacred trust, for recognition and understanding.
    That the cultivation of disciplined minds is the primary function of education; therefore intellectual growth, in range and powers of thought, must be given priority in the academic process.
    That the central aim of creative teaching is to recognize the individuality of persons.
    That the highest purpose in education is realized when the sensitive teacher, through word and example, is able to create within each student a desire to become free and fully human by accepting a sense of personal responsibility for his own destiny.
    That the quality of student conduct, both public and personal, on and off campus, is a valid concern of the educational institution.
    That a complete education will liberate man from mere existence by fusing eternal hope into his spirit.

    From Burch's second version, I wrote the final draft as it appears in the text. Subsequently, two additional changes affected line two. In 1975, Vice President James R. Wilburn suggested adding the word "uniquely," to signify Christ as one of a kind. In 1988, President David Davenport, responding to gender correctness criticism, changed "that *He* is revealed uniquely in Christ" to "that *God* is revealed uniquely in Christ." Therefore, the affirmation is the work of several of us. Walter Ellis Burch, who made early Malibu miracle contributions, died January 29, 2009.

26. Philip P. Bliss, "Let the Lower Lights Be Burning," *Songs of Faith and Praise* (West Monroe, LA: Howard Publishing, 1996), 642.

"But we have this treasure in jars of clay to show that this all-surpassing power is from God and not from us."

II Corinthians 4:7

A BRIEF PEPPERDINE
BIBLIOGRAPHY

Banowsky, William S., ed. "Christ Our Contemporary," *The Pepperdine College Bible Lectures* (August 1962 and March 1963). Nashville: Christian Family Book Club, 1963.

Clark, Richard L., and Jack W. Bates. *Faith Is My Fortune: The Life Story of George Pepperdine*. Los Angeles: Pepperdine College Press, 1963.

Gardner, Audrey. "A Brief History of Pepperdine College." Master's thesis. George Pepperdine College, 1968.

Henegar, Bill, and Jerry Rushford. *Forever Young: The Life and Times of M. Norvel Young and Helen M. Young*. Nashville: 21st Century Christian, 1999.

Hughes, Richard T. and William B. Adrian. *Models for Christian Higher Education: Strategies for Success in the Twenty First Century*. Grand Rapids: William B. Eerdmans Publishing Company, 1997.

Jones, Candace Denise. "White Flight? George Pepperdine College's Move to Malibu, 1965–1972." Master's thesis. Pepperdine University, 2003.

Meeks, Catherine. *I Want Somebody to Know My Name*. New York: Thomas Nelson Inc., 1978.

Pullias, E. V. *A Search for Understanding: Thoughts on Education and Personality in a Time of Transition*. Dubuque: Wm. C. Brown Company Publishers, 1965.

Rushford, Jerry, ed. *Crest of a Golden Wave: Pepperdine University, 1937–1987*. Malibu: Pepperdine University Press, 1987.

Watson, Jane Werner. *The Seaver Story*. Claremont, CA: Pomona College Press, 1960.

Young, M. Norvel. *A History of Colleges Established and Controlled by Members of the Churches of Christ*. Kansas City: Old Paths Book Club, 1949.

Youngs, Bill. *Faith Was His Fortune: The Life Story of George Pepperdine*. Malibu: Pepperdine University Press, 1976.

———. *The Legacy of Frank Roger Seaver*. Malibu: Pepperdine University Press, 1976.

INDEX

(Note: Entries in italics refer to photo captions.)